Charles Bodman Rae (b. 1955) is a composer and pianist. After private piano studies with Fanny Waterman, he read music at Cambridge (including studies in Oxford with Robert Sherlaw Johnson, and in Cambridge with Robin Holloway), and was then appointed at the age of 23 to a lecturership at the City of Leeds College of Music, where he taught composition and analysis. In 1981 he was awarded a two-year postgraduate scholarship in composition by the Polish Government, which enabled him to live and work in Warsaw, attached to the Chopin Academy of Music. After returning to Leeds he was appointed Head of School of Creative Studies. He is currently Director of Studies at the Royal Northern College of Music. He is married to the Polish actress Dorota Kwiatkowska; they have one daughter and now live in Cheshire.

The Music
of Lutosławski

CHARLES BODMAN RAE

OMNIBUS PRESS
LONDON · NEW YORK · SYDNEY

To my wife, Dorota

This third edition copyright © 1999 Charles Bodman Rae

ISBN: 0.7119.6910.8
Order No: OP 48072

First published in 1994 by Faber and Faber Limited
3 Queen Square, London WC1N 3AU

Exclusive Distributors
Book Sales Limited,
8/9 Frith Street,
London W1V 5TZ, UK.

Music Sales Corporation,
257 Park Avenue South,
New York, NY 10010, USA.

Five Mile Press,
22 Summit Road,
Noble Park,
Victoria 3174,
Australia.

To the Music Trade only:
Music Sales Limited,
8/9 Frith Street,
London W1V 5TZ, UK.

Photo credits:
Every effort has been made to trace the copyright holders of the photographs in this book but one or two were unreachable. We would be grateful if the photographers concerned would contact us.

Printed and bound in Great Britain by MPG Books Ltd, Bodmin, Cornwall

A catalogue record for this book is available from the British Library.

Visit Omnibus Press at http://www.omnibuspress.co.uk

Contents

Preface to the Third Edition

The first edition of this book (published by Faber and Faber, at the beginning of 1994) was written and completed while the composer was still alive, in good health, and busy composing. When I showed him a final draft of the text, in order to verify some biographical details, he remarked, jokingly, that all the book seemed to lack was a photograph of his grave in Powązki Cemetery in Warsaw. Little could one have known, least of all the composer himself, that only months later he would be diagnosed with a cancer which, in the space of just a few short weeks, would ravage his body and end his life.

Naturally, my comments at the end of the first edition were written in the present tense. At that time all the indications were that he would live to complete further, major works (in particular, a violin concerto which he was writing for Anne-Sophie Mutter). It seemed premature, therefore, to attempt an overall assessment of his creative achievement, an assessment which would have had an inappropriate suggestion of finality. Ironically, however, the tragic news of his death, on 7 February 1994, came while the book was literally being printed. The only alteration which I was able to make at that stage, therefore, was a very brief addition to the end of the preface, simply to mark his passing.

This new, paperback edition of *The Music of Lutosławski* is the second version to appear in English, but it is actually the third edition overall. For the second edition, published in a Polish translation by the composer, Stanisław Krupowicz (*Muzyka Lutosławskiego*; Warsaw, Wydawnictwo Naukowe PWN, 1996), I was able to take the opportunity to extend and slightly revise some aspects of the book. The eighth chapter (which had previously ended with a discussion of the Fourth Symphony), was extended in order to cover the period up to the composer's death, and includes reference to his last completed piece, *Subito*, for violin and piano. I also added an Epilogue (written, like the Preface, in the first person), which covers the aftermath of his death, including the poignant last weeks of his widow. In this ninth chapter I discussed (and included two music examples from) the sketches for a violin concerto, copies of which (some 160 pages of them) Danuta Lutosławska had given to me shortly before her own death. I then concluded with an attempt to evaluate his position in relation to other major figures of the twentieth century, particularly some of his close contemporaries. This and other additional material from the Polish edition is published here for the first time in English.

Fortunately, it has also been possible, as with the Polish edition, for me to include twice as many photographs as were included in the first edition. This has enabled me to present a number of significant photographs of the composer's family which have hitherto only been published in the Polish edition. I am grateful to the composer's stepson, Marcin Bogusławski, for allowing me access to the composer's archives after his death, and for allowing me to reproduce these materials.

Inevitably, perhaps, the critical reception of the first edition tended to be divided between those who found the level of musical analysis a little intimidating and those for whom it was insufficiently detailed. I stand by my original decision, however, to present the essential features of my analytical findings, but without necessarily including all the densely technical analytical 'evidence' on which the findings are based. In any case, those with 'a professional curiosity in such matters' (as Steven Stucky so elegantly phrased it in his earlier study) can make full use of all the bibliographical references, to writings by myself and others, if they wish to probe even more deeply.

I am grateful to several friends and colleagues for kindly pointing out a few errors and omissions: for example, Martina Homma and Zbigniew Skowron have reminded me that there *is* a twelve-note row present in *Grave*; Adrian Thomas has drawn attention to a 'slip of the pen' relating to a music example from *Mi-Parti* (Ex. 5 : 8, where black-headed notes indicate pitches that have been displaced from the *preceding*, rather than the 'following' chord; and Krzysztof Meyer has pointed out that I had omitted to mention the popular songs and dances which Lutosławski wrote under the pseudonym 'Derwid'. The latter topic has now been well researched by Adrian Thomas, in the archives of Polish Radio and elsewhere, and has resulted in a most interesting article published in *The Musical Times* (August 1995). For the present edition I have appended a listing of the known 'Derwid' pieces collated from the information published by Thomas and by Jadwiga Paja-Stach, and I am grateful to both of them for their permission to do so.

Perhaps the most substantive criticism of the first edition (made by

Zbigniew Skowron, writing in *Muzyka*) was that a merely 'select' bibliography seemed inappropriate for the first book to cover the composer's complete works. The first edition, of course, had not been intended as the final word on the subject, but nonetheless I readily acknowledge the validity of this criticism. Accordingly, I have provided for the third edition (and for the entry in the forthcoming seventh edition of *The New Grove Dictionary of Music and Musicians*) a more comprehensive bibliography. I would not claim, however, that it is exhaustive; I have still been selective and have excluded many of the numerous secondary sources (such as concert reviews, and other journalistic writings). At this point I would like to pay tribute to the bibliographic work done by the late Maria Stanilewicz, and particularly to Jadwiga Paja-Stach who completed her work for publication as a mammoth appendix to the commemorative double issue of *Muzyka* published in 1995. My expanded bibliography owes much to their splendid work which collates other bibliographies (including my own) and provides an invaluable resource for future scholars.

Since the first edition of this book appeared several significant contributions to what we might now call 'Lutosławski studies' have either been published or planned, variously in Polish, English and German. Two books which also appeared in 1994 were referred to in my Epilogue to *Muzyka Lutosławskiego*: a monograph tribute by Tadeusz Kaczyński, and a volume of conversations between the composer and Irina Nikolska. More recently there has been a published version of Martina Homma's long-awaited doctoral dissertation on Lutosławski's use of 12-note rows. This has been followed by two books from Jadwiga Paja-Stach: the first was a short but useful handbook; the second is a study of the composer's style, and includes some interesting additional information on the composer's family and his childhood home at Drozdowo. Thanks to the initiative of Dr Zbigniew Skowron, these, and other scholars, from various countries, were brought together for the first time, under the auspices of the Musicology Institute of Warsaw University, for a conference in June 1997 on the composer and his music, held at the Ostrogski Palace in Warsaw (home of the Chopin Society). The purpose of the conference was to allow for an exchange of ideas between the various contributors to a volume entitled *Lutosławski Studies* (Oxford, OUP, due in 1999), including: Andrzej Tuchowski, Martina Homma, Jadwiga Paja-Stach, John Casken, Irina Nikolska, Anna-Maria Harley, Adrian Thomas, Steven Stucky, and myself.

In addition to those individuals whom I have already thanked above, I would also like to express my gratitude to the following: Dr Paul Sacher, for his kind permission to reproduce material from sketches now owned by the Sacher Foundation (held at his archive in Basel), and also for his financial support for the Polish edition; Malcolm Crowthers for his excellent photographs; Tadeusz Kaczyński, Dr Martina Homma, and Dr Jadwiga Paja-Stach, for continuing to send me copies of their own, significant publications; Robert Dimery, of Omnibus Press, for steering this new edition through to publication; and to Anna Markwandt, whose twenty-five years of devoted service to the Lutosławskis, as their housekeeper, must not go unrecorded.

Finally, it is perhaps worth noting that, since his death, public attention towards Lutosławski's music has undergone a change which is curious, but not altogether unexpected. It is not uncommon for there to be a lull, a period of relative neglect (at least by orchestra managements, concert promoters, and broadcasters), immediately following the death of a composer who has been very widely performed during his lifetime. Thus it has been with Lutosławski, with the exception of a few, notable festivals and retrospectives. It is certainly not that his music is valued any less since his death. On the contrary, his music seems already to have achieved a kind of undisputed modern 'classic' status. It hardly seems necessary to argue that he was a 'great' composer, or that this is 'good' music; the more important questions are 'What makes it good?', and 'How was it made?' This book, from the point when it was conceived in the late 1980s, was always intended to reflect the standpoint of one composer trying to retrace the steps of another, in an attempt to reveal some of the authentic processes of conception and composition through which this superbly crafted, multi-layered and multi-faceted music came into being. I hope that, in a modest way, it may have helped readers to gain some extra understanding of what they experience as listeners from the beauty and the drama of Lutosławski's music.

J.C.B.R.
Bowdon, August 1998

Preface to the First Edition

The moment of discovery is a precious experience in our exploration of music. One such moment occurred when, as a teenager, I heard the radio broadcast of a powerfully expressive piece for string orchestra that hinted at Bartók, yet was not a work that I knew. As happens with the radio, I had switched on during the piece and had missed the announcement of composer and title. By the time it finished I was ready for the information to be indelibly engraved in my memory: *Musique funèbre*, in memory of Bartók, by Witold Lutosławski. I spent weeks devouring all the scores and recordings of Lutosławski's music that I could find. Such periods of intense enthusiasm are common currency in the adolescence of a composer, however, and their lasting significance can only be measured over time. The more crucial test came ten years later with the British première of *Les espaces du sommeil*. My response to this piece was to be the catalyst for an eventual move to Warsaw that, in turn, has led me to a closer understanding of both the man and his music.

When I lived in Warsaw during the austere period of martial law from 1981 to 1983, Lutosławski was working on his Third Symphony. In spite of the pressures and concerns of that time, he produced a piece that seems to be an affirmation of optimism, rich in expressive melody. At that time I was busy with my own music and had not intended to write a book about Lutosławski; but during our frequent informal conversations it became apparent that significant aspects of his compositional technique, particularly concerning harmony and melody, had not been addressed in sufficient detail. In 1987 these discussions became more formalised, and over a ten-day period that April I recorded a series of conversations in the study of the composer's home in Warsaw, which resulted in over twenty hours of taped material. The transcripts of those conversations have been used as primary source material for this book, whether by direct quotation or paraphrase. Since then we have had many further meetings and conversations, and I am very grateful to the composer for his co-operation and candour. While there is inevitably some overlap with previous published conversations, there are significant aspects of his harmonic language that Lutosławski disclosed for the first time. Not all of that information is presented here; much of it is too detailed, and some relates to elements of his compositional technique that are still evolving. Mindful of a responsibility towards preserving some privacy for work presently in gestation, I have tried to balance the demand for disclosure against a need for discretion.

Certain events and turning points have defined stages in the development of Lutosławski's music. The need to account for the characteristics of each stage, particularly the most recent, has not only prompted this book but also determined some of the divisions between chapters. External political events mark the ends of the first two chapters at 1945 and 1956, respectively. These dates were chosen not for mere historical convenience, but because they represent considerable changes of condition that genuinely bear on Lutosławski's life and career. Thereafter, the dividing lines are determined by purely musical changes arrived at by Lutosławski alone: the introduction of twelve-note chords in the late 1950s; the adoption of aleatory procedures in 1960; and the development of simpler harmony after 1979, which marks the beginning of what now appears to be his late style.

I have been in the fortunate position of building on a secure foundation of previous writing, much in Polish, some in German or French, and some in English, including the critical survey by Steven Stucky, *Lutosławski and his Music* (Cambridge University Press, 1981), which discusses works up to and including *Mi-Parti* (1976). I have taken the opportunity of correcting some minor errors and omissions made by Stucky, but, more important, of reassessing his identification of Lutosławski's 'late style', which he applied to works composed since 1960. By 1981 Lutosławski was already two years into a new stylistic phase.

The present study is not intended as a biography; a comprehensive account of the composer's eventful life remains to be written. In the first two chapters, however, it was necessary to clarify the sequence of contemporary events, as the path of his early and early-middle years is traced against a background of the fate and fortunes of Poland up to 1956. Subsequent chapters consider the development of his career primarily through the music, but linked by some biographical narrative.

Similarly because of considerations of space and scope, the main focus of this book is necessarily critical rather than analytical. Yet I have been guided by the conviction that penetrating analysis is a necessary precondition for the formulation of properly informed criticism. While it has not been possible to include my detailed analyses here, much of the critical discussion stems from close examination of Lutosławski's compositional technique: *Pitch Organisation in the Music of Witold Lutosławski since 1979* (Ph.D. thesis, University of Leeds, 1992). An effort has been made to minimise the use of analytical and technical jargon in favour of discussing the music in as familiar terms as possible. Even so, some technical vocabulary has been unavoidable, such as the terminology and numbering of 'interval-classes' (although the more common musical vocabulary of intervals is also used).

I acknowledge permission from the following to reproduce music examples from works in which they hold copyright: Chester Music Ltd of London, in association with Polskie Wydawnictwo Muzyczne (PWM) of Kraków; Moeck Verlag of Celle (Five Songs and *Jeux vénitiens*); and not least the composer himself, for permission to reproduce examples and facsimile extracts from published and unpublished scores, manuscripts and sketches, and for permission to quote from various unpublished lectures. (I was fortunate in having access to all the composer's autograph manuscripts and sketches then still in his possession; in May 1990 most of these were acquired by the Paul Sacher Stiftung, so future investigators will have to travel to Basel to view them.) I also acknowledge permission from Chester Music to quote from the two books of conversations with the composer compiled, respectively, by Tadeusz Kaczyński and Bálint András Varga.

I acknowledge assistance from the following libraries in providing access to various source materials: the Library of the Polish Composers' Union (ZKP) in Warsaw, particularly the invaluable assistance of the former librarian Kazimierz Nowacki; the Polish Library of the Polski Ośrodek Społeczno Kulturalne (POSK) at Hammersmith in London; the music manuscripts section of the Polish National Library at the Krasiński Palace in Warsaw; and the Polish Film Archive in Warsaw, for allowing me a private screening in April 1987 of the two films of 1945–6 for which Lutosławski composed scores.

I am grateful to the following individuals: Professor Julian Rushton; Professor Arnold Whittall; Dr Caroline Rae; Martina Homma; Helen Sprott, formerly of Faber and Faber; James Rushton and the late Sheila MacCrindle of Chester Music; and especially my wife, Dorota Kwiatkowska, not only for sharing her knowledge of Polish literature and helping with the translation of Polish texts, but also for her constant support and encouragement.

Finally, I offer my warmest thanks to Witold Lutosławski and Danuta Lutosławska, for welcoming me to their home on so many occasions, and for allowing me continually to invade their privacy with endless questioning.

While this book was actually being printed, tragic news came from Warsaw. Witold Lutosławski died at 10 p.m. on Monday the 7th of February 1994, aged eighty-one.

We have lost one of the greatest creative artists of our time.

J.C.B.R.
Ilkley
8 February 1994

Guide to Polish Pronunciation

The Polish alphabet contains thirty-two letters:

a ą b c ć d e ę f g h i j k l ł m n ń o ó p r s ś t u w y z ź ż

Unlike English, Polish is a phonetic language with consistent rules of pronunciation. The stress falls on the penultimate syllable, with the exception of a few foreign words. All vowels are simple and of even length, as in Italian, except two nasal vowels – ę and ą (as in French: ę = un; ą = on). At the ends of words 'ę' loses its nasality in colloquial Polish and is pronounced as oral 'e'; the 'ą', however, preserves its nasality. Other vowel sounds are contained in the following English words: sum (a); ten (e); heat (i); lot (o); book (u); sit (y). Most single consonants behave the same way as in English except for 'c' (ts), 'j' (soft, as in 'yes'), and 'w' (v). As in German, some consonants are softened when they fall at the end of a word, hence 'b, d, g, w, z' become 'p, t, k, f, s', respectively.

Polish		Equivalent		
ą	as in sąd	on	as in French :	on
ę	as in kolędy	un	as in French :	un
c	as in taniec	ts	as in English :	its
ch	as in Lech	ch	as in Scottish :	loch
cz	as in Iłłakowicz	ch	as in English :	church
ł	as in Lutosławski	w	as in English :	why
ń	as in Toruń	nu	as in English :	inured
ó	as in Kraków	oo	as in English :	woof
rz (ż)	as in żałobna	su	as in English :	pleasure
sz	as in Szymanowski	sh	as in English :	show
szcz	as in Szczecin	shch	as in English :	pushchair
ś	as in Solidarność	sh (soft)	as in English :	sheep
ć	as in Solidarność	ch (soft)	as in English :	cheese
w	as in Witold	v (hard)	as in English :	vase
w	as in Kraków	f (soft)	as in English :	roof
y	as in muzyka	i	as in English :	ill

Examples of English (approximate) phonetic transliteration:

Lutosławski	= Lootoswavski	Iłłakowicz	= Iwakovitch
Solidarność	= Solidarnoshch	Łomża	= Womzhah
Muzyka żałobna	= Moozika zhawobna	Endecja	= Endetsia
Szymanowski	= Shimanovski	Wałęsa	= Vawensa
Górne Drozdowo	= Goorne Drozdovo		

List of Illustrations

Nos. 1–10 from the composer's collection; nos. 11 & 12 by Malcolm Crowthers.

List of Tables

I
Formative Years
(1913–1945)

1913 was a good year for the birth of a composer. Even the most concise selection of premières from that *annus mirabilis* in the history of European music conveys extraordinary resonance: Schoenberg's *Gurrelieder* (Vienna, 23 February); Webern's Six Pieces op. 6 (Vienna, 31 March); Debussy's *Jeux* (Paris, 15 May); Stravinsky's *Le sacre du printemps* (Paris, 29 May); Rakhmaninov's *Kolokola* ('The Bells', St Petersburg, 13 December). These and other contemporary musical events held the promise of a challenging and invigorating creative climate; but for Lutosławski, born in the centre of Europe, the turmoil of contemporary political events would prove both more immediate and perhaps ultimately more decisive in determining his character and temperament at the most fundamental level.

Witold Lutosławski was born on 25 January 1913 in what we now know as the capital of Poland; but although he was born in Warsaw, strictly speaking it is an anachronism to say that he was born in Poland. Her ancient territories were then still divided politically and militarily in the wake of the Congress of Vienna (1815) between the three partitioning powers: Prussia, Russia and Austria. Hence he was born not within the boundaries of an independent Polish state but in the Imperial Russian province of 'Privislinskiy Kray' (Vistulaland), and was thus a subject of the tsar. Unduly extended discussion of Polish history would be out of place in a musical study; yet some knowledge of events is essential for a proper understanding of the way Lutosławski's life has been repeatedly haunted by powerful and inescapable forces of circumstance.[1] The Second World War and its aftermath left problems for Poland that were finally resolved as late as 1991; but the effect of the First World War on the composer's family was no less great.

His parents both came from cultured families of the Polish *ziemiaństwo* (landed gentry), and his father's family owned estates at and around Drozdowo on the River Narew, a few miles upstream from Łomża, in the Kurpie region north-east of the capital. His mother, a qualified medical doctor, had chosen to give birth at a maternity clinic in the centre of Warsaw (in Moniuszki Street), and afterwards she and her youngest son returned to the Górne Dwór (upper manor) at Drozdowo. Other members of the family lived at Dolne (lower) Drozdowo; a photograph taken when he was about nine shows the composer at his late grandfather's piano in the Dolne Dwór.

Józef Lutosławski, his father (whom the composer resembles), was born at Drozdowo on 28 March 1881, the youngest of six brothers.[2] He studied agricultural science in Zurich, where he met Maria Olszewska, a fellow medical student of his brother Kazimierz. She was born at Kursk in the formerly Polish lands of the Podolian Ukraine on 15 June 1880. They married in early 1904 before moving to London, where Józef continued his scientific studies and where their eldest son, Jerzy, was born in December of the same year.[3] In Poland Józef and four of his brothers, Wincenty, Jan, Kazimierz and Marian, had all been politically involved with Endecja, the National Democracy Party, so while in London, Józef acted as correspondent for the Endecja paper, *Gońca*. After returning to Warsaw in 1905, he continued to involve himself closely with National Democracy politics as one of the editors of *Myśl Polska*. In 1908 he assumed management of the family estates at Drozdowo, where their second son, Henryk, was born in 1909. After the birth of their third and youngest son, Witold, they were to enjoy only a few more months of family life together at Drozdowo before the First World War erupted.

On 3 August 1914 Imperial Germany declared war on Imperial Russia. Initially, the various Lutosławski families remained at Drozdowo, but in May 1915 Hindenburg's forces in East Prussia broke through the Russian defences and began to drive south towards Warsaw. The Lutosławskis had little choice but to leave their home, which lay directly in the path of the advancing army. Only the composer's uncle, Stanisław, remained.

Previous accounts of Lutosławski's life have overlooked the fact that the early years of his childhood were spent not in Warsaw or Drozdowo, or even in Poland, but in Moscow.[4] His family's removal to the east was due not only to their close involvement in the politics of the National Democracy Party, but also to their intimacy with its founder Roman Dmowski (1864–1939). As Dmowski was one of the first delegates to the Imperial Russian *Duma* (Parliament) in 1905, it was natural that he, and the many thousands of other Poles associated with his policy of alignment with tsarist Russia against Germany and Austria, should seek temporary refuge in Moscow during the First World War.[5] Thus the Lutosławskis escaped the occupation which engulfed not only their estates and the Łomża region but also Warsaw, which German forces occupied by 6

August. What they did not know, and could not have foreseen, was that they would find themselves removed from the proverbial 'frying pan' into the fire of revolution.

Dmowski's memorial in St John's Cathedral in Warsaw commemorates him as 'father of the Polish nation' (although 'Polish state' would be more appropriate). During the First World War he served as Chairman of the Polish National Committee, which took the side of the Allied Powers during the conflict, unlike his arch rival Piłsudski, who served for the Central Powers. On 28 June 1919 Dmowski was the Polish signatory to the Treaty of Versailles, which formally established the Republic of Poland as an independent state, albeit with borders that were to remain the subject of dispute during its brief twenty-year existence. He outlined (in English) his views on the European conflict in a lecture given at Cambridge in August 1916, as part of a conference on 'Russia and Poland':

The present war has brought into prominence the name of Poland and the fact of existence of the Polish nation ... It was only after the outbreak of the War, when the Polish problem reappeared ... that questions began to be asked: what was the Polish problem, what was Poland herself, what her frontiers ... and what the role of this nation in central Europe? ... close analysis of the political situation of the whole of Poland revealed ... that the greatest danger threatening the national existence of the Poles came from Germany; for the German view was that ... to assure for themselves their position on the Baltic coast, they must ... look to the future destruction of the Kingdom of Warsaw. That means the total destruction of the Polish nation ... When the Poles realised that political situation, they employed all their force to come to a reconciliation with Russia ... But there was a very great difficulty because ... between the Poles and the Russians there was a sea of blood shed in secular struggles ... if the country is to be saved from German conquest ... Polish civilisation must be given freedom to develop ... The truth is understood by many enlightened and thoughtful men in Russia, and at their head we see the august person of the Russian Emperor ...[6]

As a result of his friendship, not only with Józef Lutosławski, but with his brothers and their families, Dmowski remained a frequent visitor to Drozdowo throughout his life.[7] In 1938, knowing he did not have much longer to live, he chose to spend his last few months with his 'adopted family' at Dolne Drozdowo. In view of the close personal and political ties with Dmowski, it is possibly no mere coincidence that Józef chose the name Roman as the middle, baptismal name of his youngest son.

Lutosławski's earliest childhood memories inevitably date from the period spent in Moscow, and include vivid recollections of his father playing the piano. In later years he was to learn that his father's pianistic accomplishments had been more than those of an amateur. He played many works of Chopin and Beethoven, and had apparently taken private lessons with Eugène d'Albert (1865–1932), possibly during the period of his scientific studies either in London or in Zurich.

For much of the time in Russia, however, his father was not with the family, but was politically and militarily active, organising Polish Legions in preparation for the anticipated counter-offensive that might liberate the Polish territories and lead to the establishment of an independent Poland.[8] According to the strategy of Dmowski and Endecja, Imperial Russia was to be the guarantor of security for this long-awaited Polish state; but the February Revolution of 1917, and the consequent abdication of Tsar Nicholas II on 13 March, put an end to any such plans. Worse was to follow. The October Revolution culminated in the storming by Bolsheviks of Kerensky's Provisional Government headquarters in the Winter Palace at St Petersburg on 6 November. The hurriedly arranged armistice between the new Soviet administration and Germany was confirmed on 5 December, followed on 3 March 1918 by the Treaty of Brest-Litovsk.

Meanwhile, Józef and his brother Marian were at Murmansk, organising the transportation of Polish military forces. This inevitably brought them into conflict with the Bolsheviks. Only weeks before the British and French landings, the two brothers were arrested at Murmansk in April, accused of counter-revolutionary activities and alleged falsification of secret diplomatic documents. After their arrest they were transferred to the notorious Butyrki (Butyrskaya) prison in central Moscow, where Józef occupied himself by writing a strongly nationalist essay, 'Chleb i ojczyzna' ('Bread and Fatherland'), dated 28 May 1918.[9] On 5 September, without being brought to trial, Józef and Marian were taken by Bolsheviks to just outside Moscow, where they were executed by firing squad.

Naturally, the composer's recollections of these years are mostly very hazy, but certain strong images have remained, particularly the painful memory of visiting his father in Butyrki prison shortly before the execution. Lutosławski was only five-and-a-half years old. He does not readily discuss these events, and it has become part of his nature not to dwell on recollections from the past, precisely because so many of his memories are acutely painful.

German occupation of Warsaw ended on 13 November 1918, and the remaining members of the family were then able to return home to

Drozdowo. They found the estates ravaged and the economy of their various agricultural and light industrial enterprises ruined. Without either Józef or Marian to restore order and prosperity, Kazimierz Lutosławski employed a succession of estate managers under whom the lands fell into further decline. Initially Maria Lutosławska chose to stay with her three young sons in Warsaw, where they lived at 21 Marszałkowska Street, near Plac Uni Lubelskiej. Although her position was financially austere, she made the necessary sacrifices to pay for her youngest son to have two years of piano lessons with Helena Hoffman, a well-known teacher in the capital. Thus his musical training began at the age of six.

After his father's death, Lutosławski's aunts, uncles and cousins played an important part in his childhood. It would be foolish, therefore, to underestimate the significance of the cultural, literary, philosophical and artistic background of the family as a whole. Wincenty Lutosławski (1863–1954), Józef's half-brother (their mothers were sisters), was a distinguished (albeit controversial) philosopher who published works in Polish, German, French and English.[10] Wincenty's first wife was the Spanish poet and writer Sophia Pérez Eguia y Casanova (1861–1958). The eldest of their four daughters, Maria, and her husband Mieczysław Niklewicz, remained among Dmowski's closest confidantes until his death.[11] Their second daughter, Izabela, wrote and published an intimate account of Dmowski's friendship with the family.[12] Of Józef's other brothers who survived the war, Jan (1875–1950) was a land economist, while Kazimierz (1880–1924), a doctor of medicine and philosophy, became a priest in 1912 (and a doctor of theology in 1914). Kazimierz was also very active in National Democracy politics, and from 1919 to 1922 served as an elected member of the first post-war Polish Parliament (*Sejm*), as representative of the Podlasie region.[13]

On 14 February 1919 the Soviet Army engaged Polish forces at Bereza Kartuzka in Byelorussia, thus starting the Polish–Soviet War. Drozdowo again found itself in the path of advancing and retreating armies, particularly during the Red Army's drive towards Warsaw in July 1920. In the decisive Battle of Warsaw (13–19 August), the Soviet 15th Army was routed by Polish forces under the command of Piłsudski and Sikorski, and by late August had been driven back across the Narew.[14] The Treaty of Riga, signed on 18 March 1921, ended the Polish–Soviet War, and confirmed the boundaries of 12 October that gave Poland a large slice of Byelorussia. On 21 March 1921 the *Sejm* enacted the 'March Constitution'; the introduction to which was drafted by Father Kazimierz

Lutosławski, who also wrote and administered the oath of allegiance to the new Republic, sworn by the President and Deputies. By this time the family was able to return once more to Drozdowo (yet again ravaged by troop movements), and Lutosławski's piano lessons with Helena Hoffman were discontinued as a result. His mother, however, soon arranged for him to have lessons with a local teacher, under whose guidance he had composed his first fully notated little piano piece by the time he was nine. Running and attempting to rebuild the estates proved to be a mammoth undertaking, and after two years or so Maria Lutosławska surrendered responsibility for these tasks to the succession of estate managers engaged by Kazimierz and returned once more with her sons to Warsaw. In 1924, at the age of eleven, Lutosławski entered the prestigious Stefan Batory *gimnazjum* in Myśliwiecka Street, while continuing his piano studies with a new teacher, Józef Śmidowicz (1888–1962). The most significant musical experience of this period in his childhood was at a concert in Warsaw, where he first heard Szymanowski's Third Symphony, op. 27, 'Song of the Night' (1914–16).[15] Although this musically intoxicating experience had a strong impact on Lutosławski at the time, it would nevertheless be misleading to suggest that the music of Szymanowski determined the development of the young composer's style.

As for the possible similarities with Szymanowski, perhaps they're an echo of my childhood experiences. I first heard Szymanowski's Third Symphony when I was a boy of eleven, and the occasion was a real revelation to me ... Then came a strong reaction against the whole somewhat over-delicate aesthetic of that period, and my work never again showed the direct influence of Szymanowski.[16]

In 1926, at the age of thirteen, Lutosławski began a course of violin lessons with Lidia Kmitowa (1888–1967) which was to last until 1932. During that time he progressed to the stage of playing solo sonatas of Bach, two or three Mozart concertos (with piano), and the Franck Sonata. Meanwhile, the situation in Poland remained volatile, and on 12 May 1926, impatient with the impotence and inefficiency of Poland's fledgeling democracy, Marshal Piłsudski staged the *coup d'état* that began the period of his dictatorship.

Karol Szymanowski (1881–1937) was appointed *Rektor* of the Warsaw Conservatory in February 1927, an appointment he resigned only two years later, frustrated by what he regarded as the provincialism of Warsaw musical life. Also in 1927, Lutosławski entered the Conservatory as a part-time student, while still attending the Stefan Batory *gimnazjum*.

By the following year, however, the combined pressures of schoolwork and the violin made it necessary to suspend his studies at the Conservatory. In the meantime, he had written a *Poème* for piano, on the strength of which he was accepted as a private pupil of Witold Maliszewski, under whose guidance in 1930 he wrote his first publicly performed piece. *Taniec Chimery* (Dance of the Chimera), for piano. His first attempt at an orchestral piece, a Scherzo, also dates from this year.

After passing his final *gimnazjum* examinations in 1931, Lutosławski proceeded to enrol at the University of Warsaw to study mathematics. During the same year he composed incidental music for a dramatisation by Janusz Makarczyk of *Haroun al Rashid*. In 1932, while still maintaining his course of study in mathematics at the university, he formally entered the composition and analysis class at the Conservatory taken by the recently appointed professor of composition, Maliszewski.

Witold Maliszewski (1873–1939) had studied with Rimsky-Korsakov at the St Petersburg Conservatory from 1898 until 1902. During this period he appears to have attended the course on musical form given by Glazunov, and to have absorbed an approach to the psychology and perception of musical structure that Lutosławski recalls as being disseminated as Russian rather than Germanic in origin. In his classes at the Warsaw Conservatory Maliszewski apparently devoted much time to applying this allegedly Russian approach to the analysis of first-movement sonata-form schemes from the Viennese Classical period, including many works of Haydn and Beethoven. The significance of these analyses in relation to Lutosławski's treatment of large-scale forms cannot be over-emphasised. He vividly recalls the content of those classes and is aware of the lasting impression they made:

I attach great importance to playing with the listener's perception. I always reckon with his power of anticipation or thinking about what *could* happen, I always purposely disappoint my listener, surprising him by giving something which he couldn't expect. All those are tricks which I learned mainly from the sonatas of Beethoven. The course in musical forms that was given by my professor of composition, Maliszewski, has remained in my memory for my whole life. In his analyses of the sonatas of Beethoven, he explained the psychological factor in perceiving a form ... To my mind, it is much more to the point to treat perception of music psychologically than just describing the sound phenomena and their order, independently from the perception of them. So I think the psychological approach to form is absolutely essential in my work. All that I really learned then ... To give you an example of how the psychological approach works, I can give you the terminology he used. He used four different words of 'character'; Introductory, Narrative,

Transitional and Concluding. In each large-scale form there is always the use of those four characters ... only in the Narrative is content the most important thing to be perceived, while in all the other three the role of the given section in the form of the music is more important than the content.[17]

This focus of his studies, directed primarily towards issues of form rather than content, structural schemes rather than techniques of pitch organisation, provides an important clue to his subsequent development. Although he later found it necessary to expend much time and compositional effort in redefining his harmonic language, the question of form does not appear to have been as problematic for him.

Time was at such a premium for Lutosławski in those teenage years that he found it difficult to maintain all his various studies, not only of composition and the violin, but also of mathematics. This was partly resolved when he accepted Maliszewski's advice to abandon the violin order to concentrate on the piano. The way was now clear for him to join the conservatory piano class of a newly appointed and highly regarded professor, Jerzy Lefeld (1898–1980). The problem was more fully resolved a year later, in 1933, when he finally made the decision to give up his mathematical studies at Warsaw University so that he could concentrate entirely on music. The most immediate result was his first performance of an orchestral piece: a revised version of a dance from *Haroun al Rashid* was conducted by Józef Oziminski at the Warsaw Philharmonic Hall. Although this event could be regarded as his compositional début, Lutosławski does not acknowledge it as such and prefers this label to be reserved for the Symphonic Variations. In any case, the score of *Haroun al Rashid* did not survive the war. The most significant extant work of these early years, from which we can assess the development of Lutosławski's musical language, is his Sonata for Piano. The score of this piece still exists only in the composer's original manuscript and bears the completion date: 'Warszawa, 29 xii 1934'.

Of Lutosławski's student works the Piano Sonata reveals most clearly his feeling for harmony, predilection for exploiting several levels of sonority, and an attachment to the sound world of Debussy and Ravel. The three-movement fast–slow–fast scheme lasts a substantial twenty-four minutes in performance; nine, six and nine minutes, respectively, are the composer's own performance timings marked in the autograph score. The architecture is defined as much by management of tonal relationships as by thematic features; these centre around B♭ minor and D♭ major in the first and third movements, and F minor in the second. The first movement, cast in classically proportioned sonata form, contains many passages that illustrate how even at this early stage in his career, Lutosławski was able to succeed, pianistically, in superimposing several levels of sonority that suggest orchestral thinking. Such effects occur in bars 216–21 during a gesturally expansive passage that leads towards the end of the recapitulation (Ex. 1 : 1). From bar 217 there are four layers: two melodic parts, in canon, are played by the right hand; while the left hand supplies a low A♭ in the bass, and oscillating chords in the tenor register. There are also some harmonic features that can be found in the composer's later musical vocabulary; for example, the major/minor four-note chord played by the left hand on the first, third and fifth quavers of bar 218 (its triadic ambivalence resulting from the presence of both major and minor thirds). The significance of this and other types of four-note chord configuration will be considered fully in Chapter 3 (see Ex. 3 : 4).

EX. 1 : 1   Piano Sonata, first movement, bars 216–21

There are some obvious similarities with the Sonatine of Ravel, particularly in the pianistic figurations and general harmonic colour of the opening. One is also reminded of Debussy's *Suite bergamasque*; both the five-flat key-signature and a propensity for chromatically descending bass lines evoke strong aural connections with *Clair de lune*. There are also some distant echoes of Rakhmaninov; but surprisingly, in view of Lutosławski's own experience as a pianist, there is no obvious influence from Chopin, either in pianism or in harmony. Also surprising, in view of his later harmonic style, is the absence of Stravinskian harmony made from superimposed chords. Neither do there appear to be any strong traces of Szymanowski. If one is to indulge in the game of spotting (or imagining) influences, it is important to balance the exercise by registering the significance of their absence as well as their presence:

> In my youth, when I composed my first works, I was surrounded by a world of 'violated tonality'. In other words, tonal music with false notes, such as early Hindemith, or some of the works of Les Six. That is what I found to have no future ... alien to my nature, for I longed for order. I tried to create order in my very first compositions, but that was of course very difficult in that period of my life. Perhaps not a tonal order, yet some kind of order.[18]

Lutosławski performed his Piano Sonata during 1935 at both Riga and Wilno (Vilnius) Conservatories, in student exchange concerts with the Warsaw Academy. In Riga he had his one and only meeting with Szymanowski, a brief but none the less historic encounter between the two most influential figures in Polish music of the twentieth century. A few months later, in 1936, Lutosławski received his Piano Diploma from Warsaw Conservatory after performing the following final recital and concerto programmes:[19]

Recital:	J. S. Bach	Prelude and Fugue in D major, BWV 874
	Mozart	Sonata in A Minor, K.310
	Schumann	Toccata, op. 7
	Liszt	Paganini Caprice in A minor
	Chopin	Study in C♯ minor, op. 10 no. 4
	Chopin	Study in C♯ minor, op. 25 no. 7
	Chopin	Ballade no. 4 in F minor, op. 52
	Debussy	*Reflêts dans l'eau*, from *Images*, Book I
	Maliszewski	Dance, from the ballet *Syrena*
Concertos:	Beethoven	Piano Concerto no. 4 in G major, op. 58
	Prokofiev	Variations from Piano Concerto no. 3

During the same year he completed an orchestral Double Fugue and a Prelude and Aria for piano, both for his forthcoming portfolio submission, and began work on the Symphonic Variations. In 1935–6 he experimented with musical montage for three short films produced by the

Institut Spraw Społeczych (Institute for Social Affairs), two of which were directed by Eugeniusz Cękalski (*Gore* and *Zwarcie*), and one by Stefan and Franciszka Themerson (*Uwaga*). He was awarded his Composition Diploma in 1937, on submission of two fragments of a requiem, *Requiem aeternam* and *Lacrimosa*, of which only the latter survives. Then he began a year of military service, training in signals and radio communications at the officer training school at Zegrze near Warsaw. Good memory for rhythmic patterns, and a pianist's manual dexterity enabled him to achieve fast speeds in transmitting morse code, skills which would come into their own during the September Campaign of 1939.

Lutosławski gave the first broadcast performance of his Piano Sonata on Polish Radio in 1938. He also began a set of pieces making use of folk music from the Kurpie region near Drozdowo: *Suita Kurpiowska* (Kurpian Suite). It is important to note that he was already attempting to find a way of combining elements of folk material with his own emerging language before the war. Accounts of his career can give a misleading impression, by implying that his use of folk music in functional pieces composed after the war represented a gesture towards Stalinist socialist-realism. Work on the Suite was interrupted, first by military service, then by the war, after which it was abandoned. He did not, however, abandon the general idea of using such material, which can be detected in the highly effective score for the 1946 film, *Suita Warszaswska*, and later in the Little Suite of 1951.

While 1938 also saw the première of *Lacrimosa*, a more significant signpost for his compositional development came with the completion of the Symphonic Variations. Like many of his later orchestral works, the instrumental forces required are large but not unusual: triple woodwind and brass, four horns, percussion, harp and strings. The ten-bar theme is simple and tonal (Ex. 1 : 2a), and is followed by variations that unfold seamlessly to generate a nine-minute time-span without obvious structural subdivisions. The variation principles are primarily melodic, motivic and rhythmic, and exploit instrumental colouring rather than harmonic transformation. Stravinskian superimposition of chords and motoric ostinato patterns are much in evidence, and the influence of his early ballets is clear. Although the sound world of *Petrushka* permeates the score, there are equally strong suggestions of *Le chant du rossignol* (Song of the Nightingale), particularly in the *adagio* section (bars 152–77) which features a flute solo (Ex. 1 : 2b) derived from the first four bars of the theme, accompanied by celesta, piano, and the texture of strings playing *sul ponticello*.

EX. 1 : 2 Symphonic Variations: a) theme, bars 1–11; b) variation 6, bars 155–60

Lutosławski's liking for woodwind counterpoint, particularly the single- and double-reed sound of clarinets, oboes and bassoons in various combinations, can be traced throughout his career. In the Symphonic Variations an imitative passage for two oboes and piccolo clarinet (from bar 205) anticipates the canonic technique that was to become a significant feature of the First Symphony.

Harmonically, a clear distinction is made between chords having the open sonority of perfect fifths in the lowest register, and those with the more unstable sound of tritones placed at the bottom, such as the chord which underpins the beginning of the first variation (Lutosławski acknowledges that this chord contains some vestige of harmonic influence from Szymanowski, even though his general aesthetic was apparently already alien at this stage). Contrast between the sonority of perfect fifth and tritone can also be detected in the First Symphony (see Ex. 2 : 2b) and continues to influence his choice of chords, particularly in the twelve-note chord-aggregates he has developed and exploited since 1957 (see Ex. 3 : 5). Other details attract one's attention; for example, the passage in bars 188–9 that hints at the converging progression of chord-aggregates later used in the Apogeum of *Musique funèbre*. Here the top line descends sequentially in minor thirds, while the low parts rise by semitones. Although the chordal convergence is not followed through, it none the less demonstrates the composer's fondness for a harmonic procedure often found in later works.

The Symphonic Variations received their first performance in a broadcast by Polish Radio from Warsaw in April 1939; the first concert performance was given at the Wawel Festival in Kraków on 17 June by the Polish Radio Symphony Orchestra, conducted by Grzegorz Fitelberg. By this time, political tensions had grown to fever pitch, and Lutosławski was among those mobilised during the summer. It had previously been his intention to continue compositional studies in Paris, possibly with Nadia

Boulanger (to whom four of the Five Songs of 1957 were later dedicated). He was aware of the need to continue developing his own, more personal language, and had not envisaged ending his studies so soon. Not for the first time in his life events affecting the destiny of Poland were to decide the matter.

Meanwhile, Roman Dmowski had died at Dolne Drozdowo on 2 January 1939, surrounded by those he referred to as his 'adopted family'. After a funeral service at Drozdowo, his body was transported ceremonially to Warsaw where he was buried with full state honours in Bródno cemetery. Dmowski's early political strategy for the future of Poland, formulated before the First World War, had been for a solution that would stop short of complete independence, forgoing sovereignty for the sake of alignment with Imperial Russia. His aim had been to safeguard against German territorial expansion. The two revolutions of 1917 put an end to such schemes, but had he lived to witness the catastrophic events of September 1939, some essence of his strategy might have been vindicated.

The fate of the short-lived Polish Republic was sealed by the infamous Secret Protocol contained within the Nazi–Soviet Non-Aggression Pact of 23 August 1939. Accordingly, Germany invaded western Poland and the Polish Corridor on 1 September while unleashing the Blitzkrieg, particularly on Warsaw. On the outbreak of hostilities Lutosławski was an Officer Cadet (*Sierżant Podchorąży*) commanding the signals and radio unit of the Polish First Army at Kraków. Driven back by the speed of the German offensive, the First Army had withdrawn to a position near Lublin by the time he was eventually taken prisoner later that month. Throughout the September Campaign, his signals unit had been the only communications link between the First Army, the neighbouring army groups and Polish Central Command. Observing a strategy often dubbed the 'hyena principle', the Red Army invaded eastern Poland on 17 September, prompting Winston Churchill's memorable observation that 'Russia is a riddle wrapped in a mystery inside an enigma'. A Nazi–Soviet convention of 28 September confirmed the division and dual occupation of the country, establishing *de facto* the 'Seventh Partition' of Poland. Later, the composer was to hear that his mother had been left alone at Górne Drozdowo, now just on the Soviet side of the demarcation line; fortunately, some friends were later able to spirit her to the comparative safety of occupied Warsaw. In less than two years, Drozdowo was again to be caught on the front line. After Hitler launched 'Operation

Barbarossa' on 22 June 1941, beginning his thrust into the Soviet zone of occupied Poland and his drive deep into the Soviet Union itself, Drozdowo was incorporated within the new Nazi administrative district centred on Białystok.

In retrospect, it is fortunate that, in 1939, Lutosławski was captured by the *Wehrmacht* rather than the Red Army; otherwise he would not have survived. His brother Henryk, already commissioned as an officer in the Polish reserves, suffered the worse fate. He did not perish with the 15,000 Polish officers murdered by the Soviets, 4,321 of whom were later exhumed from the mass graves in Katyń Forest, but was among those transported deep inside the arctic circle to the 'Gulag Archipelago' labour camps in the Kolyma region of north-eastern Siberia, where they were forced to mine for gold. There, on 7 October 1940, he died of typhoid, hunger and exhaustion. A moving account of his death was published in London (in Polish) after the war, by a fellow prisoner who managed to survive until the 'amnesty' declared in 1941. In order to provide a measure of protective anonymity for those still in Poland, the author chose partially to conceal Henryk's identity by altering the surname to 'Sierosławski'.[20]

After only eight days in German captivity Lutosławski managed to escape. Unlike the commissioned officers, who were immediately transported to prisoner-of-war camps in Germany, officer cadets were grouped with other non-commissioned ranks and taken on foot to their (as yet unknown) places of confinement. During their march, he escaped through woods with several members of his platoon. Together they proceeded to walk the 400 kilometres back to Warsaw, a journey that had to be made across country and under extremely hazardous conditions. They reached their destination by late October. During the dark and dangerous years of Nazi occupation, Lutosławski maintained a precarious existence, supporting himself and his mother by playing in clandestine concerts and performing at various cafés in the capital, initially with a cabaret group, then in a piano duo with fellow composer, Andrzej Panufnik:

It didn't begin with Panufnik. It began much less interestingly, when I sought some job to earn a living. I came across a group of cabaret singers; a group of four gentlemen who were famous before the war. Their boss, a pianist and composer who was the originator of the group, was not in Poland but abroad. So they looked for someone to revive the ensemble. I don't remember in what way they found me, but they proposed that I should take his place. So I had to make some arrangements for four male voices of cabaret songs, and also to accompany them. I also accompanied some soloists of the cabaret genre. We performed in the café *Ziemiańska* on Mazowiecka [street]. Before the war it was a very famous café where the cream of Polish literature and poetry met. We performed there for a few months. It was just on the opposite side to *Aria*, the first café in which I played with Panufnik. In early 1940 Panufnik proposed that we form a duo. Of course, it was much better for me as a job, because I was not compelled to play exclusively light music. For instance, our repertoire of over two hundred arrangements contained organ toccatas of Bach, waltzes of Brahms and Schubert, ballet music of Tchaikovsky and so on. The only original arrangement for two pianos that we played was Debussy's *Prélude à l'après-midi d'un faune*. First we played in *Aria* then in *U Aktorek*, and finally in *Sztuka i Moda* [*SiM*]. *U Aktorek* was where the Swiss embassy now is, on the corner of Aleje Ujazdowskie and Piękna [the Ślesiński Palace]. The café was on the first floor. *SiM* was almost in the same place where the Victoria Hotel now stands, on Plac Saski [Plac Zwycięstwa]. We finished in *SiM* because it was already 1944, but we had played pretty long there. Beginning with *Aria*, then *U Aktorek* and *SiM* there were also some soloists . . . the violinist Eugenia Umińska for instance . . . played Szymanowski's Second Concerto with us. We also made some arrangements for the famous soprano, Ewa Bandrowska-Turska.[21]

During the war Lutosławski met his future wife, Danuta, sister of the writer Stanisław Dygat (1914–78) and daughter of the prominent architect Antoni Dygat (1886–1949). Panufnik's later account of these events suggests that he introduced Lutosławski to both Dygat and his sister;[22] but Lutosławski's recollection differs.

I had known her brother earlier. Before the war he worked a lot with film-makers . . . I had the occasion to write some music for some avant-garde films,[23] and in those circles I met Stanisław Dygat. After the war he was a very famous novelist. . . . He was a man very sensitive to music and a great music lover. He used to come to *Aria* to listen to our duo. He knew both Panufnik and me before the war. One day, he decided to bring Danuta to let her hear us.[24]

The Two Studies for piano were composed over several months in 1940–41, and provide an insight into his musical thinking during this difficult time. Although he completed only two pieces, they were originally intended to form part of a longer set of studies, modelled on the example of Chopin. Hence the arpeggiated patterns of the first piece allude to Chopin's C major Study, op. 10 no. 1. This gestural reference apart, Lutosławski did not model either his harmonic or melodic language on that of his composer compatriot. As well as being studies in pianistic technique they are studies in composition. Just as some of Debussy's *Etudes* (dedicated to the memory of Chopin) focus on certain intervals, so Lutosławski concentrates on a particular interval or combination of two intervals. The second study, for example, continually emphasises the juxtaposition and alternation of perfect fourths and perfect fifths, moving chromatically. As compositional studies they helped him to develop the language and techniques for his First Symphony, which he began to sketch in 1941. As pianistic studies they not only testify to his considerable youthful prowess at the keyboard, but also acknowledge and extend a tradition that links his work with that of Chopin and Debussy.

The set of Variations on a Theme of Paganini, for two pianos, also written in 1941, has become one of Lutosławski's best-known and most frequently performed pieces. The essential features of the variations are not original to Lutosławski, however, but are based on a transcription of Paganini's own variations from the Caprice no. 24 for solo violin. Even so, the degree of compositional craftsmanship shown by Lutosławski in translating them into idiomatic pianism reveals his understanding both of the piano and the violin. In 1978 he made a revised and slightly extended version of the piece for solo piano and orchestra. Whereas in the original, the melodic and harmonic material is continually interchanged between the two players, for the orchestral version Lutosławski found it necessary to extend some of the variations to allow for a similar interchange between the soloist and orchestra. Of the 200 or so pieces and arrangements made for performance with Panufnik, only the 'Paganini' Variations were to survive the occupation and the final conflagration of 1944.

In response to encouragement from the Allies, on 1 August 1944 the Polish patriots who made up the Armia Krajowa (AK, 'Home Army', as opposed to AL, the much smaller, Soviet-backed Armia Ludowa, 'People's Army'), launched the Warsaw Uprising. Over the ensuing sixty-three days of valiant resistance, the remaining population of the already blitzed city was subjected once more to the full force of the Nazi war-machine, while the supposedly 'liberating' Soviet Red Army maintained its infamously cynical, passive role encamped within the city limits on the east bank of the River Vistula. Three days before the beginning of the Uprising, Lutosławski and his mother had left the city to seek refuge at Komorów, eighteen kilometres south-west of Warsaw, where they stayed with a maternal aunt and her husband, Janina and Józef Zaporski. In the heat and haste of the moment, unable to take with them more than literally a handful of belongings, Lutosławski managed to save only his sketches for the First Symphony, a few student works, the Two Studies, and the 'Paganini' Variations. All the other scores were left in Warsaw where they subsequently perished by fire.

Some of the time spent in Komorów was devoted to continuing the preliminary work for the First Symphony, which included a series of contrapuntal studies (mostly for woodwind instruments) that Lutosławski had begun in 1943. Most are canonic (including nine Canons for three clarinets[25] and ten Canons for two clarinets), some are not (ten Interludes for oboe and bassoon). There is also a collection of twenty-one canons in four parts notated in short score, with no instrumentation specified (divided into two sets, with ten canons in the first and eleven in the second).[26] The seventh of the Interludes for oboe and bassoon (Ex. 1 : 3a) plays with certain chromatic twists in the upper line, often sequentially linked. This reveals an approach to melodic shaping that relates not only to the First Symphony but can also be found in some of Lutosławski's later works, for example in the Largo theme from the slow movement of the Piano Concerto (see Ex. 8 : 4). By far the most obvious example, however, of material from these pieces being transplanted elsewhere occurs with the tenth of the Canons for two clarinets (see Ex. 2 : 6a) which bears a striking resemblance to the parodied march theme in the slow movement of the First Symphony (see Ex. 2 : 6b).

The set of nine Canons for three clarinets provides a partial chronicle of the extraordinary life shared by mother and son in Komorów during the late autumn of 1944. As Lutosławski completed each little piece on the

EX. 1 : 3   a) Interlude no. 7 for oboe and bassoon, bars 1–5;   b) Canon no. 5 for three clarinets, bars 1–5;   c) Canon no. 6 for three clarinets, bars 1–6.

few scraps of manuscript paper left, they were passed to his mother who then copied them into a tiny six-stave pocket manuscript book that the composer still has in his collection of autograph scores and sketches. After each canon there is a date: the first was composed on 20 October and the last was completed on 4 November. The fifth (Ex. 1 : 3b), dated 30 October, opens with an angular, disjunct line emphasising a minor ninth. The first five notes are drawn from a three-note cell of adjacent semitones which is thoroughly characteristic of Lutosławski's music, not only of his early works (note that the entry points of the three parts also correspond to the notes of this cell – C–C♯–D). The sixth canon (Ex. 1 : 3c), dated 31 October, also exploits similar three-note cells, but treated as a motoric device to achieve perpetual rhythmic activity in fast quavers.

It may seem bizarre to picture Lutosławski composing canonic miniatures while surrounded by death and destruction. Yet such abstract activity can provide a vital mechanism of intellectual and emotional protection, as the mind turns inward in order to block out the horror and distress of external events. Lutosławski's life has passed through several such episodes, which he has endured only by maintaining the intellectual discipline, emotional control, and compositional rigour which have insulated and preserved his inner creative world.

On 2 October, General Bór-Komorowski formally capitulated the remnants of the Armia Krajowa to the *Wehrmacht*, whereupon the entire civilian population of Warsaw was evacuated and the final phase of destruction implemented, watched by the Red Army from across the river. By 12 January, the Second Byelorussian Front was established along the River Narew. As a result the estates at Drozdowo were laid waste and the composer's home, the Górne Dwór, was razed to the ground. Soviet troops did not try to cross the Vistula until 17 January 1945. When they entered what had been a city there was nothing and nobody left to 'liberate'. The fate of Poland in the post-war era was sealed at the Yalta Conference in February. On 21 April a Polish–Soviet 'Treaty of Friendship, Mutual Aid and Co-operation' was signed, valid for twenty years (renewed in 1965 and 1985 for further twenty-year periods). A formal declaration of peace was made on 9 May, by which time Lutosławski could return with his mother from Komorów to the smouldering rubble and ruins of the utterly devastated capital.

2
Functional Music and Formalism
(1945–1956)

Survival in the difficult political climate of post-war Poland required Lutosławski to divide his work into two separate, parallel strands of compositional activity. The work he regards as 'serious' was centred on the First Symphony, which he eventually completed in 1947. Meanwhile he supported himself and his family by writing what he calls 'functional' music. The term invites comparison with Hindemith's concept of *Gebrauchsmusik*, but there is the important distinction that Lutosławski was obliged to engage in this form of professional activity for purely practical and financial reasons, rather than ideological or philosophical ones. Lack of familiarity with the bulk of his work from the post-war years has led to a distorted 'received opinion', outside Poland, that his musical output has been relatively small. Yet if one adds to his list of major works composed since 1960 the enormous quantity of different types of functional music composed prior to that date, including incidental music for the theatre, music for radio plays, film scores, many songs, and simple pieces based on folk material, the overall picture is entirely transformed and received opinion is confounded.

Immediately after the war, his first new piece to be performed was a three-movement Trio for oboe, clarinet and bassoon, related to the various Canons and Interludes of 1943–4. It was played at a Festival of New Music in Kraków, held there to coincide with the first Congress of the new Związek Kompozytorów Polskich (ZKP – Union of Polish Composers) from 29 August to 2 September. Lutosławski was elected to the offices of ZKP secretary and treasurer, honorary positions he was to hold until the political and cultural deterioration of 1948.

So soon after the end of hostilities, Warsaw was still in no condition to host such gatherings. During the initial period of rebuilding, not only of the capital but of the state as a whole, documentary films were made to record this regeneration; for two of these Lutosławski composed scores.[1] *Odrą do Bałtyku* (Along the Oder to the Baltic) was made in late 1945. It shows the newly acquired (former German) industrial territories of *Śląsk* (Silesia), and traces the ancient trade route along the River Oder to the Baltic port of Szczecin (Stettin). Its prime purpose appears to have been to clarify public perception of Poland's new western border with the then East Germany and Czechoslovakia along the Oder–Neisse line. Unfortunately, the music is swamped by the superimposition of propagandist narration.

Suita Warszawska (Warsaw Suite) was made in 1946 and rises well above the level of mere propaganda material, presenting an historically valuable record of the devastated capital and the early stages of its rebuilding. Structurally, the twenty-minute symphonic score unfolds according to the film's three sections (five, six and nine minutes, respectively). *Klęska* (Disaster) begins with a desolate moonscape of smouldering ruins, devoid of human inhabitants (only stray dogs remain). In *Powrót do Zycie* (Return to life) people are seen gradually returning to the city during the early spring of 1945 as the music becomes more active and warmer. Poignant, symbolic images among the ruins include a one-legged man on crutches slowly making his way through the rubble; another, showing an old man playing the fiddle, is literally represented in the score. Musically the most original is the final section, *Wiosna Warszawska* (Warsaw spring), particularly in the colourful orchestrations and modernist textures that accompany images of trees in blossom. Stylistically there are similarities with the First Symphony and the Little Suite, and some features, such as the treatment of flutes and celesta, that anticipate the Concerto for Orchestra. It is easy to view documentary material of the post-war period with cynicism, but one should remember that the task facing Varsovians was truly horrendous, and there was a genuinely heroic story to be told. The musical result is far more satisfactory than the Silesian film, largely because of the absence of spoken commentary. Dramatically, it succeeds through the powerful conjunction of memorable visual images and music.

On 26 October 1946 Lutosławski married Maria Danuta Bogusławska (née Dygat). Theirs was destined to be an exceptionally happy marriage and a highly effective working partnership; her meticulous drafting can be seen in most of the scores that are reproduced from hand-drawn transparencies. Graphic skills came naturally to the daughter of the well-known architect Antoni Dygat (1886–1949), but her own architectural studies at Warsaw Polytechnic were interrupted by marriage to an architect, Jan Bogusławski,[2] and the birth of their son, Marcin, who is also an architect and now lives in Oslo. As a result of his marriage, Lutosławski added to the responsibilities of (surviving) son those of husband and stepfather.

Immediately after the war there was not yet an official requirement for composers in Poland to write according to the Stalinist principles of socialist-realism. So when Lutosławski embarked upon his earliest folk-based pieces, he was returning to plans made before the war, rather than responding to sinister political influences. If politics are to be taken as a background for understanding the use of folk material in the brief post-war honeymoon period, before the establishment of a Soviet-style socialist state in 1947, it should be remembered that all manifestations of Polish national culture, including the music of Chopin, had been suppressed during the Nazi occupation. Under these circumstances, it is natural that there was a spontaneous and entirely sincere affirmation of national identity expressed in many ways, including music.

Lutosławski composed his set of twelve *Melodie Ludowe* (Folk Melodies) for piano in 1945, fulfilling a commission from the new state-owned music publishing house based in Kraków, Polskie Wydawnictwo Muzyczne (PWM).[3] Unlike Bartók, whose folk materials were gathered through his own ethno-musicological travels and research, Lutosławski drew upon tunes gathered by others, in this case a collection by Jerzy Olszewski.[4] The first public performance was given in Kraków by Zbigniew Drzewiecki in 1947, but they were not intended as concert works. Their true value was recognised through their adoption as prescribed texts for Poland's specialist music schools; separate decrees of 24 December 1958, 21 December 1959, and 31 October 1961, from the Ministry of Culture, ensured that several generations of young Polish musicians would learn to play the *Melodie Ludowe* as an integral part of their studies.

Several different areas of Poland are represented by the twelve pieces. The first, *Ach, mój Jasieńko* (O, my Johnny), uses a tune from Łowicz in the western region of Mazovia. As the title of the second piece makes explicit, *Hej, od Krakowa jadę* (Hey, I come from Kraków), its tune is from the ancient capital. The third and fourth pieces, *Jest drożyna, jest* (There is a path, there is), and *Pastereczka* (The little shepherdess), both use melodies from the Podlasie region due east of the modern capital. The tunes of the fifth and sixth pieces originate from the town and area of Sieradz in Wielko Polska('Great Poland'): *Na jabłoni jabłko wisi* (An apple hangs on the apple tree), and *Od Sieradza płynie rzeka* (A river flows from Sieradz). Hence the title of the sixth refers to the River Warta, which continues its journey to Poznań and later forms a tributary of the Oder. The origin of the seventh piece, *Panie Michale* (Master Michael), relates to the composer's own childhood at Drozdowo; it is a waltz from the widely forested Kurpie region, an area defined by the River Narew and its various tributaries. The eighth piece, *W polu lipieńka* (The lime tree in the field), takes its tune from the Mazurian lake district in the north-east of Poland, bordering on the territories of East Prussia (which in 1946 were within the Soviet Union). Mazuria has indirectly given us the Mazurka, but the piece in question uses a melody typical of the region rather than the more famous dance rhythm. The last four pieces are all dances from Silesia: *Zalotny* (Flirting), *Gaik* (The grove), *Gąsior* (The gander), and *Rektor* (The schoolmaster).

Certain recurring features can be identified as characteristic of the composer's treatment of these and other simple, tonal melodies: Bartókian chromatic counterpoints which alternate and interlock minor thirds with semitones and tones; supporting harmony that opposes, either by semitone or tritone, the chord function implied by the tune; chord substitution a third (minor or major) below the implied tonal function; and the frequent disposition of three harmonic layers, consisting of the tune at the top, chromatic part(s) in the middle, and the clear, open sonority of a perfect fifth at the bottom. Even though they are unpretentious little pieces, composed to fulfil a limited function, it would be a mistake to overlook those hallmarks of Lutosławski's technique that can be identified in the *Melodie Ludowe* and in the accompaniments to his Twenty Carols.

As far as is known, Christmas songs were first introduced to Poland by Franciscan monks in the thirteenth century.[5] These examples of nativity celebration were Latin church songs rather than the secular folksongs we tend to associate with yuletide; but even from this early stage, the Franciscans cultivated stories that emphasised the manger as the focal point for identifying with the humble birth of Christ. The earliest surviving sources of Latin texts date from the fifteenth century, but they do not contain the melodies, which were passed down through an aural rather than written tradition. By the sixteenth century, widespread popularity of Christmas songs had led to increasing secularisation, with texts in the vernacular, improvised instrumental accompaniments, and tunes that owed more to folk music than the church. The addition of archetypal pastoral characters to the stories, with slavonic rather than biblical names (e.g. Bartos and Kuba), led to a great increase in their popularity.

For his set of *Dwadzieście Kolęd* (Twenty Carols), Lutosławski took traditional texts and melodies from several collections gathered during the nineteenth century by Michał Mioduszewski and Oskar Kolberg.[6] His settings for voice and piano were made in 1946, in response to a commission from PWM, and treat the traditional, diatonic melodies with accompaniments which complement rather than correspond to their harmonic implications. As in the *Melodie Ludowe*, a pervading harmonic principle is the chromatic interchange of major and minor thirds, which modifies and confuses the diatonic functions without destroying them. The high degree of compositional ingenuity and invention shown in these accompaniments places them more on the level of miniature studies than mere arrangements. Close inspection of individual carols reveals a sophistication of harmony behind their apparent simplicity, which brings to mind Ravel's axiom: 'Complexe, mais pas compliqué'.

Example 2 : 1 shows extracts from six of the Carols (in short score) and illustrates techniques that can be found in other functional works of the period up to the Concerto for Orchestra, and in some cases beyond. *Anioł pasterzom mówił* (Ex. 2 : 1a) has a chord progression rising by semitones in the middle register; the pedal note, on G, is placed a tritone away from where one would expect it to be, on D♭, the dominant; the functional progression of the piano (ii⁷–IV⁹–I) complements but does not strictly correspond to the implied functions of the tune. *Gdy się Chrystus rodzi* (Ex. 2 : 1b) does employ an obvious dominant pedal (on A♭) but accompanied by a curling pattern of major thirds in the middle register; the cadence functions of the harmony in this case almost correspond to those of the melody (except for the substitution of chord ii⁹ in place of the more obvious Ic). *Przybieżeli do Betlejem* (Ex. 2 : 1c) shows the substitution of mediant and submediant chords in place of the tonic: beginning on a chord of C major (the flat submediant), it then moves through G♯ major (the mediant major) before reaching the tonic (E major). *Północ już była* (Ex. 2 : 1d) uses a chromatic progression of minor thirds rising by semitones in the middle register. Where the tune repeats, from bar 13, the bass drops to the submediant, thus substituting chord vi⁷ for I; this downward move of a third used to harmonise melodic repetition can be found frequently in Bartók's folk-music pieces. *Hola hola, pasterze z pola!* (Ex. 2 : 1e) is propelled by a motoric staccato line, twisting around semitones, major seconds and minor thirds, above which there is a middle part of chromatically descending minor thirds. *A cóż z tą dzieciną?* (Ex. 2 : 1f) is a particularly interesting setting as it provides an early illustration of Lutosławski pairing two classes of interval in order to generate a distinctive kind of horizontal line. Here this technique is applied to the middle

EX. 2 : 1   Carols: a) *Anioł pasterzom mówił*, bars 10–13;   b) *Gdy się Chrystus rodzi*, bars 13–20;   c) *Przybieżeli do Betlejem*, bars 1–3;   d) *Północ już była*, bars 5–10;   e) *Hola, hola, pasterze z pola!* bars 5–8;   f) *A cóż z tą dzieciną?* bars 3–6

part which is woven from major thirds and semitones. Elsewhere in the Carols and the *Melodie Ludowe* one can find the more common pairing of semitones and minor thirds. Such patterns were undoubtedly borrowed from Bartók, but their significance is not merely that of an oblique stylistic reference. The principle of horizontal interval pairing that Lutosławski developed while working on these functional pieces was to become one of the most crucial elements of his compositional technique (see Chapter 3 and Table 5).

Unfortunately, the Carols are little known outside Poland. This is mostly because of the difficulty of pronouncing the Polish texts, but is also because the settings were conceived as a collection of separate pieces for publication rather than as a cycle for professional performance. In 1985 the composer agreed to orchestrate seventeen carols from the collection, which were performed (in Polish) in December of that year by the London Sinfonietta and Chorus. In order to facilitate their performance outside Poland rhyming English translations of verses selected (by the composer) from the original Polish texts were then prepared (by the present author), and the complete orchestral version of all twenty Carols was first performed by the Scottish Chamber Orchestra and Chorus in December 1990.[7]

Symphony no. 1

Lutosławski took six years to complete his First Symphony. While many of his works have undergone a long gestation period (e.g. the Concerto for Orchestra 1950–54, *Musique funèbre* 1954–8 and others), in this case the reasons were entirely exceptional and external. Since it was begun in 1941 during the Nazi occupation of Warsaw, at a time when there was no prospect whatsoever of it being performed, one may marvel that it was planned at all. This should not be misinterpreted as optimism on the composer's part about the likely outcome of the conflict, but rather demonstrates his determination to fulfil an inner need by confronting the problems of large-scale symphonic form in spite of the conditions around him.

Structurally, the symphony follows the four-movement plan of the Classical tradition, but this alone does not justify a 'neo-Classical' label. One should at least distinguish between neo-Classicism of style and that of form, as they do not necessarily go together. Lutosławski's orchestral forces are those of the late Romantic, rather than the Classical, era. Yet it

would be equally misleading to label the work as neo-Romantic, a notion
that remains anathema to his musical aesthetic.

EX. 2 : 2   a) Symphony no. 1, first movement, opening 8-note chord;
b) Symphony no. 1, first movement, selected chords

The opening gesture is a *fortissimo* eight-note chord that leads to an
emphatic chord of D major (with added eleventh) in the third bar. The
interval structure of this harmony deserves close inspection (Ex. 2 : 2a), as
it reveals Lutosławski's practice of superimposing four-note chords, thus
anticipating the type of chord-aggregate structures he has used since 1957
(see Chapter 3). Essentially a Stravinskian pianistic procedure, here the
harmony results from the superimposition of two similar four-note chord
configurations placed a minor ninth apart, each of which supplies a
half-diminished-seventh chord: C♯–E–G–B and D–F–A♭–C. The
aggregate of these chords is characterised by the adjacent use of only two
kinds of interval: major and minor thirds. The same chord reappears at
the beginning of the recapitulation from bars 109–12.[8] Another harmonic
feature worth noting is the contrast between extended chords with either
a perfect fifth or a tritone placed strategically in the lowest register (Ex.
2 : 2b). The former can be found in bars 3,6,7,9,10 and 109, while the
latter occur in bars 15,40,45 and 134.

EX. 2 : 3   Symphony no. 1, first movement, second theme in canon, bars 32–7

The first movement is in clear sonata form and bustles with rhythmic
energy generated by motoric motifs and a brisk harmonic rhythm. The
second subject has a type of melodic line where minor thirds, minor
sevenths and perfect fifths combine to emphasise angular minor ninths.
First appearing in the violins between bars 32 and 38, with a canonic

26

complement in the lower strings (Ex. 2 : 3), it reappears between bars 95 and 108, and again in bars 125–33, where the canon is between horns and violins. The interval structure of this theme can be compared with the expansive string line that begins at Fig. 86 in the Third Symphony (see Ex. 6 : 10).

EX. 2 : 4   Symphony no. 1, canonic treatment of first theme, bars 58–61

Chromatic transformation of the first theme begins the compact development section (Figs. 13–25). The theme had originally been announced by solo trumpet at Fig. 1, and here it is played in canon between two flutes and piccolo up to Fig. 16. The melodic transformation is entirely typical of Lutosławski and reveals his predilection for twisting chromatic lines produced by manipulating three-note cells of interlocking tone and semitone (Ex. 2 : 4).

EX. 2 : 5   Symphony no. 1, second movement, bars 1–12

While the first movement recalls the Symphonic Variations through the shared influence of early Stravinsky, the second contains allusions to the music of three other composers who influenced Lutosławski at that time: Bartók, Roussel and Prokofiev. It opens with a bass line (Ex. 2 : 5) that suggests the chromatic stealth of the first movement of Bartók's Music for Strings, Percussion and Celesta; the subsequent canonic treatment of this line reinforces the connection. (Similar chromaticism can be found in the accompaniment of the carol *Hej, hej, lelija Panna Maryja*, where it is used to generate an ostinato in the middle part.) The last three bars of the opening nine-bar horn solo contain a repeated motif emphasising two falling tritones (E–B♭; F–B), in which Lutosławski himself acknowledges some analogy to the slow movement of Roussel's Third Symphony (Ex. 2 : 5 provides a reduction into short score of bars 1–12). Later, from bar 95, the movement builds towards its *fortissimo* climax (at bar 113) by continual and intensified repetition of the same motif. A corresponding motif in the slow movement of Roussel's Third Symphony fulfils an equivalent function; first introduced towards the end of the first theme (bars 22–3), it is also repeated and intensified (bars 95–102) in the passage leading to the climax of the movement (at bar 110). Hence Lutosławski's allusion to Roussel is not merely melodic and harmonic, but displays dramatic and structural similarities:

I heard the Third Symphony of Roussel for the first time in the Warsaw Philharmonic shortly after its first performance [Boston, 24 Oct 1930] . . . later, during the war, a record of it made a strong impression on me. . . . the richness of harmony in Debussy's and Ravel's music had a strong influence on me; but I was never happy because it was used for suites or ballets or some symphonic poems, but never for more serious forms like symphonies. Roussel's Symphonies, especially the Third, filled that gap. He used the richness of the French world of harmony . . . in a form which makes us think about Brahms. He is a sort of French Brahms of the twentieth century.[9]

One can also hear more than a passing allusion to Prokofiev in the second theme of the slow movement. From bar 37 a solo oboe plays a parody of a march (Ex. 2 : 6b), and is subsequently joined by other woodwinds. Lutosławski now regrets the directness of this allusion, even though the theme is not derived from Prokofiev, but from the tenth of his own Canons for two clarinets (Ex. 2 : 6a). Similar allusive association of double-reed tone-colour with a parodied march surfaces many years later in the final movement (*marciale e grotesco*) of the Double Concerto.

The traditional functions of scherzo and trio are performed by the third movement, albeit without literal repeats. It opens with a *pizzicato* bass

EX. 2 : 6   a) Canon no. 10 for two clarinets, bars 1–5;   b) Symphony no. 1, second movement, march theme, bars 38–40

line delivering a twelve-note row (the earliest example of a row to be found in Lutosławski's music), comprising two six-note sets where the second inverts the first: D♯,A,C,B,D,C♯; E,B♭,G,G♯,F,F♯,D♯ (Ex. 2 : 7). The row contains only three types of interval: semitone, minor third and tritone (interval-classes 1, 3 and 6). Of these, the semitones and minor thirds are paired to form isomorphic three-note cells (marked with slurs in Ex. 2 : 7). Canonic treatment of the row introduces other intervals vertically between the contrapuntal parts (e.g. bars 54–80). Although a row is used to supply the full chromaticism of all twelve notes, this is only one element used in building a movement that is not serial. When we hear the twelve-note theme treated canonically between clarinet and oboe between Figs. 92 and 95, technique and timbre are again reminiscent of the woodwind canons, rather than conveying any kind of reference to the Second Viennese School. Some typically Lutosławskian combinations of orchestral tone-colour occur in the third movement and anticipate the sonic palette of later works; for example, the combination of harp, piano, celeste and glockenspiel at Figs. 95–6.

EX. 2 : 7   Symphony no. 1, third movement, 12-note row

In the fourth movement, one can again observe the ubiquitous three-note melodic cells of interlocking tone and semitone. These occur in the solo violin line from bars 42–8 before passing to the violin section as a whole from bar 67. A brief reminiscence of this idea reappears played by solo flute between Figs. 142 and 143, soon after the climax. Interlocking tone/semitone cells are also applied to the bass line from Figs. 123 to 126, played by lower strings (including violas). The final movement also provides an illustration of Lutosławski's general approach to the dramatic shaping of a large-scale form. Here six distinct stages can be observed as the work reaches and leaves its overall climax: approach; climactic harmony; exit; aftermath; coda and cadence. In this case the immediate approach to the climax is achieved through symmetrically divergent chords in bars 161–8 (emphasising minor thirds and diminished triads), and rhythmic elongation in bars 166–8 (comparable with the end of the Partita for violin and piano composed some forty years later). The climactic harmony at bar 169 is a massive eighteen-note tutti chord, played *fortissimo*, containing nine different pitches with octave doublings. Lutosławski leaves this climactic point in a highly characteristic manner, used in several later works, whereby the dynamic suddenly drops to *pianissimo* as some parts stop while others evaporate. The aftermath of the climax is often, as in this case, a brief episode of calm and repose as the dramatic level subsides. A fast coda propels the symphony towards its final cadence on D.

Curiously, if one looks through the pages of the symphony for signs of the folk material or functional music of the immediate post-war years one draws a blank. Equally, one searches in vain for any obvious signs of its origin during the Nazi occupation. Yet, in assessing the First Symphony one must acknowledge the extraordinarily difficult circumstances afflicting the composer during the initial stages of its composition. The work displays a very high degree of craftsmanship, particularly in its treatment of counterpoint and the handling of orchestral colour; but the composer's main achievement was in building and sustaining a large-scale form that is genuinely symphonic rather than merely orchestral. Lutosławski's own assessment of his First Symphony, however, was severely critical. Dissatisfied with the post-tonal language he had been using up to this stage in his career, he subsequently began a long and painstaking search for fresh means of harmonic organisation, which was to lead to the language of twelve-note chords he has used since 1957.

The First Symphony received its première at Katowice on 6 April 1948, conducted by its dedicatee, Grzegorz Fitelberg. A performance at the Kraków Festival followed on 15 June. Meanwhile, an All-Union Congress of [Soviet] Composers had been held in Moscow from 19–25 April, closely followed by the Second International [i.e. Soviet-bloc] Congress of

Composers in Prague, at which a declaration was made on 29 May, ostensibly on behalf of the Polish Composers' Union, promising to uphold the principles of socialist-realism in Polish music. The political climate had now changed, and in November Lutosławski was dropped from the committee of the Polish Composers' Union.

The First Symphony bears the distinction of having been the first major musical work in Poland to be proscribed, denounced as 'formalist' by the strident cultural commissars of the Stalinist era. Tracing the sequence of events requires a review of the political changes which had been taking place in Poland since the war. Like most of Poland's post-war ills, the notion of formalism was imported from the Soviet Union. Perhaps the most notorious case was the fate which befell Shostakovich's opera *Lady Macbeth of the District of Mtsensk*, first performed in Leningrad on 22 January 1934, and later dropped after its denunciation in the infamous article published in *Pravda* on 28 January 1936. Stravinsky was denounced *in absentia*, while Prokofiev's prodigal return to the Soviet Union in 1932 was rewarded by a struggle with Stalin so stressful that it was resolved only by their respective deaths, ironically on the same day (5 March) in 1953.

Mutually supporting concepts of socialist-realism (*socrealizm*) and formalism were imported to Poland (by Communist Poles trained in the Soviet Union) at a conference in early August 1949 held at the ancient castle of Lagów in the Lubuskie district of the 'recovered territories' in western Poland, a favourite haunt of the vice-Minister of Culture, Włodzimierz Sokorski. A simple explanation of formalism would be 'elevation of form over content', a deliberately vague specification designed to allow for blanket condemnation of any works that failed to please the authorities of the time.

Active promotion of socialist-realism in the field of music would not have been feasible without the collaboration of certain strategically appointed arbiters of musical aesthetics masquerading as critics. One of the most influential players in this absurd, tragi-comic drama of Orwellian totalitarianism was the Marxist–Leninist musicologist Zofia Lissa (1908–80).[10] As the Polish signatory to the declaration made in Prague on 29 May 1948 at the Second International Congress of Composers and Musicologists, which committed the Polish Composers' Union to the official line established by its Soviet counterpart, she thus condemned her Polish colleagues to aesthetic assessment according to the following four aims: avoidance of subjectivism; cultivation of national character in music; adoption of well-known forms; and increased involvement by composers and musicologists in music education. Appointed to the Institute of Musicology at Warsaw University as a professor in 1951, she became Director of the Institute in 1954, remaining in that position until 1975. According to one's political point of view Lissa might be judged either as aesthetic arbiter or critical commissar. It is hard to comprehend now just how damaging and dangerous was the influence exerted by such engineers of socio-political attitudes either under the guise of academic peer-pressure or cloaked as musical criticism.

Elections held in January 1947 (without secret ballot) were duly rigged to give 80 per cent of the vote to the Communist-led so-called 'Democratic Bloc'. By October the political situation had deteriorated to such an extent that Stanisław Mikołajczyk, Prime Minister of the London-based Polish Government in Exile from 1943–4, fled Poland in fear of his life. Thus ties with the legitimate pre-war Polish Government were severed, creating a political schism that was resolved only with the inauguration of President Lech Wałęsa in December 1990. In 1948 Władysław Gomułka was ousted as First Secretary of the Polish Communist Party and replaced by the Stalinist stooge, Bolesław Bierut.[11] On 22 July 1952 a new constitution was proclaimed, a mechanism for conferring the identity of a Communist state on the renamed 'Polish People's Republic' (Polska Rzeczpospolita Ludowa). As the Stalinist 'cult of personality' descended on Poland, among the many changes of name, statues and symbols that followed, the Silesian city of Katowice (home of the Polish National Radio Symphony Orchestra) was renamed 'Stalinogród'.

Against this turbulent and increasingly totalitarian background, the First Symphony received its first Warsaw performance in the autumn of 1949, at a gala concert to mark the beginning of the fourth Chopin Piano Competition. During the performance at the Philharmonic Hall, several Russian jury members who, significantly, had been sitting in the government box, ostentatiously displayed their disapproval of the work by standing up and walking out. After the concert, the vice-Minister of Culture, Sokorski, is reputed to have said to the artistic director of the Philharmonic Hall, Raczkowski: 'Such a composer as Lutosławski should be thrown under a street-car.' Thus the symphony was proscribed. It was not performed again in Poland until ten years later.

Lutosławski aired his views on the Stalinist period during a speech on 'The Role of Truth in Art' delivered to the Congress of Culture, which was convened in Warsaw by the organisers of Solidarity in the winter of 1981, immediately prior to the sudden imposition of martial law on

December 13. As a result of his candour, Lutosławski became *persona non grata* in the Soviet Union during the remainder of the Brezhnev/Andropov/Chernenko era, until the advent of the thaw in attitudes attributed to Gorbachev.[12]

This Congress was organised by people of art and science. So I begin by stating straight away that the highest purpose of art is beauty, just as the highest purpose of science is truth. However, just as in mathematics, astronomy, and many other fields of science we can see their own kind of beauty, so in art we inevitably encounter the question of truth. . . . I should remind you briefly of the 'Fight Against Formalism', as it was then officially called. It was decreed that the twentieth century had contributed to the total degeneration of art as a creation of bourgeois culture. The works of Stravinsky, Bartók, Schoenberg, Prokofiev (those from between the wars), and many others, were to be regarded as Formalist, and we were to break with everything that those pieces represented, eradicating and forgetting them. The prescribed way to create music of our time was by returning to a simple nineteenth-century tonal language, which would reach wide masses by conveying our time in a 'realistic' way. Vocal music based on carefully chosen propaganda texts had priority over instrumental pieces . . . The intellectual crudity of such thinking was probably less harmful than the fact that for years this dismal picture was placed before our eyes prior to every discussion, official meeting and official criticism. . . . This perfidious, primitive operation, which was a form of attack on the truthfulness of art, had terrible consequences. Composers were forced to hide their most important pieces in a drawer, while their previous works were not performed. The whole situation in the musical world was falsified. Critics aimed to destroy all signs of individuality, or investigation of new styles and techniques. For many of us, it was all the cause of deep psychological depression.[13]

In the meantime, while conditions under Stalinism were so severe and the available choices so limited, Lutosławski attempted to maintain a low profile and continued to compose functional music, particularly for the radio and theatre. Modest but regular requests came from the radio for simple children's songs which he was happy to provide without feeling that this could be misconstrued as indicating collaboration with the regime.

He composed forty-five Children's Songs over a twelve-year period from 1947 to 1959. Although implacably opposed to the ideas of socialist-realism, he has indicated that he was 'not averse to the idea of composing pieces for which there was a social need'.[14] Certain poets figure prominently, in particular, Julian Tuwim (1894–1953) and Lucyna Krzemieniecka (1907–55). The first eight songs, composed in 1947 and 1948 are all settings of Tuwim's poems for children, which are known in Poland much as the poems of A. A. Milne are to English readers (it must be said that the works of Milne are also hugely popular in Poland, and there is even a street in the heart of Warsaw named after Winnie the Pooh: Ulica Kubusia Puchatka, which runs parallel to Nowy Świat).

Piosenka o złotym listku (Song of the golden leaf), the second of four songs in the set under the title *Wiosna* (Spring) composed in 1951, displays Lutosławski's technique of melodic interval pairing which occurs with increasing significance in his later works (Ex. 2 : 8). Throughout the song there is a contrapuntal line in the middle register that complements the tune by shadowing it with only two kinds of interval used horizontally: in this case, semitones and minor thirds. This principle of establishing a pairing of two types of interval has already been observed in the Carols; here we have another early example, thus confirming that such modest little pieces were used, whether consciously or not, as compositional studies or exercises during the years 1948–58 when Lutosławski was redefining his musical vocabulary and language.

In 1954 Lutosławski was awarded the Prime Minister's Prize for his Children's Songs. This came as both a surprise and a considerable shock. While he had regarded this avenue of compositional activity as a

EX. 2 : 8   Children's Song, *Piosenka o złotym listku*

34

politically harmless means of providing for his family, unwittingly he had in fact become the victim of a deliberate ploy from the Ministry of Culture to misrepresent his position as collaborating with socialist-realism:

Later on, it was for those functional compositions of mine that the authorities decorated me because they mistakenly believed that I had composed them to obey the guiding principles. That was another shock because I realised that I was not writing innocent, indifferent little pieces, only to make a living, but was carrying on an artistic creative activity in the eyes of the outside world.[15]

After the First Symphony, the first concert piece to be completed was a short Overture for Strings. Written in 1949, the same year as the Łagów conference and the formalism affair surrounding the First Symphony, it received its first performance not in Poland but in Prague, from the Prague Radio Symphony Orchestra, conducted by Grzegorz Fitelberg. In the Overture for Strings the influence of Bartók is paramount; the main technical similarity lies in manipulation of three- and four-note melodic cells that are used to generate longer lines as well as short motifs. The Overture opens with a four-note melodic curve: B–A♯–G♯–A. Discounting octave and unison doublings, this motif appears no fewer than 132 times during the total of 188 bars that constitute the work's five-minute time-span. Thus the listener will inevitably recall the motif rather than the synthetic mode that acts as the underlying material of the piece. Although the modal pitch organisation used in the Overture was not a method Lutosławski was to pursue (he admires but had no wish to emulate the approach of Olivier Messiaen), the treatment of modes reveals his liking for intervallic patterns generated by three-note cells. The octatonic mode is made from two tetrachords, each comprising tone–tone–semitone, as in a major scale, but here linked (in its basic form) by a semitone (i.e. E,F♯,G♯,A + B♭,C,D,E♭). The tetrachords themselves do not give rise to three-note cells of interlocking tone–semitone, but the various ways Lutosławski links the four-note segments to each other frequently produces these ubiquitous patterns.

Although the avenues in Poland for concert performance of serious, abstract orchestral works were closed to Lutosławski (and many others), he continued to receive some modest commissions for the radio in which he was able to apply the techniques he had been developing in his functional pieces. In this category we can place the Little Suite, written in 1950 for Polish Radio, who had requested a piece for a small orchestra that was used to playing programmes of light music. The thematic material is based on folk melodies from the Rzeszów region, and the style is uncomplicated, with transparent textures and sonorities. Stylistic similarity between the Little Suite and Lutosławski's music for the 1946 film, *Suita Warszawska*, has already been noted, but whereas the film has only three sections, the Little Suite contains four pieces: *Fujarka* (Fife), *Hurra Polka*, *Piosenka* (Song), and *Taniec* (Dance). The first piece features the piccolo representing a fife, suitably partnered by side drum; the third piece shows traces of the chromatic counterpoints used to complement tonal melodies in the Carols. In 1951 he made a revised, concert version, scored for a symphony orchestra with double woodwind (rather than the large orchestra of triple woodwind that he usually favours). This version was first performed in Warsaw on 20 April 1951 by the Polish Radio Symphony Orchestra, conducted by Fitelberg. *Silesian Triptych*, for soprano and orchestra, was also written in 1951, but it does not defer to light music, and hence shows more imaginative treatment of the orchestra.[16] For example, the typically Lutosławskian combination of harp and celesta gives a delicate background texture at the beginning and end of the second piece. When the Suite and the Triptych were written, Lutosławski was already collecting ideas for a more substantial orchestral work that might incorporate the techniques he had learned during the post-war years. This project eventually grew far beyond its original conception and resulted in the Concerto for Orchestra. Cross-connections between these works can be heard, such as similarity between the opening of the Concerto's *Capriccio Notturno* and Figs. 31–3 in the third piece of the Triptych.

The five *Bucolics* for piano, written in 1952 to a commission from PWM, use tunes from the Kurpie region, which Lutosławski drew from a collection by Father Władysław Skierkowski.[17] The first performance was given in Warsaw by the composer in December 1953. Because the medium was instrumental rather than vocal, Lutosławski was able to take more liberties with his treatment of the tunes than was possible with the Carols. Even so, there are many stylistic similarities, particularly in the use of chromatic counterpoints. The second piece, for example, has an extended sequence of minor thirds and semitones, paired in alternation, as the supporting line descends chromatically in bars 1–9 (Ex. 2 : 9) and again in bars 17–21. One of the most interesting aspects of the *Bucolics*, and their principal difference from the *Melodie Ludowe* and the Carols, is their concentration on metrical contradictions. Superimposed metres oppose each other, thus greatly contributing to the rhythmic energy of the faster pieces (first, third and fifth), while also enlivening the more reposeful second and fourth pieces. Rhythmic patterns are often notated across and through the bar lines; the latter are determined by the tune and only notional for the counterpoints.

EX. 2 : 9   Bucolic no. 2, bars 1–9

The Three Pieces for Young People were commissioned by PWM in 1953. In technical terms the first may be a four-finger exercise, but in compositional terms is an exercise in interlocking major and minor thirds. It is also a kind of simple study in perpetual semiquaver motion. The second piece makes use of a triadic ostinato pattern that oscillates continually between major and minor. The final piece of the set is a March that throws more than a passing glance in the direction of Prokofiev.

Concerto for Orchestra

When Witold Rowicki suggested to Lutosławski in 1950 that he might write something for the recently formed Warsaw Philharmonic Orchestra, the composer considered producing a piece based on folk material, perhaps more ambitious than the Little Suite, but not a work of the grand proportions it turned out to be. His initial idea was to make use of techniques he had learned from little functional pieces such as the Carols, but this time in a concert work. Having accumulated many sketches, he found himself unable to prevent the project growing in size and scope and was carried along by an unconscious sense of large-scale form, as he later experienced with *Livre pour orchestre*. The gestation period of the Concerto for Orchestra eventually spread over four years, and the autograph score in the Polish National Library bears the completion date of 1 August 1954. At the first performance, given by Rowicki and his new orchestra at the Warsaw Philharmonic Hall on 26 November, it was enthusiastically received, and it has remained one of his most enduringly popular works. In Poland it secured his position as the most distinguished composer of his generation, and was honoured with state prizes in 1955.

The overall scheme of the Concerto for Orchestra reveals Lutosławski's preoccupation with forms structured so that the main dramatic weight falls in the final movement. The First Symphony has a similar thirty-minute time-span, but is subdivided into four movements with the main weight in the slow movement rather than in the finale. In the Concerto for Orchestra, however, we encounter an approach to the relationships between the movements that has more in common with Lutosławski's later music: the finale leads to the culmination of the work, and in this case is longer than the first two movements combined; the functions of the earlier movements, expressed in the terms favoured by Maliszewski, are introductory and transitional, respectively.

The title of the first movement, Intrada, makes explicit both its introductory character and function. Lutosławski takes the opening theme, apparently a Mazovian folk melody from Czersk (according to Zofia Lissa, *A czyje to kuniki*),[18] places it above the constant pulsation of a low F♯ pedal and makes it grow from within, stretching the second and third phrases by making sequential insertions (Ex. 2 : 10). By this means the line is carried higher so that the three phrases span intervals of a minor sixth, minor seventh and minor ninth, respectively. Successive entries of the theme appear in a rising pattern of fifths beginning on the following notes (the modal 'tonic' is shown in brackets): F (D), cellos, bar 2; C (A), violas, Fig. 1; G (E), second violins, Fig. 2; D (B), first violins, Fig. 3; A (F♯), woodwind, Fig. 4. Example 2 : 10 shows the entry of the cellos on F in bar 2 and the entry of the violas on middle C in bar 9. The process of gradual thematic growth from the outset conveys to the listener that the Concerto is to be genuinely symphonic. In view of the composer's dependence on harmonic procedures in several of his later works, it is worth noting that here the burden of development is carried primarily by the melodic line.

EX. 2 : 10   Concerto for Orchestra, opening theme, bars 2–10

Table 1 sets out the structural unfolding of the first movement. It is interesting to observe that once the movement has passed the centre of its arch-like scheme, the further appearances of the C and B material are double their previous length. The listener is aware of a process of continuing growth up to the point where the first theme returns for the magical closing section, also extended.

TABLE 1   Concerto for Orchestra Intrada, formal scheme

Stage	Bars	Length	Material
A	1–39	39 bars	first theme grows over low F♯ pedal
B	40–51	12 bars	*cantando*
C	52–63	12 bars	interval classes 4 + 5; then tritone F/B
B¹	64–74	11 bars	*cantando*
C¹	75–99	25 bars	interval classes 4 + 5; then tritone E/B♭
B²	100–123	24 bars	*cantando* extended
A¹	124–172	49 bars	first theme below high F♯ pedal

The middle section of the Intrada is dramatically more expansive, and introduces thematic material that is later transformed and developed in the toccata of the finale. By comparison with the opening and closing sections of the movement, where low and high F♯ pedals (respectively) produce harmonic stasis, the middle section is more harmonically active, although the leading role is still taken by the melodic line. A *cantando* theme first appears in the horns, from Figs. 5–6, then horns and strings from Figs. 7–8, the violins with woodwind and brass doubling from Fig. 11. In between these phrases of the *cantando* theme is a contrasting chordal and rhythmic passage from Figs. 6–7 and 8–11, two features of which are arresting: first, there is a descending sequence of minor sixths and perfect fourths, linked by major thirds (interval-classes 4 and 5 only, F♯–A♯–D♯–G, B–D♯–G♯–C, and E–G♯–D♭–F); then, at the arrival on F, the strings play pounding repetitions of an F minor chord on the down-bow, *pesante*, similar to Fig. 13 in *Le sacre du printemps* (tritonal opposition is provided by a low B♮ repeated by trombones and tuba). When the sequence of interval classes 4 and 5 returns at Fig. 11, it has been transposed up a minor third. After initial delivery by strings and brass in descending sequence, the idea is extended by brass and woodwind in bars 79–85 in ascending sequence by inversion, still using only interval-classes 4 and 5.

Whereas the opening of the Intrada is underpinned by a long pedal F♯ sustained through the first thirty-seven bars in the lowest register (by double-basses, harps, timpani and bassoons), for the magical final section the same pitch is transferred to the highest register where it is sustained during the last forty-nine bars by piccolo, celesta, and violins (harmonic). Successive entries of the theme balance the pattern of ascending fifths, used in the first stage of the form, with a sequence of descending fourths: F (flute, Fig. 14); C (oboe, Fig. 15); G (clarinet in A, Fig. 16); D (cor anglais, Fig. 17); and A (clarinet in A, Fig. 18). The haunting quality of this closing section arises from the orchestration, in particular the combination of celesta with harp, strings sustaining a harmonic background against which the woodwinds play out their melodic phrases. Each entry in the sequence of descending fourths adds a new note to the sustained string harmony, which thus builds up a quartal sonority. Finally it resolves onto (or 'into') an F♯ major-seventh chord.

The second movement, Capriccio notturno e Arioso, adheres to the formal scheme of scherzo and trio:

Capriccio	(quasi-scherzo)	bars 173–236 (64)	*mormorando*
	(integral repeat)	bars 237–310 (74)	*mormorando*
Arioso	(quasi-trio)	bars 311–342 (32)	*cantando*
Capriccio	(single repeat)	bars 343–417 (75)	*mormorando*

'Murmuring' is the suggestive term given by the composer for the scherzo music (*mormorando*), and on which its nocturnal character depends. The dynamic level is mostly *pianissimo*, rising to *mezzo-piano* and disappearing to *ppp*; only a few isolated *pizzicato* notes are marked up to a notional *mezzo-forte*. By complete contrast, the Arioso begins *fortissimo* with a chord played by the whole orchestra that signals the beginning of the *cantando* theme. This is also played *fortissimo*, initially by four trumpets before transferring to an exchange between strings and horns. The climax is reached at bar 331 with the whole orchestra playing *fff*, followed by gradual subsidence as the *cantando* theme is passed to the flute and then the clarinet, against a shimmering harmonic background of chromatically descending string trills.

EX. 2 : 11   Concerto for Orchestra, opening of second movement, bars 173–85

Momentum is generated at the outset of the Capriccio with a repeated-note chromatic turn on F, extended by adding and manipulating modal segments, mostly tetrachords of semitone/tone/tone (Ex. 2 : 11). The end of each chromatic phrase is punctuated by the harmonic highlight of a minor triad on the last note. This effect was later used in the second movement of *Chain 2*. Six-note chords are used for the second idea of the Capriccio at Fig. 22 (bar 189), a developing rhythmic pattern that alternates pairs of superimposed triads: A minor on G minor; and B♭ major on A♭ major; in both cases the roots are a tone apart. When this second idea returns in the scherzo repeat at Fig. 29 (bar 255) the string chords are densely doubled, but still as superimposed triads: G minor on F minor; and A♭ major on G♭ major. The final statement of the scherzo music, following the Arioso, murmurs at a murky register in the low strings, with triadic punctuation provided by low woodwinds. Hence the effect is more subdued than before. *Pianissimo* drum rolls end the movement enigmatically.

For the finale, Lutosławski uses a formal scheme in two stages: first a Passacaglia, then a Toccata interwoven with a chorale-like theme. The Passacaglia provides an early example of Lutosławski adopting a structural procedure that aims for unbroken continuity by overlapping strands of material, as opposed to the more conventional approach of placing phrases or sections end to end (in the 1980s he was to refer to this principle as 'chain technique'). During the course of eighteen statements the passacaglia theme passes through all sections of the orchestra and exploits many different instrumental combinations. A simplified summary of these is shown in Table 2, together with the overlapping episodes (these coincide with the beginning of the theme only at Figs. 55 and 59).

The passacaglia theme is eight bars long (Ex. 2 : 12), except for the final version, which is extended to nine bars. As the successive repetitions

TABLE 2   Concerto for Orchestra: Passacaglia

Theme			Episodes		
No.	Bars	Instrumentation	No.	Figs.	Feature
1	418–424	dbs 2, harp 1			
2	425–433	(no change)			
3	434–441	+ dbs 1, harp	I	48–49	pf, vcs/vas
4	442–449	(no change)	II	49–50	cor anglais solo
5	450–457	+ b cl	III	50–51	ww, 3-note cells
6	458–465	+ bn 1	IV	51–52	rising str line
7	466–473	+ bn 2, harp 2	V	52–53	ww, hns
8	474–481	+ str, timp	VI	53–54	ww/brass *frullato*
9	482–489	+ vns 1	VII	54–55	ww modal motifs
10	490–497	+ hns, brass, xyl			
11	498–505	+ pic, fls, pf	VIII	55–56	str, *fortissimo*
12	506–513	+ hns, tpts	IX	56–57	str, *espressivo*
13	514–521	+ hns, tpts	X	57–59	fast repeated chords
14	522–529	+ fls, pf			
15	530–537	+ ob, cl	XI	59–60+	*poco più agitato*
16	538–545	+ xyl, bells, vns 1	XII	+60–61	climactic tutti
17	546–553	vns 1 only	XIII	61–	pf
18	554–562	(no change)	—		

EX. 2 : 12   Concerto for Orchestra, passacaglia theme of third movement

unfold, it passes from the lowest register of the basses upwards through the orchestra by octave doublings, and reaches its widest registral span of six octaves during the tenth repetition. Thereafter it gradually contracts by dropping the lower doublings until it remains only in the highest register, played by violin harmonics for the eighteenth repetition. The sections of contrasting material that overlap with the passacaglia theme can be styled 'episodes', signifying their free composition and lack of relationship to each other (the term 'variation' would be misleading as it would imply connections between the episodic sections). Most of the episodes are also eight bars long; for the most part they do not coincide with the beginning or end of the passacaglia theme, except for the eighth and ninth at Figs. 55 and 59, respectively. Altogether there are thirteen episodes and each is invested with a different character.[19]

EX. 2 : 13   Concerto for Orchestra, third movement, episode 2, bars 447–54

The second episode consists of a solo for cor anglais (Ex. 2 : 13) that stretches a highly expressive line against a harmonic background of strings (note how Lutosławski treats the repetition of the quintuplet group and makes intervallic changes to extend the compass of the line). The fourth episode is a much simpler idea, but none the less of interest: a chromatically rising line played in octaves, *pesante*, by second violins and cellos (Ex. 2 : 14). Both of these episodes illustrate the pervading influence of Bartók in their manipulation of three-note intervallic cells of inter-locking tone and semitone. The sixth episode has a grotesque character, like a sonic grimace; this kind of effect occurs in other works where the

EX. 2 : 14   Concerto for Orchestra, third movement, episode 4, bars 463–70

composer uses effects of woodwind and brass *frullato*. Overall, the formal scheme of the Passacaglia and overlapping episodes is cumulative, and reaches its highpoint in the twelfth episode, just after Fig. 60.

It is the toccata section of the final movement that propels the work towards its culmination. Its rhythmic energy derives from motoric repeated-note figures introduced at Fig. 62, whose thematic outline relates to the passacaglia theme, but transposed to the dominant pitch level (A). First appearing at Fig. 75 in a four-part woodwind choir of oboes and clarinets, the chorale idea alternates with a *cantabile* countermelody from solo flute against harmonic accompaniment provided by harp. The chorale thickens to six parts when transferred to a brass choir of trumpets and trombones, over which two solo violins project the countermelody supported harmonically by the piano. When the chorale passes to the strings, it is heavily doubled, thickening the texture to fourteen parts spread over five octaves; the countermelody passes round the woodwind section, set against harmony provided by the scintillating combination of celesta, harps and piano. The woodwind countermelody acts as a link to the Toccata, overlapping with the string chorale as it converges into a range of only two octaves; hence one cannot draw a straight line through the score, as the sectional division is deliberately obscured. From the return of the Toccata up to the overall point of destination where the chorale reappears *fortissimo* in the brass, the music passes through several stages of transformation, often strongly reminiscent of Ravel's *La valse* in its orchestral gestures. A fast coda ends the work.

Comparing the Concerto for Orchestra with the First Symphony or the Symphonic Variations, one observes a marked decline in reference to the orchestral sound world of early Stravinsky. This is not because the influence has been replaced by others, even that of Bartók. In spite of the fact that the Concerto grew from Lutosławski's work in the field of functional music, with modal treatment of folk melody as raw material, both the style and compositional technique are genuinely his own. Traces of Bartókian chromaticism endure; but if one were to draw a meaningful parallel with Bartók, it should be with Music for Strings, Percussion and Celesta, rather than his own Concerto for Orchestra.

Although the Concerto for Orchestra represents the end of an era in which Lutosławski composed as he was able to (rather than as he wished), it is worth noting that several features have a significant bearing on particular late works: the opening bars of the second movement (Ex. 2 : 11) anticipate a memorable passage in the second movement of *Chain 2* (see Ex. 7 : 11); the Passacaglia in the finale (Ex. 2 : 12) is akin to the rhythmic chaconne in the last movement of the Piano Concerto (Ex. 8 : 5); the Passacaglia is also the earliest example of his technique of overlapping sections which he was later to exploit in all three works that bear the title of *Chain*, as well as in the Piano Concerto; the toccata material used in the final movement corresponds to the similarly motoric section of the Third Symphony (from Fig. 49). Few connections are apparent between the style and technique of the Concerto for Orchestra and Lutosławski's subsequent works composed in the late 1950s and 1960s; but if one takes a longer view it can be seen that his handling of the orchestra and his treatment of form alone justify the inclusion of this piece among the most significant works of his career.

The Concerto for Orchestra also displays the composer's typical preoccupation with triple metre. Only sixty-seven of the work's 956 bars are not in some kind of triple metre; of these, sixteen are in the first movement and fifty-one in the third. But if clarity and consistency of metre are hallmarks of Lutosławski's style in the Concerto, then contradiction and deliberate confusion of metre are as characteristic of his next composition as they were in the case of the *Bucolics*.

The set of five Dance Preludes was composed in 1954 and was the last of Lutosławski's works to make use of folk material; the composer referred to it soon afterwards as his 'farewell to folklore'. There are three versions. The original, for clarinet and piano duo, was first performed in Warsaw on 15 February 1955. Later that year the composer produced a *concertante* version for clarinet and orchestra to be broadcast on Polish Radio, although its first concert performance was not given until the 1963 Aldeburgh Festival, when it was played by Gervase de Peyer with the English Chamber Orchestra and conducted by Benjamin Britten. The version for nine instruments differs from the others by not featuring the clarinet in a solo role, but instead, integrating it as an equal member of the ensemble. Scored for wind quintet and solo strings, this third version was first performed by the Czech Nonet at Louny (north-west of Prague) on 10 November 1959.

Superimposition of different metres is the main feature of these pieces, resulting in metrical and rhythmic contradictions (Ex. 2 : 15). This technique is most noticeable in the first, third and fifth pieces and invests them with much of their rhythmic vitality. So great was the transformation in his language after 1957 that few connections can be drawn between the style of the Dance Preludes and subsequent works. Certain traits can be

EX. 2 : 15   Dance Prelude no. 3, Fig. 2

observed, however, such as the generation of melodic lines by pairing two types of interval; the fourth piece opens and closes with a bass line characterised by melodic pairing of semitones and minor thirds (Ex. 2 : 16).

EX. 2 : 16   Dance Prelude no. 4, bass line in bars 1–10

In the same year that Lutosławski was making his farewell to folklore, his erstwhile piano-duo partner, Andrzej Panufnik, defected to England.[20] There was an additional shock when Lutosławski unexpectedly received the Prime Minister's Prize for his Children's Songs. After this attempt to compromise his position had been made he composed no more Children's Songs until 1958, by which time the regime in Poland had changed considerably. In February 1956 Bolesław Bierut died in Moscow under mysterious circumstances while attending the twentieth Congress of the Soviet Communist Party. Sokorski was then removed from his highly sensitive position as Minister of Culture in April 1956, although he was transferred to the Commission for Polish Radio and Television, where he continued to exercise influence, albeit in a diminished capacity. In October, Gomułka was elected First Secretary of the Polish Communist Party, an appointment that marked the beginning of a new era perceived as more liberal, at least by comparison with what had just been endured.

The year 1956 is also considered to be a landmark in Polish musical history because of the inauguration of the Warsaw Autumn Festival of Contemporary Music. Organised by the Polish Composers' Union, it was held from 10 to 21 October 1956. Although it had originally been planned to take place every two years, from 1958 it has been held annually, with only one fallow year. In 1982, during the period of martial law (in Polish, *Stan Wojenny*, literally 'State of War') imposed with the intention of crushing the dissent represented by Solidarity, the central council of the Polish Composers' Union declined to organise a festival until repressive measures were lifted. A programme was put together hastily for the autumn of 1983 after martial law was formally rescinded in July.

It has become a commonplace critical observation that the Warsaw Autumn Festival provided both an international platform for new Polish music and a window on current musical developments outside Poland, a window that awakened Polish composers to new ideas. While the latter may have been true for Polish composers of a younger generation such as Penderecki (b. 1933), it was far less significant for composers of Lutosławski's generation, whose formative years had been spent in the comparatively liberal artistic climate of the pre-war Polish Republic. It was an understandable reaction for composers in Italy and Germany to catch up after the war with music that had been denied to them, in Germany's case from 1933 to 1945, but in Poland the situation was entirely different. If one inspects the chronicle of performances given at the Warsaw Autumn Festival since its inception (as listed in an appendix to the 1990 programme), it is surprising to note that only one of Lutosławski's works has received its 'world première' at the Festival: the complete four-movement version of *Jeux vénitiens* in 1961 (although three movements of that work had already been performed in Venice the previous April).

For a parting glance at the dark, Stalinist years, we can turn once more to Lutosławski's speech to the Congress of Culture in December 1981, in which he referred to the events of 1956 opening up new possibilities, but also alluded to painful memories:

It is already a long time since the cutting edge of official music criticism became blunt and left composers alone. We have to acknowledge that since then, which means since about 1956, music has enjoyed a privileged position by comparison with other fields of art. Worldwide acclaim of Polish music has assisted this situation, giving our country some element of originality in this field by comparison with others of Eastern Europe. Naturally we should be glad of this, but it should not obscure the sad truth about the years before 1956, because the wounds then inflicted still hurt today.[21]

3
Sound Language and Harmony
(1956–1960)

At the end of the four years it took Lutosławski to complete the Concerto for Orchestra, the difficult political conditions in Poland were soon to show signs that might point to change. The events of 1956, which relaxed the unwelcome grip of Stalinism, and released it as far as music was concerned, enabled him at last to consider bringing into the open the radical revision of sound language that had occupied him since 1947. For the remaining four years of the decade his music was to pass through a period of transition and remarkable transformation. His decision to embrace the full chromaticism of twelve-note harmony after 1956 proved to be the most significant turning-point in his career, yet it would be misleading to suggest this was brought about by the post-Stalin cultural thaw. Lutosławski had been experimenting with polychords for many years, although with fewer than twelve notes, and he had explored various possibilities of pitch organisation since completing the First Symphony. Some of these experiments had been tested in the informal and flexible medium of incidental music for the theatre and radio plays, rather than closed-form pieces for publication or concert performance; others had been confined to the composer's private sketches.

Twelve-note pitch organisation can be used to govern three dimensions of a musical score: the vertical plane (chords and harmony); the horizontal plane (lines and melody); and a plane tangential to chords and lines that can be described as 'oblique' (counterpoint and polyphony).[1] Before moving to discussion of individual works, it is necessary to present a concise classification of the various kinds of twelve-note chords that Lutosławski has used and which he continues to exploit.

There are many different ways of constructing twelve-note chords. As used by Lutosławski such chords fall into two main groups: those that can be classified according to the number and types of intervals they contain; and those that can be classified as chord-aggregates (or chord complexes), according to the combination of complementary chords they contain. Each of these broad groups can be subdivided into more precise categories; in the case of the former, such sub-classification depends primarily on the number of different interval types present:

49

One rule which it is possible to formulate about my experiments with twelve-note chords is that the fewer different intervals between neighbour [ie. adjacent] notes the chord contains, the more characteristic the result is. If, for instance, you use all possible intervals in one chord, the final result is, in a way, faceless, something which has no character, which in colour is grey ... I began with the elementary ones containing only one kind of interval between neighbour notes ... Then I tried to find some simple but not elementary chords which would contain only two different intervals.[2]

One can add to the composer's terms of 'elementary' and 'simple', those 'complex' chords that contain three or more different types of interval. It is helpful in analysing these chords to use the numbering of 'interval-classes', which treats intervals, their inversions and compounds as equivalent, and labels all those of a given type with a single digit, representing the distance between notes expressed as the notional number of semitones:

Interval-class 0: unison, perfect octave, perfect fifteenth, etc
Interval-class 1: minor second (semitone), major seventh, minor ninth etc
Interval-class 2: major second (tone), minor seventh, major ninth, etc.
Interval-class 3: minor third, major sixth, minor tenth, etc
Interval-class 4: major third, minor sixth, major tenth, etc.
Interval-class 5: perfect fourth, perfect fifth, perfect eleventh, etc
Interval-class 6: augmented fourth, diminished fifth (tritone), etc

Normally, this labelling is not extended beyond interval-class 6; but in some contexts it will be seen that Lutosławski uses perfect fifths as distinct from perfect fourths, particularly when combined with minor thirds. In such cases, fifths will be shown as interval-class 7, and the pairing with minor thirds will be represented by the integer code 3 + 7.

Elementary twelve-note chords can be generated only by interval-classes 1 or 5. Lutosławski has often used eleven adjacent semitones clustered together within one octave; the earliest examples occur fleetingly in the second of the Five Songs, *Wiatr*, and the earliest emphatic examples can be found in the Apogeum of *Musique funèbre* (Ex. 3 : 1a). One of the most dense harmonic effects used by Lutosławski is found at Figs. 44 and 45 in the first movement of the Second Symphony, *Hésitant*, where *pizzicato* strings play a chord of thirty-nine adjacent semitones covering forty notes across a range of just over three octaves.[3] Even more dense is the harmonic texture between Figs. 41–4 of *Chain 3*, where one can find fifty-five adjacent semitones covering fifty-six notes over a span of four and a half octaves. The composer, however, does not like the expression 'cluster' used for these or other chords, recalling with dismay its indiscriminate use by critics, particularly in the 1960s, to describe any harmonic effect containing many different notes. Clearly, it is valid to describe a twelve-note chord of eleven or more adjacent semitones as 'clustered', but the term is crude and misleading if misapplied to other kinds of interval structure. In the final movement of *Jeux vénitiens*, for example, one can find twelve-note chords containing only interval-class 1 between adjacent notes, but where there is a subdivision into distinct harmonic layers separated by minor ninths (Ex. 3 : Ib). For such a sonority the term 'cluster' is inappropriate.

EX. 3 : 1   Elementary 12-note chords: a) clustered; b) widely spaced

Simple twelve-note chords can be generated by only eleven of the fifteen possible pairings of interval-classes 1 to 6. Expressed as integer codes these pairings are: 1 + 2, 1 + 3, 1 + 4, 1 + 5, 1 + 6, 2 + 3, 2 + 5, 3 + 4, 3 + 5, 4 + 5 and 5 + 6. A selection of such chords is shown in Example 3 : 2. The first is also drawn from the last movement of *Jeux vénitiens* (Ex. 3 : 2a) and shows a similar configuration to the clustered chord from *Musique funèbre* quoted above (Ex. 3 : 1a), but with major seconds exposed at the top and the bottom. The same section of *Jeux vénitiens* also provides an illustration of semitones combined with major thirds (Ex. 3 : 2b) in a layout that emphasises subdivision of the twelve notes into four three-note cells (a similar approach to the chord in Ex. 3 : 1b). Two examples of the 2 + 3 pairing are given (Ex. 3 : 2c), one that occurs almost at the end of Preludes and Fugue (at Fig. 60), and another that occurs immediately after the climactic harmony of *Les espaces du sommeil* (at Fig. 97). Two examples are also given of the 2 + 5 pairing (Ex. 3 : 2d), from the second movement of Symphony no. 2 (at Fig. 124) and the succession of three chords that diverges to form the final cadence of Preludes and Fugue (only the last contains all twelve notes). The 4 + 5 pairing (Ex. 3 : 2e) is shown as a ten-note chord from *Livre pour orchestre* (at Fig. 102), and the climactic harmony of the Second Symphony (at

Fig. 153) demonstrates the vertical pairing of interval-classes 5 and 6. It is worth noting that many of Lutosławski's simple twelve-note chords are vertically symmetrical, around either an axis note, or an axis interval. Vertical interval symmetry is typical of his twelve-note chords from compositions of the 1960s, but is found less in the later works.

EX. 3 : 2   Simple 12-note chords; selection of vertical interval pairings

Complex twelve-note chords are those containing three or more different types of interval. Obviously, there is an enormous range of possibilities for constructing such chords. Some are rather 'simple', predominantly of only two interval-classes, but with perhaps one linking interval of another type (interval symmetry also occurs in such cases). As already noted, Lutosławski tends to be wary of harmonies containing many interval-classes, finding them lacking a distinctive character. Hence he has developed a technique of subdividing complex (and some simple) interval constructions into clearly defined harmonic 'strands' (the composer's own term), each of which can be invested with a distinctive harmonic character. The term 'chord-aggregate' will be used here to refer to such pitch collections that contain two or more superimposed chords. The principle can be traced back to Stravinsky; for example, the tritonal triad contradiction (C/F♯) associated with the character of Petrushka, and the repeated seven-note aggregate of F♭ and E♭[7] chords introduced at Fig. 13 in *Le sacre du printemps*. Lutosławski takes the principle further and makes twelve-note chord-aggregates by superimposing three complementary four-note chords in separate harmonic strands. The word 'complementary' is here used to mean having no notes in common and providing all twelve notes when combined.

Subdivision into three harmonic strands can also be observed in some chord-aggregates that are of the simple variety combining only two interval-classes. Pitch collections of this sort make use of the four-note diminished-seventh chord in each strand; five such aggregates are shown in Example 3 : 3. The first three (Ex. 3 : 3a) are from *Rycerze*, the fourth of the Five Songs, and they show interval-pairings 3 + 4, 3 + 5 and 2 + 3, respectively. Here there is a genuine sense of linear progression (as opposed to unrelated succession of chords) because of the patterns of sequential transposition: the upper strand descends by perfect fourths; the middle strand descends by major seconds; and the lower strand rises by semitones. The fourth and fifth chords are both drawn from the third movement of *Paroles tissées* (Ex. 3 : 3b) and demonstrate interval pairings 3 + 4 and 1 + 3.

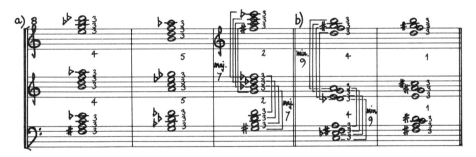

EX. 3 : 3   Simple chord-aggregates made from diminished-seventh chords

It is important here to note that Lutosławski often distinguishes between the different aural properties of major-seventh and minor-ninth intervals, even though, theoretically, they are of the same interval-class. He attributes to the presence of these intervals, between neighbouring strands of a twelve-note chord-aggregate, an effect comparable to magnetic poles in either attracting or repelling. To his ear, the major seventh tends to attract, pulling the interval closer, while the minor ninth tends to repel, pushing outwards. The third and fourth chords of Example 3 : 3 show this difference; the former gives rise to major sevenths between the respective four notes of each adjacent strand, while the latter gives rise to minor ninths.

Taking the diminished-seventh chord as the point of departure, ten four-note chord configurations are identifiable in Lutosławski's complex chord structures. Their classification can be determined by the intervals they contain when in close position. Table 3 shows them labelled from A to K in four categories: the first contains only the minor third; the second has the three patterns that combine two minor thirds with one major third; the third contains those that combine two major thirds and one minor third; and the fourth category has those with two minor thirds and one perfect fourth.

TABLE 3   Classification of four-note chords

1	2			3			4		
min 3	maj 3	min 3	min 3	maj 3	maj 3	min 3	min 3	per 4	min 3
min 3	min 3	maj 3	min 3	maj 3	min 3	maj 3	per 4	min 3	min 3
min 3	min 3	min 3	maj 3	min 3	maj 3	maj 3	min 3	min 3	per 4
A	B	C	D	E	F	G	H	J	K

Example 3 : 4 shows all ten types of chord, each rooted to the same note, E (an arbitrary choice), simply for convenience of comparison. Although they are used in a purely abstract way, divorced from any tonal context, most of them are readily recognisable as extended triads. Hence it will be helpful if they are also described as individual chords, although these should not be taken as implying tonal functions: type A, diminished-seventh chord; type B, half-diminished-seventh chord; type C, minor-seventh chord; type D, dominant-seventh chord; type E, minor triad with major seventh; type F, major-seventh chord; type G, major-seventh chord with augmented fifth; type H, major/minor chord; type J, diminished triad with added fourth above; type K, diminished triad with added fourth below. They are shown here in close position, but can be inverted (in the traditional, chordal sense) and spaced more widely within each strand; for example, type J appears either as a diminished triad with added major seventh, or a major triad with added minor ninth.

A   B   C   D   E   F   G   H   J   K

EX. 3 : 4   Ten 4-note chord types used to build chord-aggregates

Hierarchy between the four groups is determined by the ways of combining them, with themselves or each other, to make twelve-note chord-aggregates. The diminished-seventh chord is the only one which can provide a twelve-note chord on its own, by complementation in all three harmonic strands. The three chords of group 2 are the only ones which can be used at the same time in two strands (the diminished-seventh chord can be used in either all three strands or in only one, but not in only two, because the principle of complementation automatically reproduces the chord in the remaining strand). The chords of group 3 occur when a different chord is used in each strand. Those of group 4 occur primarily as a by-product of using a chord from group 2 in two strands. Chord-aggregates with two or three of the same four-note chord are summarised in Table 4.

TABLE 4 Harmonic strands of chord-aggregates

High strand:	A	B	C	D	K	B	H	C	J	D
Middle strand:	A	K	H	J	B	B	C	C	D	D
Low strand:	A	B	C	D	B	K	C	H	D	J

Choice of chord for the low strand is of prime importance. As already observed in the Symphonic Variations and the First Symphony (see Ex. 2 : 2), contrast often depends on whether the low register emphasises a perfect fifth or a tritone. Intervals in the low strand are often spaced more widely than those higher in the chord, giving a more open sonority. In many cases the bottom note is doubled at the lower octave, with the next note of the chord placed a perfect fifth higher. Such sonorities illustrate that Lutosławski's approach to the building of his complex chord structures is still largely conditioned by the traditional view of harmony which works from the bottom upwards (determined by the phenomenon of the natural overtone series, and its acoustic law of decreasing intervallic distances as harmonics ascend).

Some chord-aggregates are invested with particular significance because they are deployed at strategic points in the structural unfolding of certain works. Aggregates of three diminished-seventh chords A–A–A feature not only in *Rycerze* and *Paroles tissées* (Ex. 3 : 3), but also perform a significant role in Symphony no. 2 (see Ex. 4 : 9) and are crucial to the Apogeum of *Musique funèbre* (Ex. 3 : 12). Aggregate C–H–C (Ex. 3 : 5a) is one of the most favoured harmonic sonorities used by Lutosławski; it occurs at the climax of *Livre pour orchestre, Novelette and Chain 3*; and it defines the long-range harmonic organisation of *Chain 2*, since it occurs at two structurally significant points in the second movement and returns at the overall climax in the final movement (see Ex. 7 : 15). Aggregate D–J–D (Ex. 3 : 5b) provides the final chord of *Les espaces du sommeil* and the opening chord of *Mi-Parti* (see also Ex. 5 : 8). A similar combination of chords, but with type J in the upper register, occurs at the climax of *Musique funèbre* (Ex. 3 : 12). Memorable appearances of aggregate B–K–B (Ex. 3 : 5c) include the climax of *Mi-Parti*, the beginning of the final movement of *Chain 2*, and the intentionally nonclimactic highpoint (*pianissimo*) in the first movement of *Partita* (see also Ex. 7 : 4).

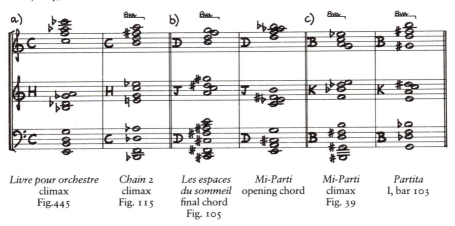

| *Livre pour orchestre*
climax
Fig.445 | *Chain 2*
climax
Fig. 115 | *Les espaces*
du sommeil
final chord
Fig. 105 | *Mi-Parti*
opening chord | *Mi-Parti*
climax
Fig. 39 | *Partita*
I, bar 103 |

EX. 3 : 5   12-note chord-aggregates

Individual chords examined in isolation are inevitably divorced from their proper context. In this brief outline of twelve-note chords and chord-aggregates, it has not been possible to show how Lutosławski establishes a sense of progression between harmonies. This issue can only be addressed with longer musical examples, and is therefore deferred to the discussion which follows, in this and later chapters, of individual works. Meanwhile, one can note that the absence of conventional, tonal functions of harmony has required the composer to explore a wide variety of unconventional means of moving from one chord to another.

One of Lutosławski's reasons for using twelve-note chord-aggregates that subdivide the chromatic whole into complementary harmonic strands, is that he is able to establish what he calls 'local harmony' in each register. These local harmonies are often associated with particular groups of instruments, and therefore invested with a distinctive tone-colour. This is one of the most telling aspects of Lutosławski's orchestral writing, and contributes to his success in achieving clear, characteristic sonorities, while maintaining a high level of chromatic density.

One thing is always undeniable to me: no sound sequence, no vertical aggregation should be composed without regard being given to every single detail of expression, colour, character, physiognomy. Even the minutest detail should satisfy the composer's sensitivity to the maximum degree . . . there should be no indifferent sounds in music.[4]

Five Songs

The set of Five Songs to poems of Kazimiera Iłłakowicz was the first work in which Lutosławski employed his harmonic vocabulary of twelve-note chords and chord-aggregates. The original version, for soprano and piano, was written in 1956–7, followed in 1958 by a version for soprano and small orchestra. All except the first song are dedicated to Nadia Boulanger, with whom he had intended to continue his compositional studies, had it not been for the intervention of the war and the difficulties of the post-war period. Although the Five Songs are among his most significant pieces, they are sometimes overlooked and have been unjustly neglected. Their performance outside Poland has been restricted by two factors: the difficulty, for most singers, of negotiating Polish pronunci-ation, and the almost inevitable inadequacy of performing them in trans-lation. The English performing translations published in the score are particularly unsuitable, and have certainly contributed to limiting their performance. As a direct result of these difficulties, Lutosławski decided in future to set the poetry of his second language, French.

Kazimiera Iłłakowicz (1892–1983) was born near Wilno (Vilnius). Her Lithuanian origins colour much of her work, which includes recurring motifs drawn from Lithuanian history and folklore. She became loosely associated with the Warsaw literary group 'Skamander', named after a reference in Stanisław Wyspiański's *Acropolis*. Another member of this group, Julian Tuwim (1894–1953), became a favourite of Lutosławski during the period when he was selecting poems for his songs for children.[5] The Iłłakowicz poems were chosen by the composer from the collection of twenty-seven *Rymy Dziecięce* (Children's Rhymes), first published in

1923. During his studies at the Warsaw Conservatory, in 1934, he had already set two other poems by Iłłakowicz for soprano and piano: *Wodnica* (Water-nymph) and *Kołysanka lipowa* (Linden lullaby), published in her collection of 1927, *Płaczący Ptak* (Weeping bird). These songs had been performed during the occupation in 1941, at clandestine concerts in Warsaw. Sadly, they were among the many manuscripts which perished during the Uprising in 1944.

Morze (The sea) gradually works through a succession of ten chords (Ex. 3 : 6). Apart from no. 9 (which has only five notes), they are all twelve-note chords. Chords 1 and 10 have the same type of vertical layout and are made up almost entirely of superimposed semitones and minor thirds (1 + 3); a perfect fifth at the bottom of both chords breaks the vertical symmetry. Both exploit opposition between white and black keys (a feature obscured in the orchestral version); for chord 1 the left hand plays all five black keys, while the right hand plays all seven white keys; for chord 10 the roles are reversed. The vocal line corresponds closely to the supporting harmony, from which it takes its interval patterns; while the first chord sounds, the vocal line uses only semitones and minor thirds when rising through the corresponding notes of the harmony. Chords 2 and 4 are both chord-aggregates (J–D–D) containing dominant-seventh chords in the low and middle strands, complemented by a major triad with added minor ninth in the high strand (see also Ex. 3 : 12).

EX. 3 : 6   Five Songs, harmonic reduction of *Morze*

The remaining six chords (nos. 3, 5, 6, 7, 8 and 9) are all of the same type, though one is incomplete (the upper parts are discontinued for no. 9). Although not strictly symmetrical, they have a slightly modified symmetrical layout which would have the following interval structure if the low strand had not been adjusted to sound a tritone at the bottom: 3–2–1 (3) 2–3–2 (3) 1–2–3; this can be seen by moving the lowest note up an octave. Similar adjustment of the lowest note can be observed in the other chord-aggregates used in this song: in chord 1 only the low perfect fifth denies vertical symmetry of interval-classes 1 + 3; in chord 2 the dominant-seventh chord in the low strand is opened out by displacing the fifth down an octave. Chords 5–9 form a progression that descends chromatically by semitones until it reaches the A contained within chord 10.

Wiatr (The wind), uses twelve-note harmony based on four different subdivisions of the chromatic whole. The first three consist of complementary tetrachords (2–1–2, 2–3–2, and 1–1–1, respectively), used as chords rather than linear modal segments. At the (literal) highpoint of the song, where the singer reaches and holds a high G for seven bars, *fortissimo*, the harmonic support comes from a twelve-note chord-aggregate of three complementary and interlocking diminished-seventh chords (A–A–A). *Wiatr* and *Rycerze* show the earliest examples in Lutosławski's published work of this harmonic technique. In *Wiatr*, however, the effect of overlapping all three chords in the low register results in a harmonic texture rather than a sonority in which the component chords are aurally identifiable. The final chord has a symmetrical pattern of minor thirds, tones and semitones.

Zima (Winter) uses seven chord-aggregates, each consisting of complementary augmented triads in four harmonic strands (Ex. 3 : 7). All are vertically symmetrical structures that use only interval-classes 4 and 3: four pairs of major thirds (the four augmented triads) linked by minor thirds. Chord 5 has a similar pattern but covers a much wider range, using augmented triads spaced as minor sixths instead of major thirds.

EX. 3 : 7   Five Songs, harmonic reduction of *Zima*

59

The title of the fourth song, *Rycerze*, is usually translated into English as 'Knights'. Although accurate, it is not the most musical solution for either the singer or the listener, because of the unfortunate disruption of text underlay caused by a mismatch between the number of Polish and English syllables: 'Crusaders' would correspond more closely. *Rycerze* has fourteen twelve-note chord-aggregates (Ex. 3 : 8); eight of one type followed by six of another, the change corresponding to contrast between the poem's two stanzas. The first verse is optimistic and depicts the knights and their chargers setting out for battle. The second relates their homecoming, not in glory, but wounded and dejected. The more sombre interval disposition of chord 9 marks this change of mood.

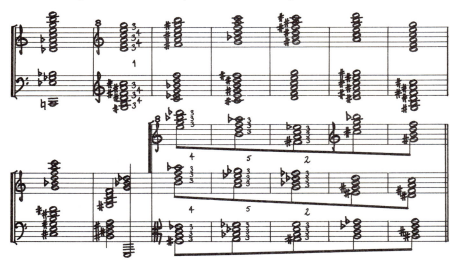

EX. 3 : 8   Five Songs, harmonic reduction of *Rycerze*

Chords 2–8 are all symmetrically constructed from complementary hexachords of major and minor thirds, linked by a semitone. Chord 1 is essentially of the same type, although its interval structure differs through the displacement of a central note (A) to the low register. Chord 7 duplicates chord 2, and chords 3–6 form a progression that rises by semitones, counterbalanced by chords 6–8 which fall by perfect fifths. Chords 9–14 are all aggregates containing three diminished-seventh chords in distinct harmonic strands (A–A–A). The last five form a progression which converges until the strands overlap: the low strand rises by semitones; the middle strand falls by tones; the high strand falls by perfect fourths. All five chord-aggregates are vertically symmetrical.

The title of the last song, *Dzwony cerkiewne*, has continually been mistranslated as 'Church bells', 'Cloches d'église', or 'Glocken'. Even the published scores printed in Poland and Germany show the title, simply and incorrectly, as 'Church bells'. Yet the Polish adjective *cerkiewne*, stemming from the noun *cerkiew* (meaning 'onion dome'), refers specifically to the distinctive tradition of rhythmically co-ordinated and highly dissonant *zvon*-ringing, as practised in the Russian Orthodox Church. The consequence of this mistranslation is that the true character of these bells has been overlooked and misunderstood.[6] Lutosławski is probably the only composer living today who has heard the pre-revolutionary *zvon*-ringing of Moscow; the October Revolution of 1917 not only silenced its critics and opponents, its militant atheism also silenced the bells.

He uses two different kinds of twelve-note chord-aggregate (Ex. 3 : 9) to evoke the contrasting bell sounds described by Iłłakowicz. In the first verse the bells are sweetly singing: *Lubimy dzwony cerkiewne, kiedy są śpiewne . . .* ('we like the orthodox bells when they are singing . . .'). The sonic image of the second verse is quite different: *Ale lubimy także dzwony cerkiewne, kiedy są gniewne . . .* ('but we also like the orthodox bells when they are angry. . .'). 'Singing' bells are represented by a chord-aggregate in which thirds predominate: a diminished-seventh chord played in the high strand as two interlocking and alternating tritones, a half-diminished-seventh chord (enharmonically) in the middle strand, and a dominant-seventh chord in the low strand. There is also a process of rhythmic layering designed to represent the controlled striking of each bell.[7]

Two Italian words appear in the score, stressing the change of character

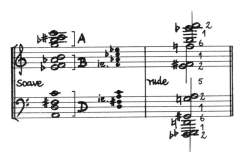

EX. 3 : 9   Five Songs, harmonic reduction of *Dzwony cerkiewne*

and mood: *soave* suggests the euphony of 'singing' bells; *rude* marks the change to 'angry' bells. At the point of division the interval content is abruptly transformed. Replacing third-based harmony, Lutosławski uses a symmetrical construction in four harmonic layers, each containing a three-note cell, laid out to maximise the dissonance of major sevenths and minor ninths. The same Italian terms were to be used many years later in the second movement of *Chain 2*, where they are associated with the strongest contrast of interval pairings; major seconds and perfect fourths/fifths (2 + 5), *soave*; minor seconds, major sevenths and tritones (1 + 6), *rude* (see Ex. 7 : 10). The vocal line of *Dzwony cerkiewne* also matches the contrast between the two verses. As the first chord-aggregate sounds, the melodic line curls through interlocking semitones and tones, then extending to include minor thirds. The combination of interval-classes 1, 2 and 3 is also used for the beginning of the second verse, but opened out to produce wide, angular interval-leaps.

Lutosławski's instrumentation for the orchestral version of the Five Songs anticipates sonorities and textures he was to explore in *Paroles tissées*. The ensemble is a small group of strings (9, 4, 4, 4), without woodwind or brass, with some percussion, piano and two harps. The combination of harps and piano (with celesta) has already been noted in the finale of the Concerto for Orchestra, where the chorale first appears. Similar sonorities and tone-colour combinations later form an important part of the orchestral sound world of works such as *Livre pour orchestre* and *Mi-Parti*. Background harmonic texture in *Zima* is provided by sustained, muted strings playing *pianissimo* and sliding between notes of the chord, glissando. The overall effect of this treatment of strings is strikingly similar to the opening of *Mi-Parti*, composed nearly twenty years later.

The original version of the Five Songs did not receive its première until 25 November 1959, at Katowice, while the orchestral version was not performed until 12 February 1960. Before either was heard, Lutosławski had already received international recognition for the other outstanding work of the transitional years, *Musique funèbre*. As this piece is well known for its use of a distinctive kind of twelve-note row, it is necessary at this stage to survey his methods of linear pitch organisation.

Naturally, Lutosławski's methods of organising pitch do not apply solely to the vertical dimension of twelve-note chords and chord-aggregates. He also employs various methods of organising the horizontal dimension, both as featured melodic lines and as underlying linear patterns. To some, the notion of planning or 'organising' a melodic line may suggest undue compositional contrivance. For this reason there is an inherent danger that a purely technical explanation of the composer's methods may convey a false impression of artificial rather than artistic creation. Hence it must be stressed that, while it is possible to examine individual components of the musical vocabulary, and even to observe how they combine as a language, there are also phenomena which resist explanation. Melodic features often come into this category.

Some works project a melodic line through exposure of a solo voice or instrument, for example the flute solo in the third movement of *Jeux vénitiens*, the tenor line in *Paroles tissées*, or the *cantando* theme in the Cello Concerto. Other works project comparatively little in the way of melody, but concentrate on orchestral textures and dense harmonic effects, the prime example of which is the Second Symphony. Later works, composed after 1979, focus much more strongly on the melodic dimension and show a significant shift in emphasis connected with simplification of harmony (see Chapter 6). In one way or another, all the works after 1956 confront a basic compositional problem: how to achieve some sense of musical logic in the unfolding of a horizontal line, without conventional diatonic or modal functions.

The temporary solution adopted by Lutosławski for *Musique funèbre* was to explore the possibilities of a twelve-note row (treated in an unorthodox way). It was not the first time he had made use of a twelve-note line; the earliest example occurs in the scherzo of the First Symphony (see Ex. 2 : 7). There, the row has very clearly defined intervallic properties, which are exploited through canonic techniques. Concern for intervallic character is also a feature of the row in *Musique funèbre*, an issue that Lutosławski feels to owe little to the tenets of Schoenbergian serial technique:

I have never been influenced by the doctrine of Schoenberg, even though I must admit that I make use of certain elements of his principles, that is to say the use of the chromatic whole ... In no case have I ever used the twelve-note technique as more than that. Even if I use twelve-note rows, this use always aims for entirely different effects ... in *Musique funèbre* ... the way of handling and certainly the choice of intervals shows clearly that what matters is the means of obtaining a harmonic result, of creating vertical aggregations, and not of employing a new functional system of intervals as is the case in the classic doctrine of serialism.[8]

Lutosławski has long been fond of employing certain interval pairings to give melodic lines of distinctive character. Attention has already been drawn to such lines in the counterpoints to the *Melodie ludowe* and the Carols (see Ex. 2 : 1), some of the Children's Songs (see Ex. 2 : 8), and in the Dance Preludes (Ex. 2 : 16). Of the fifteen possible pairings, he has used the following: 1 + 2, 1 + 3, 1 + 4, 1 + 6; 2 + 3, 2 + 5; 3 + 4, and 3 + 7 (as distinct from 3 + 5). A crucial factor in his attitude towards horizontal interval pairing is the strong contrast available between 1 + 6 and 2 + 5, as shown by the symmetry of the following diagram: opposite ends represent the strong dissonance of semitone and tritone; consonant intervals that give rise to triads are in the centre, minor and major thirds (and their inversions); the remaining pair represents the essence of pentatonicism, major seconds and perfect fourths/fifths.

Interval-classes: 1   2   3   4   5   6

The above interval pairings can be used to generate the twelve notes of a row, but they are by no means used only for this purpose. While twelve-note pitch organisation is an undeniably important element of Lutosławski's compositional technique, the principle of horizontal interval-pairing is perhaps even more significant. A select list of interval pairings discussed in the present study is given in Table 5, together with cross-references to specific music examples.

Lutosławski's use of horizontal interval pairing is one of the principal means by which he achieves linear coherence in those works that feature the technique. But it is the use of changing interval pairings, whether gradually or by strong contrast, that is particularly successful, because it provides him with a means of building sections of the form in a way analogous to the structural properties of key change in a tonal language. In some later works, the contrast of 1 + 6 against 2 + 5 is exploited by identifying these pairings with alternate sections of the form. This principle defines the relationship between the fugue subjects and the intervening episodes in the second movement of Preludes and Fugue. It also defines the cello part of *Grave* and the alternation of *rude* and *soave* passages in the second movement of *Chain 2*. In other works, the interval pairings are changed more gradually, without seeking maximum contrast, so that successive sections share one of the intervals involved. The latter procedure can be observed in the Cello Concerto (as the long *cantando* unfolds, phrases alternate between interval pairings 2 + 3 and 2 + 5),

TABLE 5   Melodic interval pairing

Pair	Work	Section(s)	Cross-ref.
1 + 2	Concerto for Orchestra	3rd mvt, episode 4 bars 463–70	EX. 2 : 14
	String Quartet	Fig. 15, vn 1 and vc	EX. 4 : 5
	Paroles tissées	2nd mvt, tenor lines	EX. 4 : 6
	Double Concerto	2nd mvt, Figs. 28, 32, 45–6	EX. 6 : 4
	Symphony no. 3	ww refrains, Figs. 10, 18, 29	EX. 6 : 8
	Chain 2	2nd mvt, Figs. 37–9	EX. 7 : 11
	Chain 2	opening of 3rd mvt	EX. 7 : 13
	La Belle-de-Nuit	violins' line	EX. 8 : 8
1 + 3	Children's Song	*Piosenka o złotym listku*	EX. 2 : 8
	Bucolic no. 2	bars 1–9 (and 17–23)	EX. 2 : 9
	Dance Prelude no. 4	bass line	EX. 2 : 16
	Epitaph	falling phrase of oboe refrain	EX. 6 : 1
	Interlude	underlying bass progression	EX. 7 : 8b
1 + 3 + 6	Symphony no. 1	3rd mvt, 12-note row	EX. 2 : 7
1 + 4	Carol	*A cóż z tą dzieciną*	EX. 2 : 1f
1 + 6	*Musique funèbre*	Prologue/Epilogue, 12-note row	EX. 3 : 10
	Preludes and Fugue	fugue subject(s), 12-note row	EX. 5 : 3
	Epitaph	oboe line in episodes	EX. 6 : 2
	Grave	vc line (alternates with 2 + 5)	EX. 6 : 6
	Chain 1	most of stage 1	EX. 6 : 11
	Chain 2	2nd mvt, *rude*	EX. 7 : 10a
	Piano Concerto	chaconne theme	EXX. 8 : 5 8 : 6
2 + 3	Cello Concerto	*dolente cantando*, Figs. 63–81	EXX. 5 : 1 5 : 2
	Mi-Parti	Figs. 24–5 and 28–9	EX. 5 : 9
	Mi-Parti	coda, Figs. 43–53	EX. 5 : 10
	Epitaph	rising phrase of oboe refrain	EX. 6 : 1
2 + 5	*Paroles tissées*	12-note tenor lines	EX. 4 : 7
	Cello Concerto	Figs. 65–77 (alternates with 2 + 3)	EX. 5 : 1
	Preludes and Fugue	episodes of the fugue	EX. 5 : 4
	Les espaces	Adagio section, Figs. 24–82	EX. 5 : 6
	Grave	vc line (alternates with 1 + 6)	EX. 6 : 6
	Partita	1st mvt, bars 84–98	EX. 7 : 3
	Partita	final mvt, bars 9–12	EX. 7 : 6
	Chain 2	1st mvt, Fig. 15	EX. 7 : 9
	Chain 2	2nd mvt, *soave*	EX. 7 : 10b
	Chain 2	2nd mvt, Figs. 38–48	EX. 7 : 12
	Piano Concerto	1st mvt, pf episodes	EX. 8 : 1
	La Belle-de-Nuit	vocal line	EX. 8 : 8
3 + 7	Symphony no. 3	Figs. 84–6	EX. 6 : 9
	Symphony no. 3	Figs. 86–7	EX. 6 : 10
	Chain 2	Figs. 67–9, 72–4, 86–90	EX. 7 : 14
	Piano Concerto	2nd mvt (major 3rd links)	EX. 8 : 4

and it also acts as a means of gradual progression between the refrains, episodes and coda of *Epitaph*. In the mid-1950s, however, Lutosławski was much more preoccupied with matters concerning harmony than with the relationship of the melodic dimension to form. Here his most rigorous application of horizontal interval pairing during these transitional years was designed to obtain a clear and consistent harmonic outcome. The interval-pairing in question was the sombre combination of semitones and tritones; the work was *Musique funèbre*.

Musique funèbre

In 1954 the Polish conductor, Jan Krenz, suggested to Lutosławski the idea of composing a work to commemorate the tenth anniversary of Bartók's death (26 September 1955). The resulting piece for string orchestra, dedicated to the memory of Bartók, took four whole years to complete; Krenz conducted the first performance with the Polish Radio Symphony Orchestra at Katowice on 26 March 1958. A major landmark in Lutosławski's career, it brought him international acclaim, winning joint first prize from UNESCO in May 1959, having already won the annual prize of the Polish Composers' Union.

In English-speaking countries the work is commonly known as 'Funeral Music', an inaccurate translation from the French title, *Musique funèbre*. Referring to the original Polish form, *Muzyka żałobna*, the composer makes his preferred translation as 'Music of mourning'. This is unlikely now to oust the more familiar form, but is closer to his original intention. Both *żałobna* and *funèbre* are adjectives, hence the grammar of the English title should at least be corrected to 'funereal music'; use of the noun falsely implies music for a funeral rite, rather than a memorial tribute.

Although the score of *Musique funèbre* is subdivided into four sections, in performance these follow one another without a break to unfold as a single, unbroken arch that spans one of the most powerfully dramatic shapes ever composed by Lutosławski. Its progress is remarkably reminiscent of the first movement of Bartók's Music for Strings, Percussion and Celesta: after beginning with a subdued, chromatic solo line, it builds through canonic, quasi-fugal polyphony towards a decisive climax, then subsides through inversions of the earlier canons. Although there are no quotations from Bartók, the intervallic vocabulary, chromatic language and strategic placing of the climax allude to Bartók in a way which is so clear, and yet original, that the work forms a telling tribute from one composer to another.

The Prologue consists of canons in 2, 3, 4, 6 and 8 parts using a twelve-note row coupled with its tritone inversion (Ex. 3 : 10). While the pitch organisation is governed by an idiosyncratic treatment of the row that owes little to Viennese serialism, the rhythmic organisation is perhaps indebted to some aspects of Renaissance polyphony. The canons are delivered by an isorhythmic scheme that uses a pattern of seventeen rhythmic values. Canonic technique, also used in the Epilogue, conforms to an established convention of such memorial tributes (for example, Stravinsky's *In memoriam* Dylan Thomas: Dirge-Canons and Song, composed in 1954). The pitch organisation of *Musique funèbre* has often been discussed in terms that are rather misleading, and that convey the false impression Lutosławski was pursuing serial techniques. The real significance of the opening theme lies in its intervallic properties, chosen to generate a specific kind of harmony. Containing only semitones and tritones horizontally, the counterpoint of isorhythmic canons is strictly controlled to produce chords that contain only interval-classes o, 5 and 6 in vertically adjacent combination:[9]

It is the only piece where I have used a twelve-note row methodically – in the outer two sections ... But what matters in these two sections is the vertical result of using this row. It is composed solely of tritones and minor seconds. Used canonically it gives certain harmonic results which, containing neither third nor sixth, produces a certain atmosphere of open sonority which corresponds particularly to the title of the piece.[10]

EX. 3 : 10   *Musique funèbre*, 'double' 12-note row

Pitch organisation is altogether a more complex matter, however, in the second section of the piece.[11] The subtitle, 'Metamorphoses', refers primarily to the gradual transformation of the twelve-note row. Twelve versions are used, one for each metamorphosis, beginning with the prime form at its original pitch level followed by eleven transpositions which move anti-clockwise round the cycle of perfect fifths, beginning on F (it is also worth noting that fifth transpositions also feature in the first movement of Bartók's Music for Strings, Percussion and Celesta, where the entries fan out symmetrically on either side of the starting pitch). With each metamorphosis a growing number of additional notes is inserted between the notes of the row. Example 3 : 11 illustrates this process up to and including the sixth stage (these passages occur in bars 65–76, 77–85, 86–100, 101–13, 113–28 and 129–40 respectively). The process is not unlike the treatment of an underlying cantus firmus which is woven into the polyphonic texture and gradually transformed by trope. The additional notes inserted are derived as segments from the Locrian mode (B–B); a significant choice because of the tritone between its first and fifth degrees.

Transformation of the row is only one of three elements which constitute the pitch organisation of the second section. In addition there is what Lutosławski calls a 'harmonic continuo' (i.e. a freely composed layer which lends harmonic support to the horizontal line), together with a supporting melodic line which begins a few bars before each metamorphosis (e.g. the double-basses from bar 59). As the piece progresses, the separation between these three layers becomes less clear; as it pushes towards the climax they become enmeshed and analytical distinction between them purely notional. Systematic rhythmic quickening also plays an important part in the dramatic development of the Metamorphoses and there is an acceleration of rhythmic energy which assists in driving towards the point of culmination.

Although the melodic material and harmonic effects of the outer sections are governed horizontally by a twelve-note row, the full chromatic density of vertical twelve-note harmony is reserved for the moment of arrival at the climax of the work, Apogeum. There are thirty-two chords (Ex. 3 : 12), most of which are conceived in three harmonic strands corresponding to the following grouping of subdivided strings: violins I–IV (high strand); violas I and II (middle strand); cellos I and II, and basses I and II (low strand). Chords 1 and 5 have a similar construction (J–D–D), with dominant-seventh chords in the low and middle strands, and a major triad with added minor ninth in the high strand. Note the widely spaced intervals used for the G⁷ chord in the low strand, and the octave reinforcement of the low G. Lutosławski often opens out the low harmonic strand in this way, thus acknowledging the acoustic properties of the natural overtone series. Chords 3 and 4 are both of the elementary type, being densely clustered adjacent semitones (containing twelve and ten notes, respectively). Although chords 25–32 all result in clustered semitones, they contain only 8, 11, 5, 8, 7, 5, 4 and 2 notes, respectively.

EX. 3 : 11 *Musique funèbre*, Metamorphoses 1–6

69

EX. 3 : 12 *Musique funèbre*, harmonic reduction of Apogeum

The remaining chord-aggregates (2, and 6–24) all contain complementary diminished-seventh chords.[12] From chord 6 they form a genuine
progression (as opposed to mere succession) which drives inexorably
towards the intense unison A at the beginning of the Epilogue. Example
3 : 12 shows how this progression causes the chords to fold inwards,
compressing the harmony and thus increasing the dramatic tension by
maximising the dissonance. The interval structure of the chords used in
the outer strands appears either as superimposed minor thirds or interlocking tritones; the exchange of notes between chords 6–7, 8–9, 10–11,
and 12–13 emphasises this feature. The progression is driven by converging patterns of intervals in the top and bottom lines; the top descends
sequentially by alternating minor thirds and semitones, while the bottom
ascends sequentially by alternating minor thirds and tones. Gradually, the
component chords overlap and interlock to such an extent that their
separate identities become less and less clear. Eventually, the subdivision
into four-note groups is no longer audible as the harmonic texture
becomes that of densely clustered semitones.

Whereas the twelve-note chords of the Apogeum provide climactic
density, the Epilogue opens with the idea of greatest emotional intensity,
a statement of the twelve-note theme in unison, *fortissimo*. The piece
subsides as the canons reappear, inverted. Gradually the number of parts
is reduced, leaving the last phrase to the cellist who began the Prologue.
By this stage the piece has come full circle and if the cello were to play just
one more note it would begin the whole piece again.

Musique funèbre lasts about thirteen-and-a-half minutes in most performances conducted by the composer. If one calculates how long it takes
to reach the climax at the beginning of the Apogeum, the highpoint
occurs after eight-and-a-half minutes in a relationship of 0.63 to the
overall duration. This is remarkably close to the point of Golden Section,
which would be approximately 0.618 of the whole. In view of this
intriguing phenomenon it is worth emphasising the dedication. The significance of Golden Section proportions in the music of Bartók has been
extensively researched,[13] with some convincing examples drawn from
precisely those works of the 1930s so much admired by Lutosławski:
Music for Strings, Percussion and Celesta, and the Sonata for Two Pianos
and Percussion (not forgetting the slow movement of the Divertimento
for strings). This is not to say Lutosławski calculated the proportions to
produce this result (at least not consciously); but whether they formed
part of his precompositional plan or not, one should not overlook the

connection. A similar proportion occurs in *Paroles tissées*; an even more intriguing case, as the *ad libitum* sections would have rendered precise precompositional calculation impossible. Even closer to the Golden Section proportion than either of these examples is the piece which immediately followed *Musique funèbre*: Postlude no. 1.

Postludes

The Postludes proved severely problematic for Lutosławski. In fact, the work we now know under the title of Three Postludes for orchestra, was originally planned to extend to a four-movement scheme. His inability to realise the full scope of the original conception highlights the transitional nature of the stage Lutosławski had reached by the end of the 1950s. His dilemma was not one of harmonic language (that problem had already been solved in the Five Songs and *Musique funèbre*), it was a complex issue of time and rhythm, polyphony and form. The solution was eventually reached in *Jeux vénitiens*; but once this breakthrough had been made it was too late to go back. Hence the orchestral work which led Lutosławski to a crossroads in his career was abandoned. Precisely because it was left incomplete, one should not underestimate the significance of this episode, as it marks another of the decisive turning-points in his creative development.

Postlude no. 1 was written between 1958 and 1960, and eventually received its first performance at a concert in Geneva on 1 September 1963 to celebrate the centenary of the International Red Cross, when it was played by the Suisse Romande Orchestra, conducted by Ernest Ansermet. The second and third pieces, composed in 1960, were later salvaged from the abandoned symphonic work. Together with no. 1, they were performed under the title Three Postludes at Kraków on 8 October 1965.

The most remarkable feature of Postlude no. 1 is its shape. It is the most simply and obviously structured of all the composer's many goal-orientated pieces; lasting only about three-and-a-half minutes in performance, it moves directly to a point of climax, from which it subsides. Here it is comparatively easy to calculate the structural proportions, in particular the position of the climax in relation to the overall time-span. As all the bars are subject to an unchanging triple metre, and the tempo does not alter, the proportions can be calculated simply in terms of bar numbers, without any need for more complicated procedures. One finds that the climactic moment occurs just over a bar's distance from the point of Golden Section. Lutosławski claims not to calculate such matters, so it is remarkable that the piece should correspond so closely to this proportion. One might conclude that his admiration for the music of Bartók has exerted a profound influence that unconsciously affects his approach to form; perhaps so, but it is more likely that these proportions manifest themselves in his work independent of any particular influence, as a deeply lodged structural archetype.[14]

Postlude no. 2 provides plenty of evidence to demonstrate that Lutosławski was searching for means of achieving harmonic blurring, particularly in the melodic lines. This can be observed throughout the piece wherever there are two or more parts playing similar phrases in the same register: for example, the string parts at the beginning of the movement. Here, as elsewhere, similar parts play variants of the same intervallic cells and rhythmic motifs, but the composer ensures a result which is always harmonically out of synchronisation. Instead of forming co-ordinated unison lines, the polyphonic parts are composed in order to be slightly astray. This effect was soon to be established as one of the most important characteristics of Lutosławski's technique of 'controlled aleatory counterpoint', and he later used the term 'bundles' to describe such disaligned polyphony. At bar 115 we reach the first twelve-note chords of the movement and of the work as a whole. They are aggregates of superimposed diminished-seventh chords, of the kind already observed in *Rycerze* and the Apogeum of *Musique funèbre*.

Postlude no. 3 is the most curious of all. Its opening is signalled by a *fortissimo* chord which recurs as a point of reference for the whole piece. All sections and episodes of the form are defined by its return, a procedure Lutosławski was soon to adopt in the first movement of *Jeux vénitiens*; similar referential features were later used in the first movement of the String Quartet and in the Third Symphony. Here, however, the numerous statements of the same chord gradually assume a negative rather than positive role, not so much signalling the beginning of something new as an abrupt termination that prevents further development. This punctuating chord is extensively doubled but contains only three pitches (B, E, A) linked by interval-class 5. Altogether it is stated thirty-six times during the course of the piece, up to bar 214, always *fortissimo*. In bars 215–17 the dynamic level reaches *fff* as chords 37–9 change to interval-class 2 (F–G–A), the first two each followed by a four-second pause. Chord 40 contains interval-class 4 (D♭–F–A), followed by chord 41 with interval-class 3 (E♭–G♭–A). Chords 42–6 are all played *fff* with interval-class 1 stretched out and presented in minor ninths. The last six chords (47–52) all contain interval-class 1 as a single clustered three-note cell played in all registers. With each of the six statements of this last chord, the dynamic level drops: *ff, f, mf, mp, p, pp*. A dramatic device which could have been used as a mechanism for structural growth instead becomes an instrument of intractability that impedes development. The harmonic object becomes an insurmountable obstacle; Lutosławski had created his own impasse. One could describe it as a 'block' chord, with irony fully intended.

Although he had already established the main elements of his new harmonic language, the Postludes show that Lutosławski had not yet found for himself a satisfactory way of harnessing the resources of fully chromatic harmony to the vivid orchestration already developed in the Concerto for Orchestra. This problem was finally resolved in *Livre pour orchestre*. With hindsight, we are aware that he had not yet succeeded in applying the principle of separate harmonic strands to different instrumental groups within the orchestra. At its simplest, this would later involve assigning the top harmonic strand, for example, to the woodwind section, the middle strand to the brass and the low strand to the strings. In practice, there are far more subtle and sophisticated solutions than this simple subdivision. Yet the principle, once observed, enables one to trace the development of his treatment of twelve-note chords as an integral part of his orchestral sound world.

The title of the Postludes is apt, because they represent the end of an era as far as Lutosławski's treatment of ensemble rhythm is concerned. He was about to turn his attention from problems of harmony and chords to those of polyphony and pulsation. In retrospect we can see that the period from 1954 until 1960 was a transitional phase in his development. The next milestone was to be the introduction of an element of chance, and his exposure to the idea also came by chance.

4
Chance and Polyphony
(1960–1968)

Jeux vénitiens relates to Lutosławski's organisation of time as the Five Songs relate to his organisation of pitch. Each was a decisive turning point marking the introduction of new elements that have remained central to his musical language and compositional technique ever since. Though these elements have been developed and refined, both changes were radical and neither has been reversed. But whereas the issue of harmony occupied him over a decade before a solution to the problems of pitch organisation was unveiled, the change in rhythmic technique occurred suddenly, while Lutosławski was still working on the Postludes. The catalyst for change came in 1960, when he heard a radio broadcast of the Concert for Piano and Orchestra[1] by John Cage, which gave him the idea of using 'chance' procedures (he later expressed his gratitude to Cage by presenting him with the autograph score of *Jeux vénitiens*). In spite of the significance of this event as a breakthrough for Lutosławski, one must beware of overstating the notion of direct influence; he was certainly stimulated by the ideas of Cage, but was not influenced by the sound of the music itself. He later recalled his experience of first hearing the Cage *Concert*: 'Composers often do not hear the music that is being played . . . we are listening to something and at the same time creating something else.'[2]

Chance has been central to Lutosławski's vocabulary since 1960, yet the word leads to misunderstanding, especially if his gratitude towards Cage is misread as signifying gravitation towards orientalism. Lutosławski's approach remains thoroughly European. Closely connected with chance is the adjective 'aleatory', which has entered the musical lexicon primarily by translation from various French and German sources (French: *aléatoire*, German: *aleatorisch*).[3] Misleading accounts persist, unfortunately, about the application of these principles to the music of Lutosławski.[4]

Aleatory is defined as depending on the throw of a die or dice (from the Latin *alea*; hence *aleator*, dice-thrower). Lutosławski's use of the term, and application of the concept in his music, recognises a framework of limitation, a restricted range of possibilities. The throw of a single die produces one of only six results, while the throw of two dice is subject to only twenty-one possible results; in both cases the full range of possible outcomes is foreseen. Hence the aleatory aspects of chance should not be confused (as they often are) with things which are random; games of chance depend on hazard, but need not be haphazard. In a lecture originally intended for presentation at Darmstadt, 'Rhythm and the organisation of pitch in composing techniques employing a limited element of chance', Lutosławski began by defining 'aleatory' (in German), quoting the leading proponent of Information Theory as applied to music, Werner Meyer-Eppler:

'Aleatorisch nennt man Vorgänge deren Verlauf im groben festliegt, im Einzelnen aber von Zufall abhängt.' [By 'aleatory' one means a procedure whose broad outcome is defined, but whose details depend upon chance.][5] Compositions written within the terms of this definition do not really go beyond the basic conventions and traditions of European music where a piece of music is, typically, an occurrence rather than a state ... The work will continue to be 'an object in time' so long as the play of chance is held sufficiently in check by the composer and it does not become the controlling impulse of the work, but is kept subservient to the composer's design ... Conceived in this way, aleatorism does not appear to be much of an innovation. But although it is true that it makes no fundamental change in the treatment of a music-work as 'an object in time', it has an utterly radical effect on its rhythmic and expressive physiognomy, and this is enough to give music composed in this vein a totally different sound from that in which chance makes no appearance whatsoever.[6]

Before discussing individual works affected by chance and aleatory techniques, it is necessary to consider both how the radical effect on 'rhythmic and expressive physiognomy' is achieved, and how it relates to compositional control over pitch organisation.[7] The essence of aleatory technique lies in ensemble co-ordination: in cueing the beginning and end of *ad libitum* sections; and in cueing the entry of individual parts within these sections. In most cases the ensemble is directed by a conductor; but in Lutosławski's String Quartet an elaborate system of written instructions, with aural and visual signals, enables the group to function (see Ex. 4 : 5). Apart from this unusual case (and later chamber pieces such as *Epitaph*, *Grave* and *Partita*), the role of the conductor is crucial to an understanding of Lutosławski's work.

Notational signs for ensemble co-ordination in the later works differ from those used in the earliest aleatory pieces of the 1960s. Most of these changes arose from the composer's experience of conducting his own music. Since returning to the podium for the première of *Trois poèmes* in 1963, he has been increasingly in demand with orchestras worldwide to realise his works in performance. Hence, the notation of *Jeux vénitiens*, and other works of the 1960s differs from the more standardised notation evolved by the mid-1970s. Sections of 'collective *ad libitum*' (the composer's term) are defined by the absence of pulsation common to all parts (i.e. not conducted). Once the performers have been cued to begin such a section, they play as individuals without co-ordinating with other parts, except when directed by another cue from the conductor. It follows that *ad libitum* sections do not require time-signatures or bar lines, although approximate metronome marks may be given.

It is ironic that Lutosławski's explanation of his aleatory technique was intended for presentation at Darmstadt, because he was drawn in the direction of chance procedures partly as a reaction against the over-complex scores of the Darmstadt school in its post-Webernian serialist phase of the 1950s. Others were to react in a similar way, notably Ligeti. Lutosławski's controlled aleatory technique relies for its rhythmic sophistication on the complex combination of relatively simple individual parts. Rather than being rhythmically strict and intellectually exhausting, it tends to be rhythmically subtle and intellectually refreshing. Lutosławski has expressed his dislike for the idea of performers being required to execute music with the rhythmic precision of a machine, preferring to derive his complex ensemble rhythms from the interaction of individual parts that are flexible rather than rigidly fixed:

The rhythmic structure developed by collective *ad libitum*, being the sum of all the rhythmic structures of the individual parts, is a far more complex texture than any polyrhythmic structure to be found in traditional music. One of the reasons for this is that there may be . . . accelerandos and rallentandos within each part. There are many other similar possibilities. All of them spring from the composer's assumption that each of the performers will, within a specified time-unit, play as though he were on his own, without worrying whether he is in time with the others. In this way the rhythmic structure acquires a distinctive suppleness not attainable otherwise.[8]

Because of the absence of bar lines, which would cancel the validity of accidentals, sharps and flats apply in aleatory sections only to the notes which they immediately precede (conventionally metred pieces, however, such as the first, third and fifth movements of *Partita*, are notated in the traditional way). Natural signs are thus rendered redundant, although for added clarity they are provided in the orchestral parts. Multiple repetition of a single note governed by a sharp or flat is usually abbreviated to show the first note followed by rhythmic flags without note heads, in order to avoid the necessity of repeating the accidental. These features, together with the conducted cues, contribute to a distinctive page-image that makes Lutosławski's scores instantly recognisable; but it is also necessary for him to make all decisions concerning the pagination and layout. Hence the production of the final score is a very time-consuming operation, in many cases taking longer than the compositional process itself. Fundamental issues are inevitably confronted in the application of aleatory techniques. To what extent does a composer exercise and maintain compositional control over the resulting performance? Can the composer foresee and determine the outcome?

In principle I should make allowance for all the possible versions that can arise out of my text as a result of the introduction of simultaneous *ad libitum* performance and compose the text in such a way that all the versions meet the planned requirements. To visualise all the possible alternatives is usually impossible, but then it is not really necessary either. It is enough to compose just one version of a particular section of the form ... which might be called 'the least advantageous' from the point of view of the original intention.[9]

Differences between performances of the same work are usually slight, and in many cases not discernable. This is because aleatory technique as used by Lutosławski does not affect the form as a whole. All such decisions are made and strictly controlled by the composer. Nowhere in Lutosławski's music can the individual performers choose which sections they play or the order in which they play them. It must also be stressed that there is no indeterminacy or improvisation in Lutosławski's music, although some critics have mistakenly suggested otherwise.[10] The title of Lutosławski's lecture on 'Rhythm and the organisation of pitch ...' made explicit his conviction that aleatory procedures could be acceptable to him only if carefully limited in extent and always subject to pitch control. In spite of this and other attempts over the years to clarify the nature of his aleatory technique, misunderstanding still persists on the crucial question of how aleatory principles have affected his harmony:

When I first discovered chance as an element of my music, my main problem was not so much the organisation of time, as it was superficially interpreted by some, but the organisation of pitch. I think this is the basic problem of music: the vertical and horizontal organisation of pitch.[11]

Vertically planned aleatory sections can be built on a single chord, either containing all twelve notes, or a subdivision of the chromatic whole. Collective *ad libitum* is then used merely to elaborate only the notes of that unchanging harmony, similar to the broken-chord patterns used in music of the Classical period. This approach is also embellished by introducing non-harmony notes to the individual parts which relate to the basic chord much in the same way as passing notes and auxiliary notes (neighbour notes) in tonal harmony. All such aleatory sections, however, share the disadvantage of being harmonically static. In order to mitigate the static quality of chordally conceived aleatory sections, Lutosławski has developed a technique of composing some passages that move gradually from one chord to another. In such sections there are three stages: where only the notes of the first harmony will be heard; where notes of the first and second harmonies will mix and overlap; and where only the notes of the second harmony will be heard.

Horizontally planned aleatory sections can consist of the projection of a monodic line delivered as a polyphonic 'bundle' of individual parts which play slight rhythmic variants of the same line. Bundles may deliver the notes of a twelve-note row (see Ex. 5 : 3), or may be more freely composed according to a particular horizontal interval pairing (see Ex. 5 : 10). The effect is one of blurring the single line (note that the composer also uses this principle of blurring in some passages that are controlled by conventional metre, such as the cycle of chords at the beginning of *Mi-Parti*, and the whole of *Interlude*).

Subdivision of the chromatic whole into complementary groups of notes (set complementation) is used where the composer wishes to combine several horizontal lines in a polyphonic texture that maintains strict separation of pitch material between the constituent parts (see Exx. 4 : 5, 4 : 10, 6 : 4). In most cases the sum of the parts will provide all twelve notes, while the individual lines contain complementary sub-sets, usually of between three and six notes. In other cases, the sum of the parts may provide less than twelve notes, perhaps only six. The latter method is employed in cases where successive aleatory sections derived from complementary pitch-sets are overlapped and thus harmonically superimposed, for example in *Chain 3*. Before evolving these comparatively sophisticated methods, however, he first had to test the aleatory medium; the resulting experiment interrupted his work on the Postludes and charted a new course for his career.

Jeux vénitiens

The title of *Jeux vénitiens* (Venetian Games) refers both to the aleatory game played by the composer, and to the location of its incomplete first performance in Venice. The première (without the third movement) was given on 24 April 1961 in the Teatro La Fenice by the Kraków Philharmonic Chamber Orchestra, conducted by Andrzej Markowski. The first complete performance, including the third movement (and slight revision of the others), was given at the Warsaw Autumn Festival on 16 September 1961 by the National Philharmonic Orchestra, conducted by Witold Rowicki. The work is scored for a relatively small wind section, four percussion players with a comprehensive battery of instruments, harp, piano (two players at one instrument), and a small string section (4. 3. 3. 2.); the number of string players required was obviously conditioned by the need to score twelve-note chords.

At first glance, the opening movement appears to have been affected most by aleatory principles (in fact the last movement is more radical). It is divided into eight sections notated in self-contained boxes and labelled A–H, inclusive. Each begins with a percussive aural signal (played *fortissimo* by side-drums, claves and xylophone) which decisively marks the beginning of a section, and therefore abruptly terminates the preceding one. The form may be described as refrains (or ritornelli) and episodes, a typical procedure for an introductory movement in Lutosławski's work. Sections A, C, E and G represent the refrain (the instrumentation is increased each time), while sections B, D, F and H are the episodes. The refrains are rhythmically active and intervallically angular, while the episodes are reposeful, slow and sustained.

EX. 4 : 1 *Jeux vénitiens*, first movement, harmonic reduction of refrain

The refrains are based on two superimposed twelve-note chords (Ex. 4 : 1). The first is heard each time (played in angular, arpeggiated figurations by a seven-part woodwind section of two flutes, oboe, three clarinets and bassoon), and contains only interval-classes 2, 3 and 5. It is a vertically symmetrical construction of major seconds and minor thirds around the axis of a perfect fourth. The second twelve-note chord is fully overlaid on the first in section G and partially in section E. In the latter, three brass instruments play a four-note semitone cluster (G–B♭) that fills the axis interval of the first twelve-note chord (i.e. the perfect fourth F♯–B). In section G the piano delivers a widely spaced symmetrical pattern of superimposed minor thirds that complement the brass cluster in order to complete the second twelve-note chord. Thus the whole idea is based on vertical interval symmetry, an aspect of harmonic design that is typical of Lutosławski's works from the 1960s, but less common in the later works. He has explained his method of organising rhythmic motifs and pitch in the refrains:

There are seven woodwinds here, each of them playing a number of motifs divided by caesuras. Altogether there are nine such motifs. They appear in a different order in each of the instruments . . . The 'least advantageous' situation is when the same motif is played by all the instruments at once. But even should this happen, there would be no sameness of rhythm because each of the motifs appears in various rhythmic variations [see Ex. 4 : 2 for variants of the first motif], one version being reserved for each instrument . . . The four notes of the brass strand and the eight notes of the piano strand combine to form a twelve-note chord having no notes in common with the previous chord [i.e. at the same octave register]. In this way twelve octave doublings are produced . . . In the perception of the whole passage there is something that might be called a division into local harmonies, that is a disintegration of the perception of the harmonies into three separate strands and an elimination of the harmonies arising between the notes belonging to different strands.[12]

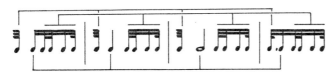

EX. 4 : 2 *Jeux vénitiens*, first movement, rhythmic motifs in refrain

In episodes B, D and H of the introductory movement, strings quietly sustain eight-note semitone clusters; each begins with one and then transposes gradually to another (in episodes B and D the transposition is upwards, while the last episode transposes the cluster down and dies away as parts gradually stop). The harmony of episode F contains only one eight-note vertically symmetrical, extended chord, of superimposed minor and major thirds. This results in two minor-seventh chords placed a minor ninth apart. At the end of episode H, Lutosławski plays with the listener's expectation: another percussion signal suggests another refrain, but it does not return. The percussion players try again, three times with a reduced number of participants and a quieter dynamic: *ff, f, mf, p.* A solitary side-drum has the last word.

Whereas the first movement refrains are directed *ad libitum,* the second is a very brief scherzo in triple metre throughout. The notation slightly obscures the metre, as the bar lines are shown as dotted. In fact, there appears to be no reason why the score could not have been notated in a conventional manner; all instruments are subject to metred control, except for one brief passage in the piano part. This movement lasts only about one-and-a-half minutes, and is textural in conception with little that could be described as melodic. The fast rhythmic pace is generated by fragmentary motoric motifs. Dynamic level is low throughout, mostly *pianissimo,* but rising to *mezzo-forte* in the bassoon and first clarinets parts where they develop a slightly more expansive phrase. The character of this fleet scherzo is similar to the second Postlude, and in both cases they fulfil a transitional function in the structural scheme.

The third movement is the most memorable of the four. Here the piano carries a continually unfolding twelve-note row of a very simple type, containing only perfect fourths and perfect fifths as adjacent intervals, delivered (in full) thirteen times. In the first section of the piece the prime-form of the row (G, C, F, B♭, E♭, A♭, D♭, G♭, B, E, A, D) appears in full eight times, plus the first note at letter L of what would be the ninth statement. The central section, from L to Q, does not use the row. After Q the inversion of the row is given five times, plus the first two notes of what would be the fourteenth statement. The piano part, however, is only one of several independent strands of the whole texture, and it simply provides harmonic colour against which a solo flute plays out a melodic line. The latter gradually expands, from tight little three-note cells of tone/semitone, to a wide-ranging interval span. The other woodwind parts sustain notes as a residual harmonic trace of prominent notes in the flute melody. The harp fulfils a similar supporting role, but with clustered motifs becoming gradually more active and expansive. The strings, unlike the other supporting parts, do not accompany the flute, but punctuate the movement with sixteen chords, mostly of twelve notes. These become successively louder up to Q, and then gradually quieter until the end. The succession of dynamic levels assigned to these chords shows clearly that the movement is planned in order to build towards a climax at Q from which it then subsides. Both the flute melody and its various supporting layers, including the piano's row, begin with small interval patterns contained in the middle register. By octave displacements in the piano part (and the introduction of different interval patterns in the flute solo) they move towards the climax of the movement between M and Q. From Q the intervals of the flute melody contract until they return to three-note cells, but played in the highest register.

So far, we have a formal scheme that treats the first movement as fragmented and inconclusive, the second movement as fast-moving and rather featureless, and the third as carrying the main melodic focus. The final movement completes the scheme by building to a decisive climax and then subsiding. Thus we have a four-movement design that provides a perfect illustration of the formal principles that Lutosławski so vividly recalled from his studies with Maliszewski. In *Jeux vénitiens* we have each of Maliszewski's four 'characters' precisely identified with the individual movements: introductory, transitional, narrative and concluding. The flute solo that delivers the content of the third movement is the only narrative feature of the work. Each of the other movements is defined by its function in relation to the scheme as a whole.

The final movement is the one most affected by aleatory principles. As it unfolds, contrasted instrumental blocks are overlapped and super-imposed. Although the aleatory counterpoint within each textural block is controlled, there is much scope for discrepancy between different performances in the co-ordination of these blocks. The effect is of dense sound-mass. This is a far more radical chance procedure than the straight-forward sectional construction of the first movement, where the divisions are clear. In the last movement the collage superimpositions are obscured in order to assist the cumulative build-up towards the climax. The latter is reached where strings, woodwind and brass all coincide in a *fortissimo* collective *ad libitum* section on p. 42 of the score. In the 1978 recording conducted by the composer the work's duration was 12'45", with the climax occurring after 10'12" at eight-tenths of the duration. This is much later than preceding works such as *Musique funèbre* and Postlude no. 1, and is also much later than in subsequent pieces of the 1960s such as the *Trois poèmes d'Henri Michaux* or *Paroles tissées*.

Harmony in the final movement is dominated by twelve-note chords emphasising either tritones (with perfect fifths or semitones) or minor thirds. It is arguable, however, whether the harmonic sonorities are heard, because the level of harmonic and textural density is so great that one tends to perceive the dramatic gestures rather than the character of chords. The composer has outlined the harmony from J to the end:

there are four strands played *ad libitum*. Each is constructed of notes belonging to a separate twelve-note chord ... First and foremost, we register the 'local harmonies', that is, those occurring within the particular levels and not between them. The lowest level is constructed around a twelve-note chord of minor seconds contained between C and B. The double-basses and cellos play C, C♯, F, F♯, G, and B, the other notes being taken by the harp. The next twelve-note chord is played by a motorless vibraphone and is contained between G♭ and F. Its three top notes are also played by a group of three brass instruments. The third chord has a different structure; its notes are played by a group of woodwinds and celesta. The highest chord is an eleven-note chord of minor seconds ... played by three violins, three violas and piano. Each of the four levels has its own rhythmic physiognomy. On the other hand, the time-density of the sounds varies in each of the levels in a corresponding way ... Since the instrumental groups representing each of the levels do not enter at once, but successively, the moments of the highest density of sound do not occur simultaneously. The listener's attention, caught by these peaks of density, is switched from one level to the next, and this also tends to make for a perception of 'local harmonies' rather than a summing-up of all the sounds into a single harmony.[13]

In practice, the texture of the final movement is probably too dense for the character of these 'local' harmonies to be perceived. Instead, one is left with an impression of shifting textures within sound-mass. All this was an experiment for Lutosławski, one that stimulated him to explore various applications of aleatory technique in other works of the 1960s. Although the Second Symphony and *Livre pour orchestre* use some harmonically dense (and static) sound-masses, he was also to use conventionally metred passages in order to achieve greater pace and dramatic drive. Before fully addressing the problem of harmonic stasis, however, he was to go even further with chance procedures, exploring the potential of aleatory technique in the fields of chamber and vocal music.

Trois poèmes d'Henri Michaux

Standing conspicuously alone as the only choral work of Lutosławski's mature years, the *Trois poèmes d'Henri Michaux* (1961–3) provide an invaluable insight into his approach to text setting for vocal ensemble. Having decided to set French poetry (as a result of translation problems with the Iłłakowicz songs), he spent several years searching for poems that might suit the abstract ideas of form already in his mind. In a Polish literary journal he eventually found two poems by Henri Michaux

(1899–1984): *Pensées* and *Repos dans le malheur*, originally published in Paris in 1938, as part of a collection entitled *Plume*. The remaining text needed for the climactic, central movement of his dramatic scheme, he found in an earlier collection of Michaux's poems, *Qui je fus* (1928).

Lutosławski has described in detail his enthusiasm for the poetry of Michaux in conversation with Jean-Paul Couchoud.[14] Their discussions were wide ranging, but no aspect of his work was more sensitively addressed than the choice and treatment of French poetry: by Michaux, Jean-François Chabrun (*Paroles tissées*), and Robert Desnos (*Les espaces du sommeil*). The conduct of these interviews in French appears to have encouraged the composer to express his feeling for that language. (By contrast, the interviews in Polish prompted by the questioning of Tadeusz Kaczyński were notably less revealing.)

from the very first I was fascinated by the poetry of Michaux. I discovered it in a monthly Polish revue, translated into Polish. Immediately I began to study his poetry. I must say that he is one of those rare poets with whom contact is immediately created, without any preparatory stage ... He is a very profound poet who handles eternal themes, common to all humanity. And he always expresses himself with very great originality. Take the end of *L'époque des illuminés*. The description of the end of time is a poetic discovery worthy of the greatest poets of humanity.[15]

Although Pierre Boulez had already made use of a Michaux text in *Poésie pour pouvoir*, first performed at Donaueschingen in 1958, there is little similarity between his treatment of the vocal medium and that adopted by Lutosławski, who, in coded criticism of some of his composer contemporaries, has declared himself to have been thoroughly disillusioned with the choral works of that time. In referring to serial and post-serial choral music in negative terms, Lutosławski was no doubt thinking in particular of the kind of angular vocal writing which had taken Webern as its point of departure. Boulez's concerts with the Domaine Musical typified this sort of approach, as did many performances at Darmstadt and Donaueschingen during the 1950s and early 1960s.

in the development of instrumental music of recent decades ... many approaches to writing have interested me. But, in general, that which has been composed for choir during the same period ... seems unacceptable to me. In these diverse kinds of choral writing there have been extremely complex structures, chords, sequences of intervals which are very difficult to sing and very doubtful as a resulting sound. Even in works by those of great renown. ... I speak of ... serial and post-serial writing. And it is just because I didn't find anything there that struck me as satisfactory, in the realms of choral writing, that I decided to write something for choir.[16]

Irregular prosody is a decisive consideration for Lutosławski when choosing a text. The poetry of Henri Michaux seems to have supplied him with what he regards as an ideal combination of irregularly metred verse and prose. The following comments can be regarded as illuminating not only his attitude towards prosodic and poetic rhythm, but also the wider question of rhythm in general:

of great importance for the composer's work is the form of his [Michaux's] poetry, which is mostly written in a mixture of verse and prose, and the verses themselves are irregular. The sameness of rhythms in traditional poetry, and even in contemporary poetry ... is an insurmountable obstacle for a composer these days. To avoid the monotony of a rhythm which repeats incessantly, it is necessary to do unexpected things ... With Henri Michaux, on the contrary, it is possible as a musician to remain completely natural in following faithfully the form of his poetry, because of his rhythmic and formal variety.[17]

Audibility of the text is frequently problematic in the *Trois poèmes*, largely because of the textural treatment of the vocal ensemble. Lutosławski considers this aspect of the work to be unsatisfactory:

I always strive to make the text audible and intelligible. Unfortunately, here I have not always succeeded and I deplore that ... I could even say that if I were to compose the *Trois poèmes* by Michaux again, I would profit from all the experience I have had as listener, and as conductor of the chorus, and I would certainly do some retouching, aiming to render the text more completely audible.[18]

In his search for natural effects of vocal expression, in this piece he makes use not only of singing, but also of monotone recitation, speaking, whispering, and shouting. These sounds are used particularly in the second movement, *Le grand combat*, where there is no singing at all. Although the effects are quite natural for each individual voice, when they are used in sections of collective *ad libitum* co-ordination the resulting rhythmic and textural complexity often obscures the text. Such passages are mostly notated without any indication of pitch other than a general indication of medium, high or low. This should not be confused, however, with principles of chance applied to the pitch of sung notes, an aspect of compositional control which Lutosławski does not surrender.

Aleatory independence between the vocal and instrumental ensembles is such that separate scores are provided and two conductors needed, one for the chorus, the other for the orchestra. Instrumental requirements are for woodwind (3, 2, 3, 2) and brass (2, 2, 2, 0), with harp, two pianos, and four percussion players commanding a large battery. There is a notable absence of strings. Instead, the two pianos are used to generate the harmonic sonorities that strings might otherwise have provided. Lutosławski's methods of organising pitch in this work are quite simple compared with some of those he was later to evolve. His continual use of twelve-note chords (as opposed to chord-aggregates), particularly those with clustered semitones, leads to a kind of harmony that is heard in terms of general texture, with little opportunity for the projection of melodic lines. The question of melody does not seem to have been confronted in this work, so the problems and limitations of texturalism remain.

The first movement, *Pensées*, opens with a symmetrical twelve-note chord (two hexachords of interval-classes 2 + 5 linked by a semitone), played by the two pianos. This sets in motion a long, babbling section for wind instruments which gradually contracts in register to reach a twelve-note chord of clustered semitones at Fig. 28. There the voices enter to deliver the first verse unaccompanied: 'Penser, vivre, mer peu distincte; Moi – ça – tremble, Infini incessamment qui tressaille.' For the second verse ('Ombres de mondes infimes . . .'), there is an instrumental context provided simply by ascending and then descending chromatic scale segments treated in various ways. These are notated without rhythmic stems, but with their relative positions within the polyphonic texture clear. The instrumentation for the third verse ('Pensées à la nage merveilleuse, qui glissez en nous . . .') has woodwind textures juxtaposed against the scintillating, typically Lutosławskian combination of vibraphone, celesta, harp and two pianos at Figs. 103–8, 113–28, and 132–42 (where the vibraphone is replaced by xylophone and glockenspiel). The fourth verse refers back to the clustered harmony of the first before the voices conclude the text, again unaccompanied: 'poussières pour nous distraire et nous éparpiller la vie.'

In stark contrast to the delicate intimacy of *Pensées*, the mood of the second movement, *Le grand combat*, lives up to the desperate struggle described through the poem's savage imagery. The chorus are onlookers to the contest and one accepts as entirely appropriate that their speaking and shouting should be delivered with the degree of individual freedom afforded by Lutosławski's technique of collective *ad libitum*. The instrumentation, strongly featuring the battery of percussion, reinforces our awareness of the brutality of the conflict.

Although there is no pitch dimension to the vocal parts in the second movement, this does not mean that the result is chaotic. The harmony of the orchestral dimension is very carefully organised to give a sense of direction to the form. Several different types of interval combination are used to generate chords, not necessarily of all twelve notes. At Figs. 28 and 34 a symmetrical eight-note chord of major thirds connected by major sixths emphasises minor ninths between the four harmonic strands. Just after Fig. 50 there is a twelve-note chord with a symmetrical arrangement of minor thirds and minor sevenths, connected at the axis by a minor second. This chord provides an illustration of the minor-ninth principle that is so important an aspect of the characteristic interval physiognomy in many of Lutosławski's twelve-note chords (see Ex. 3 : 3). In the final push towards the orchestral climax of the work (Figs. 55–6), there is a succession of fourteen chords (Figs. 52–3): seven eight-note chords (emphasising major thirds) played by the woodwinds, alternating with seven six-note chords (emphasising minor thirds) played by the brass (Ex. 4 : 3). In addition to this clear definition and contrast of vertical interval-pairing, there are also linear connections of voice-leading created by a pattern of rising semitones, first at the top (A♯–C♯), then at the bottom (C–E). These patterns are linked by the sequence of descending perfect fourths that can be traced through the bottom notes of chords 1, 3, 5 and 7. Whether these vertical and horizontal connections are perceived by the listener is another matter. But it is interesting to observe that, even in a work as texturally and gesturally based as the *Trois poèmes*, Lutosławski was at pains to establish a secure harmonic framework. *Le grand combat* ends as it began, unaccompanied, but quietly as the chorus confides: 'On cherche aussi, nous autres, le Grand Secret.'

EX. 4 : 3 *Trois poèmes d'Henri Michaux*, chords from 'Le grand combat'

At the beginning of the third movement, *Repos dans le malheur*, after the harp intones the first of four focal pitches (initially D♭/C♯, then E♭, F and finally on F♯), the two pianos play a harmonic pattern of gradually changing interval structure which illustrates the importance to Luto-sławski of the various horizontal interval pairings outlined in Chapter 3. First, only perfect fourths/fifths are used (interval-class 5); these are then combined with tritones (5 + 6); the tritones are retained but the fourths/fifths are replaced by semitones (6 + 1); eventually the tritones are eliminated, leaving simply a chromatic scale treated with octave displacements. A similar passage occurs later between Figs. 12 and 13. In both cases a distinctive intervallic 'progression' is produced: 5;5 + 6;6 + 1;1. After the work has reached its conclusion on F♯ ('Je m'abandonne'), the two pianos finish with a repeated six-note pattern (G–C–G♯–B–A–B♭) of intervals that contract: 5–4–3–2–1.

Obviously, Lutosławski places his rigorously organised harmony at the service of the text, in order to enhance the psychological moods, gestures and images of the three poems; but one must not forget that the texts were chosen to serve a design rather than to provide one. The strength and clarity of this design ensure that, even if the poems are neither heard nor understood by the listener, the dramatic scheme is experienced and a level of abstract meaning will have been conveyed. In any case, Lutosławski is aiming for a much more complex end result than simply a literal comprehension of the text:

For me, the meaning of Michaux's poems does not stay within the narrow confines of the concrete. They are not merely a sceptical reflection on human thought (*Pensées*), or a description of a battle between two men (*Le grand combat*), or an act of resignation (*Repos dans le malheur*). The outward appearance of these poems hides a wealth of meaning, imagery, thought and emotion which allows us to live through the poems and to interpret them subjectively. That complexity of meaning brings some poems very close to music, which contains more meanings than any other art, or – to be more precise – has *no* definite meaning, which comes to the same thing.[19]

The *Trois poèmes* were completed on 17 April 1963 and first performed at the Zagreb Music Biennale on 9 May. This performance marked Lutosławski's professional return to the podium (conducting the orchestra) and the beginning of a long and productive period during which he gained invaluable experience from conducting his own work, first-hand experience that has played a crucial role in determining his treatment of the orchestral medium. In November 1963 Lutosławski received a prize from the International Music Council of UNESCO and the Gesellschaft der Musikfreunde in Vienna, for a recording of the Concerto for Orchestra. But soon the *Trois poèmes* would attract international acclaim that was to focus attention on his new, more radical language and technique. For the recording made at the Warsaw Autumn Festival of 1963 he received the Koussevitsky Prix Mondial du Disque in May of the following year. In Poland, on 22 July 1964, Lutosławski's international eminence was recognised by the award of the State Prize for music, first class, for the second time. He had received the same award (on the same day) in 1955, for the Concerto for Orchestra (this was a Communist anniversary, celebrating the proclamation and constitution of Polska Rzeczypospolita Ludowa – the 'Polish People's Republic' – on 22 July 1952). It is interesting to contrast the Polish government's intent behind these awards. In 1955 the old Stalinist nomenklatura was still firmly in charge of the Ministry of Culture; Sokorski was not removed from his position as Minister until April 1956. There is little difficulty, therefore, in interpreting this as a gesture cynically designed to imply that Lutosławski's use of folk material was done in accordance with the principles of socialist-realism. The award made in 1964, however, illustrates the profound change that had taken place (at least in outward policy, if not in basic attitudes of manipulation), a change enabling the authorities to align themselves with music whose modernist aesthetic they would previously have condemned.

The *Trois poèmes* were commissioned for the Zagreb Radio Choir by their conductor, Slavko Zlatić. This was the first of Lutosławski's works to be composed in fulfilment of a commission from outside Poland. It was also to be the last of his works whose copyright would be assigned exclusively to the Polish music publishers, PWM. His first relationship with a publisher based in Western Europe had been with Moeck Verlag of Celle in Germany; both the Five Songs and *Jeux vénitiens* were assigned to them, although the *Trois poèmes* were not. As his career developed, and his international reputation became enhanced, so the need for a Western publisher that could provide representation in many countries became increasingly acute. The next composition would be his first to be assigned to the Chester/Hansen publishing house before it was issued in Poland.

String Quartet

During the thirty years between the Dance Preludes (1954), and *Partita* (1984), Lutosławski's only substantial piece of chamber music was the String Quartet (the only other chamber pieces are short *pièces d'occasion*). It has become one of his most frequently performed and recorded

works, securing a position as one of the few truly outstanding contributions to the repertory since the quartets of Bartók. Commissioned by
Swedish Radio, it was first performed in Stockholm on 12 March 1965, in
the contemporary music concert series 'Nutida Musik', played by the
LaSalle Quartet.

The principal reason for his comparative neglect of chamber music
forces after 1960 was simply that they could not offer the same oppor-
tunities for exploiting aleatory techniques and textures that were to be
found in an orchestral medium. Yet in the String Quartet, we find aleatory procedures carried further than in any of his other works, composed
before or since. This does not mean that aleatory techniques are applied
to parameters other than rhythm, but the extended length of some *ad
libitum* sections creates the potential for differences between performances that are greater with this work than any other.

In relation to the *ad libitum* writing of the String Quartet, the composer
has used the word 'mobiles', a term borrowed from the movable, pendant
sculptures of Alexander Calder. Coincidentally, the spring of 1965 wit-
nessed the première of at least two other pieces influenced by Calder:
Gunther Schuller's *American Triptych: Three Studies in Texture* (New
Orleans, 9 March); and Earle Brown's *Calder Piece* (Paris, 8 April). Their
close proximity to the première of the String Quartet rules out any
question of cross-influence between the composers concerned, but it does
demonstrate the general appeal of such ideas during the 1960s. Edward
Cowie later took this aspect of aleatory technique to provide the title of
an article on Lutosławski's music.[20] The composer has explained his use
of the term:

The term 'mobile' refers to the variable length of sections in different instrumental
parts, which is connected with group playing *ad libitum*. The work contains a number
of very long sections, lasting several minutes each, which leads to great differences
between individual performances. That is why I coined a phrase which suggests the
mobility of various layers within the work, depending on the way they are performed.
I would like to stress that I was not aiming specifically at this variability within the
long sections. I wanted merely to loosen the time connections and to achieve a specific
texture, which we might call a 'fluid' texture. This kind of composition could be
compared, paradoxically, with sculpting in non-solid, almost liquid material.[21]

He also explained the idea of mobiles, and gave a comprehensive
commentary on the unusual treatment of ensemble co-ordination, in a
letter to Walter Levin, leader of the LaSalle Quartet:

The piece consists of a sequence of mobiles which are to be played, one after another, without any pause if there is no other indication. Within certain points of time particular players perform their parts quite independently of each other. They have to decide separately about the length of pauses and about the way of treating ritenutos and accelerandos. However, similar material in different parts should be treated in a similar way ... each particular player is supposed not to know what the others are doing, or, at least, to perform his part as if he were to hear nothing except that which he is playing himself. In such sections he must not bother about whether he is behind or ahead of the other. This problem simply does not exist, because of measures which have been taken to prevent all undesirable consequences of such freedom. If each performer strictly follows the instructions written in the parts, nothing could happen that has not been foreseen by the composer. All possible lengthening or shortening of the duration of the sections as played by each particular performer cannot affect the final result in any decisive way.[22]

Levin had made a particular plea for some kind of score which might assist the LaSalle Quartet in their preparations for the first performance; but because the work had been composed in separate instrumental parts, Lutosławski was resistant to the idea of contriving a score, for fear of misrepresenting or 'falsifying' the notation of collective rhythm and aleatory polyphony:

You may ask me why I attach such importance to the non-existence of a score of my piece. The answer is quite simple: if I did write a normal score, superimposing the parts mechanically, it would be false, misleading, and it would represent a different work. This would suggest, for example, that the notes placed on the same vertical line should always be played at the same moment, which is contrary to my intention ... That would deprive the piece of its 'mobile' character, which is one of its most important features.[23]

Eventually, this apparently intractable problem was solved not by the composer but by Danuta Lutosławska, who not only drew but also designed the study-score. She devised a workable scheme by cutting up the individual parts and pasting together the corresponding sections on large-format pages. The problem of rhythmic and polyphonic 'falsification' was overcome by enclosing aleatory sections for each instrument in boxes that overrule the conventional reading of a score according to vertical rhythmic alignment. A similar solution had been adopted for the first page of *Jeux vénitiens*, but there the change from one section to another is cued by the conductor. In the String Quartet there is a verbal instruction at the end of each section informing the players how and when to give or receive co-ordinating signals to or from each other (see Ex. 4 : 5).

The String Quartet is the first of several works in which Lutosławski has explored a personal approach to large-scale form, through subdivision into two movements. According to this scheme, the first is introductory and loosely episodic, while the second is cumulative and ultimately climactic. Subtitles for the two movements of the Quartet are simple and self-explanatory: 'Introductory Movement' and 'Main Movement'. The structural scheme of *Jeux vénitiens* had already shown signs of moving in this direction, although there the subdivision was into four movements (effectively operating as three plus one); a similar plan was later realised in *Livre pour orchestre*. After the String Quartet, the two-movement design was also explored in the Second Symphony, Preludes and Fugue, and even in the underlying shape of the Third Symphony.

The introductory movement is episodic in character and construction, opening with an extended solo for the first violinist. The composer has described this solo as a 'monologue', although its hesitant, introspective quality might be better styled as a 'soliloquy': the soloist plays without regard to the other three players. Terms such as 'soliloquy' or 'monologue' aptly allude to theatrical situations, since the String Quartet is a piece for which extra-musical, theatrical analogies are not inappropriate (the Cello Concerto is another). The material delivered by the violinist in this discursive solo consists of fragmented intervallic and rhythmic motifs generated by the horizontal pairing of interval-classes 1 and 6, mostly semitones with only a few tritones. This interval combination suggests a similarity with the outer sections of *Musique funèbre*, but here the effect is whimsical rather than funereal.

The structure of episodes in the introductory movement is defined by a recurring motif consisting of repeated octave Cs. Altogether, these appear nine times during the course of the movement, and act as an instantly recognisable aural signal that the composer is able to exploit and manipulate as a psychological device. The signal aids the performers in their task of negotiating the aleatory polyphony by marking the ends and beginnings of sections. Studied avoidance of octaves (and the note C) elsewhere, greatly reinforces the referential potency of the signal which appears for the second time (Ex. 4 : 4a) just before Fig. 5. Although the signal is static in its unchanging pitch, it is not static in terms of rhythmic or dramatic gesture. Motivically it develops, changing the pattern of repetitions each time it reappears. At its ninth appearance (Fig. 12), it extends to fifty-four repetitions before the octaves are distorted into superimposed major sevenths (with prominent minor ninths). Here the function of the signal breaks down. It can no longer operate in the way we have come to expect. After an attempt to continue the distorted version of the signal (from Fig. 13), the movement can go no further. It ends with a reference to the opening soliloquy, played this time by the cello.

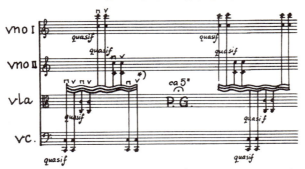

EX. 4 : 4   a) String Quartet, Introductory Movement, signal before Fig. 5

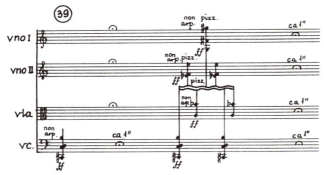

EX. 4 : 4   b) String Quartet, Main Movement, signal at Fig. 39

The main movement brushes aside the hesitant character of the introductory movement and plunges straight into music of rhythmic vigour and directional dramatic purpose. The formal unfolding is defined primarily by changes in the mode of playing: *arco* (to Fig. 14); *pizzicato* (Figs. 14–24); *arco* again (Figs. 24–9); *sul ponticello* (Figs. 29–35); *arco flautando*, for the violins (Figs. 35–9). A decisive moment in the form is reached between Figs. 39 and 40, with a *fortissimo* reappearance of the distorted *pizzicato* signal transplanted from the introductory movement (Ex. 4 : 4b).

Much of the String Quartet is composed according to a method of pitch organisation where the chromatic whole is subdivided into complementary sets. The *pizzicato* section of the main movement between Figs. 14 and 23 is entirely composed in this way, mostly with mobiles drawn from three pitches assigned to each of the four parts. For example, for Figs. 23 to 24, violin I has A♯, B and F, and the viola has C, F♯ and G; these mutually invertible three-note cells both give rise to interval-classes 1, 5 and 6. On the other hand, violin II has D♭, E♭ and A♭, while the cello has E, D and A; each of these cells produces interval-classes 2 and 5. Thus the chromatic whole is partitioned to produce complementary three-note cells which will invest each harmonic strand with a particular intervallic character, usually emphasising some form of contrast. Another example is provided by the aleatory section beginning at Fig. 15 (Ex. 4 : 5). Here, violin I has A, A♯ and B, while the cello has E, F and F♯; both parts contain a three-note cell of adjacent semitones giving rise only to interval-classes 1 and 2. These outer layers contrast with the interval patterns of violin II and the viola: G, C, D♭, and D, E♭, A♭, respectively; mutually invertible cells giving rise to interval-classes 1, 5 and 6. Naturally, the sum of intervallic relationships, produced by the polyphonic interaction of parts in such an aleatory section, will actually be much more complex than suggested by the interval profile for each individual cell.

Once the distorted signal has been reached at Fig. 39 (Ex. 4 : 4b), the piece pushes towards its climactic, *appassionato* section beginning at Fig. 42. The climax itself is reached just prior to Fig. 43, and is unusual in that each player reaches an individual highpoint without collective co-ordination. The way of moving beyond the climax is also unusual in that each part subsides independently, with the result that the climax is gradually reached and passed without the listener being aware of a precise moment when this happens. Proportionally, the climax occurs at just over seven-tenths of the work's duration, thus inviting comparison with the similar proportions of the Third Symphony. In both cases, significant material is introduced after the climax, although the psychological effects are quite different. Whereas the later stages of the Third Symphony reach a thematic plateau of broad, expansive melody, the String Quartet descends into a state of exhaustion and a mood of resignation.

Immediately following the climax there is a quiet, harmonically reposeful aftermath, played without vibrato (Figs. 43–5), that leads to an epilogue with the sectional heading 'Funèbre'. For such expression one might expect interval-pairing of semitones and tritones, as in *Musique funèbre*, but here the bleak, funereal atmosphere is conveyed by other means: an emphasis on the non-expressive sonority of the violins' open G strings; similar effects from natural harmonics of the viola and cello G

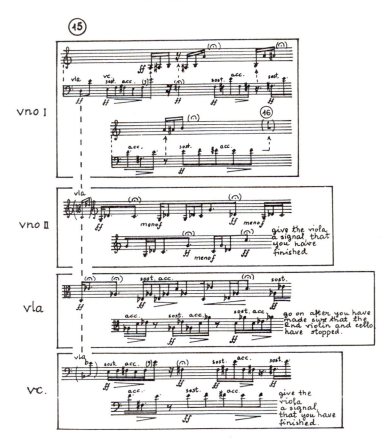

EX. 4 : 5   String Quartet, Main Movement, Fig. 15

strings: and three-note cells of interlocking semitones and tones as the bundle of *cantabile* lines makes its gradual descent. The remaining aleatory sections return to fragmented motifs, as in the introductory movement. As in *Musique funèbre*, there is a sense of the drama having turned full circle to end much as it began.

In one respect the quartet is a conundrum. In spite of the extensive application of aleatory technique, a feature ensuring each performance will differ to some degree, the composer praised the LaSalle Quartet at a rehearsal shortly before the première with the exhortation: 'keep it just the same'. This confounds the notion that his main purpose in using a chance procedure was to ensure differences of outcome between various performances, and there is no real contradiction or aesthetic conflict between the means employed to realise the work in live performance and 'definitive' preservation on a gramophone recording. In a superficial sense there may appear to be some similarity of compositional approach with the techniques of early polyphony, whereby contrapuntal lines were written as separate, melodic parts without a score; but this would be to overlook the rhythmic mensurations governing the time dimension in such pieces. A specific intention of Lutosławski, however, was precisely the opposite: to obviate the need for collective pulsation, and thereby to obtain a degree of rhythmic flexibility that would enable him to compose a kind of textural polyphony based on gestural motifs rather than lines.

While he was in Stockholm for the première of the String Quartet in March 1965, Lutosławski delivered a lecture (in English) at the Swedish Royal Academy of Music on 'The role of the element of chance in compositional technique'. This was his first structured attempt to explain the fundamental differences between his use of aleatory counterpoint and the more extensive applications of chance procedures and indeterminacy that were common at the time, and with which his technique has often been confused. By this time he had already been working intensively for several months on a new work for soloist and orchestra in which the focus of his attention had shifted from polyphony back towards melody.

Paroles tissées

After completing the Iłłakowicz Songs, Lutosławski spent several years searching for a suitable text which might serve to compose a work for solo voice and orchestra. Eventually he found what he needed in *Poésie*, an anthology published in 1947, containing the 'Quatre tapisseries pour la Châtelaine de Vergi' by Jean-François Chabrun. Delighted with his find, he entered into correspondence with the poet, partly in order to find a shorter title for his musical setting. *Paroles tissées* (Woven words) was one of two alternative titles suggested by the poet in response to the composer's request, and it can be interpreted as referring to the verse structure whereby certain poetic images are repeated from one poem to another, thus weaving a complex network of surreal allusions by cross connection and unexpected juxtaposition of ideas.

I have always had some idea, if only a very vague one, of what my vocal compositions were going to be like, even before I found a suitable text. That was the case here . . . Poetry which states everything openly has no room for music. Chabrun's surrealistic work allows many interpretations and I found mine straight away. I saw the text at once as the basis for a composition in four movements. Each of them has its own individuality and is at the same time integral to the work as a whole . . . It's difficult to talk about the content of Chabrun's poem because there's no definite action. But there is a hidden inner logic in the sequence of apparently disconnected images. It's certainly not a logic of realistic events, but rather the logic of dreams. Even though the work seems absurd from a realistic point of view, one can detect the outline of some action, some dramatic conflict and a catastrophe. Though the first line of the last stanza reads, 'Dormez cette pâleur nous est venue de loin', it is quite clear to me that the poet is speaking of the pallor of death. I am further confirmed in this by the original title of the work, which alludes to the medieval romance between the Lady of Vergi and the Duke of Burgundy, a romance which ended in the death of both lovers.[24]

The poems are full of vivid sound-images that could easily lend themselves to effects of word-painting, but Lutosławski deliberately avoids anything too obvious or potentially banal, preferring to allow the poetic images to operate in the imagination of each individual listener, rather than to impose a single interpretation that might pall on repeated hearings (this approach was later also to govern his setting of *Les espaces du sommeil* by Robert Desnos). The clearest illustration of Lutosławski avoiding too literal an interpretation of the text can be found in his treatment of the second three-line stanza of the first poem: 'Le cri du bateleur et celui de la caille / celui de la perdrix celui du ramoneur / celui de l'arbre mort celui des bêtes prises' (The cry of the juggler and of the quail / that of the partridge and of the chimney-sweep / that of the dead tree and of captured beasts). Lutosławski's view of this passage is that it would be ridiculous to depict these sounds by direct musical imitation. Instead, he composed this passage of the first movement by using twelve-note chords, played *pianissimo* by the strings at Figs. 16–17 and 18–19, to provide a harmonic and textural background against which the listener is free to imagine the sounds described by the soloist.

The first movement opens with a twelve-note chord-aggregate of four-note chords in three harmonic layers; a minor-seventh chord in the low strand, a major-seventh chord in the middle strand, and a diminished triad with added major seventh in the high strand. This widely spaced sonority converges onto a unison C♭ via an *ad libitum* section in which all parts except the double-bass play arpeggiated patterns drawn from notes of the twelve-note chord. It is worth observing in the score how Lutosławski achieves conducted control of Figs. 1, 3, 19 and 25 by using a single metred bar in order to set an approximate tempo for the aleatory sections that follow. Apart from these four isolated bars, both the first and second movements are directed entirely according to *ad libitum* technique.

The second movement opens with an expressive and expansive line for unaccompanied voice, which lingers in the memory of the listener as one of the most potent melodic ideas of the whole work: 'Quand le jour' – 'quand le jour a rouvert' – 'a rouvert les branches du jardin' (Ex. 4 : 6a). The textual repetition is particularly telling, as it binds the phrases together, contributing to the effect of growth in the melodic line. The phrase builds gradually, ascending through three, six and then nine notes. The ascent is from low F to high F♯, thus outlining an augmented octave, remarkably similar to the solo oboe refrain that Lutosławski was later to use at the beginning of *Epitaph* (see Ex. 6 : 1), although there the line climbs through the melodic pairing of tones with minor thirds (here the tenor line winds upwards using only tones and semitones). The same phrase is used at the end of the movement, with the words: 'Au dire des merveilles / l'ombre en deux s'est déchirée' (Ex. 4 : 6b). The vocal setting of the second movement is almost entirely syllabic, except for a three-note melisma at the end of the movement, introduced so that the melodic line will correspond to the opening phrase.

EX. 4 : 6 *Paroles tissées*, second movement: a) Opening phrase; b) Closing phrase

After the initial phrase, the harp enters with a modal pattern drawn from the preceding tenor line. Throughout the rest of the movement the voice takes its cue from the harp, which changes from one modal pattern to another. With the leading role played by this canonic partnership between harp and tenor, the remaining instruments are cued in to provide *ad libitum* mobiles that add harmonic colour to the melodic line. There are no passages in either the *Trois poèmes* or the String Quartet where a melodic line takes the lead in this way. Only the flute solo in the third movement of *Jeux vénitiens* is even remotely comparable.

Whereas the second movement is played entirely according to *ad libitum* co-ordination, much of the third is conventionally conducted in metre. The harmonic pace of the third movement is consequently more brisk than either of the preceding ones, and enables the movement to build up and drive towards the climax of the work. The twelve-note chords that open the third movement are chord-aggregates containing superimposed and interlocking diminished-seventh chords (Ex. 3 : 3), of the type already encountered in the Five Songs (Ex. 3 : 8), and the Apogeum of *Musique funèbre* (Ex. 3 : 12).

Dramaturgy in *Paroles tissées* is obviously a natural consequence of the poetry, but one suspects that the choice of text was influenced to a large extent by the need for a dramatic scheme that would eventually lead to a climax. There is more than one highpoint in this work. The orchestra reaches its *fortissimo* climax on a twelve-note chord played *ad libitum* between Figs. 62–3. Because of the problems of balance with the soloist that would have occurred, however, it was not feasible for the tenor to compete with the orchestra at this point. Hence, the voice reaches the highpoint of its tessitura and the emotional climax of the work at Fig. 70 on the word 'peine': 'Mille coqs hurlent ma peine' ('A thousand cockerels scream my sorrow'). As the vocal setting of the work has been almost entirely syllabic up to this point, it is a gesture of expressive and emotional significance when the tenor sings a thirteen-note melisma (Ex. 4 : 7a) that descends a full octave from high B♭ through a twelve-note row comprising major seconds and perfect fourth/fifths (interval-pairing 2 + 5). Later, at the end of the movement, there is a similar melismatic phrase (Ex. 4 : 7b), this time unaccompanied and ascending an octave from E♭–D♯ through the same pairing of intervals, as the tenor sings: 'toutes mes peines'. Here the dramatic gestures of Lutosławski's music perfectly match the expressive quality of Chabrun's poetry.

After the emotional climax reached in the third movement we find tranquillity in the final movement associated with the lines: 'Dormez cette pâleur nous est venue de loin', and 'Dormez cette blancheur est chaque jour nouvelle'. The nocturnal mood comes from a twelve-note 'sleeping' chord appearing four times: at the beginning, on each occasion the soloist sings 'dormez', and finally at the very end of the work, where the chord collapses as all twelve notes converge on to a central pair, F/F♯. The interval structure of this chord, particularly in its

EX. 4 : 7 *Paroles tissées*, third movement: a) Climactic 12-note tenor line;
b) Concluding 12-note tenor line

low-middle register, is remarkably similar to the harmony at the beginning of the slow, somnolent section that lies at the heart of *Les espaces du
sommeil.*

Paroles tissées is without doubt one of Lutosławski's most hauntingly
beautiful works. Much of its beauty derives from the third-based harmony, which is mostly subtle, but at times strong and powerful. The
instrumentation is a critical element contributing to the work's success
and is closely allied to the harmonic world; this is because of the association of particular instrumental tone-colours with distinctive intervallic
patterns drawn from the harmony. The small orchestra of seventeen
strings (10, 3, 3, 1), harp, piano and percussion, was undoubtedly chosen
in order to avoid problems of balance with the soloist (for the Five Songs
he had used a remarkably similar combination, and in both cases the
percussion is used sparingly). Above all, the presence of the solo voice
encourages Lutosławski to develop lines of a lyrical quality not found in
his other works of the 1960s. Not until *Les espaces du sommeil* (1975)
will we encounter an equally successful relationship between the projection of melodic line and transparent harmonic sonorities.

From the outset the work was conceived for Peter Pears, to whom it is
also dedicated. The first performance was given at the 1965 Aldeburgh
Festival, on 20 June, sung by the dedicatee with the Philomusica of
London conducted by the composer. For the 1963 festival Lutosławski
had already produced a *concertante* version of the Dance Preludes which
Benjamin Britten conducted; this was to be the beginning of a friendship
between these exact contemporaries which was to last until Britten's
death in 1976. Lutosławski returned to the Maltings at Snape for a
symposium on his work in November 1980, and was also invited back to
the Aldeburgh Festival as featured composer in June 1983, although by

that time, sadly, Pears was already too ill to perform *Paroles tissées*.

1965 not only saw the première of the String Quartet in the spring and that of *Paroles tissées* in the summer, but also the first 'complete' performance of all Three Postludes in the autumn, at Kraków on 8 October. Having brought these pieces to fruition Lutosławski was then able to concentrate his attention and creative energies on the mammoth project that had been dominating his thoughts for some time. It was to be his first attempt at a large-scale work for full orchestra since the discovery of chance procedures had interrupted the composition that was later salvaged as the Postludes. Not since 1947 had he composed a symphony.

Symphony no. 2

The Second Symphony was commissioned by North German Radio in Hamburg, for the hundredth concert in their series 'Das neue Werk'. Lutosławski began work on the second movement, 'Direct', during the summer of 1965 and completed it in time for the première on 15 October 1966, conducted by Pierre Boulez. The first movement, 'Hésitant', was not completed until early the following year, so the first complete performance was not given until 9 June 1967, played in Katowice by the Polish Radio Symphony Orchestra under the composer's direction.

The durations of the two movements as timed from the composer's 1978 recording are fifteen-and-a-half and sixteen-and-a-half minutes, respectively; but these apparently equal and balanced pillars fulfil entirely different structural functions. Lutosławski has usually been reluctant to discuss or analyse his works in detail, and has rarely provided any more than the briefest of programme notes. In the case of the Second Symphony, however, we have the benefit of an extended article by him, from which the following extract is taken:

Symphony no. 2 is composed in two movements that are not separated from each other by a pause. The last phrase of the first movement still echoes when the second movement has begun. The composition, therefore, constitutes an indivisible whole . . . The first movement . . . comprises a series of episodes performed by various small instrumental groups. Despite the clear distinctions between them, the episodes are united by certain common traits . . . something like diffidence, indecision (hence the movement is titled 'Hésitant') . . . Each of the episodes is followed by a short, slow refrain which is always played by three instruments . . . which do not take part in the episodes. The last episode . . . is longer than the preceding ones, and the different instrumental groups are heard in succession ... as it approaches the point which seems to bode the climax it stops abruptly. The final version [of the refrain] is considerably developed, forming a bridge to the second movement.[25]

Formal schemes of episodes and refrains can also be observed in several other works, including the first movement of *Jeux vénitiens*, *Epitaph*, and the first movement of the Third Symphony. In *Livre pour orchestre*, the separation of movements by interludes can also be regarded as a variant of the same procedure. In the String Quartet the episodes of the introductory movement are separated by a signal of repeated octaves Cs, rather than by refrains; but still there is a similarity of formal approach.

Each episode of the first movement is characterised by a different combination of instrumental tone-colours, and invested with a distinctive harmonic property produced by exploiting subdivisions of the chromatic whole.[26] The hesitant quality is achieved by interrupting each episode twice: first, just after it has begun, giving the effect of a false start; secondly, just before the end, with a general pause followed by a brief abortive attempt to continue.

The first episode is an introductory fanfare for the ten-part brass section, and is generated entirely by the bright sound of major seconds combined with perfect fourths/fifths and resulting in a twelve-note row (E♭, F, B♭, C, G, A, D, E, B, C♯, F♯, G♯). This positive beginning, with its harmonic overlap of a major second between E♭ and F, is crucial to the long-range harmonic organisation of the work. The same notes later reappear at Fig. 158 as a major ninth played by the entire orchestra, *tutta forza*, and act as the ultimate destination point of the second movement, and therefore, the dramatic culmination of the work as a whole. Episode 1 is abruptly terminated by a twelve-note chord of clustered semitones played *pizzicato* by the strings at Fig. 2. There is a half-hearted attempt to continue before another statement of the string chord ends this introductory section. Apart from these two *pizzicato* chords near the beginning, and another two which bring about its end, the string section does not feature in the first movement.

The second episode is scored for three flutes, celesta and five tom-toms.[27] Lutosławski assigns nine notes to each of the four main parts. Eight of these notes are common to all four instruments, but each line also contains one other note exclusive to that part; thus all twelve pitches are used. The eight common notes are linked horizontally in all four parts by interval pairing 2 + 5. The other four notes, B (celesta). B♭ (fl. I)], A (fl.

II), and G♯ (fl. III), are announced at the beginning of the episode at Fig. 4; thereafter they are separated from the other eight notes by being isolated in the top register.

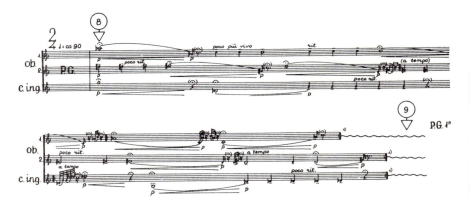

EX. 4 : 8   Symphony no. 2, *Hésitant*, Figs. 8–9

After episode 2 we hear the refrain for the first time (Ex. 4 : 8). On each of its six appearances, it is played by three double-reed instruments: two oboes and cor anglais (1–2); cor anglais and two bassoons (3); oboe, cor anglais and bassoon (4–5); two oboes and cor anglais (6). These double-reed woodwinds are specifically excluded from the episodes; thus the composer is able to exploit contrast of instrumental tone-colour between successive sections, as well as identifying the refrain with a particular timbre. Pitch organisation is also carefully controlled. Each refrain uses only six notes, partitioned as three-note cells: for example, F♯–G–G♯ and C–D♭–D in refrain 1; the two other implied three-note cells of the complementary hexachordal set (A–A♯–B and D♯–E–F) are left unstated. Similar pitch patterning of two three-note groups is used for the other five refrains, but transposed by a semitone each time so they span G–A and C♯–E♭, G♯–B♭ and D–E, A–B and D♯–F, B♭–C and E–G♭, B–D♭ and F–G, respectively. There is also a distinctive disposition of intervals in the refrains. Each individual part plays only two pitch-classes, assigned so that two lines give interval-class 4, while the remaining line gives interval-class 6. Recognition of the refrains on each repetition rests on these three factors: distinctive intervallic content in the individual lines, identification with a particular instrumental tone-colour, and a restricted harmonic palette.

Episode 3 is scored for four horns, harp, two side-drums and bass drum. Gradually, the range of each line making up the five-part polyphony is extended until, collectively, they have outlined a chromatic scale ascent from G♯ to G, enclosing a semitone cluster within one octave. In the fourth episode, for three clarinets, piano and vibraphone, subdivision of the chromatic whole corresponds to the contrast of instrumental tone-colours. The three clarinets each play only two notes, paired by interval-class 3 and linked by semitones: F/D, C♯/E, and E♭/C (in descending order). Vibraphone and piano provide the remaining six notes: B, A♯, A, G♯, G, and eventually F♯ after Fig. 17. Episode 5 shows Lutosławski's predilection for the combination of piano, harp and celesta, and also has two suspended cymbals and tam-tam. Here the repertory of pitches subdivides into three four-note groups: E, F, F♯, G (piano); G♯, A, B♭, C♭ (harp); C, D♭, D, E♭ (celesta). Most of the instrumental resources already used for episodes 2–5 are combined in the sixth: three flutes, three clarinets, three horns, celesta, harp with piano, and five tom-toms. It starts at Fig. 27 with nine parts building up a nine-note chord, then re-starts at Fig. 28 with the addition of the three flutes, and reaches a full twelve-note chord by Fig. 29.

Episode 7 is the longest and brings back each of the instrumental combinations already used in the previous episodes (including the brass section from the introductory fanfare), although not all at the same time. Initially (Figs. 32–3), the three flutes and three clarinets combine in a twelve-note chord, consisting mainly of thirds, which emphasises minor ninths. The flutes and clarinets are in distinct harmonic strands that contain four and eight notes, respectively. The lower strand, played by clarinets, extends upwards from middle C in a pattern of major and minor thirds as two half-diminished-seventh chords, placed a minor ninth apart. The remaining four notes are given to the flutes (G♯, D, F, A), stressing the minor ninth G♯–A. At Fig. 33, the woodwinds are replaced by four horns with harp, celesta, piano, xylophone and tubular bells. This group plays a twelve-note chord, also subdivided into patterns of four and eight notes. Extending upwards from a low G♯ played by both piano and harp, the interval structure of the eight-note segment contains only minor thirds and perfect fifths. It is worth noting that this pairing of intervals appears elsewhere in Lutosławski's music, also with interval class 5 used as perfect fifths rather than perfect fourths. In order to show this significant distinction, the interval-pairing can be coded as 3 + 7, rather than 3 + 5 (see Table 5).

Further subdivisions of the twelve available pitch-classes are applied as the instrumental groupings change, some overlapped. By Figs. 42 and 43, a dense polyphonic texture has been built up before the percussion parts take over and continue to Fig. 44, where they are abruptly truncated by a forty-note chord, played *pizzicato* by the string section, consisting of thirty-nine adjacent semitones across a range just over three octaves. The purpose of the chord is to signal the end of the first movement; but this does not happen immediately. Against a delicate harmonic sonority provided by celesta, harp and piano, the percussion begin again, but another forty-note semitone cluster stops them. They make one more attempt to continue before finally surrendering. The sixth and last refrain, unlike the others, covers all twelve notes by passing from one hexachordal set to its complement, so that all four three-note cells are heard. Various trio combinations are used, alternating double-reed woodwind timbre with brass, as the changing instrumentation assists downward transposition of refrain material: two oboes and cor anglais; trumpet, trombone and tuba; three bassoons; trumpet and two trombones transferring to two trombones and tuba; and finally, three bassoons, which also overlap into the second movement.

The subtitle of the second movement, 'Direct', describes its function in driving inexorably towards a decisive climax. The composer continued his commentary on the symphony by giving an account (here condensed) of the formal stages through which the second movement passes:

> The second movement, unlike the first, unfolds continuously without any pauses. Individual musical ideas overlap one another frequently, creating uninterrupted discourse. This development proceeds directly, without any digressions, to its ultimate destination . . . The form . . . is composed of five successive evolutionary stages . . . Sustained notes and a slow tempo prevail in the first stage . . . The second stage comprises a superimposed *cantilena* of the string instruments . . . with increasingly long interventions of instrumental groups playing in a fast tempo . . . The fast tempo triumphs ultimately . . . At this moment the form enters the third stage of its evolution: the fast tempo prevails, the tension mounts . . . The fourth stage is the only part of the composition . . . conducted in the traditional manner . . . the fifth stage marks the highpoint of the work . . . collective *ad libitum*, with the whole orchestra playing at full force. What follows is an attempt of sorts to end the composition with a *fortissimo* accent. This attempt is 'unsuccessful', for in the pauses between the triumphal enunciation of the E♭/F major ninth by the entire orchestra, one can already hear . . . the background for the epilogue that is to follow . . . It ends with E♭/F, the same notes which began the composition . . .[28]

Although the composer refers to a *cantilena* played by the strings (i.e. the *cantando* beginning at Fig. 123), the whole passage produces an effect of considerable harmonic density, a sound-mass of complex polyphonic texture, rather than the projection of a melodic line. In fact, there is very little either in the second movement or in the work as a whole, that could be regarded as melodic. For some, this may be a failing, because it means that there are few melodic features to provide and sustain aural focus. But there is ample compensation as one's attention is directed towards the harmonic, textural, and especially rhythmic events through which the powerful symphonic drama gradually unfolds.

EX. 4 : 9   Symphony no. 2, Direct, Fig. 147

Interval-classes 2 and 5 predominate in the early stage of the second movement, and are used to build full twelve-note chords at Figs. 104, 112 and 124 (see Ex. 3 : 2d). The passage from Fig. 147 provides an excellent example of Lutosławski's treatment of twelve-note chord-aggregates (Ex. 4 : 9). Here the strings play in two discrete harmonic strands, each delivering a progression of diminished-seventh chords: the upper strand initially ascends through two whole-tone scales, then descends chromatically; the lower strand descends in sequential chromatic-scale segments. Superimposed on the strings is a third strand, played first by four horns, then transferring to woodwinds; this strand contains the diminished-seventh chords that complement the other two. It is significant to note that this fast passage is conventionally metred (in $\frac{3}{4}$), and that it occurs where the music is propelled towards the climax. The first metred section in the work, at Fig. 133, lasts only five bars; but after a brief interruption from wind and percussion at Fig. 134, metred co-ordination resumes at Fig. 135 to begin the fourth stage in the formal scheme. Gradually the harmonic pace quickens to give a sense of composed accelerando, until, by Fig. 147, the pace reaches a rate of one chord per beat. Thus we sense that the destination point of the work cannot be far away, and it is reached at Fig. 153 with a stunning *fortissimo* twelve-note chord of superimposed tritones and perfect fifths (see Ex. 3 : 2f).

Proportionally, the moment of climax occurs at close to nine-tenths of the symphony's duration (calculated from the composer's 1978 recording). Similar climax positioning is shown by *Livre pour orchestre* (0.85), *Les espaces du sommeil* (0.85), and Preludes and Fugue (0.88). Significantly, the climax of the Second Symphony occurs later in the form than the equivalent highpoint in earlier works such as *Musique funèbre* (0.63), *Jeux vénitiens* (0.8), *Trois poèmes* (0.56), the String Quartet (0.72), or *Paroles tissées* (0.6). Perhaps the most interesting contrast is with the climax of the Third Symphony (0.72), which reaches a plateau with a vista beyond, rather than a peak from which the ground falls steeply away.[29]

There remains what the composer referred to above as an 'unsuccessful attempt' to end the work with a *fortissimo* accent. The two notes used, E♭ and F, are those which open the first movement. Thus the work has, at least in one limited sense, come full circle, but psychologically it has not. After the strenuous exertion of the second movement, the listener is aware of having been taken far from the point of departure. Lutosławski's masterly control of this psychological journey fully justifies the enthusiastic assessment of the second movement by Edward Cowie as 'one of the most powerful symphonic arguments composed in the twentieth century'.[30]

Lutosławski's achievement in the Second Symphony has been to make a substantial contribution to the symphonic repertory even though neither the musical language nor the form looks to the past for the re-creation of any obvious model. It is a symphony only in the most general sense of being a large-scale, non-concertante orchestral work, yet the composer's decision to give the piece its generic title inevitably invites comparison with the symphonic tradition. His First Symphony and Concerto for Orchestra are both traditional in the sense that they are defined primarily by the projection and development of thematic, melodic material. The Second Symphony, on the other hand, extends and adds to the symphonic tradition without conforming to established procedures; the absence of thematic material throws the burden of development on rhythm, and the rhythmic management of dense harmonic and polyphonic textures. Ironically, in view of the First Symphony's proscription as formalist, the Second would be a more deserving candidate for description in terms of 'elevation of form over content'. It is an abstract essay in form. The

Second Symphony manages to be both monumental (in the static, sculptural sense) and dramatic, and it confirms Lutosławski's place as one of the few committed symphonists of our time.

The time spent working on the Second Symphony was not only busy but also eventful. In 1966 Lutosławski finally signed an agreement with J. and W. Chester Ltd, then the London-based division of the Scandinavian publishing house, Wilhelm Hansen. This was to make a considerable difference to his career, particularly in promoting and co-ordinating the performance of his music by leading orchestras in the West. One must remember that at that time, at the height of the Cold War, symbolised by the renewal in 1965 of the Polish–Soviet 'Treaty of Friendship, Mutual Aid and Co-operation' for a further twenty years, it was crucial for a Polish artist to have effective representation outside the Soviet sphere of influence.

In 1966 Lutosławski received the Alfred Jurzykowski Prize from the foundation of that name based in New York. A few weeks before going to Hamburg for the première of the Second Symphony's final movement, he travelled to Stockholm for a strenuous week of jury service for the International Society for Contemporary Music (he had also been on the International Jury for the ISCM Festivals of 1959 in Rome and Naples, and 1964 in Copenhagen). While in Hamburg he was elected an Honorary Member of the Freie Akademie der Künste. Other prizes followed in 1967: the Gottfried von Herder Prize from the University of Vienna, and the Léonie Sonning Prize presented in Copenhagen. The Second Symphony itself was honoured in 1968, earning first prize for Lutosławski from the Tribune International des Compositeurs administered by UNESCO, the third time he had received this particular award.

At a time when Lutosławski's international reputation was developing rapidly, a fact marked not only by performances of his work by leading orchestras and at prestigious festivals in many countries, but also by a stream of honours, prizes, and awards, it is surprising to find that his next major composition was written for a relatively obscure orchestra. The explanation is an interesting one, for it sheds light on the approach to commissions that he has since maintained throughout his career. Because he was being offered far more commissions than he could possibly accept, he was able to choose only those that corresponded with his own creative plans. One of these intentions was to attempt a successful realisation of the orchestral design he had failed to complete in the Postludes.

Livre pour orchestre

Livre pour orchestre was composed to fulfil a commission from the German town of Hagen. Their request for a new piece was made in 1962, through their Generalmusikdirektor, Berthold Lehmann, who had been a long-standing admirer of Lutosławski's work. The first performance was given at Hagen on 18 November 1968 by the Städtisches Orchester conducted by Lehmann, to whom the work is also dedicated. It represents a highly successful realisation of the four-movement scheme employed in *Jeux vénitiens*. In both cases, the first three movements are self-contained pieces which provide preliminary stages in the form leading to a final movement that is considerably more extended and drives to a collective climax.

The title was chosen as an intentional allusion to the collections by Couperin (*Livre pour clavecin*) and Bach (*Orgelbüchlein*) that contain separate pieces rather than representing a unified cycle. In the event, however, Lutosławski was unable to resist the inner need for development, hence the final movement became much more extended than originally intended. By the time this was apparent, he realised that his original title was no longer appropriate and contacted the commissioners in order to change it; but the first performance had already been publicly announced and so the title had to remain. It is revealing to note that the underlying archetype governing his approach to large-scale forms, symphonic and other, is apparently so strong that he was unable to avoid it, even when making a conscious effort to move in a different direction. His experience with the composition of *Livre* forms a fascinating case study in the strength of the underlying model.

The work is divided into four *Chapitres*, separated by three *Intermèdes*, although without any break in performance. His purpose in providing these interludes was to give the listener an opportunity to relax the level of concentration, thereby refreshing the ear and the mind for what is to follow. He was later to apply a similar formal principle of intervening interludes with the five-movement scheme of *Partita*.

The first two *Intermèdes* are associated with woodwind sound: the first has three clarinets, while the second has two clarinets and harp (the third is for harp and piano). A similar association of interlude material with woodwind sound has already been observed in the first movement of the Second Symphony (Ex. 4 : 8), and also occurs in the first movement of the Third Symphony (see Ex. 6 : 8). All three *Intermèdes* have similar

The Lutosławski family at the Dolny Dwór, Drozdowo (1888). Back row, standing, from left to right: Wincenty; Stanisław; Marian; Jan. Front row, from left to right: Sofia Casanova (first wife of Wincenty) holding her baby daughter Maria (later Niklewicz); Kazimierz (standing); Franciszek (sitting), the composer's grandfather; Józef (standing), the composer's father; Paulina, the composer's grandmother.

The composer's family home, the Górne Dwór at Drozdowo. This house no longer exists; it was destroyed by Russian troops in 1940.

The composer's parents, Józef Lutosławski and Maria Lutosławska (Olszewska). (c. 1910)

The composer's father, Józef Lutosławski (c. 1916).

Ks. dr. med. Kazimierz Lutosławski (1919). 'Kochanej Mateńce w smutniejsze powrotu rok z smutnego wygrania, Drozdowo 18/IV/1919'. (Photograph by A. Mazlowski, Hotel Bristol, Warszawa). In this dedication to his mother, Kazimierz is making a reference to the tragic events in Moscow, a few months earlier, when his brothers Marian and Józef were executed (without trial) by Bolsheviks.

The composer aged about three (centre) with his brothers, Henryk (left) and Jerzy (right). (c. 1916, photograph probably taken in Moscow.)

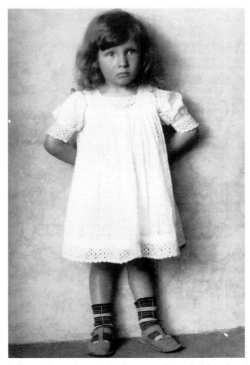

The composer (standing) aged about three. (c. 1916, photograph probably taken in Moscow.)

The composer aged about nine (c.1922) at the Becker piano in his late grandfather's house at Dolne Drozdowo.

Maria Danuta Dygat with her brother, Stanisław Dygat (c. 1923, photograph © by Drewiński of Nowy Świat, Warszawa).

The composer with colleagues at the Stefan Batory gymnazjum (c. 1925). Lutosławski is second from left, sitting on floor, smiling.

Danuta Lutosławska (1950, photograph © by B. J. Dorys of Nowy Świat, Warszawa).

The composer (1950, photograph © by B. J. Dorys of Nowy Świat, Warszawa).

The composer and his wife sailing on the Mazurian lakes (c. 1950).

The composer standing at the piano in his apartment in the east-bank Warsaw district of Saska Kępa, ul. Zwycięzców 39 m. 10 (c. 1950, photograph © by Marek Holzman).

distribution of pitch into four complementary and overlapping tetrachords, giving twelve pitches (with four duplications) spanning a major
seventh from G to F♯. Vertically, each tetrachord forms a symmetrical
pattern of tone/minor-third/tone, although they are actually used horizontally with interval pairing 2 + 5 rather than 2 + 3. The first interlude
(Ex. 4 : 10a) has three rhythmic layers: clarinets I and II make use of one
tetrachord, while the third clarinet has two tetrachords; inevitably there is
an overlap of pitches between these layers. Even though *Intermède* 1
delivers all twelve notes within the span of one octave, the harmonic
result is quite different to a semitone cluster, because of the choice of
intervals and the way the chromatic whole is partitioned. The second
interlude retains the first two clarinets which play the same tetrachords as
before; but the seven pitches previously played by the third clarinet are
assigned to the harp (whose pedal mechanism permits only seven pitch-
classes to be played at the same time). Unlike the previous interludes,
Intermède 3 (Ex. 4 : 10b) develops without any break into the final
movement. The harp plays as before, but the five pitches previously
played by the tetrachords given to first and second clarinets are now
assigned to the piano. The leading developmental role, in moving from
the third interlude into the main discourse of the final *Chapitre*, is
performed by the piano.

EX. 4 : 10 *Livre pour orchestre*: a *Intermède* 1, Fig. 110 b *Intermède* 3, Figs.
401–2

Lutosławski's notation for *Livre* differs from that used for the orchestral works of the 1970s and beyond. It should be borne in mind that, even in the late 1960s, he was still exploiting ways of using aleatory techniques and trying different ways of notating them. In *Chapitre* 1 there is an uncharacteristic example of Lutosławski deciding not to specify pitch and giving only an abstract contour of the required line (at Fig. 109); a footnote in the score explains that 'The xylophone plays arbitrarily, merely approximating the indicated pitch and duration'.

Chapitre 1 begins by outlining a perfect fifth E–A in the strings; this interval then curls back on itself to imply the minor triad E–A–C. Throughout the opening string section, glissandi are used in an expressive manner, recalling moments of the String Quartet and anticipating both the early stages of *Mi-Parti* and central Adagio in *Les espaces du sommeil*. In spite of the string glissandi, the effect is not merely textural. The intervallic profile of the harmony is too specific to be regarded as mere texturalism. As the first *Chapitre* begins with strings playing in quarter-tones, one should note Lutosławski's attitude towards subdivisions of the chromatic scale into units of less than a semitone. They are not exploited for harmonic purposes (because he feels they would simply sound out-of-tune), but they are used melodically, as chromatic passing-notes.

Between Figs. 102 and 103 the strings diverge for a succession of five widely spaced chords; the second contains six notes while the others contain ten. The first and third are the same, and result from vertical interval pairing 4 + 5, in a symmetrical layout (see Ex. 3 : 2e). The second covers a narrower range of pitch with only six notes, but still with the same interval pairing. The fourth chord is also symmetrical, but combines interval-classes 3, 4 and 5. The last is similar to the first and third. Similar interval patterns characterise the eight-note string chords from Fig. 104, and the brass chord just before Fig. 109. At that point the attempt by the brass section to take over is arrested and terminated by a *fortissimo* stroke on the bass drum, accompanied by a splintered gesture from tom-toms and xylophone (not unlike the final gesture of *Les espaces*). The eight-note string chord which emerges, *pianissimo*, from this interruption is one of the most beautiful sonorities in the whole work, and results from a symmetrically arranged pattern of perfect fifths and major seconds. This chord gradually converges, by glissandi, onto another eight-note chord of similar interval configuration but a perfect fourth lower. The notes of this chord are gradually cleared, but as they leave they are taken up by the piano, which also supplies the four pitches that complement the eight-note chord: D, G, A, A♭. Gradual transfer of pitches from the harmonic to the melodic dimension is a technique that Lutosławski was to develop and use increasingly in the works of the 1980s.

Perhaps the most distinctive feature of the second *Chapitre* is the role played by the combined tone-colours of harp, piano, celesta, vibraphone, tubular bells and glockenspiel. Throughout this scherzo-like movement, Lutosławski exploits the contrast between instrumental families: wood-wind, brass, percussion and strings. This does not mean they are used purely for textural purposes, because the harmony is still clear. At Fig. 212 we reach the first clearly stated twelve-note chord of the work. Played by strings, it is a chord-aggregate (B–F–D) containing a different type of four-note chord in each of the three harmonic strands: a dominant-seventh chord at the bottom (A, D, F♯, C), a major-seventh chord in the middle strand (E♭, A♭, B, E), and a half-diminished-seventh chord at the top (G, B♭, D♭, F). It gradually converges onto a unison middle C, at which point the movement ends with a master-stroke: piano, harp, celesta, bells and vibraphone combine to deliver a vertically symmetrical twelve-note chord of interval-classes 2 + 3, centred around a perfect fifth. Technical explanation cannot do justice to the enchanting effect of this ending. The middle C held by violas then dies away.

After the second interlude, the third *Chapitre* develops the melodically blurred quarter-tone string sonorities of the opening movement. Between Figs. 308 and 310 there is a sense of building towards some goal, but having encouraged this expectation the composer denies it by preventing the strings from reaching a climax (at least for the time being). Once implanted in the unconscious memory of the listener this expectation remains, to be reactivated and fulfilled in the final movement.

Intermède 3 leads directly into the final *Chapitre*, where the strings gradually develop a complex network of *ad libitum* polyphony, all with a rich, warm *cantabile* sound. The effect of this glorious string *cantilena* is basically one of harmonic and polyphonic texture, rather than emphasis on a particular profile of melodic lines. Later, in *Chain 3*, Lutosławski was also to exploit the strings in a long, growing *cantilena*, but one conceived primarily as a melodic line. Here, other textural blocks from the contrasting sonorities of woodwind and brass are gradually overlap-ped and superimposed, until this stage is brought abruptly and decisively to a close by a *fortissimo* eight-note brass chord at Fig. 419. After that,

the process is of a different kind altogether. The eight-note harmony is the
first in a succession of ten such chords (Ex. 4 : 11) played *fortissimo* by
the brass from Figs. 419 to 428, repeated from Figs. 429 to 438, and then
also used from Fig. 439 in the final push to the climax. The vertical
interval structure of these chords is very distinctive, and is generated by
the superimposition of interval-classes 1, 5 and 6. Horizontally, each
individual part making up the eight-note chords is linked by only two of
these interval-classes (1 and 5), and this linear progression can be seen
clearly in the outer parts in Example 4 : 11. Initially, these chords fulfil
the function of aural signposts that separate episodes of contrasting
instrumental tone-colour. But as the distance between them is gradually
reduced, so that each intervention comes sooner than the last, the episodes become successively shorter. The dramatic acceleration achieved by
telescoping the eight-note chords in this way is similar to the psychological principle adopted first in Postlude no. 3, and again in the Second
Symphony. Here, the structural foreshortening propels the music
inexorably to its point of culmination, the climactic harmony at Fig. 445.

EX. 4 : 11   *Livre pour orchestre*, 8-note chords from Figs. 419–38

Lutosławski's choice of chord-aggregate for the climactic harmony is a
matter of significance in each work. Certain favoured combinations of
four-note chords recur. In this case, he chooses a vertical design that is not
only symmetrical in its disposition of intervals (7–3–5–3–3–5–3–3–5–3–
7), but also in its layout of chords (C–H–C; see Table 4), having minor-
seventh chords in the outer strands with a major/minor chord in the
middle strand (shown as the first chord in Ex. 3 : 5a). This type of
chord-aggregate occurs at the climax of *Novelette*, and also defines the
long-range harmonic organisation of *Chain 2*, including the climactic
harmony in its final movement (see Exx. 3 : 5a and 7 : 15). In *Livre*,
similar chord-aggregates are also used for the slow-moving twelve-note

chords in the coda, where octave doubling generates a rich, dense harmonic texture of strings subdivided into twenty-eight parts. Yet the chord configurations can still be identified in the outer harmonic strands; the middle strand contains the overlapping of all three chord types caused by the doubling. Horizontal progression between the three twelve-note chords that alternate throughout the coda is determined by a single three-note cell in the top part: E♭, D, E. With this cell playing the leading role, all three harmonic strands exchange their chord configurations. Against this hypnotic harmony, a flute duet gradually ascends to a high E, where it meets the strings. The penultimate chord of the final movement is subdivided into quarter-tones; yet this is for horizontal rather than vertical reasons. It is simply a chromatic passing-chord leading to the final, symmetrical four-note chord: E, F♯, A, B.

Livre pour orchestre is undoubtedly one of the landmarks of Lutosławski's mature style. For sheer beauty of orchestral sound, and richness (as opposed to density) of harmonic sonorities, it is equalled (perhaps surpassed) only by *Les espaces du sommeil* and *Mi-Parti*. Yet its true significance lies in the magnificent achievement of its form. The four-movement scheme that had been tried and abandoned in the Postludes, then tested and adopted in *Jeux vénitiens*, here reaches a masterly realisation. The fact that this scheme imposed itself on the composer, in spite of his different original conception for the piece, testifies to the enduring strength of an underlying formal archetype.

The period spent working on *Livre* was no less eventful for Lutosławski than the time devoted to the Second Symphony, but the changes were more personal than public. His mother, Maria, died on 18 October 1967. She had lived with Lutosławski and his wife since they had moved to the Saska Kępa district of Warsaw, on the east bank of the Vistula, shortly after the end of the war. A few months after her death, with the proceeds of his mounting number of performances and conducting engagements, Lutosławski was able to finance the family's move from their small apartment into an elegant, detached house with a large garden in a leafy part of Żoliborz, a district of the city slightly north of the Nowe Miasto and close to the Cytadela. This has been their home ever since.

The year 1968 was also busy and eventful in other respects. Lutosławski received an important commission from the Royal Philharmonic Society in London for a concerto for cello and orchestra, and he began to accumulate the sketch material for the new piece, although he was not able to work on it intensively until the following year. In September he was chairman of the ISCM International Jury held in Warsaw during the Autumn Festival. In the meantime, Warsaw had been racked by political unrest and student protests. The catalyst for the long summer of disturbance was the suppression, by the Soviet ambassador to Poland, of a theatre production of *Dziady* (Forefathers' Eve) by Adam Mickiewicz. Readers and audiences unfamiliar with the Polish Romantic tradition, of expressing through symbols and literary metaphor the strong nationalist aspirations for independence, may find it hard to grasp why a cancelled theatre performance should result in such a storm of protest. But those acquainted with Poland's recent history will understand how the metaphors of the nineteenth century, intended to fan the flames of anti-Russian sentiment, were able to ignite the imagination of a new generation born during the era of Soviet control. Then came the backlash. On 21 August 1968 Warsaw Pact forces from five countries, including Poland, invaded Czechoslovakia to suppress the liberal reforms of the Dubcek government. One should not underestimate the significance of this event for many Poles; the bitter irony of helping to crush neighbours whose aspirations for greater freedom mirrored their own.

It is tempting, but potentially misleading, to imply that these events in some way coloured or influenced the nature of Lutosławski's music. They may have affected the man, but this does not necessarily mean that the anxieties caused by external events would touch his creative work. It has already been observed in relation to Lutosławski's experiences during the war, and through the post-war Stalinist period, that he has developed a protective reflex that successfully shields his inner world from the interference of unwelcome tensions and pressures. In spite of this separation, could there sometimes be a connection?

Lutosławski's new concerto for the Royal Philharmonic Society was to prove a work containing expressions of harsh conflict in a medium normally emphasising co-operation. The relationship between soloist and orchestra is based on opposition and struggle. Whether or not there is any valid connection to be drawn with contemporary events in Poland and neighbouring countries, it is certainly possible, with hindsight, to regard the Cello Concerto as a potent musical metaphor of a turbulent time.

5
Mastery of a Mature Language
(1969–1979)

Dramaturgy has been a crucial feature of Lutosławski's approach to large-scale musical forms throughout his career. During his studies with Maliszewski, much emphasis appears to have been placed on the psychology of how the gradual unfolding of a work is perceived. Although these lessons were absorbed primarily through studying scores of the Viennese Classical period, particularly Haydn and Beethoven, it would appear that Lutosławski may also have learned a great deal directly from the theatre, through observing dramatic conventions, treatments of plot and sub-plot, and functional principles governing relationships between characters. Lutosławski may be dismissive about the musical significance of his many scores of incidental music for theatre and radio plays composed during the post-war years from 1947 to about 1960, but one should not overlook or undervalue such a clear indication of his exposure to the underlying structure of dramatic works.

If one resorts to discussing music in terms of analogy or metaphor, then the most appropriate parallels for Lutosławski's work lie in areas relating in some way to phenomena occurring over or through a span of time, as that is how music of the Western European tradition is experienced and perceived. Analogies are often drawn between music and visual arts, usually painting or sculpture; but such parallels as exist are severely limited in validity because of the absence of a time dimension. The temptation to draw analogies with theatrical situations thus becomes almost irresistible. Even this, however, must be approached with considerable caution, lest misleading notions of 'meaning' are introduced and applied.

In a lecture originally intended for presentation at Darmstadt, 'Notes on the construction of large-scale closed forms' (still unpublished), Lutosławski discussed the problems facing a composer of the later twentieth century in shaping the abstract drama of music without the established conventions associated with tonal language. From the outset, he made clear his commitment to the idea of composing each work as an entity, including not only the notes but also the perception of the listener:

When composing large-scale closed forms, I always remember that what I am principally engaged in doing is organising the process of perception of my work. To my
mind, a piece of music is not only an arrangement of sounds in time but also the set of
impulses transmitted by these sounds to the listener and the reactions those impulses
then awaken in him.[1]

He went on to distinguish between active and passive kinds of musical
perception. The latter he considers to be where the listener's attention is
totally absorbed by what is heard at a given moment; whereas the former
(his main concern) relates to the process of assimilating what has been
heard earlier, and in anticipating and waiting for what might occur:

it would be wrong to assume that large-scale closed forms are a hopeless proposition
for the modern composer. His only problem is to find ways of activating the listener's
memory and anticipation, despite the absence of recognised conventions which could
serve as a cue, or of a congenial soil of listening habits. It is such devices that I have
been hunting for over the past years ... My explorations in this field can be divided
roughly into two groups. The first is a matter of providing a purchase for the listener's
powers of recall and anticipation through the creation of 'once-only conventions' ...
The second, much less important, area ... lies in the direction of borrowings from the
other arts, principally the theatre. This can be fruitful when the aim is to create more
intricate formal situations in which the elementary once-only conventions ... are no
longer enough.[2]

The simplest kind of 'once-only convention' used by Lutosławski is
where he establishes in a given work a repeated idea, in order to play with
the listener's expectation that it will recur. This effect can be produced by
a ritornello or refrain, as already observed in the first movements of both
Jeux vénitiens and the Second Symphony (the same principle will later be
identified in relation to other works such as *Epitaph*, the Double Concerto, and the Piano Concerto). The listener's capacity for expectation
can also be primed and manipulated by a referential signal, as observed in
the String Quartet (also to be discussed in relation to the Third Symphony). It is worth noting that Lutosławski's continuing search for varied
treatments of the dramatic, psychological principles of expectation, fulfilment, denial and surprise has been brought about by a desire to simulate
effects typical of music composed within the framework of tonal conventions. Without the referential potential offered by tonal organisation
(such as returning to particular keys), Lutosławski has tried to find his
own substitutes within the non-tonal harmonic language he has used
since 1957.

Cello Concerto

No piece of Lutosławski has been discussed more extensively in terms of analogy to theatrical situations than the Cello Concerto. The general idea for such a *concertante* piece had been in his mind for some years, but once he had begun to concentrate on the project the intensive compositional work occupied him for a period of about eighteen months in 1969 and 1970, not long after writing the above lecture (which refers to works up to and including the Second Symphony).

The Cello Concerto was commissioned in 1968 by the Royal Philharmonic Society for its 1970–71 season. At the first performance, in London on 14 October 1970, Mstislav Rostropovich was presented with the highest accolade of the Royal Philharmonic Society, its Gold Medal commemorating their commission of Beethoven's Ninth Symphony. The work was written for and is dedicated to Rostropovich, who is fond of finding possible extra-musical interpretations in order to make more vivid the task of projecting the performance. Many of the quasi-theatrical situations and gestures which can be found in the work had, particularly at that time in Rostropovich's life, significant allusions to the personal conflict he had long experienced with Soviet institutions of state 'security'.[3] This certainly does not mean that the work was composed with such matters in mind; these interpretations were formulated after it had been completed, during rehearsal. In one respect, however, Rostropovich's individual mode of identification corresponded with the composer's original intention: the principle of conflict.

The traditional role of the orchestra in a solo concerto is accompaniment, dialogue or orchestral *tutti* which separate passages played by the soloist. The relationship between soloist and orchestra in my composition is rather different. I built it by borrowing analogies from other arts, the theatre in particular. The relationship is one of conflict. The situation should be quite clear to the listener from the very first orchestral note, because the orchestra provides the element of intervention, interruption, even disruption. This is followed by attempts at reconciliation: dialogues. But these are in turn interrupted by a group of brass instruments, which in fact provide the element of intervention in the work. My aim was to find some justification for employing these two contradictory forces: the solo instrument and the orchestra. The relationship between these two forces undergoes a change in the course of the concerto. There is even a moment of complete harmony in the *cantilena*, but this provides the opportunity for the most violent of the interventions, this time from the whole brass section.[4]

The concerto begins with a discursive monologue for the soloist, lasting some four minutes. Clear comparison obtains with the similarly theatrical principle underlying the violin soliloquy that opens the String Quartet. During the long cello introduction, the score shows several expressive markings which assist gestural presentation of the line and its changing moods: *indifferente*; *grazioso*; *un poco buffo ma con eleganza*; *marciale*. After a group of strident interruptions from trumpets, there follows a sequence of four episodes where the soloist collaborates with various concerted combinations drawn from the orchestra (the composer describes these as 'attempts at reconciliation: dialogues'). Each in turn is interrupted and terminated by harshly conflicting sounds from the brass instruments. Throughout these early stages of the work, the orchestral strings play only *pizzicato*, thus their lyrical and expressive voice is not heard, either individually or collectively (obvious extra-musical associations may be drawn from this observation). After the fourth episode has been forcefully broken off, the soloist cajoles the orchestral strings to enter the discourse, provoking their participation by changing to *pizzicato*; here the basses enter, *arco*. The developing *cantilena* which ensues eventually reaches an intense unison line: the composer's 'moment of complete harmony'. Table 6 summarises how these and later events occur in the four stages of the formal scheme.

TABLE 6   Cello Concerto, formal scheme

Figs.	Stage	Material	Character
0–7	1	soloist's introductory monologue	capricious
1–9		first brass interruption	conflicting
10–24	2	episode 1	concerted
23–25		second brass interruption	conflicting
26–38		episode 2	concerted
37–39		third brass interruption	conflicting
40–48		episode 3	concerted
48–49		fourth brass interruption	conflicting
49–61		episode 4	concerted
61–63		fifth brass interruption	conflicting
63–81	3	*cantilena* develops in solo line	concerted
77–81		*cantilena*; all strings in unison	co-operation
81–83	4	sixth brass interruption	conflicting
83–134		build-up towards climax	contested
134		orchestral tutti on 9-note chord	climactic
135–137		aftermath of climax; *dolente*	post-climactic
137–end		fast coda and soloist's climax	concluding

Although the action of the concerto is defined primarily by its gestural, quasi-theatrical elements, the string *cantilena* raises the profile of express-ive melody to a level not encountered in previous works such as the String Quartet or the Second Symphony (*Paroles tissées* is exceptional among Lutosławski's works of the 1960s in this respect). For the listener, there is inevitably a sense of disappointment that melodic lyricism does not prevail; but this response is an integral part of the abstract 'plot'. Example 5 : 1 shows the solo line (only) from Figs. 64–6. After a brief return to 'indifference' (after Fig. 63) gives way to increasing insistence (Figs. 64–64d), the *cantilena* gradually unfolds against a growing textural background of polyphonic bundles developed by the orchestral strings.

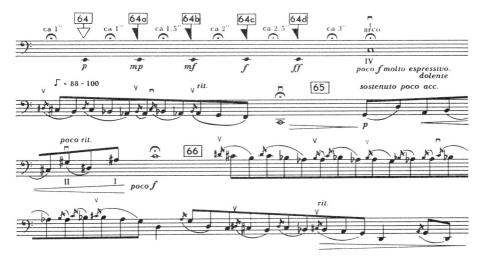

EX. 5 : 1   Cello Concerto, cello line Figs. 64–6

This *cantilena* comprises one of the most striking appearances in Luto-sławski's music of a *dolente* melody using the horizontal interval pairing of major seconds and minor thirds (2 + 3). In the gradual build-up from Fig. 63 towards the brass *fortissimo* at Fig. 81 Lutosławski exploits the difference between particular interval pairings as a means of articulating phrases within the melodic line. The use of interval pairings contrasted in this way in order to generate sections of the form is an aspect of his technique that becomes more highly developed in later works. Here the soloist plays *molto espressivo* (*dolente*) when the melodic line is derived from the 2 + 3 interval pairing. *Dolente* expression alternates with phrases of the 2 + 5 pairing which is initially marked *sostenuto*. There are also two passages of the semitone/tone pairing (1 + 2). Table 7 outlines the intervallic scheme of the solo part during the third stage:[5]

TABLE 7   Cello Concerto, solo part (Figs. 63–81)

Figs.	Interval pairing(s)	Expressive character
63–64d	1 + 2	*indifferente*
64d–65	2 + 3	*dolente, molto espressivo*
65–66	2 + 5	*sostenuto*
66–67	2 + 3; 2 + 5; 2 + 3; 2 + 5	*dolente*, then *sostenuto*, etc (implied)
67–68	2 + 5	*sostenuto*
68–69	2 + 3	*dolente* implied
69–76	1 + 2	no expression mark
76–	2 + 5	*sostenuto* implied
–77	2 + 3	*dolente, molto espressivo*
77–81	2 + 3	*dolente, molto espressivo*

The only, slight deviations from the maintenance of strict intervallic differentiation between these sections are where there is a quasi-cadential falling perfect fourth at the end of a 2 + 3 line. This occurs, for example, just prior to Fig. 65 and between Figs. 66 and 67. In each case, the falling perfect fourth provides a link leading into a 2 + 5 line. Example 5 : 2 shows the final stage of the *cantilena* from Figs. 77–81. The unison intensity of this string line calls for comparison with the powerful unison statement of the twelve-note theme in the Epilogue of *Musique funèbre*.

Blow-by-blow description of the ensuing contest between soloist and orchestra in the fourth stage of the form is unnecessary, as the theatrical situations are self-evident in performance. Suffice it to note that Rostropovich's personal identification with the unequal struggle, of the individual against the collective, has undoubtedly been a major contribution to communicating the work in performance, and has been a model for other cellists' subsequent interpretations. One recurring feature worth observing is the use of *frullato* chords from brass and woodwind; these act as grotesque grimaces punctuating the contest. Similar *frullato* interruptions can be found in other works, including the 'First Event' of *Novelette*, and the second movement of *Chain 2*.

The orchestral climax is reached at Fig. 134, on a nine-note chord played *tutta forza* by all except the soloist (who obviously cannot

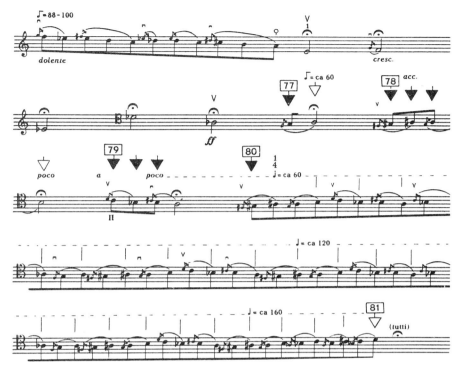

EX. 5 : 2   Cello Concerto, cello line Figs. 77–81

compete, or even participate). Symbolically, the soloist reaches a separate climax, at the very end. After a bitter struggle against overwhelming odds, the resilience of the individual triumphs. If one seeks political metaphors they can easily be found. Yet the strength and potentially universal appeal of this music lies in its independence from such specific interpretations. The powerful drama can be perceived and understood in abstract, purely musical terms.

The political analogies that helped Rostropovich with his interpretation of the Cello Concerto were obviously those that related to his difficulties with the Soviet system in Russia. On 31 October 1970 he made public his support for the increasingly embattled Aleksandr Solzhenitsyn, whose Nobel Prize had been announced earlier in the month. This was to bring Rostropovich into direct conflict with the Soviet administration and would soon lead to his emigration. Exactly two months (to the day) after the première of the Cello Concerto in London, events in the north of Poland were to provide an equally apt parallel for the representation of conflict. On 14 December an ill-fated strike was called at 'Stocznia Gdańska', the Gdańsk shipyards named 'fraternally' after Lenin. During the accompanying civil unrest the Gdańsk headquarters of the Polish Communist Party were burned to the ground, and on 15 December shipyard workers were shot by the security forces. The political shock-waves of these events had an immediate effect in the resignation of Gomułka as head of the Party on 20 December and his replacement by the reformist Edward Gierek. But the bitterness, anger and distrust engendered during that December were to simmer for another ten years until the same shipyards (and some of the same people, including one Lech Wałęsa) gave birth to the Solidarity movement in the summer of 1980. In the early 1970s there was not yet a clear focus for uniting Polish resistance to the totalitarian regime. Neither was there yet the powerful alliance of workers and intellectuals that was to sustain the Solidarity movement. In the 1980s Lutosławski was destined to play his part in that alliance and would be honoured by Solidarity. But in the meantime his life and career developed outside Poland.

In the summer of 1971 Lutosławski visited the United States to receive an honorary doctorate of music (the first of many) from the Cleveland Institute of Music. He also received the Prix Maurice Ravel in Paris the same year, together with a special cultural award from the French President. His main compositional effort at that time was directed towards the fulfilment of a commission from Mario di Bonaventura, originally intended for performance at the Dartmouth Festival in New Hampshire, but eventually unveiled at the Styrian Autumn Festival in Austria. This new piece, for strings, would evoke some of the sound world of *Musique funèbre*, but its most striking feature was to be its unusual approach to form.

Preludes and Fugue

Preludes and Fugue, for thirteen solo strings, provides another example of the two-movement form already exploited in the String Quartet and the Second Symphony, where the first is introductory and episodic, while the second is cumulative and ultimately climactic. Paradoxically, its form is fixed, yet flexible. The structure is not 'open'; neither is it determined by aleatory procedures. Simply, there are alternatives for performing the work either in its entirety or shortened. The composer provides the following explanation in the score:

The work can be performed whole or in various shortened versions. In the case of performances of the whole, the indicated order of the [seven] Preludes is obligatory. Any number of Preludes in any order can be performed with or without a shortened version of the Fugue. The Preludes are always to be played without rests between them. They are composed in such a way that the overlapping of the ending of any Prelude and the beginning of any other one is possible.

It must be stressed that any shortened version must be decided by the conductor in advance, and that no opportunity exists for individual players to select any options during the performance. Thus there is a limited element of choice, rather than chance, in determining the time-scale of the work, all of which is foreseen and controlled by the composer. In practice, most performances present the work in its entirety, without omitting any Preludes or shortening the Fugue. When performed complete, it is the longest of his large-scale works; lasting between thirty-four and thirty-six minutes, it slightly exceeds the duration of all the symphonies and the Concerto for Orchestra.

The seven Preludes are composed to interlink with each other in any order. This is made possible by overlapping all endings and beginnings with the same group of six parts: violins 2,4,6; violas 1,3; and cello 1. Linking the Preludes provides an effective mechanism for passing from one formal stage to another without the listener being aware of sectional subdivisions. Here, the points of overlap have a distinctive division of the chromatic whole into two complementary hexachords: each ending is drawn from the notes D♯,D,B,B♭,A and G♯; while each beginning is drawn from the remaining six notes. Thus there is no duplication of pitches between strands during periods of overlap. Material had already been overlapped in this way as early as the finale of the Concerto for Orchestra, and this 'chain' principle was to be explored more fully in the three *Chains* and the finale of the Piano Concerto.

The first Prelude begins with a fanfare-like pattern of tones and perfect fifths/fourths. Its interval pairing (2 + 5) suggests similarity with the opening of the Second Symphony, and reappears in the introductory episode which begins the Fugue, as well as in each of the subsequent episodes and the final cadential flourish. Hence this interval pairing provides a distinctive 'frame' for the work as a whole. The second and third Preludes contain superimposed layers or strands of material: in the second, these are respectively *pizzicato* and scurrying *arco*; in the third, a bundle of parts marked *molto cantabile e espressivo* (for seven violins), is placed against another bundle playing *pizzicato* (the six lower strings).

Prelude no. 4 opens out from a unison F to become chordal. A note is added to each chord, until a succession of twelve-note chords is reached (just before letter C). Against this *pianissimo* harmonic background, violin 1 introduces disruptive repeated notes, *fortissimo*, which gradually appear in the other parts as they play in an increasingly frenetic manner. This quasi-theatrical situation invites comparison particularly with the String Quartet and the Cello Concerto. In Preludes 5 and 6 the leading role is fulfilled by a horizontal line or lines. No. 5 features the double-bass, while no. 6 features a duet for the two cellos. Prelude no. 7 gives the impression of moving towards a climax, although the composer deliberately denies this expectation. At the point where the listener expects a climax to be reached (letter I), all players break off at once. After attempts to regain momentum, the piece subsides into harmonic stasis not unlike the passage following the climax of the String Quartet.

The Fugue begins, not with the main subject, but with an introductory bridge passage linking it to whichever Prelude comes before. After this link, characterised predominantly by interval-classes 2 + 5, the initial entry of the first fugue subject appears at Fig. 1 (Ex. 5 : 3). Although composed as a single line, this subject is delivered in a polyphonic bundle of three parts: viola 3; cellos 1 and 2. Subsequent entries of the theme in

EX. 5 : 3   Preludes and Fugue, first fugue theme

this section, equatable with alternating entries of subject and answer, are presented in similar three-part bundles, gradually building a complex polyphonic texture of twelve string lines. The most significant feature of the fugue subject is its use of interval pairing $1 + 6$ (semitones and tritones), which contrasts strongly against the $2 + 5$ pairing used for the episodes. Table 8 summarises the Fugue's structural scheme, and emphasises the principle of intervallic differentiation that defines contrast between alternate sections of the form.

TABLE 8   Fugue, formal and intervallic scheme

Figs.	Episodes	Subjects	Character	Horizontal	Vertical
0–1	episode 1			$2 + 5$	
1–5		subject 1	*cantabile*	$1 + 6$	
5–6	episode 2			$2 + 5$	
6–9		subject 2	*grazioso*	$1 + 6$	
9–10	episode 3			$2 + 5$	
10–13		subject 3	*lamentoso*	$1 + 6$	
13–15	episode 4			$2 + 5$	
15–17		subject 4	*misterioso*	$1 + 6$	
17–18	episode 5			$2 + 5$	
18–20		subject 5	*estatico*	$1 + 6$	
20–21	episode 6			$2 + 5$	
21–24		subject 6	*furioso*	$1 + 6$	
24–29	episode 7			$2 + 5$	12-notes
29–47		stretto 1	(layered)		
47–48	episode 8			$2 + 5$	
48–49		stretto 2	(layered)		
50–51		stretto 3	(layered)		
51–53		stretto 4	(layered)		
53–54			climactic		$3 + 4 (+5)$
54–58			subsides		$2 + 3$
58–60			static		$2 + 3$
+60	cadence			$2 + 5$	$2 + 5$

Altogether, there are six fugue subjects, each with a different character of expression. All are based on a twelve-note row (Ex. 5 : 3) of similar interval structure to *Musique funèbre* (see Ex. 3 : 10). In the first formal stage (up to Fig. 24), which functions as fugal exposition, the designated character of each fugue subject is kept within a discrete section. In the second stage, however, the six characters are superimposed to create even more complex polyphony, not only of individual lines but also of contrasting textures and differing gestures. This procedure may be equated with the technique of stretto in conventional fugal writing; but the degree of contrapuntal complexity is far greater than anything to be found in previous fugal forms.

After Fig. 24 the pitch organisation ceases to be conceived horizontally, and greater attention is paid to the vertical dimension. Throughout this second formal stage the effect is of dramatic intensification. This change of approach is shown in Example 5 : 4, a facsimile of a passage occurring between Figs. 24 and 25. A blurred horizontal line (of interval pairing 2 + 5) expands outwards in pitch to produce a sustained twelve-note chord-aggregate (B–F–D) that has a dominant-seventh chord in the low strand (E♭,B♭,G,D♭), a major-seventh chord in the middle strand (E,A,C,F), and a half-diminished-seventh chord in the high strand (G♯,B,D,F♯). Table 8 inevitably over-simplifies this process of development, which is neither purely linear nor simply chordal, but an oblique combination of both.

From Fig. 24, four shortened versions of the Fugue are possible. The composer marks in the score which segments can be omitted: I, Figs. 24–50 (episodes 7–8 and stretti 1–2); II, Figs. 24–47 (episode 7 and stretto 1); III, Figs. 29–50 (episode 8 and stretti 1–2); IV, Figs. 29–47 (stretto 1 only). Whether sections of the Fugue are cut or not, the formal principle remains the same: from Figs. 50–54 there is an inexorable move towards the climax of the work. This is played *tutta forza* by all thirteen solo players who combine to produce a complex network of differentiated lines derived from a vertically symmetrical twelve-note chord (of interval-classes 3 and 4 around the axis interval of a perfect fifth). Here there are some similarities to the String Quartet. In both cases the climax is individual to each part within an aleatory section, rather than being co-ordinated by a downbeat from the conductor (as in the Second Symphony, *Livre pour orchestre*, and many other works). The way out of the climax is also unusual, although here there is no direct correspondence with the String Quartet. The sense of winding down is gradual and the period of subsidence is lengthy, repose being reached between Figs. 58 and 60. The final gesture is a fast, quasi-cadential burst of activity related to the 2 + 5 interval pairing of the earlier episodes of the Fugue and also to Prelude no. 1. This final succession of *fortissimo* chords is built entirely

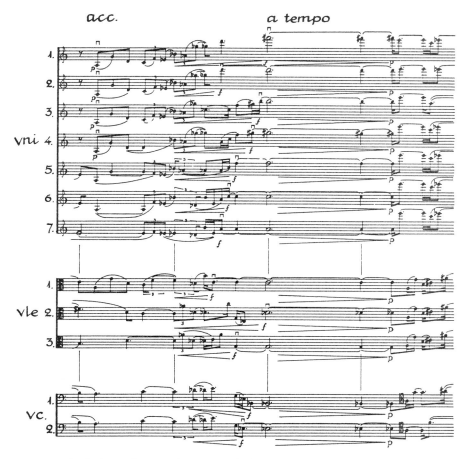

EX. 5 : 4   Preludes and Fugue, fugue episode showing the 2 + 5 interval pairing

of interval-classes 2 + 5, ending on a widely spaced twelve-note chord
(see Ex. 3 : 2d).

Preludes and Fugue is dedicated to its commissioner, Mario di
Bonaventura, and the first performance was given at the Styrian Autumn
Festival in Graz, on 12 October 1972. After its completion, Lutosławski
spent almost two years working on a projected Third Symphony. Dissatisfied with the results, he temporarily put the project to one side. His
problem was fundamentally one of the relationship between the harmonic
and melodic dimensions, a problem not solved until the emergence of his
late style after 1979. During the same period he also worked on a

concertante piece for the oboist Heinz Holliger, and in March 1973 he was able to describe his plans in conversation with Bálint András Varga (see Chapter 6). He also had problems with this project, but in this case it was because of an ambitious scheme for extensive application of chance procedures in the second movement. The work was eventually completed in 1980, but only after Lutosławski had put aside his apparently unworkable design for the slow movement. The early 1970s, therefore, constitute the high watermark of his experimentation with aleatory principles.

The most intractable of his problems with *ad libitum* technique had always been that of harmonic stasis, a shortcoming that can be mitigated but not completely solved. There is also the problem of aleatory sections being perceived in terms of textural and gestural effect, rather than in harmonic or melodic terms. Lutosławski has developed varied treatments of the harmonic dimension, and the differentiation he achieves between the harmonic strands of his complex twelve-note chord-aggregates must be counted a success in addressing this particular compositional difficulty. But the problem of impoverished melody remains. Of Lutosławski's pieces dating from the 1960s, only *Paroles tissées* shows a concern for the projection of melodic lines. This is largely due to the tenor soloist, who provides a *concertante* focus for horizontally generated material. Similarly, *Les espaces du sommeil* was to stand out from the other works of the 1970s. In both cases the vocal line provides a thread of continuity, against which comparatively short aleatory sections are cued by the conductor. In neither case does the composer choose to apply chance procedures to the horizontal unfolding of the solo line (presumably because of the textual confusion that would result). It is important to note that although the rhythmic and polyphonic aspects of Lutosławski's music had been greatly enriched by his pursuit of limited aleatorism up to and including Preludes and Fugue, the melodic aspect had been greatly impeded.

The way out of his *impasse* with both the Third Symphony and the Double Concerto was provided by the stimulation of a memorable musical event. On 2 October 1973, Dietrich Fischer-Dieskau and Sviatoslav Richter gave a recital in Warsaw. Not for the first time Lutosławski was to find compositional inspiration in the artistry of a performer, and he turned his attention to a medium in which the projection of a melodic dimension would be explicit: baritone and orchestra.[6]

Les espaces du sommeil

French surrealist poetry had provided Lutosławski with the inspiration for both vocal works of the 1960s: *Trois poèmes d'Henri Michaux* and *Paroles tissées*. Searching for a text to serve a large-scale work for Fischer-Dieskau, he once again turned to surrealism, this time a poem by Robert Desnos:[7] *Les espaces du sommeil* (The spaces of sleep).

Desnos was born in Paris on 4 July 1900. On returning to Paris in 1922, after completing two years of military service in Morocco, he plunged into the literary world of surrealist friends such as André Breton, Louis Aragon, Paul Eluard, Philippe Soupault, and René Crevel. Until 1929, Desnos took part in all the activities of this group, which even organised meetings to experience the unconscious world of dreams through hypnotised sleep. *Les espaces du sommeil* dates from this period, and is part of a group of poems under the collective title 'A la mystérieuse' written in 1926. Much of this early, surrealist poetry was published in the collection *Corps et biens* of 1930; but in that year he made a decisive break with surrealism. In a polemic pamphlet he wrote: 'Le surréalisme est tombé dans le domaine public, à la disposition des hérésiarques, des schismatiques et des athées' ('Surrealism has fallen into the public domain, at the service of leaders of heresy, schismatics and atheists'). This was later to provide an appropriate title for the collection of (most of) his poetic works, *Domaine public*, published posthumously in 1953. Like many writers, Desnos had been active in the Resistance. He was arrested by the Gestapo in February 1944 and taken initially to Buchenwald. On 8 June 1945 he died of typhoid in the concentration camp at Terezin in Czechoslovakia, only a few hours after its liberation.[8]

Les espaces du sommeil was chosen by Lutosławski both for its surreal images and its inherent musical form, which corresponded closely to a scheme already in the composer's mind. It has already been noted in the cases of the *Trois poèmes d'Henri Michaux* and *Paroles tissées*, that he tends to begin with an abstract outline and to choose a suitable text which enables the underlying formal archetype to be realised. Structurally, the piece is cast as an unbroken, fifteen-minute movement that evolves through three stages. The first is episodic, corresponding to the first four verses of the poem, its subdivisions determined by a recurring idea between verses. The second stage is slow, and corresponds to the fifth and sixth stanzas. The third stage builds towards the orchestral climax relatively late in the form (0.85), while the individual climax for the soloist occurs at the very end, and is determined by an unexpected twist at the conclusion of the poem. Table 9 summarises the formal scheme.

TABLE 9   *Les espaces du sommeil*, formal scheme

Figs.	Stage	Section	Text	Pitch organisation
[0]–2	1	intro.		basic set B, C, D♭, F (str/timp)
2–10		episode 1	verse 1	
10–12			*Il y a toi*	G, F, C (voice); D, E, F, G (hns, harp)
12–15		episode 2	verse 2	
15–17			*Il y a toi*	A, G, B (voice); E♭, F, G, A (hns, harp)
17–20		episode 3	verse 3	
20–22			*Il y a toi*	B, A, B♭ (voice); E, F♯, A, B (hns, harp)
22–24		episode 4	verse 4	
24–33	2	phrase 1	verse 5	12-note row of interval pairing 2 + 5, in prime/
33–40		phrase 2		inverted 24-note cycles, stated two-and-a-half
40–50		phrase 3		times, with transposition by perfect fifths
50–63		phrase 4	verse 6	
63–82		phrase 5		
83–92	3		verse 7	vocal part continues 2 + 5 row
92–96			verse 8	
96–97		climax		12-note chord-aggregate F–J–K
97–104		aftermath	verse 9	
105		cadence		12-note chord-aggregate D–J–D

Repetition of two images defines the structure of the poem: 'Dans la nuit', and 'Il y a toi'. The former conveys the nocturnal, somnolent world of dreams, through which the surreal images manifest themselves. Each of the first three verses begins with 'Dans la nuit', which also returns at the beginning of the eighth and ninth verses and in the penultimate line of the latter. Example 5 : 5a shows the patterns of intervals used for the initial vocal entry on 'Dans la nuit'. This grows naturally out of the preceding four-note melodic pattern played on timpani, which in turn is an extension of the opening four-note chord played by the strings. The soloist repeats 'Dans la nuit' three times in different ways derived from the same four-note cell (B,C,D♭,F), emphasising semitone/tritone, a three-note cell of semitone/tone, and then semitone with rising minor ninth. Example 5 : 5b

EX. 5 : 5   *Les espaces du sommeil*, vocal settings of: a) 'Dans la nuit';   b) 'Il y a toi'

shows the expanding pattern of intervals used for repetition of 'Il y a toi' after each of the first three verses.

For Lutosławski, obvious word-painting of sound-images would seem banal. Consequently, in *Les espaces* he adopts a principle already applied in *Paroles tissées*, where he treats poetic sound images in a neutral way that allows for the imagination of the individual listener, rather than imposing a fixed interpretation. Such a passage occurs in *Les espaces* at the beginning of the fourth verse, between Figs. 22 and 23 in the score, against background harmony from a twelve-note chord sustained by the strings. Here the text evokes four sounds: 'un air de piano, un éclat de voix, une porte claque, une horloge'.

When a poet describes a sound, this poses a problem for a composer: how is he to treat it? In my case, it is inconceivable that I should provide musical illustrations to the sounds described in a poem. However, I have introduced a certain device which allows me to keep them. I imagine the singer is telling us about his dreams. It is a first person narrative, after all. If the story teller is describing the sounds that occur in his dream, it does not necessarily follow that we should be able to hear them. I imagine the sounds are imprinted on the narrator's memory or consciousness. My device amounts to creating a situation where the singer conveys, in a fairly rapid recitative with pauses, the presence of the inner voice that is intelligible to him but not to the listener. The pauses . . . symbolise the moments of silent absorption in the sounds he is describing. Obviously, all this cannot take place in total silence. The silence is also symbolically expressed: it is conveyed by the static *pianissimo* of the strings.[9]

Verses 5 and 6 form the slow, second stage. Underlying this central period of calm and repose, a distinctive kind of twelve-note row is used to provide exquisite harmony in the strings. The subtle harmonic sonorities change very slowly, each new note being introduced individually. Although the row is fully chromatic in linear terms, the vertical harmony is more transparent, and only builds up a full twelve-note chord in the dense, semitone cluster sustained at the end of the Adagio section, prior to Fig. 82. The composer has commented on the harmony of this passage:

In my most recent works I have tried to make use of simple aggregations containing a limited number of pitches. This is already apparent in *Les espaces du sommeil* where there is a long passage, *adagio*, in which I wanted each new note appearing in the orchestra to have its own meaning. It is built on a series which comprises only two kinds of interval: major seconds and perfect fourths or perfect fifths.[10]

As notes of the row are delivered one at a time, the major seconds and perfect fourths/fifths produce a pentatonic effect, both horizontally and vertically, which is one of the most distinctive aspects of the sound in evoking the desired mood of tranquillity. Example 5 : 6 is a facsimile of the composer's original sketch for this section. Here, the twelve-note row can be seen above the short score, the prime form followed in each case by its inversion, with the composer's own circled numbering (1,2,3) labelling a simple cycle of transposition by perfect fifths. Notes are assigned to particular registers by octave displacement. Although the horizontal line contains only two interval-classes, the vertical harmony is not restricted in the same way. While the first five versions of the row are used for the Adagio section, the sixth begins the baritone line of the next section, from Fig. 82, and extends the 2 + 5 interval pairing to govern the vocal part up to Fig. 92. On the sketch the composer also shows the corresponding phrases of the poem.

The strings' harmony is only one of three layers during the Adagio. Melodic focus is provided by the vocal line, which uses notes drawn mostly from the string harmony. The third layer is provided by various trio combinations of two woodwind instruments and one tuned percussion instrument that add colouristic embellishments in an upper register. The relationship of pitch organisation between the strings and woodwind/percussion represents what the composer calls 'local harmony', and demonstrates his developing concern for clear differentiation between superimposed layers of the musical texture. Notes which are not (at a given moment) used in the strings, provide a repertory of pitches to be used by the woodwinds and percussion. Hence, as notes are gradually added to the string harmony within each phrase, there are fewer notes available for the woodwinds' local harmony. In most cases the sum of these layers gives all twelve pitches (by set complementation), although sometimes there are only ten. With each phrase the instrumentation of woodwind/percussion trios changes: two piccolos and glockenspiel (Figs. 24–32); two oboes and piano (Figs. 33–9); two flutes and celesta (Figs. 40–46); two clarinets and piano (Figs. 50–62); two horns and harp, then two trumpets and harp (Figs. 63–77).

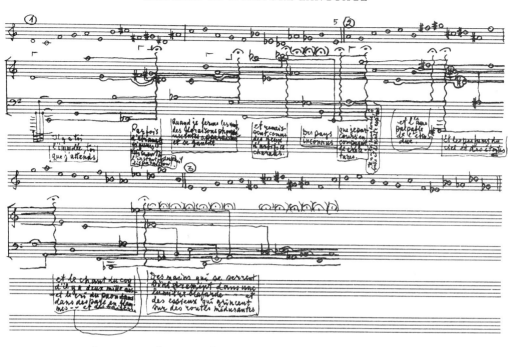

EX. 5 : 6 *Les espaces du sommeil*, composer's autograph sketch for the Adagio

Interval pairing of major seconds and perfect fourths/fifths continues in the vocal line through the next stage of the form, from Figs. 83–92. Example 5 : 6 includes twelve notes of the row (the inverted form of cycle no. 3) that are projected beyond the end of the Adagio and provide material for continuation. Thus the same method of twelve-note pitch organisation is used in both the vertical plane, for sustained harmony, and then in the horizontal plane, for the baritone line. The melodic 2 + 5 interval pairing ceases at Fig. 92 for the eighth verse prior to the climax of the work as the vocal line climbs ever higher with each phrase: C–C♯–D–D♯–E–F–F♯. Thereafter, the orchestral sound is so powerful that the voice would be unable to make itself heard. For the climactic harmony, played *ad libitum*, Lutosławski uses a twelve-note chord-aggregate with a different four-note chord in each harmonic strand (F–J–K). This is followed by an abrupt change to a *pianissimo* string chord at Fig. 97 made from the contrasting sonority of major seconds combined with minor thirds (see Ex. 3 : 2c), against which the soloist begins to deliver the final stanza: 'Dans la nuit, il y a les merveilles du monde. Dans la nuit il n'y a pas d'anges gardiens, mais il y a le sommeil'.

Throughout the work, the vocal setting is nearly all syllabic. Only five words from the entire poem are treated with vocal melismata. Of these, by far the most important occurs in the ante-penultimate line on the word 'sommeil', which is repeated four times (Ex. 5 : 7). It is worth noting that this is only the second place in the work where the composer adjusts the original text (the other was at the very beginning). In keeping with the post-climactic mood of gradual subsidence, the melodic line falls by interval contraction on each repetition; hence the rising intervals at the beginning of each phrase alter. Each time, the phrase descends through a pattern comprising only major seconds and minor thirds, thus matching the harmonic accompaniment of low strings which is derived from the same interval pairing.

EX. 5 : 7   *Les espaces du sommeil*, vocal line Figs. 103–5

After such strong, continual emphasis on nocturnal dream images, even in the penultimate line ('Dans la nuit il y a toi'), the final line comes as a wonderfully uplifting surprise: 'Dans le jour aussi'. At this point the baritone soloist, who did not participate in the collective, orchestral climax at Fig. 96, reaches his own highpoint. On a high E, the vocal line intones the last line unaccompanied, *piano,* with a crescendo to *fortissimo* on the final note. Such separation between collective and individual climax points has already been observed in the Cello Concerto. The parallel is close. In both cases the soloist finishes on a high, repeated note, as a gesture of expressive exultation. In *Les espaces*, however, there is one more event to come. The soloist's high E is taken up by strings and brass who continue and further intensify the crescendo, with a composed rhythmic accelerando that leads to the final chord. This *fortissimo* twelve-note chord-aggregate (type D–J–D; see the first of the two chords in Ex. 3 : 5b) provides one of the most original, exhilarating conclusions to be found in any of Lutosławski's works. After the initial attack by the entire orchestra, the chord simply evaporates through rhythmically elongated arpeggio patterns in the woodwind and percussion. No verbal account can do justice to this spellbinding ending.

If one is tempted to indulge in expressions of hyperbole, with *Les espaces du sommeil* such temptations become irresistible. It contains some of the most beautiful sonorities ever composed by Lutosławski and must be counted as one of his supreme achievements. Taken in isolation it is impressive; but even more remarkable is its close proximity to the next work he was to complete, *Mi-Parti*, which is its equal.

Although it was completed in 1975, because of difficulties in planning Fischer-Dieskau's schedule, *Les espaces* did not receive its première until 12 April 1978, when it was performed at the Berlin Phiharmonie, with the composer conducting the Berlin Philharmonic Orchestra. Hence the chronology of composition may be confusing to the observer. More significantly, in the absence of any feedback from performances of *Les espaces*, it was *Mi-Parti* that enabled Lutosławski to focus on the aspects of his harmonic language that he would soon seek to refine and to simplify.

Also in 1975 Lutosławski composed a short *pièce d'occasion* for the seventieth birthday of Paul Sacher. This was done at the request of Rostropovich, who had invited several composers to contribute celebratory pieces. The resulting three-minute piece for solo cello, *Sacher Variation*, makes cryptic use of notes drawn from the letters of Sacher's surname: E♭ (i.e. 'Es' [S] in German musical terminology), A, C, B (i.e. 'H' in German usage), E, and D (as 'Re' in solfeggio). The piece is based on contrast between the six pitches representing 'Sacher' and the complementary hexachordal set: F,F♯,G,A♭,B♭,D♭. Rostropovich gave the first performance of this and other birthday pieces for Sacher in Zurich on 2 May 1976. For Lutosławski, of course, it was a mere bagatelle, and the prime focus of his creative energy was the composition of *Mi-Parti*.

Mi-Parti

Like *Les espaces du sommeil*, *Mi-Parti* is a single movement piece unfolding in several stages across a time-span of about fifteen minutes.[11] The title is a French term and refers to bipartite division into two equal but not identical parts. Although it seems to suggest an interpretation of the work's form, the composer has stressed that this is not the case:

having found a suitable title, I realised it didn't match the work completely . . . it refers to the structure of the musical phrases to be played in the first, slow part of the piece. These phrases, performed as a solo by the wind instruments, can be heard against the pianissimo of the strings. Each phrase is repeated, and the beginning of the next phrase occurs during the repetition. Hence the title.[12]

Table 10 summarises the formal scheme. Note that the climax occurs comparatively early, leaving a considerable portion of the work still to come.

TABLE 10   *Mi-Parti*, formal scheme

Figs.	Section	Stage	Material	Pitch organisation
[0]–8	part 1	1	emerging lines	12-note chord-aggregates
8–14		2	emerging lines	12-note chord-aggregates
14–19		3	emerging lines	12-note chord-aggregates
19–24		4	polyphonic	overlapped harmonic strands
24–28	part 2	5		initially 2 + 3 interval pairing
28–39		6		passages of 2 + 3 interval pairing
39–40	climax		tutti, *fortissimo*	12-note chord-aggregate (B–K–B)
40–43	aftermath			
43–53	coda		str *cantilena*	horizontal interval pairing 2 + 3
52–53			final chord	12-note chord-aggregate (J–K–F)

The first of nine solo lines appears in the subdued tone-quality of the bass clarinet in its low register at Fig. 1. and plays without a break through to Fig. 7 (bars 10–37). Eight other lines then follow, played by two horns, two clarinets, two oboes and two flutes. Although there are nine instruments used, this does not indicate the true number of composed parts, since the horns, clarinets, oboes and flutes are used in pairs. This pairing enables the individual players to rest while a melodic line is passed to the other member of the pair. Thus the resulting network of nine lines really represents five layers of (metred) counterpoint, with the top four layers played by pairs of instruments and the lowest played only by the bass clarinet. There is also a gradual process of foreshortening produced by the introduction of successive layers at progressively shorter time intervals. Thus the first stage breaks down into eight units with the following numbers of bars: 9,7,6,5,4,3,2,1. The last bar in this metred passage, which is also the first *ad libitum* section of the work, is thus an inevitable consequence of the foreshortening of phrases.

The network of melodic lines grows out of the background harmony provided by the strings. This harmony consists of a succession of eight twelve-note chord-aggregates (Ex. 5 : 8) repeated cyclically with simple upward transposition of a semitone between cycles. Some of these chord-aggregates have the same type of four-note chord in both the outer strands (1,2 and 7), others have a different chord in all three strands (3,5 and 6), while only one has the same type in all three strands (8). Only the fourth aggregate has chords that do not belong to one of the ten classified chord types (see Table 3 and Ex. 3 : 4). The process governing the gradual change from one chord to another, as Steven Stucky has shown, is by selective octave transfer.[13] Example 5 : 8 shows all the chord-aggregates, with black notes marking the pitches that will be displaced to a different register in the following chord.

EX. 5 : 8   *Mi-Parti*, harmonic reduction of opening chord-aggregates

Lutosławski treats the succession of eight chord-aggregates as extending the cycle of repetitions across the *ad libitum* subdivisions that separate the first three stages; thus each stage begins and ends with a different chord-aggregate. Each of these three stages establishes its own pattern of foreshortening, the chords coming closer together as the rate of harmonic change increases. In each case this foreshortening has the effect of pushing towards the ensuing *ad libitum* section. Comparing the three stages with each other, one can also see another process of foreshortening as they take, respectively, thirty-six, twenty-one, and ten bars of metred playing before reaching an *ad libitum* section. The last of these is extended and acts as a link to the second, main section of the work.

Stages 5 and 6 each begin with nine-note sets played by three trumpets and three trombones. The line is divided between the six parts with notes sustained in each part for a short time so that the melody leaves behind a residual harmonic trace, akin to playing a single line on the piano with the sustaining pedal depressed. At certain points these harmonic by-products of the melody are changed, just as if the piano's sustaining pedal had been lifted and the resonance cleared. Example 5 : 9a shows the passage of twelve bars, from Figs. 24 to 25, which begins the fifth stage. There are fifty-one notes all linked by the 2 + 3 interval pairing. It is the particular pairing of intervals that matters, rather than the presence of any kind of row. Intervallically there is a nine-note pattern that repeats five times (3, 2, 3, 2, 3, 2, 2, 3), the sixth rotation being incomplete; the repetition of pitches operates on an eleven-note cycle. Example 5 : 9b shows the equivalent passage of forty-nine notes that begins stage six, the eleven bars between Figs. 28 and 29.

EX. 5 : 9 *Mi-Parti*, 2 + 3 interval pairing: a Figs. 24–5; b Figs. 28–9

The function of stages five and six is to propel the music towards its climax, which occurs relatively early in the form. The climactic harmony is a distinctive type of twelve-note chord-aggregate (B–K–B; see the first of the two chords in Ex. 3 : 5c), similar to the seventh chord-aggregate in the succession occupying the first part of the work. Few of Lutosławski's large-scale forms reach their highpoint at such an early stage. Here the proportion is almost exactly two-thirds of the overall duration (0.67).

The coda is supplied by a long *cantilena*, first for three solo violins then for a bundle of twelve solo violin lines (from Fig. 44), which winds its way in a leisurely ascent from G♯ at the bottom of the instruments' compass to the high C at the top of their range. A melodic reduction of the *cantilena* is shown in Example 5 : 10, presented as a single line rather than a bundle of polyphonic voices. Against this unbroken *cantilena* there are some moments of punctuation provided by chords on the lower strings, *pizzicato*, with colouristic mobiles in the woodwind and percussion parts. The pitch organisation of these embellishments is vertical rather than horizontal and is conceived as an independent layer of 'local harmony'. The *cantilena* itself unfolds entirely according to melodic interval-pairing of major seconds and minor thirds (2 + 3). This governs the forty-three notes of the winding ascent from G♯ to high C (Figs. 44–53), as well as the smaller bundle of three parts from Figs. 43 to 44. At Fig. 53, the typically Lutosławskian combination of celesta, harp and piano (with timpani) enters to play harmonic fragments that complement each other to produce the final twelve-note chord-aggregate (J–K–F), which is also sustained by the lower strings. The sounds conjured by Lutosławski in the coda of *Mi-Parti* are pure magic, and unforgettable for the listener; but for precisely this reason they were also to be unrepeatable.

Curiously, while *Mi-Parti* remains one of the most highly regarded of all Lutosławski's works, acclaimed by many commentators as a masterpiece of orchestral writing, it engendered considerable dissatisfaction on

EX. 5 : 10   *Mi-Parti*, string *cantilena* Figs. 43–53

the part of the composer not long after its first performance. The unease he has experienced concerns the first section in particular and its relationship between the harmony and melody. One could refer to notions of harmonic background and melodic foreground, but it is precisely the absence of such differentiation that troubles the composer:

> I consider melodies derived from harmonies as rather poor. That's the way I composed the beginning of *Mi-Parti*, which I think I will avoid in the future . . . especially the solo instruments which more or less repeat the sounds of the chords. I find it an unsatisfactory solution. It was a piece that I composed before I discovered the possibilities of composing in another way, and if I were to write this section of *Mi-Parti* again, I should do it in an entirely different way which would be a more accurate realisation of my sound-vision.[14]

Mi-Parti had been commissioned by the Amsterdam Concertgebouw Orchestra, with whom Lutosławski conducted the first performance on 22 October 1976. He then turned once more to the sketches for the Third Symphony and the Double Concerto and devoted most of 1977 to working on these projects. He was still unable to find a satisfactory solution to the problem of foreground and background, so yet again these works were temporarily shelved while he concentrated on a new piece for Rostropovich, this time not as cellist but as conductor.[15]

Novelette

Whereas the vocal line in *Les espaces du sommeil* had given Lutosławski an opportunity and a purpose for projecting a melodic line, the purely orchestral medium of *Novelette* did not. Compared with the other full orchestral piece of the 1970s, *Mi-Parti*, it does not shine; but then the comparison is unfair, since *Mi-Parti* is one of his master-works.

The title may appear to be French but is originally German. Usually used in the plural (*Novelletten*, anecdotes or sketches), it was first borrowed from the world of literature and applied as a musical title by Schumann.[16] Lutosławski used the title in order to suggest something rather light in weight, a narrative comprising several episodes. The schematic principle underlying the five-movement form can be regarded as an extension of the four-movement plan of both *Jeux vénitiens* and *Livre pour orchestre*, in which the first three were preparatory episodes, and were followed by a final section bearing the main dramatic weight. Here the approach is similar, with the cumulative and culminating material placed in the fifth movement, although this time preceded by four episodes rather than three. The composer gives each movement a pragmatically functional subtitle, signifying nothing more than the order in which they appear: Announcement, First Event, Second Event, Third Event, and Conclusion. As one would expect with Lutosławski, the last movement is the longest (about six-and-a-half minutes); the first is the shortest (about one-and-a-half minutes). Each of the three 'Events' lasts about two-and-a-half minutes in performance.

An abrasive opening gesture of loud, repeated chords announces the beginning of the musical action. Fifteen repetitions of a harshly dissonant major-seventh dyad (F against E) alternate with fifteen seven-note chords played in an ascending progression by woodwinds and brass. The harsh, almost brutal dissonance of these chords is reminiscent of the *Danse sacrale* of *Le sacre du printemps*, but dramatically the effect is entirely different. In the Stravinsky work the dissonance level is perceived in the context of the whole work, and a lot of other material has gone before; but in *Novelette* there is no such preparation, hence the listener may experience a degree of disaffection from the outset. This is quite a risk for a composer to take. Softer material follows, played delicately by strings without vibrato from Fig. 1. The loud chords reappear three times to interrupt the strings' gentle harmonic texture of eight-note semitone clusters. Against this background, two ideas of melodic significance are set in relief: first a repeated motif from the piccolo; then another, played by the xylophone. The latter is a seed sown early in the listener's unconscious memory and will reappear in the Third Event.

Horizontal interval pairing of semitones and tritones predominates in the First Event. The strings begin with a twelve-note row comprising these intervals which leave a residual harmonic trace within each phrase. A brief, but none the less welcome melodic line comes between Figs. 7 and 9, played by solo clarinet. Intervallically it is unrelated to the row, and therefore stands out in greater relief. Its character provides a fleeting foretaste of the kind of freely composed rhapsodic lines that were later evolved in *Partita* and *Chain 2*. This line is developed by the whole woodwind section and marimba from Figs. 13 to 14. At this point the semitone/tritone row returns in the top line above a succession of twelve-note chords, played tutti but without percussion. In the First Event, *frullato* chords from woodwinds and brass act like the grotesque grimaces encountered in the Cello Concerto and the second movement of *Chain 2*.

The Second Event also exploits the semitone/tritone interval pairing in a way that is immediately engaging. A woodwind trio of cor anglais, clarinet and bassoon pass the line from one to another, punctuated by textural highlights from the two harps, piano and marimba. This trio gives way to a bassoon solo (up to Fig. 18), then a network of woodwind lines from Fig. 19, growing to eight parts with the participation of two horns up to Fig. 20. All the lines exclusively use the semitone/tritone pairing, as does the piccolo solo that ends the movement.

The Third Event is driven by fast, motoric patterns and also witnesses the return of the motif first stated by the xylophone at Fig. 3. This motif is derived from a three-note cell of tone/semitone (D♯,F,E), made disjunct to emphasise angular major sevenths. Later, its rhythmic pattern is retained although the intervals are transformed and compressed in various ways (for example, the violins after Fig. 32).

The final movement, Conclusion, is the longest of the five. It begins in the lowest, murky depths of the harps' bass strings, as a three-note cell (F♯,E♯,G) gradually expands, creeping upwards chromatically through the lower reaches of clarinets and bass clarinet. The leading role in this movement is played by a pair of *cantabile* violin lines which enter, *pianissimo*, in the sixth bar on a unison F. No consistent interval pairing is used, and the line does not generate a row. Instead, it is freely composed in a way that Lutosławski was later to adopt in *Chain 3*. The violins are conducted *a battuta* from their entry and gradually climb higher and higher, until Fig. 45. From Fig. 46 they subdivide into seven-part polyphonic bundles in the high register, first *cantabile*, then scherzando (Fig. 47), then *poco appassionato* (Fig. 48).

At Fig. 52 we reach the collective climax on a twelve-note chord-aggregate of type C–H–C. This point of culmination occurs comparatively late in the form, at just over nine tenths of the work's duration (0.92 in Heinz Holliger's recording made at the 1984 Warsaw Autumn Festival). After the climax of *Novelette* there is a brief period of winding down, followed (after a clear break) by a quasi-cadential ending of repeated chords similar to the opening of the work. Here, the major-seventh dyad of F against E is repeated six times by most of the orchestra and alternates with a descending progression of five eight-note chords played by the brass, which also add the final five-note chord. The effect of this ending is as abrasive as the opening.

Novelette was the last of Lutosławski's works to be composed before he entered a new stylistic phase. Begun in 1978, it was completed on 5 May the following year. The first performance was given in Washington on 29 January 1980 by the National Symphony Orchestra under

Rostropovich, to whom it is also dedicated. Between the completion of *Novelette* and its first performance, the première had also been given in London of a *pièce d'occasion* that can now be seen as the decisive turning-point leading into the late style: *Epitaph*, for oboe and piano.

6
Emergence of the Late Style
(1979–1983)

Maturity as a composer had come comparatively late in Lutosławski's career, with the synthesis of his personal methods of pitch and rhythmic organisation: a harmonic language of twelve-note chords and chord-aggregates, together with the rhythmic sophistication provided by controlled aleatory counterpoint. Eighteen years after this maturity had been established through the completion of *Jeux vénitiens*, he was ready to progress into what can now be seen as a new stylistic phase.[1]

Lutosławski's dissatisfaction with the lack of differentiation between foreground melodic lines and background harmony in *Mi-Parti* has already been noted; this was to act as the catalyst for change. Yet the change did not come immediately. He gradually came to terms with the sound of *Mi-Parti* through practical experience of conducting the work in performance; hence it took three years, from 1976 to 1979, before he was able to compose the piece which, in retrospect, the composer has identified as the decisive turning-point:

I have been trying to work out a simpler harmony for some time now and, as to a turning point, the future will show. I rather think this point has already been reached, and the first attempt at the new solution which, I hope, will simplify matters a great deal, is a short work composed in 1979: *Epitaph* for oboe and piano.[2]

It is interesting that such a significant turning-point should have been made in what at first appears to be rather a modest piece. But it is precisely because of its brief time-scale and instrumental requirements that *Epitaph* provided the opportunity for Lutosławski to test his language through a compositional study. He had done the same thing many years before, during the war, when he worked on woodwind Canons and Interludes, and a woodwind Trio, all of which served as studies for the First Symphony. Later, in the Five Songs, he tested his experiments with twelve-note chords before applying them to a large-scale form in *Musique funèbre*. It is also intriguing to consider why the turning-point came with *Epitaph* rather than *Novelette*. The answer surely lies in the absence of orchestral resources. With a piece for only two instruments there can be little purpose in applying *ad libitum* techniques of controlled aleatory counterpoint to any great extent. Hence sophisticated orchestral texture was obliged to give way to exposed instrumental line; vertically conceived harmony thus gave way to horizontally conceived melody.

There are signs in *Novelette* that Lutosławski was already trying to simplify his harmonic language, for example with eight-note rather than twelve-note chords; but the absence of either a solo line or *concertante* focus for melodic expression seems to have been a missing ingredient. Lutosławski's late style is closely connected with concentration on *concertante* works. In turn, each of these has been preceded by a chamber piece acting as an essay for the larger work to follow. *Grave* prepared the way for *Partita* (in both duo and *concertante* versions), while *Partita* stands in a similar relationship to both *Chain 2* and the Piano Concerto. *Epitaph* began this sequence of events; its treatment of the oboe line prepared the way for the completion of the Double Concerto.

The composer has often remarked about his experience of composing during the post-war period, up to and including the Concerto for Orchestra: 'I could not compose as I wished, so I composed as I was able.' Although this remark can easily be interpreted against the background of political constraints obtaining in post-war Poland, it also has another level of significance, and refers to his awareness of limitations and lacunae in his compositional technique. Gradually, some of these problems were solved: twelve-note harmony; melodic interval pairing; controlled aleatory counterpoint; but others remained.

Refinement rather than reversal has been the path to the realisation of Lutosławski's late style.[3] Like all over-simplifications, this one also has weaknesses, but it does draw attention to a crucial point: that new elements have been added without previous ones having been abandoned. Features of the mature style have remained, to be refined rather than replaced, developed rather than discarded. Essential features of his late works include: simpler, more transparent harmony using fewer than twelve notes; twelve-note chords and chord-aggregates reserved for significant staging posts in the form; restraint in the use and extent of aleatory technique; greater rhythmic pace and energy achieved by writing a larger proportion of each work in conventional metre; allusion to some aspects of Baroque music; allusion to earlier works (pre-1960); realisation of compositional projects which had remained unfulfilled in his youth; and, above all, lyrical, expressive melody projected as thematic foreground material, a feature that is facilitated, in turn, by the simplification of harmony.

By comparison with earlier periods of his career, the years since 1979 have been more productive for Lutosławski. He has always been aware of the need to resolve the compositional and performance details of each score, but this fastidious approach has limited his output. Whereas in the 1950s both the Concerto for Orchestra and *Musique funèbre* underwent a four-year gestation period, his new-found security of technique has led to the late works being composed much more quickly. In the 1960s the extensive use of aleatory techniques caused progress on the production of each finished score to be very slow, while practical problems of ensemble co-ordination were solved and 'least advantageous solutions' anticipated. In the late works the more limited extent of aleatory technique largely obviates such difficulties.

Not all the works completed after 1979 fully represent the late style. Both the Double Concerto and the Third Symphony, as pieces conceived, sketched and shelved several times during the 1970s, are partial throw-backs to his earlier, mature style. Although they were both completed after *Epitaph*, newly composed material was combined with some earlier ideas. Thus the result, in each case, is a kind of stylistic hybrid of mature and late elements. The first substantial pieces to be conceived and composed in their entirety after 1979 were *Partita* (1984) and *Chain 2* (1985), both of which encapsulate the late style and must be counted among the most significant works of Lutosławski's career.

While Lutosławski was busy working on refinements to his language and technique, others in Poland and elsewhere were making radical changes to their style, which would reverse the modernism of their 1960s reputations. The most obvious case is Penderecki, whose self-confessed 'Affair with Romanticism' reveals an aesthetic somersault hard to reconcile with his modernist stance of the 1960s.[4] No such somersault has been turned by Lutosławski, who still expresses a need to move forwards, without looking to the past. His rejection of the neo-Romantic wave is consistent with his independence from modernist excesses of the avant garde. In his speech to the Congress of Culture held in Warsaw in early December 1981, he referred to the importance of establishing and maintaining independence from trends:

[the] situation until quite recently, can be described as a permanent revolution. It would be more accurate to call it a parody of a revolution, and could be described briefly as follows: 'What was yesterday is bad; only what is today can be good; that which is good will be good if it happens tomorrow; so what is good today will tomorrow already be bad.' . . . Paradoxically, I would suggest that the most revolutionary move in a situation

of pseudo-revolution is to ignore it, to exclude oneself from the dialogue with the world of critics and managers of music and those concert and festival goers who are interested primarily in continual changes of fashion and trends. Instead, one should concentrate effort on creating work that might stand a chance of a longer existence and function independent of immediate historical context.[5]

Epitaph

Epitaph was written for the oboist Janet Craxton, and dedicated to the memory of her husband, the composer Alan Richardson; she gave the first performance in a memorial concert at the Wigmore Hall in London on 3 January 1980. The piece lasts just over five minutes in performance and has a simple form based on alternation of contrasting sections which may be designated as refrain and episodes. This formal principle has already been observed in the first movements of *Jeux vénitiens* and the Second Symphony, and was also to be adopted for the early stages of the Third Symphony. In *Epitaph*, contrast between successive sections is achieved in four ways: by alternating a refrain which (initially) does not develop, with episodes that are extended and developed; by using a slow tempo for the refrain and faster tempos for the episodes; by using the same static, sustained three-note chord for the refrain, while the episodes have a variety of harmonic treatments; and, most important of all, by adopting different melodic interval pairings for the refrain and the episodes.

Contrast between static repetition of the slow, haunting refrain and dynamic development of the faster, growing episodes determines the unfolding of the piece up to and including the climax. The first two appearances of the refrain are identical. The next two are truncated: the third is slightly shortened, while only the beginning of the fourth is stated. The psychology of this process of shrinking phrases is simple but effective. After the second refrain, the listener has been conditioned to expect its recurrence; but having established this expectation the composer denies its fulfilment, deftly avoiding redundant literal repetition. There is nothing, however, which leads us to expect extension or development of the final refrain in the coda.

EX. 6 : 1   *Epitaph*, oboe line of opening refrain

The oboe line of refrains 1–3 has two phrases, one rising through nine notes, the other falling through eight notes (Ex. 6 : 1). The rising phrase uses interval pairing 2 + 3, whilst the falling phrase uses interval pairing 1 + 3, except for the quasi-cadential perfect fourth dropping back to F. Whereas the rising phrase is unaccompanied, the falling phrase is supported by a three-note chord from the piano, whose *forte* entry marks the dynamic highpoint of the refrain and divides the two phrases. The first phrase of the refrain closely resembles the tenor solo already observed in *Paroles tissées* (compare Ex. 4 : 6), although the interval pairing is not the same. Oboe and tenor lines both ascend through nine notes and span a minor ninth. Both have a four-note segment transposed for notes 6–9. In each case the first five notes rise, while the sixth turns downwards. In both phrases major seconds predominate: in the tenor line they interlock as whole-tone segments; in the oboe line they give pentatonic patterns. The pivotal role of the fifth note is differentiated in the oboe line as an acciaccatura. The second phrase of the oboe refrain retains the minor third as one half of the interval pairing but changes from major to minor seconds; thus there is a partial rather than complete change in intervallic character. There is a similar link between the falling phrase and each of the ensuing episodes, provided by semitones within the interval pairing. Grace-note inflections are typical of Lutosławski's *dolente* melodic lines, and although the word *dolente* does not appear in *Epitaph*, the dedication means that such melodic expression is implicit.

EX. 6 : 2   *Epitaph*, oboe line of episode 1 (first two phrases only)

Each episode is generated by melodic interval pairing of semitones and tritones (1 + 6) in the oboe part. Two other pieces also have dedications *in memoriam*: *Musique funèbre* and *Grave*. In each case the semitone/tritone pairing largely determines their mournful quality. In *Epitaph*, the first episode (Ex. 6 : 2) consists of five short oboe phrases accompanied by four figurations on the piano, with no simultaneous duplication of pitches between these separate layers. Episode 2 shows further application of the pitch-complementation principle, but also reconciles the oboe and piano parts on certain notes, usually either at the beginning or end of a phrase.

Episode 3 is the shortest and leads to the most concise statement of the refrain; here the oboe line uses only interval-class 1 (semitones, major sevenths and minor ninths) and does not duplicate notes of the piano.

Episode 4 accelerates to the climax of the piece on repetitions of the oboe's high F♯, played *fortissimo*. The oboe line determines the course of this section and evolves through two stages consisting entirely of interval pairing 1 + 6. The first stage (dotted crotchet = c. 176) is supported in the piano part by a ten-note ostinato pattern of two five-note groups. Only one pitch (E♭) does not occur in the first stage; its arrival marks the beginning of the second (crotchet = c. 184). As the piece moves towards the climax the piano part rises chromatically, its simple scale outline distorted by octave doublings and octave displacement. After the climax, semitone-tritone interval pairing does not reappear. Instead, the last refrain is extended upwards, leading into the coda (Ex. 6 : 3).

Just as there is an intervallic connection between the two phrases of refrains 1–3 (continued presence of minor thirds), and a similar link between the second phrase of the refrain and the episodes (continued presence of semitones), refrain 5 and the coda are linked by the major second. Conventional notation is adopted, with bar lines and time signatures. Regular pulsation in the first five bars enables the composer to achieve hemiola contradictions of metre typical of his music from the 1940s and 50s. Continuing from the end of refrain 5, the coda begins with the piano intoning C♯, and then continues in two parts with a repeated chromatically descending sequence of major sevenths. The harmony changes in bar 5 to chromatically descending minor thirds, thus anticipating the oboe's interval pairing at the point marked *tranquillo*. Chromatic descent in minor thirds continues for a further six bars, until the parts meet on a three-note cell (C,B♭,B) four bars before the end. The oboe line in the coda's first five bars is strongly reminiscent of the third movement of *Paroles tissées*, where the tenor sings a melisma on a twelve-note row of major seconds and perfect fourths/fifths (see Ex. 4 : 7). Here, however, the oboe line is not required to supply a twelve-note row, because the composer is concerned with the sound of the particular interval combination rather than maintaining the presence of the chromatic whole.

The last ten bars of the coda, marked *tranquillo* for the oboe, return to the 2 + 3 pairing heard in the refrain. Here the line makes a gradual and unbroken ascent, twisting chromatically through thirty-six notes, and reaches its final resolution on a high F. In view of the dedication, one

EX. 6 : 3   *Epitaph*, coda

might reasonably suppose there to be some spiritual meaning to this ending. Almost the whole of this concluding passage is subject to pitch-complementation between the melodic line and its harmonic support, the only exceptions being the B grace-note three bars before the end, and the F in the last bar. The latter, placed at the bottom of the final chord and occurring as the destination of the oboe line, both reconciles the harmonic with the melodic dimension and enables the piece to finish on its pivotal pitch. Any feeling of tonal resolution is avoided, however, because of the harmonic ambiguity that derives from the superimposed tonic and dominant functions of the final chord. It is also worth noting that the sonority of this chord is determined by the combination of perfect fifths and a minor third $(3 + 7)$, a characteristic phenomenon of the late works.

Although the coda has been discussed mainly on the technical level of interval relationships, what really matters is that there is a coda at all. The form of *Epitaph*, with its most expressive (and impressive) ideas after the climax, shows the composer treating the latter not as the main destination, but as a threshold, which, when crossed, reveals further development of material and intensification of ideas. The Third Symphony shows this formal approach on a larger scale, and here, too, the climax is a means rather than the end.

Is *Epitaph* really the turning-point Lutosławski felt it to be? It certainly uses simpler harmony than any of his works since the Dance Preludes of 1954. This is hardly surprising, since a duo combination is far less suited to dense harmonic effects than an orchestral medium. Yet the change cannot be ascribed solely to the instrumental resources, since it was in the piano writing of the Five Songs (1957) that Lutosławski first introduced twelve-note chords. Thus it would have been possible for him to apply his dense harmonic language in *Epitaph* had he so wished, but there is not a single twelve-note chord to be found anywhere in the piece.

Double Concerto

The Double Concerto for oboe, harp and chamber orchestra was the first of several pieces to be commissioned by Paul Sacher, who also undertook to engage Heinz Holliger for the first performance. At Holliger's request, Lutosławski agreed to include an obbligato part for the harp, to be played by Ursula Holliger. Lutosławski's close association with Sacher is a significant thread running through the late works, particularly because of the commission and dedication of both *Chain 2* and *Interlude*. It is fitting that these works should form part of the illustrious roll-call of works associated with Sacher, as it establishes a connection with those pieces by Bartók that Lutosławski admires: Music for Strings, Percussion and Celesta, the Sonata for Two Pianos and Percussion, and the Divertimento.

The commission of the Double Concerto dates back to the early 1970s. Lutosławski began work sketching the piece soon after completing Preludes and Fugue. As with his work on the Third Symphony, the path to realisation proved to be long and problematic. After variously interrupting and resuming work on both projects throughout the 1970s, Lutosławski finally completed the Double Concerto in 1980. Hence it only partially represents the late style, as some of the earlier material was retained. The first performance was given in Lucerne on 24 August 1980, conducted by the dedicatee with Heinz and Ursula Holliger and the Collegium Musicum.

The concerto is scored for a chamber orchestra of two percussionists and twelve strings (7.2.2.1), although the size of the string section can be increased for performance in a large hall. The modest size of ensemble was obviously determined by practical considerations of dynamic balance with the soloists, as well as by the size of the Collegium Musicum, but the treatment of the strings, particularly the use of twelve solo parts to allow polyphonic delivery of twelve-note chords and chord-aggregates, establishes a strong connection with Preludes and Fugue.

An early (perhaps premature) account of the project was given in conversation between the composer and Bálint Varga during their interviews in March 1973. At that time, Lutosławski was evidently still preoccupied with ideas about interchangeability of sections, which he had recently applied in Preludes and Fugue. His outline of the concerto is surprising in view of the considerable differences from the eventual outcome:

In this work, chance will play a greater role than in the past. Although it may sound paradoxical, the piece is also going to be highly organised, but there might be greater differences between the various interpretations ... Perhaps one might liken it to a sculpture out of a liquid substance. This problem attracts me a great deal ... The first movement is going to be a short introduction, while the last will be a series of marches. It will start with a quick march, and end with a funeral march. The experiment concerns the second movement which will consist of short episodes. Only the beginning and end will be given, within the movement the instruments will be free to choose the duration of occurrences. Primarily it will be the pauses between the occurrences and the order of the particular sections that will be free. The movement will have to be composed in such a way that any section can be played together with any other.[6]

By the time the piece was completed, several of the above ideas had been abandoned. Such are the dangers of premature disclosure (whether by the composer himself or in critical commentary) concerning work still in progress. The first movement is not particularly short (about five minutes), neither is it merely introductory. The final movement does indeed have a brisk march, but there is no funeral march. There is no evidence in the second movement of the original plans for interchangeable *ad libitum* sections; the aleatory 'experiment' did not survive. The Double Concerto, as we now know it, is in three self-contained movements: Rapsodico, Dolente, Marciale e grotesco.

The first movement is in two clearly defined stages: Rapsodico (Figs. 1–17); and Appassionato (Fig. 17–end). Although the first stage could be described as introductory, the second goes beyond this limited function. The first stage is composed and co-ordinated entirely in short, self-contained *ad libitum* sections that alternate between the full body of strings and duo sections for the two soloists. This contrast between concertino and ripieno/ritornello passages provides an obvious allusion to the Baroque concerto grosso, particularly with the focus on double-reed sound accompanied by a polyphonic instrument. Although similarities of sonority and performance gesture suggest some validity for such a comparison, there are no allusions of style, technique or language. The contrast is not only one of instrumental colour and sonority, it also arises from the juxtaposition of two different approaches to the treatment of twelve-note harmony. Whereas the strings deliver a succession of twelve-note chords, mostly containing only one or two types of interval, the duo sections partition the chromatic whole into complementary segments of five and seven pitches, assigned respectively to oboe and harp (obviously, the pitch material of the duo passages is subdivided in this way because the pedal mechanism of the harp determines a maximum of seven pitch-classes at any given moment). The recurring problem of differentiation between melodic and harmonic layers of musical material, which pre-occupied Lutosławski during the latter part of the 1970s, here finds a ready-made solution. The differences of tone-colour and expression between the solo instruments are so great that their respective melodic and harmonic roles are inevitable and explicit. Similar set-complementation between melodic line and harmonic accompaniment is also used for many passages in *Partita* (although subdivided as 6 and 6, rather than 5 and 7), particularly the *ad libitum* second and fourth movements, together with the climactic *ad libitum* section in the final movement. Though this feature of the duo sections in the Double Concerto is typical of the late style, the intervening *ritornelli* for the strings, in which they play densely voiced twelve-note chords, represent a throwback to the style of Preludes and Fugue.

The second stage, Appassionato, extends from Fig. 17 to the end of the first movement, concluding with an *ad libitum* duo for the two soloists that functions as a kind of cadenza between Figs. 25 and 26. One layer of the Appassionato section is provided by the two soloists together with the cellos. This strand is set against a three-part bundle of polyphonic voices played by the upper strings (although the polyphony is metred rather than *ad libitum*, the effect is nevertheless one of rhythmic 'blurring' of the horizontal line). Interruptions occur when the whole string section plays three *fortissimo* twelve-note chord-aggregates (just after Fig. 21, at Fig. 23, and just after Fig. 24). Table 11 shows the horizontal pitch-organisation in twelve-note rows used to generate the three-part counterpoint of string lines, for violins and violas, that form the background layer.[7] As this whole passage is metred (in $\frac{3}{4}$) it is possible to establish reference-points according to bar numbers from Fig. 17, although these are not printed in the score.

Typically for Lutosławski, the row (an array of twenty-four notes with the prime form followed by its retrograde inversion) is treated according to a simple method of transposition, in this case by notional successive

TABLE 11   Double Concerto, 12-note rows between Figs. 17 and 23

Bars	Row	Permutation	1	2	3	4	5	6	7	8	9	10	11	12
1–3	1	P_0 (prime)	C	E	G	B	G#	Eb	D	E#	A	F#	C#	Bb
3–5	1a	RI_0	D	B	Gb	Eb	G	Bb	A	E	Db	F	G#	C
5–7	2	P_{11}	B	D#	F#	A#	G	D	C#	E	G#	E#	C	A
7–9	2a	RI_{11}	C#	Bb	F	D	Gb	A	G#	Eb	C	E	G	B
9–11	3	P_{10}	Bb	D	F	A	Gb	C#	C	D#	G	E	B	G#
11–14	3a	RI_{10}	C	A	E	C#	F	G#	G	D	B	Eb	F#	Bb
14–17	4	P_9	A	Db	E	Ab	F	C	B	D	F#	Eb	A#	G
17–21	4a	RI_9	B	Ab	D#	C	E	G	Gb	Db	Bb	D	F	A
21–25	5	P_8	Ab	C	Eb	G	E	B	Bb	C#	F	D	A	F#
25–29	5a	RI_8	Bb	G	D	B	Eb	F#	F	C	A	C#	E	G#
29–32	6	P_7	G	B	D	F#	Eb	Bb	A	C	E	C#	G#	F
34–39	6a	RI_7	A	F#	C#	A#	D	F	E	B	Ab	C	Eb	G
39–45	7	P_6	Gb	Bb	Db	F	D	A	G#	B	D#	C	G	E
45–47	7a	RI_6	G#	F	C	A	C#	–	–	–	–	–	–	–

descent in semitones. Interval patterns within the row emphasise interval-classes 3 and 4, so the harmonic result of blurring the line is that various triadic formations are sustained. This is a very different procedure to the kind of twelve-note rows exploited by Lutosławski in previous works that use horizontal interval-pairing of either semitones/tritones (1 + 6) or major seconds and perfect fourths/fifths (2 + 5). In *Musique funèbre* the twelve-note row was constructed from semitones and tritones expressly to preclude the sound of thirds as adjacent intervals within the vertical harmonic sonorities. Here, the deliberate emphasis on triadic patterns invests the harmony with a more consonant sonority.

EX. 6 : 4   Double Concerto, second movement, Fig. 28

In the slow movement, after a twelve-note chord-aggregate played *pizzicato* by the strings, the oboe enters on a high B♭ and leads into an *ad libitum* section for the two soloists (Ex. 6 : 4). The word *dolente* appears here in the oboe part, and shows that the composer associates the character of the movement as a whole with this type of lamenting melodic line. His consistent association of *dolente* expression with melodic lines emphasising grace notes may suggest some allusion to the effect of vocal sighs (see also Exx. 5 : 1; 5 : 2, and 6 : 1). Whereas the soloists' *ad libitum* sections in the first movement subdivide all twelve pitches, here only nine are partitioned: four for the harp, and five for the oboe in a narrow band of pitch initially twisting chromatically from B♭ to F♯. Later in the second movement there is a striking foretaste of the sonorities and gestures that make the slow movement of *Chain 2* so memorable. Between Figs. 35 and 45, the soloists play delicate, wistful little patterns above four-note chords sustained by tremolos on vibraphone and marimba. Typically, there is no duplication of notes between the melodic foreground and the supporting harmony, hence there is a subtle separation between the two layers.

In the final movement, the subtitle 'Marciale e grotesco' refers to two separate elements (and not to a 'grotesque march'). The main march theme (Ex. 6 : 5a) is generated by the pairing of semitones and tones. Although the character of this theme is not grotesque, there is certainly an element of parody, comic but not ironic. It would be misleading to suggest that any allusion to Shostakovich marches was intended, but there is more than a hint of Prokofiev, particularly when one recalls the thematic character of Lutosławski's wartime woodwind Canons and Interludes (Ex. 2 : 6a) and the oboe solo in the slow movement of the First Symphony (Ex. 2 : 6b).

The third movement unfolds through five formal stages. The first (to Fig. 60) corresponds to the initial march, played by oboe and orchestra while the harp remains silent. The second stage (Figs. 60–67) is played by

EX. 6 : 5   a) Double Concerto, third movement, 'march' theme

EX. 6 : 5   b) Double Concerto, third movement, canonic treatment of march theme

the harp and orchestra without the oboe. Both these stages make use of the regular duple metre. The third stage (Figs. 67–77) is played by both soloists with orchestra, and it is here that a grotesque character is represented by the oboe and strings. Although Heinz Holliger is well known for his virtuosity in avant-garde oboe techniques, Lutosławski gives little opportunity in this Concerto for the display of effects. The only passages to make use of avant-garde techniques, presumably in deference to Holliger, are in the first movement just before Fig. 23, and in the grotesque gestures of the final movement (between Figs. 68 and 74), conveyed by squeaky sounds produced by multiphonic fingerings. In conversation with Varga, the composer stressed that he was more impressed by Holliger's performances of the Mozart Oboe Concerto than by his mastery of non-standard techniques.

The Double Concerto is also unusual in its treatment of the climax, which is not marked by a *fortissimo* chord played by the whole orchestra, as one would normally expect with Lutosławski, but by a series of *ad libitum* passages (Figs. 77–81) for the two soloists without the orchestra, which assume the function of a cadenza. His decision to exclude the orchestra from this significant part of the movement was undoubtedly influenced by the potential problems of balance presented by the harp, which would have been unable to compete or participate to any effect in a collective orchestral climax.

After the culmination, the march's reappearance (at Fig. 84), played by both the soloists with xylophone, acts as a recapitulation. The canonic relationship between the oboe and xylophone is intentionally humorous, because of a stretto pattern which sounds as if one or other of the players has miscounted or entered in the wrong bar (Ex. 6 : 5b). The composer suggests that this canonic chase is akin to walking behind someone so close as to catch one's toes on their heels. At the point where the strings re-enter, to join the trio of oboe, harp and xylophone (Fig. 89), the coda begins.

Table 12 shows the twelve-note rows that perform the leading role in the pitch organisation of four-note chords in the coda. These rows occur in the top line of the strings and are governed by melodic interval pairing of major seconds and perfect fourths/fifths (2 + 5). The chords below each of these notes of the row also emphasise the same interval pairing.

The penultimate note of this horizontal projection of the twelve-note row is a C, repeated at the top of the strings' harmony between Figs. 93 and 94. When this moves up a perfect fourth to F at Fig. 95 the aural

TABLE 12   Double Concerto, 12-note rows after Fig. 90

Bars	Permutation	1	2	3	4	5	6	7	8	9	10	11	12
227–	P₀ (prime)	F#	E	A	B	Db	Ab	Eb	F	Bb	C	G	D
		2	5	2	2	5	5	2	5	2	5	5	
233–	I₁₀	E	F#	C#	B	A	D	G	F	C	Bb	Eb	G#
		2	5	2	2	5	5	2	5	2	5	5	
239–	P₇	C#	B	E	F#	G#	Eb	Bb	C	F	[G]	[D]	[A]

sensation is of dominant pedal followed by tonic resolution, even though the rest of the harmonic succession is not governed by tonal functions. There is a separate dominant/tonic effect in the bottom part at Fig. 95 when a repeated B drops to E. Thus a conflict is established between two rival tonics placed a semitone apart. This struggle is resolved in the last three bars with an angular alternation of F and E that decides in favour of the latter. At Fig. 95 just before this quasi-cadential ending, a gesture in miniature occurs, which was soon to be developed and expanded to splendid effect in the corresponding position at the end of the Third Symphony. As the strings sustain a widely spaced chord the two percussion players (on xylophone and glockenspiel) repeat brittle, sparkling patterns projected in stark relief.

The Double Concerto seems more typical of Lutosławski's style than *Epitaph* simply because it incorporates the ensemble aleatory techniques that one associates with his mature works. Yet there are strong connections between the two pieces, particularly in the use of pitch complementation between the oboe and its partner, whether piano or harp. Lutosławski's decision to simplify his harmony by assigning fewer (than twelve) pitches to accompanimental patterns was beneficial in enabling him to compose more genuinely melodic lines that are harmonically supported rather than texturally swamped.

If *Epitaph* was a turning-point in the development of Lutosławski's harmonic language, then the Double Concerto was no less important a turning-point in his attitude towards aleatory procedures. Instead of further radical experimentation he consolidated his *ad libitum* techniques, reducing the number and length of such sections, and at the same time improving the notation of conducted cues in order to exercise more careful control. This move towards consolidation is a positive feature of Lutosławski's later works and need not be interpreted either as a sign of retrenchment or a loss of creative impetus. Instead, it comes as a welcome indication that he has addressed compositional problems presented by the element of chance.

The year 1980 was not only busy and eventful for Lutosławski, with the premières of *Epitaph*, *Novelette* and the Double Concerto; it was also one of the most significant years in modern Polish and European history. The epoch-making strike at Stocznia Gdańska (the Lenin shipyards) began on 14 August, soon to be followed by the historic Gdańsk Agreement by which the independent free trade union NSZZ *Solidarność* (Solidarity) was established. The next fifteen months were to witness the most extraordinary turbulence in Polish society as the popular will challenged Communist Party authority. It has already been noted that, at the time of the Gdańsk strike in 1970, there had been no clear focus for Polish unrest, and that there had been no person to represent a higher, moral authority. This position changed dramatically with the election of Cardinal Karol Wojtyła as Pope John Paul II on 16 October 1978. One cannot underestimate the potent effect in Poland of his emergence onto the world stage, and his first official return to Poland as Pope in June 1979 can, in retrospect, be seen as a catalyst that contributed to the events of the following summer. Lutosławski's work during these months did respond to a specific event, but one of personal rather than political significance: the death of a friend.

Grave

Stefan Jarociński (b. 1912), the eminent Polish musicologist and critic, died on 8 May 1980.[8] Outside Poland, he is known principally for his writings on French music, particularly Debussy.[9] In 1967 he had published the first book devoted exclusively to Lutosławski and his music, including a biographical essay, a selection of the composer's writings, a list of compositions, and a bibliography.[10] As a contemporary of Lutosławski, a close friend of long standing, and a constant champion of his work, it was natural that the composer would wish to honour Jarociński with a musical tribute: *Grave*, Metamorphoses for cello and piano, was first performed at a memorial concert held at the National Museum in Warsaw on 22 April 1981. In the book for which he will best be remembered by English readers, *Debussy, Impressionism and Symbolism*, Jarociński declared his great admiration for the music of *Pelléas et Mélisande*: 'Debussy's vocal music and the lyric drama of *Pelléas et*

Mélisande, its crowning glory, mark the beginning of the process of renovating the language of music and its symbolism'.[11]

In his discussion of Debussy's treatment of harmony, timbre and sonority, Jarociński identified and described a principle of subdividing the sound into different layers. His account of this feature could be taken as a description of the same type of procedure in Lutosławski's music. In view of the long and close friendship between the two men, it is difficult to say whether Lutosławski's approach to the subdivision of his sound language into complementary harmonic strands influenced Jarociński's analysis and criticism of Debussy, or vice versa:

Not so long ago the notion of verticalism was always associated with harmony; and yet these two conceptions are not identical since, according to the sound-material employed, vertical structures will always be homogeneous and compact, and will either dissolve into a single sonorous stratum or, on the contrary, will be heterogeneous or 'polygeneous', and it will then be possible to distinguish two or three strata (purely sonorous, and having nothing in common with melodic lines). The horizontal structures will not necessarily present a melodic design, and the vertical ones may be decomposed or divided into separate sonorous levels, while their harmonic links may be weakened.[12]

Jarociński's observation of harmonic strata in the music of Debussy would serve as an accurate description of the disposition of harmonic strands in Lutosławski's twelve-note chord-aggregates. His attempt to distinguish between the concepts of verticalism and harmony underlines an important difference between traditionally based chord structures and more complex aggregates of harmonic timbre. Jarociński recognised, for example, that 'the horizontal structures will not necessarily present a melodic design', an observation that touches on the oblique, polyphonic dimension of horizontally projected harmonies that are planned vertically.

In deference to Jarociński's admiration for *Pelléas*, Lutosławski begins his memorial tribute with an obvious quotation from the opening forest scene: the rising four-note phrase D–A–G–A. The interval combination of perfect fifth and major second is then taken as the point of departure for Lutosławski to develop a line using the 2 + 5 interval pairing. Thus the quotation is incorporated naturally into Lutosławski's own compositional technique and does not sound out of place surrounded by his non-tonal musical language. The *Pelléas* 'forest motif' also reappears at the end of *Grave*.

In common with the twelve-note row of *Musique funèbre* and the episodes of *Epitaph*, both works also bearing dedications *in memoriam*, *Grave* also makes extensive use of the 1 + 6 melodic interval pairing of semitones with tritones. Symbolism may be found in the way the piece then unfolds in continual alternation of the 2 + 5 and 1 + 6 interval-pairings: the former representing an allusion to Jarociński's lifelong study of Debussy; the latter expressing a mood of mourning. Lutosławski adopts a consistent method of passing from one interval pairing to the other via three-note interval cells of interlocking semitone/tone. Here he applies the cell in such a way that it acts as a link from the major seconds or minor sevenths of the 2 + 5 pairing into the semitones or major sevenths of the 1 + 6 pairing. The application of three-note 1 + 2 cells in this transitional way ensures that at no point do we hear interval-classes 5 and 6 immediately adjacent within the horizontal line. Example 6 : 6 shows the cello line from bars 1–20. The 2 + 5 pairing occurs in bars 1–2 and 13–17, while the 1 + 6 pairing occurs in bars 3–12 and 18–20 (etc).

EX. 6 : 6   *Grave*, cello line bars 1–20

Unlike *Musique funèbre* the pitch is not organised by reference to a twelve-note row. Instead, the cello line dominates, supported and complemented by the piano. A strong connection exists between the two works, however, in their use of the term 'Metamorphoses'. Although in *Musique funèbre* this subtitle for the second section of the form signifies successive transformations of the twelve-note row, there is an equally important transformation of rhythm. The Metamorphoses of *Grave* may be interpreted in this rhythmic sense, as operating independently from the continual alternation of melodic interval pairings (i.e. the moments of rhythmic and intervallic change do not necessarily occur together). The effect of rhythmic quickening in *Grave* is not the result of any system, but follows a general, and informal, principle of shortening the rhythmic durations: minims; crotchets; triplet crotchets; quavers; triplet quavers; semiquavers. Thus the piece drives towards its culmination in bars 146–50, with the cello reaching its highpoint at Fig. 10. Significantly, in view of Lutosławski's conscious decision to simplify his harmony, the collective climax is not marked by a twelve-note chord. The climax here has more in common with the equivalent moment in the slow movement of *Partita* than with the harmonically dense *ad libitum* sections typical of the orchestral works. Although the cello reaches a highpoint on B♭, the focal pitch here is D, the axis point of the augmented triad B♭–D–F♯ reached in bar 148. The significance of D as a reference pitch for the piece is obviously determined by the *Pelléas* quotation.

After the climax, there is no extended coda as in *Epitaph*. Thus there is no comparable sense of crossing a threshold into a new spiritual world. The cello returns, unaccompanied, to the semitone/tritone and then (at Fig. 11) to the opening four notes of the quotation from *Pelléas* (D–A–G–A), but this time played *fortissimo*. The final, haunting harmony is provided by set-complementation between the cello and piano: a nine-note chord sustained by the piano (emphasising a Debussian dominant-seventh sonority in the low register, D♭,A♭,F,B/C♭), against which the cello plays the three remaining, complementary pitches, D–G–A, in an expansive ascent from *fortissimo* low D to a high A harmonic, *pianissimo* (note the way the final A harmonic of the cello combines with the piano upper register to complete a diminished-seventh chord).

Stylistically, *Grave* looks towards the harmonic language and rhythmic gestures of *Partita* and *Chain 2*, rather than looking back, for example to the Cello Concerto. Whereas the latter treats the *concertante* relationship between soloist and orchestra as one of conflict and confrontation, *Grave* and the late violin works illustrate the composer's more recent preoccupation with the projection of melodic line in a solo part against harmonic accompaniment. In 1982, Lutosławski produced a *concertante* version of *Grave* for cello and thirteen strings (4.3.3.2.1), first performed that summer in Paris. Concentration on *concertante* works has already been observed as a preoccupation of Lutosławski's later years; the second version of *Grave* thus consolidated a pattern established by the Double Concerto, and which continues through *Partita*, *Chain 2* and the Piano Concerto. The parallel between *Grave* and *Partita* is particularly strong:

both originated as duos and were subsequently orchestrated. In particular, the keyboard writing of *Grave* anticipates the tactile, pianistic figurations of *Partita*, while the use of continual contrast between the 2 + 5 and 1 + 6 interval-pairings as a form-building principle anticipates the *soave/rude* contrast exploited in the second movement of *Chain 2*. The orchestral version of *Grave* highlights the absence of aleatory sections: it is the first ensemble piece since the Postludes to make no use whatsoever of chance procedures affecting the polyphonic relationships between the individual parts. There are some moments that exploit simple effects of harmonic blurring, but instead of resulting from aleatory polyphonic bundles they are strictly metred, and the outcome is precisely determined by specific notation in all the string parts. The gradual metamorphosis achieved by rhythmic quickening is more akin to the second section of *Musique funèbre* than any works post-1961. At the same time there is a rapid delivery of pitches in the unfolding of the solo line (and in the pitch complementation of the harmonic accompaniment) that would be severely impeded by the operation of aleatory technique.

Perhaps because *Epitaph* and *Grave* were both unplanned they enabled Lutosławski to find fresh ways of dealing with melodic, harmonic and polyphonic problems that had troubled him throughout the 1970s. Having tested some solutions in these little pieces he was then able to return to the mammoth project whose completion had eluded him over a period of ten years.

Symphony no. 3

Lutosławski visited the Northwestern University at Evanston, Chicago, on 15 June 1974 to receive a doctorate *honoris causa*. Taking advantage of that occasion, the Chicago Symphony Orchestra management renewed an earlier request for an orchestral work. Initially, he envisaged a one-movement symphony in four sections: Invocation, Cycle of Etudes, Toccata, and Hymn.[13] This plan was eventually rejected, however, and he temporarily abandoned the project. Work was resumed in 1977, after the completion of *Mi-Parti*, and extensive sketches made, only to be set aside once more as still unsatisfactory. When he finally returned to the symphony in 1981 he began afresh, although some material from the earlier sketches was incorporated into the new scheme. It was finally completed on 31 January 1983, eight-and-a-half years after it was commissioned. In an interview published in 1983 he clarified the sequence of events:

First of all, I wrote the main movement which I then scrapped, disqualified it completely, and began a second time. In the meantime, all manner of facts came up that tore me away from this work. The first, in October 1973, was the Warsaw appearance of Dietrich Fischer-Dieskau and Sviatoslav Richter. After the concert Fischer-Dieskau asked me whether I had ever written a composition for a baritone and orchestra. That is how I came to compose *Les espaces du sommeil*. Work on that composition took up nearly the whole of 1975. That means I had stopped work on the symphony. The same thing happened again in 1979 when I sat down to write the short symphonic piece *Novelette* at the request of Rostropovich . . . Only after I wrote a new main movement of the symphony, and this came after the completion of *Novelette*, did work begin to go much more briskly. The sketch, or rather the entire music of the symphony, was composed by March 1982. After that I sat down to work on the score . . . It is this work on the final form of the score that occupies so much time and prolongs the period of its composition.[14]

The composer's programme note is typically brief, confining itself to a general commentary on the main features of the form. Although this programme note has been widely used since the première in Chicago, it can be confusing for those analysing the score, since it would appear that some words had accidentally been left out. The confusing points (shown below in italics) can now be clarified by making some corrections, approved by the composer, to restore the sense intended:[15]

The work consists of two movements, preceded by a short introduction and followed by an epilogue and a coda. It is played without a break. The first movement comprises three episodes, of which the first is the fastest, the second slower and the third is the slowest. The basic tempo remains the same and the differences of speed are realised by the lengthening of the rhythmical units. *Each episode is followed by a short, slow refrain and the last refrain leads to the short, slow intermezzo. It is based on a group of toccata-like themes contrasting with a rather singing one:* a series of differentiated tuttis leads to the climax of the whole work. Then comes the last movement, based on a slow singing theme and a sequence of rather dramatic recitatives played by the string group. A short and very fast coda ends the piece.

The italicised passage above should, in fact, read as follows:

Each episode is followed by a short, slow refrain. The third episode leads to a short, slow intermezzo which in turn is followed by the third and last refrain. The second, main movement is based on a group of toccata-like themes contrasting with a rather singing one . . .

It is of some importance to an understanding of Lutosławski's conception of the form, that he regards the Third Symphony as comprising two movements (as opposed to three or four), to which are added an introduction, epilogue and coda. This approach to the structuring of a large-scale symphonic work establishes a clear connection with the two-movement scheme of the Second Symphony, particularly as there is no break between movements in either case. It also serves to emphasise how the Third Symphony grew from his experience of other treatments of this formal archetype in his works of the 1960s and 70s:

Comparison may be conjectured with my earlier works, because the [Third] Symphony is indeed one of the series of compositions in which I have applied the principle of the two-movement form, even though ... there are more movements here. Nevertheless, it is a two-movement piece in the sense that the main movement is preceded by an introductory movement ... while the last movement is actually an epilogue. The principle of the preliminary and the main movements was applied in my other compositions, such as String Quartet, Symphony no.2, and to a certain degree also in *Novelette*, *Livre pour orchestre* and *Jeux vénitiens*.[16]

Table 13 summarises the formal scheme, taking account of the composer's remarks and the revisions to his programme note.

The listener's attention is immediately arrested at the opening by a *fortissimo*, repeated-note signal on E (a group of four quavers, with octave doubling) played by clarinets, trumpets, trombones, tuba, timpano and xylophone. Against a background of *pianissimo* strings, sustaining E across five octaves, superimposed layers of woodwind and horns are then introduced, quietly babbling in self-contained harmonic strands that make up a twelve-note chord-aggregate: F,C,A♭,B (two flutes and piccolo); A,F♯,C♯,D (three oboes); and G,E♭,B♭,E (four horns). After gradually subsiding in pitch level from Fig. 1, the *fortissimo* repeated-note motif (still on octave Es) reappears at Fig. 2 to signal a second beginning. This is to be short-lived, however, and is abruptly terminated by the repeated-note signal, at its third appearance marking the start of the first movement. As the movement progresses, the signal (always on octave Es) returns to mark the beginning of each of the three episodes.

Lutosławski had previously used the psychological device of a repeated-note signal in the String Quartet (see Ex. 4 : 4). There it is also associated with a fixed reference pitch (octave Cs). It is in this area of musical perception that he has learned much (largely via Maliszewski) from the psychological structuring of Haydn and Beethoven symphonies and string quartets (rather than those of Mozart). Apart from its obvious function of punctuating and delineating formal sub-sections, the repeated-note signal in both the String Quartet and the Third Symphony acts as a tension-building agent whose next appearance the listener will inevitably anticipate, albeit unconsciously. It is an example of what

TABLE 13   Third Symphony, formal scheme

Fig.	Movement	Section	Material	Instrumentation
[o]	Intro.		repeated-note motif	ww, brass, timp, xyl
[o]–2		1st start	static, fragmentary	
2			repeated-note motif	brass, timp, xyl
2–3		2nd start	static, fragmentary	
3			repeated-note motif	brass, timp
3–10	First	episode 1	fastest of 3	
10–11		refrain 1	slow, static, unmetred	ww trio
11			repeated-note motif	brass, timp
11–18		episode 2	slower than 1	cor anglais solo, etc
18–19		refrain 2	slow, static, unmetred	ww trio
19			repeated-note motif	brass, timp
19–24		episode 3	slowest of 3	
24–30		intermezzo	*adagio*	sustained str
30–31		refrain 3	slow, static, unmetred	ww quartet
31–	Main		repeated-note motifs	4 hns, etc
32–36		stage 1	toccata-like theme	str, harp
–37			repeated-note motifs	ww, hns, bell
37–40		stage 2	*cantando* theme (1)	str, etc
40–			repeated-note motifs	brass, str
40–73		stage 3	toccata-like themes	
73–76			*cantando* theme (1a)	str, etc – tutti
76–77			prepares for climax	tutti
77–80		climax	abortive	tutti
80–81		aftermath	static harmony	
81–84			rising unison recit.	str
84–89	Epilogue		*cantando* theme (2)	upper str
89–92			recit.	str layers
92–93		refrain 4	slow, static	ww qt
93–97			extended chord	builds to tutti
97–99			*cantando* theme (2a)	tutti
99–102	Coda		very fast	perc, tutti
102			cadence	tutti
			repeated-note motif	tutti

Lutosławski refers to as a 'once only convention'.[17] The use of a fixed reference pitch, not only to begin the work and to mark the sectional subdivisions, but also to act as the final cadential gesture, inevitably raises the issue of whether there is any tonal principle operating across the symphony. The same question could also be posed (although less convincingly) in the case of the Second Symphony, because of the strong Eb/F dyad used both to begin *Hésitant* and to end *Direct*. In the Third Symphony there is certainly a strong sense of aural focus provided by the repeated E signal, but it lacks (initially, at least) the context of other tonal features that could invest it with the functional properties of a tonic. It is possible, however, to present an argument that such features occur later, and the issue will be considered, below, in relation to the attempted climax, the epilogue and the coda.

It is also worth considering Lutosławski's choice of pitch for the signals in the String Quartet and the Third Symphony. In both cases there is a rather obvious explanation that has nothing to do with any desire to emulate tonal procedures. The choice of C for the signal in the String Quartet was determined by the range of the cello and viola, and the tuning of their respective lowest strings. Similarly, in the Third Symphony and other pieces, E was chosen simply because it corresponds to the lowest open string of the basses (on the assumption that five-string basses would not always be available).

Comparison with the Second Symphony can be made, not only with the two-movement structure, but also with the first-movement scheme of episodes alternating with a woodwind refrain. The first episode, the fastest of the three, makes much use of motoric three-note triplet patterns of adjacent semitones, close cousins of the ubiquitous Bartókian three-note cells of interlocking tone/semitone which Lutosławski has used throughout his career. These patterns are used to convey an impression of bustling activity that is carefully controlled in dynamic to maintain a subdued, low profile. There is no melody in the first episode, but a full use of contrasted instrumental tone-colour, harmonic and rhythmic texture. Not until the first refrain do we encounter a sense of line, albeit severely restricted to a narrow band of six pitches in a three-part polyphonic bundle. The two clarinets play variants of the same group of five notes between Ab and C, while the bassoon has an overlapping group of five notes between G and Cb. For this first appearance of the refrain the lines are entirely conjunct and do not move outside the band of assigned pitches.

Episode 2 begins by projecting a melodic line (cor anglais) against a background harmonic texture, in a way typical of Lutosławski's late style (Ex. 6 : 7). In the early stages of *Mi-Parti* the melodic lines had used the same notes as the harmony, and had merely doubled notes from the twelve-note chords. Here we have simpler, four-note chords from the horns, against which the cor anglais develops an expressive line without duplicating notes of the harmony, except where reconciliation is required, for example at phrase endings. There are also clustered chords sustained by the harp and piano, but these are textural effects that colour rather than overwhelm the horns and cor anglais. The latter develops a line initially from only three types of interval: semitones, minor thirds and tritones. There are no comparable melodic lines in the Second Symphony.

EX. 6 : 7   Symphony no. 3, episode 2

Each of the refrains is played by a combination of woodwind instruments: two clarinets and bassoon (refrains 1 and 2); oboe, piccolo clarinet, bass clarinet and bassoon (refrain 3). Even when the refrain idea returns later in the work (Figs. 92–3), it is associated with woodwind tone-colour: cor anglais, two clarinets and bassoon. The similarity of approach to that of the woodwind refrains in the first movement of the Second Symphony is very clear (compare Ex. 6 : 8 with Ex. 4 : 8). Here, the horizontal, melodic lines within each of the refrains are generated by interval-pairing of semitones and tones (1 + 2). Refrain 2 (Ex. 6 : 8) develops slightly beyond the harmonic and melodic stasis of the first refrain, and shows how three-note cells of semitone/tone are exploited for their curling chromaticism. The clarinets migrate downwards (from F) to meet the bassoon which has gradually risen (from F♯), and they eventually meet three-note cells that overlap. In the process of converging they cover all twelve pitch-classes within the minimum span of just less than an octave.

After the second refrain has been halted by the fifth statement of the repeated-note signal, *pizzicato* strings begin the third episode, the slowest of the three. The initial cello line is generated by melodic interval-pairing of minor and major thirds (3 + 4), a combination which has not been exploited as often as some of the other pairings. As the other strings enter, they build two alternating six-note chords that complement each other to give the effect of a vertically symmetrical twelve-note chord of superimposed minor and major thirds around the axis of a perfect fourth.

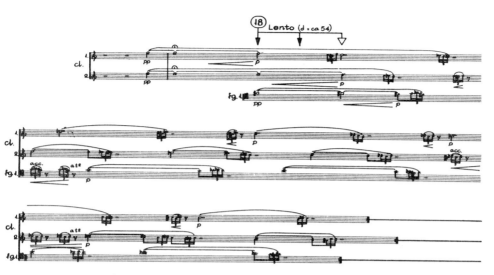

EX. 6 : 8 Symphony no. 3, refrain 2

Episode 3 is brief and leads to a slow intermezzo (Figs. 24–30) that is strongly reminiscent of the slow, central section of *Les espaces du sommeil*, with flutes against quiet, sustained harmony in the strings, which then evaporates in rising glissandi (the pitch complementation between flutes and strings is also similar to that used in the Adagio of *Les espaces*). The move from the intermezzo into the third refrain does not happen by clearly defined sectional division but by gradual transition. From Figs. 26 to 30, woodwind instruments gradually enter with linear fragments leading into the third refrain. This time, the melodic pairing of interval-classes 1 + 2 is made more expansive by opening out the intervals to emphasise more angular minor and major sevenths. Whereas the first refrain was completely static, and the second involved only very limited movement of lines converging within an octave, in the third refrain the parts migrate across a very wide span. The piccolo clarinet begins in its highest register with the bassoon on its lowest note. The bass clarinet and bassoon then migrate upwards while the upper parts gradually descend until they converge in the middle register prior to the end of the movement at Fig. 31.

Refrain 3 is interrupted by the return of the repeated-note signal (for the sixth time), played in unison, *fortissimo*, by four horns and tubular bell. At this stage the signal is extended, arousing the expectation that what follows will be developmental and directional rather than episodic and introductory. Thus the second ('main') movement is jolted into life. While the first movement was predominantly *ad libitum* in ensemble co-ordination, and hence static in character, the second movement is largely conducted in metre and thus invested with greater directional drive. Interplay between melodic and accompanimental elements is central to the unfolding of the main movement. For example, from Fig. 32, the strings develop a polyphonic texture in melodic layers (derived from disjunct treatment of motoric three-note cells) which gradually separate from the supporting harmony. As successive groups of string parts transfer from the sustained chordal background, so the balance between chord and line shifts in favour of the latter. By Fig. 35 the strings have developed into a quasi-fugato section of metred contrapuntal lines without any supporting harmony. Nothing comparable can be found in the Second Symphony, which uses the strings for dense harmonic and polyphonic textures with almost no melodic features. *Mi-Parti* represents an evolutionary mid-point between these different stages in Lutosławski's development.

Having established the fixed-pitch repeated-note signal as a 'once-only convention' operating on the listener's conscious and unconscious powers of recall and anticipation, at Fig. 40 Lutosławski exercises his prerogative to deliver it in an unexpected way. Here it marks a new stage in the form of the second movement by retaining the rhythmic motif of four repeated quavers, but abandons the reference pitch of E in favour of an eight-note chord, mostly of superimposed minor and major thirds. The effect this time is to signal impending growth and development.

Whereas the second movement of the Second Symphony was clear in its purpose, and drove inexorably towards the culmination of the work, the second movement of the Third Symphony contains so many different thematic ingredients that its progress is comparatively disjointed, often impeded. It evolves through several different stages of what the composer has described, loosely, as 'toccata-like themes'; but the effect is episodic rather than directional. It is worth noting that it was this movement of his original scheme which had given him so much trouble, and which had caused him to shelve the project several times.

There are two toccata-like themes for the strings, based on different treatments of semitone/tone cells: Figs. 32–6, and 47–9. Between these comes a brief attempt at an expansive *cantando* line, *molto espressivo* (Figs. 37–8), but at this point in the movement Lutosławski seems deliberately to prevent the strings from developing an extended *cantabile* line (reserving this idea for the epilogue). There are other features of interest, for example a 'singing' passage for the brass section after Fig. 45, which anticipates the prominent *cantabile* playing required of them in *Chain 3*. From Fig. 49 the strings build a polyphonic texture of contrapuntal layers, the lowest of which is generated by a twelve-note row of interval pairing 2 + 5. Soon, however, the aural effect of the interval pairing is obscured by the superimposition of additional layers derived from various treatments of three-note cells. These are used motorically to increase the level of rhythmic energy. The densely textural 'differentiated tuttis' that follow are reminiscent of the composer's earlier style, of the Second Symphony, *Livre pour orchestre* and the Cello Concerto, because they move towards the climax by a succession of gestures rather than by a process of linear projection (as in *Chain 3*). The earlier string *cantando* reappears at Fig. 73, developing into a startling triadic theme at Fig. 75 that gradually moves upwards by sequential shifts until reaching the putative climax at Fig. 76.

The reappearance of the *cantando* theme is significant in that it marks the end of the textural treatment of harmony in the preceding tuttis, and begins a bass line progression that defines the progress of the symphony from this point until the end of the work. The long-range significance of the bass line from Fig. 73 not only invests the earlier repeated-note signals with some of the functional properties of a tonic (on E), but also emphasises the dominant implications of B.[18]

The climax of the Third Symphony (at Fig. 77) is radically different to the equivalent moment in Lutosławski's earlier orchestral works, both in treatment and in function. Most of his pieces of the 1960s and 70s reached a point of collective *ad libitum* on a *fortissimo* twelve-note chord, or twelve-note chord-aggregate. In this case the climactic harmony is less dense. It is metred and immediately moves beyond a highpoint that is attempted rather than achieved. The position of this false climax in relation to the duration of the work suggests a different function because it occurs comparatively early in the form, at only seven-tenths. This can be compared with *Mi-Parti* (two-thirds), and the String Quartet (just over seven-tenths), both of which use the climax point as a threshold that is crossed in order to reach new material of significance. In the case of *Mi-Parti* this new material is the long, ascending string *cantando*. In the String Quartet it is the long, *funèbre* section, functioning as an epilogue. *Musique funèbre* and *Paroles tissées* both reach the climax even earlier, and each has a fourth movement of dramatic significance. Whereas the Second Symphony undertakes a journey whose destination is the climax, the Third Symphony treats this part of the form as transitional rather than concluding.

EX. 6 : 9   Symphony no. 3, melodic reduction of Figs. 84–6

After a brief post-climactic transition, the final element of the main movement is an intense unison string line, chromatically rising through horizontal interval pairing of semitones and tones. This line is delivered in several phrases, separated by dense *ad libitum* passages on a four-note chord of minor thirds either side of a perfect fifth (F,G♯,D♯,F♯). This transitional passage leads to the epilogue at Fig. 84, where the most memorable thematic idea of the work is exposed. The upper strings continue, in unison, to play a broad *cantando* theme (Ex. 6 : 9) whose main feature is the sequential pairing of minor thirds and perfect fifths (linked by five bars of twisting chromaticism). Dramatically the most potent idea of the Third Symphony is the continuation of this *cantando* theme between Figs. 86 and 87 (Ex. 6 : 10). Several features of this passage can be identified as contributing towards its powerful and memorable effect: *senza espressione* sonority of sustained open-string G, which eventually rises to G♯ after Fig. 87; tension created by the minor ninth between low F♯ (timpani) and G (strings); melodic ascent in phrases that grow by adding only minor thirds and perfect fifths; transfer of notes from the developing line into thickening string harmony as notes are sustained, building a sonority of superimposed diminished triads; melodic emphasis on minor ninths (non-adjacent); further intensification when the descending line (still interval-classes 3 + 7) eventually arrives at its destination on G♯. The psychology of this passage is masterly, particularly the inevitability of arrival on G♯, as a consequence of the melodic sequence just prior to Fig. 86 (see Ex. 6 : 9). This type of 3 + 7 melodic line is a memorable feature shared by the Third Symphony and *Chain 2* (Ex. 7 : 14).

EX. 6 : 10   Symphony no. 3, reduction of Figs. 86–7

The strings continue to dominate until Fig. 91, where they give way to a babbling texture of two clarinets, celesta and harp, each line containing three pitches that complement each other to provide twelve-note harmony. At Fig. 92 the woodwind refrain returns as a long-range reference to the first movement. The *cantando* theme also returns, from Fig. 93, this time played by solo horn against a developing harmonic background strongly rooted on E, which gradually builds a widely spaced twelve-note extended chord whose euphony derives from the seven perfect fifths embedded in the sonority. This leads to a triumphant delivery of the *cantando* theme by strings and woodwind, supported by brass and percussion from Figs. 97 to 99. The fast coda that follows reverses the kind of chordal acceleration that leads to the climactic points of the Second Symphony and *Livre*. Instead, it attenuates the repetition of chords by inserting an increasing number of beats' rest (1–2–3–5–7–9–11), while the combined forces of tuned percussion take centre stage with a jubilant display of superimposed lines that emphasise pentatonic patterns. The bright sound of this percussion polyphony conveys a psychological mood of optimism, an aspect of the Third Symphony that contrasts very strongly with the brooding, uncertain ending of the Second Symphony. After a quasi-cadential eight-note chord, complemented by the remaining four pitches in the trumpets, there is a sense of almost tonal resolution as the low D♯ rises to E for the crisply decisive ending with a return to the repeated-note motif from the beginning of the work.

The Third Symphony is a curiously hybrid work, successfully combining some densely textural passages typical of Lutosławski's earlier orchestral works with an abundance of melodic features typical of his later style. This mixture is not surprising when one considers the period of time over which the work was composed. Not all the early sketch material was discarded, however. The form bears a striking resemblance to the original outline scheme: the introductory section corresponds to the 'invocation'; the 'cycle of études' relates to the eventual alternation of episodes and refrains; the *cantando* theme of the epilogue fulfils the function of the planned 'hymn'. The original 'toccata' section did not survive, although the general intention of fast, motoric material is realised to some extent in the main movement.

The most notable omission from the Third Symphony is the kind of dense harmony of twelve-note chord-aggregates that we associate with his music after 1957. There are twelve-note chords in the symphony, but many of the original pre-compositional sketches of pitch material were discarded. In place of the chord-aggregate harmony typified by the first section of *Mi-Parti*, one finds greater use of pitch-complementation procedures that allow more scope for the generation of interesting melodic and polyphonic lines. These techniques were not new to Lutosławski in the early 1980s, but he appears to have rediscovered their potential.

The most notable addition to Lutosławski's style in the Third Symphony is the number and variety of melodic ideas. This is best appreciated if one compares and contrasts the Second Symphony with the Third. The former is a work of dense harmonic textures that inevitably are perceived in terms of their resultant sound-mass rather than specific harmonic sonorities. The latter is a work of more transparent harmonic sonorities that enable the listener to detect melodic and polyphonic detail. This difference has much to do with the more limited scope of aleatory procedures in the Third Symphony. Lutosławski's main stumbling block in the 1970s had been with the 'toccata' section of his original scheme, which was intended to be co-ordinated largely by aleatory means.

The Second and Third Symphonies deserve special attention as a pair, not because either adheres to conventions of symphonic form, but because their performing times (somewhere between twenty-nine and thirty-two minutes) present different realisations of Lutosławski's approach to long-term dramatic shaping. Whereas the Second lasts some thirty-two minutes with a decisive climax late in the form (approaching nine tenths), the Third lasts some thirty minutes with an abortive climax much earlier (at seven tenths). While the Second accelerates to an *ad libitum* climax, the Third accelerates through and beyond a metred climax. The Second has very little *a battuta* co-ordination, while the Third is largely metred; consequently, the Third has a greater sense of harmonic and rhythmic pace, while the Second is predominantly static. The Second has *ad libitum* episodes, while the Third has *a battuta* episodes. The Third ends fast and *fortissimo*, while the Second ends slow and *pianissimo*.

Lutosławski's intensive work on the Third Symphony covered the years 1981–3, a time of tremendous political tension and social upheaval in Poland. The intoxicating months of apparent liberalisation that stemmed from recognition of Solidarity in the summer of 1980 were abruptly and brutally terminated by the imposition of martial law by the Jaruzelski regime on 13 December 1981. For the next two years, until July 1983, Poland was governed by a military council. It is tempting for commentators to try and find evidence in the music that could support the notion of art reflecting the turbulent events of this extraordinary period in Polish history. Hence it is often suggested that there might be some kind of link between the Third Symphony and the events contemporary with its composition. Lutosławski recalls, for example, being questioned on the possibility of such a link during a pre-concert talk prior to a performance of the Third Symphony at the Proms in London:

there was a question: 'Did the events in Poland influence or affect your music at that time?' I said, 'No.' (Applause) 'No. Please. I can't answer such a question with one single word.' And I began speaking about it ... We live in a certain kind of world, but creative artists live a sort of double life, because several hours a day they are in another world, in the world that has (apparently, at least) nothing in common with the external world in which we really live. I think that this ideal world is the world of our dreams, of our wishes, of our notion of ideal, and we spend quite a long time every day in this ideal world. And our task, our role, our mission, is to make this ideal world available for those who are not accessed to it ... We have one psyche only. So both worlds in which we live have a certain influence on our psyche, and this psyche is the place where this ideal world is ... So, probably the external world and our life experiences must intervene in a way in this ideal world ... but it's never conscious, never wanted. I'm speaking about myself, of course, and people to whom I'm similar.[19]

This artistic credo of Lutosławski, which assigns a higher position and higher purpose to his ideal world, explains how and why his music continues to defy crude comparison and analogy with the vicissitudes of his life.

Sir Georg Solti, as musical director of the Chicago Symphony Orchestra, conducted the first performance of the Third Symphony in Chicago on 29 September 1983. Less than a week later, Lutosławski was in London to conduct the première of another new work.

Chain 1

Three of Lutosławski's late works bear the same generic Polish title of Łańcuch, which translates into English as 'Chain'. This title denotes the use of a technique, designed to achieve formal continuity, whereby successive phrases of musical material are overlapped, neither beginning nor ending at the same time. His prime purpose in exploring and exploiting this principle has been the search for alternative ways of building a large-scale form, and to replace conventional structuring in clear-cut sections. Apart from sharing this abstract technical procedure, however, the three *Chains* are not related to each other in any cyclic way and do not form a group of any kind.

Several works bearing other kinds of title also make use of what may be called 'chain technique', the earliest example being the Passacaglia in the finale of the Concerto for Orchestra. The last movement of the Piano Concerto applies the technique to a chaconne theme in the orchestral parts that overlaps with various episodes played by the soloist.

Composed in 1983, *Chain 1* was Lutosławski's response to repeated requests from Michael Vyner for a piece which the London Sinfonietta could include in their repertoire. Throughout the 1960s and 70s much of his music had been for large orchestral forces. Vyner was keen to programme Lutosławski's music in Sinfonietta concerts, but even with an enlarged ensemble most of the later works were beyond their resources. The composer was eager to provide something, although he had to wait until the Third Symphony was finished before he could embark on the new project. The resulting ten-minute piece was completed on 20 July 1983, and first performed at the Queen Elizabeth Hall in London on 4 October. Its dedication, to both the commissioner and the ensemble he nurtured until his death in 1989, made the work a natural choice for Lutosławski to conduct at the Michael Vyner Memorial Concert given at the Royal Opera House, Covent Garden, on 6 May 1990.

Chain 1 could be regarded either as a large chamber piece or as a small orchestral piece, although in reality it is somewhere between the two. The composer simply specifies 'for fourteen instruments' (i.e. fourteen players), thus emphasising the soloistic nature of the ensemble treatment. The nature of the writing itself, however, suggests that it should be considered in relation to Lutosławski's other orchestral rather than chamber works. Aleatory 'mobiles' occupy the greater part of the piece in a manner entirely in keeping with the composer's general approach to orchestral writing. It is scored for flute (doubling piccolo and alto flute), oboe (doubling cor anglais), clarinet, bassoon, trumpet, horn, trombone, percussion (marimba, xylophone, cymbals, gong, tam-tam), harpsichord, and strings (two violins, viola, cello and bass).

Although *Chain 1* unfolds as one unbroken span it subdivides into three distinct formal stages. The first is fragmented and introductory in character, and consists of overlapping links in the chain technique indicated by the title. The second stage, by contrast, delivers a continuous network of *cantabile* melodic lines. This stage builds towards and includes the highpoint of the work, which is marked by a densely clustered twelve-note chord (just prior to Fig. 47). At that point a *fortissimo* stroke on the tam-tam interrupts and abruptly concludes the second stage. The third stage is merely the aftermath, the period of winding down that occupies approximately the last fifty-five seconds of the piece.

Stage 1 opens with an introductory gesture played by almost the whole ensemble (minus double-bass). Beginning on a unison it quickly diverges to a widely spaced twelve-note chord-aggregate, laid out in three harmonic strands, before it converges on to a different unison. The effect of divergence followed by convergence, established at the outset, is a feature of the work as a whole, and operates as an underlying and unifying principle that governs the composer's treatment of the form. Stage 2 also begins on a unison (from Fig. 40, the violins' and violas' open-string G); but here intervallic expansion occurs much more gradually. Initially, the bundle of eight parts from Figs. 41 to 42 develops into a twelve-note line covering a range of slightly less than two octaves, extending upwards from the violins' open-string G. This is followed by the first of the aleatory sections marked *cantabile*, from Figs. 42 to 43, which includes all twelve pitch classes (with octave duplications) and extends upwards from the violas' open-string C over a range of two-and-a-half octaves. Thereafter, the aleatory sections are governed by vertically planned chords.

Changes to the level of harmonic density are crucial to the unfolding of the form, which is articulated primarily by the presence and strategic placing of chord-aggregates: one at the beginning of the first stage and several as stage two builds towards the climax of the piece, which is marked by a twelve-note chord of adjacent semitones densely clustered within one octave.

In assigning notes to the various chain links in the first stage, Lutosławski does not here adopt the simple method of partitioning the chromatic whole into complementary hexachords as he was later to do in *Chain 3*. Such a method would have been impractical here, as it would severely have restricted the range of lines generated by the melodic interval-pairings chosen. The predominant feature of the first stage is the pairing of semitones and tritones ($1 + 6$). In some cases these intervals are used to generate a chain link that passes from one instrument to another (and sometimes back again), for example, the thirteenth (penultimate) link which begins with the flute at Fig. 32 and then transfers to the cello for an expressive, *cantabile* line before returning briefly to the flute (Ex. 6 : 11). This cello line, falling through three octaves from high C to low open-string C, then rising again, is one of the more memorable features of the first stage.

The unfolding of the second stage has more in common with some earlier works, such as the Cello Concerto or Preludes and Fugue, than with other late works. Beginning at Fig. 40 with the open-string unison G of the violins and viola, it develops a bundle of polyphonic lines. These are variants of the same melody, combined in *ad libitum* counterpoint to give a texture harmonically thickened by residual traces of the monodic line. Notes are gradually added to the melodic phrase until it appears in

EX. 6 : 11   *Chain 1*, flute/cello line, chain 'link' 13

its complete form with all twelve pitches used in the first violin part just before Fig. 42.

Whereas the initial eight-part bundle is melodically conceived, the *ad libitum* sections that follow are harmonically based. This change to vertical methods of pitch organisation means that in stage 2 we do not find the restricted interval content to the melodic lines that formed the basis for the chain technique in stage 1. The initial bundle is comparatively restricted in its range, and spans less than two octaves. Subsequent *ad libitum* sections, however, become much more widely spaced, thus enabling the component parts to become progressively more disjunct as they derive their lines from arpeggiation of the chord-aggregates.

Chain 1 reaches its climax comparatively late in the form (at nine-tenths of its duration) within an *ad libitum* section. It creates maximum harmonic density with a widely spaced twelve-note chord converging onto a twelve-note cluster of eleven semitones within one octave. As in the String Quartet or Preludes and Fugue, there is no specific moment of climax common to all parts. Instead, there is a highpoint within each of the constituent lines of the aleatory section where the climax occurs, and these individual highpoints do not necessarily coincide with each other. Unlike the String Quartet, however, *Chain 1* has a very decisive ending to the climactic passage, at the point when the percussionist (inactive since

Fig. 40) plays a *fortissimo* stroke on the tam-tam.

Although the climax ends abruptly, the very last chord of the piece does not. It resembles a kind of evaporation, such as occurs at the end of *Les espaces du sommeil*. The chord contains only ten notes (B and G♯ are omitted), and is laid out in four rather than the customary three harmonic strands (of these, the one assigned to the viola part is the only strand that does not give a simple major triad). The psychologically inconclusive effect produced by this type of evaporating *ad libitum* ending is another feature suggesting a closer relationship between *Chain 1* and Lutosławski's work of the 1970s than with the other late works. The Double Concerto, the Third Symphony, *Partita*, *Chain 2*, the Piano Concerto and *Chantefleurs et Chantefables* all have a very clear-cut, decisive, quasi-cadential ending.

Relentless use of the semitone/tritone interval pairing in stage 1 gives a distinctive harmonic colour to that section of the piece, but it has perhaps been over-used. The fact that successive and overlapping links in the chain are generated by the same kind of interval pairing means that the ear does not detect any appreciable difference between them. This bleak uniformity of interval-pairing contrasts strongly with the approach to melody that Lutosławski had used in *Epitaph* and *Grave*, and which he was to use in the second movement of *Chain 2*.

One of the comparisons that must be made, between *Chain 1* and both earlier and later works, concerns the proportion of the piece composed in *ad libitum* sections of aleatory counterpoint. A striking feature of the late works is that they tend to have a far smaller proportion composed in this way and a correspondingly larger part is played by conventionally metred sections. Even the Third Symphony has a considerable number of metred passages that help to give pace and rhythmic energy, rather than the static quality that is usually unavoidable with the *ad libitum* technique. *Chain 1* makes very little use of metred co-ordination or *a battuta* conducting. A possible reason is that the composer's main intention was to provide an opportunity for soloistic music-making amongst the fourteen players of the London Sinfonietta, hence the consideration of rhythmic pace was subordinated to the need to generate independent melodic lines. Another explanation is that stasis may not be such an important problem in a short piece. Had *Chain 1* been conceived as a longer work, the composer would probably have adjusted the pace to fulfil the requirements of more extended dramaturgy.

By the time the Third Symphony and *Chain 1* had received their premières in the autumn of 1983, martial law in Poland had ostensibly been lifted. Although the *Stan Wojenny* (literally, 'state of war') had been rescinded on 21 July, and there was an official policy of 'normalisation' (a term of Orwellian irony that extended, appropriately, throughout 1984), the Jaruzelski regime continued to suppress all manifestations of the now outlawed Solidarity movement. Leonid Brezhnev had died on 10 November 1982, but the doctrine that bears his name continued to determine the relations between Poland and her 'fraternal' neighbour.

From the time that martial law was imposed in December 1981, until the political sea-change of 1988–9, Lutosławski fulfilled concert engagements abroad but not in Poland. This was his personal demonstration of solidarity. During this period he declined many invitations to appear on the state media and even avoided attending concerts and other public occasions, either as a member of the audience or as an official guest, where attempts would have been made to compromise his position by photographing him in the company of government ministers. He also declined repeated requests to meet successive Ministers of Culture, because he was not prepared to make the declaration of entering the Culture Ministry itself. Any such visit or other public gesture would certainly have been regarded by the government as an indication of tacit support and presented as such both within Poland and outside the country.

In the autumn of 1984, Lutosławski made a European concert tour with Heinz Holliger and the Junge Deutsche Philharmonie, and the Warsaw Autumn Festival formed part of their itinerary. Even though he was still on the programme committee of the festival, and *Novelette* had long been scheduled for its Polish première that year, Lutosławski remained steadfast to the artists' boycott and declined to appear on the podium in Poland. The performance of *Novelette* went ahead as planned, but conducted by Holliger rather than the composer. Hence it was Holliger's interpretation of the piece that was issued as part of the chronicle of recordings that year, and which was later included in volume four of the set of compact disc recordings issued by Polskie Nagrania in 1989.

For a creative artist of Lutosławski's stature and international reputation to maintain solidarity with the boycott was undoubtedly a significant gesture and one that did not go unnoticed, by either side. Late in 1983, shortly after the première of the Third Symphony, Lutosławski had sent a recording of the Chicago performance to be played in a church in

Gdańsk. There it was heard by a large and appreciative audience who understood fully the significance of such a clandestine gesture of support. In recognition of the clarity and integrity of Lutosławski's position he was subsequently awarded the Solidarity Prize of 1983. Of the many honours, awards and prizes that have been presented to Lutosławski over his long career, this is the one he acknowledges with the most pride. For a nation whose troubled history since the eighteenth century has been dominated by symbols this prize represents the highest of accolades.

7
Concertos and Chains
(1984–1986)

Several overlapping strands to Lutosławski's musical thinking can be traced through much of his work composed since 1979, and these include concertos, chains, and chamber music. It is by no means merely coincidental that the evolution of his late style has been closely connected with a focus towards *concertante* pieces, for these have assisted with the move away from dense harmony and complex polyphony towards greater clarity of melodic line. Both the Double Concerto and the Piano Concerto make use of the generic title, while *Chain 2* is a violin concerto in all but name. In turn, each of these was preceded by a chamber piece that can be regarded as an informal kind of compositional essay for the larger piece to follow. Thus the Double Concerto was preceded by *Epitaph*, and *Partita* stands in a similar relationship both to *Chain 2* and the Piano Concerto.[1] Although *Grave* and *Partita* were initially written as duos, their respective piano parts were subsequently orchestrated; hence there is an interesting overlap between Lutosławski's renewed interest in chamber music and his pursuit of the *concertante* medium.

There is also a connection between Lutosławski's application of his chain technique and the relationship between soloist and orchestra in both *Chain 2* and the Piano Concerto. The title of the former makes explicit its use of the principle of overlapping strands of musical material so that sectional divisions are blurred, and its subtitle, 'Dialogue for violin and orchestra' can be taken as referring to this kind of interactive discourse. The chain procedure was also adopted for the final movement of the Piano Concerto.[2]

Lutosławski's return to the medium of chamber music came as something of a surprise, given that his *ad libitum* technique and dense harmonic textures are more suited to orchestral than chamber forces. To a large extent this return was circumstantial rather than planned. Both *Epitaph* and *Grave* are *pièces d'occasion*, written as memorial tributes, while *Partita* resulted from a misunderstanding over the precise nature of its commission. The latter confusion turned out to be fortuitous, however, and *Partita* can be seen to occupy a central position in the evolution of Lutosławski's late style. Even more significantly, it can be seen as a breakthrough for the composer in several respects: it is his most substantial piece of chamber music since the String Quartet of 1964; its lyrical treatment of the violin paved the way for the emphasis on melody that characterises *Chain 2*; and he was able to explore ways of writing for the piano, an instrument conspicuously absent from his music of the 1960s and 1970s. Partly as a result of the advances made with *Grave* and *Partita*, Lutosławski then felt able to compose the Piano Concerto. While the latter represents the composer catching up with unfinished business from his twenties, *Partita* and *Chain 2* reveal a return to an even earlier period of his youth, the teenage years of his violin studies. Although formally these had ceased in 1932, when he was nineteen, the significance of his feeling for the violin's expressive capabilities can hardly be overstated; yet there was to be no substantial work for the violin as a solo instrument until 1984. In bringing together the two instruments that had defined the musical progress of his early years, *Partita* achieved a synthesis of idiomatic instrumental writing with melodic, harmonic and rhythmic features of the late style, which mark it as one of the most significant works of his career.[3]

Even the most cursory glance at Lutosławski's list of major works (excluding brief *pièces d'occasion*) reveals that he seems consistently to have avoided duplicating instrumental or vocal forces. Hence there is only one Cello Concerto, one Piano Concerto, one work for tenor and orchestra, one for baritone and orchestra and so on. Admittedly, there are four symphonies, although there is no real duplication between them, as they represent different stylistic phases and reveal different approaches to the question of large-scale form. Even other orchestral works such as *Livre pour orchestre* or *Mi-Parti* differ considerably in form or content, or both. The three *Chains* may share the same quasi-generic label, but have less in common than the common title might suggest. Against this background it seems curious that there are two *concertante* pieces for violin and orchestra.

Partita was composed in the autumn of 1984 in response to a request from the St Paul Chamber Orchestra in Wisconsin, but when the composer began to work on the project he sketched a piece for violin with orchestra rather than piano. Although offered the larger piece the orchestra management declined, clarifying their request for a duo. Reluctantly putting to one side the sketches that were soon to become *Chain 2*, Lutosławski honoured the commitment and so turned his attention to a piece for violin and piano. Meanwhile Paul Sacher, who had already commissioned the Double Concerto, heard of the plans for another *concertante* work and commissioned its completion. By the time *Partita* received its première on 18 January 1985, Lutosławski was already working on *Chain 2*, which he completed later that year and dedicated to Sacher. The first performance was given in Zurich on 31 January 1986, with Anne-Sophie Mutter as soloist with the Collegium Musicum, conducted by the dedicatee.

Lutosławski is known to accumulate sketches for projected works, sometimes over a long period. Hence there are cases of overlap between successive pieces, although he tends not to engage in intensive compositional activity on more than one piece at a time. There are cases, such as *Epitaph* and the Double Concerto, where overlapping chronology reveals that the pieces were composed, if not simultaneously, then at least during the same period. With *Partita* and *Chain 2* he found himself in the position of composing two similar pieces at the same time, albeit through force of circumstance rather than design.

Hearing Anne-Sophie Mutter perform *Chain 2*, Lutosławski was prompted to orchestrate *Partita* so that she could perform both works together, in the same programme. Other projects prevented him from carrying this out immediately, but after completing *Chain 3* and the Piano Concerto, he turned his attention to the orchestral version of *Partita*, which he dedicated to Mutter. Paul Sacher re-enters the story, as commissioner and dedicatee of the short orchestral piece composed to link the two works: *Interlude* was written in the autumn of 1989, and the autograph score shows 19 October as the date of its completion. The first performance of the whole scheme, embracing *Partita*, *Interlude* and *Chain 2*, was given in Munich on 10 January 1990, by Mutter with the Munich Philharmonic Orchestra, conducted by the composer.[4]

Partita

The title of *Partita* alludes to music of the Baroque period and signifies a suite of separate pieces. It consists of five movements: the first, third and fifth carrying the main weight, with the second and fourth as interludes. The three main movements are conventionally metred, while the second and fourth are both played *ad libitum*. In addition, a strategically placed *ad libitum* section near the end of the final movement acts as the climax of the work. Each of the main movements subdivides into clear formal stages: the first and third movements comprise four stages, the last of

which moves towards its highpoint and then subsides. The final movement has five stages: three preceding the climax; the climax itself; then a
fast, exuberant coda. The subsidiary highpoints reached in the first and
third movements are prevented from pre-empting or undermining the
decisive climax in the final movement. Table 14 outlines the formal
scheme.

TABLE 14   *Partita*, formal scheme

Movement	Metre	Bar/Fig.	Section	Function
1	metred	1–28	stage 1	
	metred	29–49	stage 2	
	metred	50–65	stage 3	
	metred	66–107	stage 4	build-up, highpoint, subsides
2	*ad. lib.*			interlude
3	metred	1–21	stage 1	
	metred	22–46	stage 2	
	metred	47–65	stage 3	
	metred	66–82	stage 4	build-up, highpoint, subsides
4	*ad. lib.*			interlude
5	metred	1–39	stage 1	
	metred	40–57	stage 2	
	metred	58–90	stage 3	build-up, *pp–ff*
	ad. lib.	91	stage 4	climax
	metred	92–118	stage 5	coda

Structural subdivisions in *Partita* are easier to identify than in some
other late works, as the composer does not use his chain technique of
overlapping phrases or sections. In *Chain* 2 the soloist and orchestra often
represent the links, beginning and ending at different points from each
other. In *Partita*, however, the violin and piano parts coincide at all the
main structural points without any deliberate blurring or overlapping
between the formal components. Subdivisions within the first movement
mostly correspond to the methods of pitch organisation used, of which
the most important is the principle of partitioning the chromatic whole
into complementary sets, with particular pitches assigned to each instrument. All four stages use this method to some extent, and it governs most
of the first stage, which depends for differentiation between the melodic
and harmonic planes on such separation between the two instrumental
timbres. Example 7 : 1 shows the first nine bars. The five-bar piano

introduction uses only six pitches: F, F♯, G, and B, C, C♯. In the next five-bar phrase, the piano's notes move down a semitone, while the violin supplies the complementary hexachord: G, G♯, A, and C♯, D, E♭. Subdivision of hexachordal patterns into two three-note groups of adjacent semitones is typical; these three-note intervallic cells can be seen in the violin line as part of the 1 + 6 interval-pairing of semitones and tritones. Tactile allusion to keyboard figurations of Baroque music occur through the rhythmic gestures and patterns of the piano part, although this may be seen in the score (and sensed by the performer) more than it is heard by the listener. The title's obvious reference to the Baroque period signifies an abstract connection of form (as a suite of discrete pieces) rather than evocation of style or language.

EX. 7 : 1   *Partita*, first movement bars 1–9

The beginning of the second stage of the first movement is marked by an abrupt change, both harmonically (in the piano part) and melodically (in the violin line). The melodic line for the violin is marked *cantabile* for the first time, although it is still based on the principle of pitch complementation, in this case covering six notes from B to E inclusive. A more significant change takes place in the supporting harmony, introducing a type of chord which has implications for the structure not only of this movement but of the whole work. The piano plays six notes (four pitches) superimposing two minor thirds a minor ninth apart: F♯–A (low register), and G–B♭ (middle register). The chord is both conspicuous and memorable, interrupting the hitherto fast pace and sustained for six bars. When it changes (bar 35), a gradual ascending sequence begins, arriving six bars later on a similar chord transposed a minor third higher. In each of the three main movements a chord of superimposed minor thirds appears at a comparable stage in the form: in the first and third movements it marks the beginning of the second stage: in the final movement it provides the harmony for bars 13–21, reappears in bars 35–9, is transformed in stage 2 (bars 40–57) into a chord of superimposed major thirds, governs the harmony of the climactic *ad libitum* section, and is used in the coda to conclude the work.

EX. 7 : 2   *Partita*, first movement, violin line bars 50–53

The third stage of the first movement begins with a passage of three-note cells of semitone/tone, played *pianissimo* and *dolcissimo* by the violin in its highest register (Ex. 7 : 2). Beneath this line, the piano plays a chromatically descending sequence of five-note chords with no duplication of pitches between the melodic and harmonic layers. The fourth and final stage drives towards the culmination of the first movement and includes its aftermath, a brief period of subsidence. It begins in canonic imitation between violin and piano with an angular melodic phrase arising from the horizontal pairing of semitones and tritones, with vertical interval-pairing 2 + 5 between stretto entries. The final build-up to the movement's highpoint (bars 84–98) is divided into three layers. The high harmonic strand is occupied by the violin, and comprises driving,

190

motoric triplets made from three-note cells. At the ends of phrases, where the violin line pauses briefly to 'breathe', the piano contributes cells in the same register so that the perpetual motion is almost unbroken. The middle strand, played by the piano, assumes the leading role with a line in octaves generated by melodic interval pairing 2 + 5 (Ex. 7 : 3). Harmonic thickening is achieved by retaining one or more notes from earlier in the line, thus the 2 + 5 vertical pairing of intervals (reading down through each resulting chord) corresponds with the horizontal to reinforce the distinctive character of this melodic and harmonic strand.

EX. 7 : 3   *Partita*, first movement, reduction of bars 84–98

The apparent destination of this passage is the chord at bars 99–100 and a repeated B played in the violin's top register. One would normally describe such an effect as climactic, except that the composer carefully manages this stage in the form to ensure otherwise. A whole bar's rest (102) interrupts the momentum of triplet semiquavers. At this point, instead of silence, a listener familiar with Lutosławski's work might expect to hear a twelve-note chord-aggregate played *fortissimo*; but this expectation is denied. The violin resumes repetition of B, but quietly (as a high natural harmonic), followed by a twelve-note chord-aggregate played *pianissimo* (B–K–B; see the second chord in Ex. 3 : 5b). After further repetition of B by the violin, *pianissimo* and at a lower octave, the piano plays an eight-note chord-aggregate, complemented by the remaining four notes from the violin as an arpeggiated diminished-seventh chord. Example 7 : 4 shows both chord-aggregates from the piano part, together with a slightly condensed layout (enclosed in boxes) to clarify the identity of the constituent four-note chords. The movement ends crisply with yet another application of the ever-present semitone/tone cell.

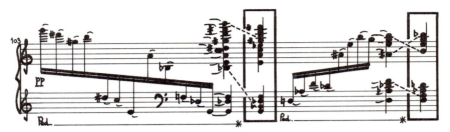

EX. 7 : 4   *Partita*, first movement, chords at and after highpoint

The *ad libitum* second movement is intended merely as an interlude between the more rigorously structured first and third movements, and provides a period of relaxation. While the first movement is rhythmically energetic and fast moving, the third is highly charged and expressive. Contrasting with the movements on either side, the second is melodically less expressive, harmonically more static, rhythmically more relaxed and emotionally more neutral. As in the String Quartet, each player reads from notes written within a self-contained box, thus the notation over-rides conventional rhythmic co-ordination of notes vertically aligned on the page. Both instrumental parts can be divided into two sections. These are clearly identifiable in each individual part, although the absence of vertical rhythmic co-ordination means that the change is unlikely to occur at the same moment in both parts. In the first section the piano has only five pitches (F, A, C, Db, E), and plays brisk demi-semiquaver patterns in high and middle registers; the second section is marked by the arrival of a sixth note, Ab, and low bass notes that underpin arpeggiated chords sustained by the pedal. In the violin part, the first section has fragmentary, scurrying figures played *pianissimo* in a high register using the six pitches that complement the piano part (F#, G; A#, B; D, Eb); the second section uses the same pitches but in phrases outlining rising arpeggios of five-note chords (B, D#, F#, G, A#; then G, B, D, Eb, F#).

In the slow, central movement of *Partita* there is a potent combination of *cantabile* line, regular rhythmic pulsation, and chromatically shifting chords, which synthesise to produce one of Lutosławski's most memorably expressive pieces. The combination of all three elements is untypical of his music from the 1960s or 70s, although similar passages can be found in other late works, particularly the coda of *Epitaph* (see Ex. 6 : 3) and the slow movement of the Piano Concerto (see Ex. 8 : 4). The chromatic movement of chords at the beginning of the slow movement may have some connection with the innovative pianistic harmony of his composer compatriot, Chopin, in whose music are many examples of such harmony, for example the A minor Mazurka, op. 17 no. 4, the E minor Prelude, op. 28 no. 4, and especially the F minor Mazurka, op. 68 no. 4.[5]

The second stage of the third movement reintroduces harmony based on superimposed minor thirds (often linked by perfect fifths) first heard in the corresponding stage of the first movement. Complementation of pitch applies throughout bars 22–32, where the static, background harmony simply repeats a four-note chord (F–A♭ and E♭–G♭) rising through two octave transpositions. In the third stage, the leading role is taken by a melodic line with grace notes using interval pairing of semitone/tone. Beginning in a low register at bar 51, the line gradually creeps higher and higher, accompanied by a chromatic rising counterpoint underneath. Eventually this long *dolente* line reaches a symmetrically spaced chord of superimposed minor thirds (linked by two perfect fifths) around an (unstated) axis of F. This, however, is not the ultimate destination of the gradual build-up which has taken place. The *dolente* line continues, leading at bar 66 to a triumphant C major chord, which announces the return of the opening material as the fourth and last stage of the movement. Both the E at the top of this C major chord, and the G at the bottom, are a logical consequence and continuation of the chromatic lines that have gone before.

EX. 7 : 5   *Partita*, third movement, set-complementation in bars 78–82

At the highpoint of the slow movement we find yet another chord of superimposed minor thirds, although here the connecting intervals are minor sevenths rather than the perfect fifths that obtain elsewhere. This six-note chord is sustained through to the end of the movement (Ex. 7 : 5), and as its resonance fades, the violin line, played without vibrato, supplies the complementary six notes (C–F, inclusive). The melodic and harmonic planes, hitherto separated, are reconciled in the violin's final three-note figure which duplicates the F♯/G♭ at the bottom of the chord.

The fourth movement, played *ad libitum*, also contrasts with the movements on either side, and achieves the composer's objective of providing a period of relative relaxation. The pitch organisation shows subdivision of the chromatic whole into complementary hexachordal sets, and into four harmonic layers, each containing patterns derived from a three-note cell: D♯, E, F (piano); F♯, G, A♭ (violin); A, B♭, B (piano); C, C♯, D (violin).[6] Although the interlude is harmonically static, there is nevertheless an impression of dynamic growth as it becomes progressively more agitated. It begins with the violin alone, *pianissimo*, playing in an expressionless way, without vibrato. The dynamic level increases as the violin climbs higher and higher. Rhythmic agitation in the violin part is set against and reinforced by obstinate oscillation of two notes in the piano part which moves from *pianissimo* to *fortissimo*. Thus, even a short, supposedly inconsequential interlude displays Lutosławski's innate feel for goal-orientated schemes as it proceeds, without a break, to lead directly into the beginning of the final movement.

EX. 7 : 6   *Partita*, fifth movement, violin line bars 9–12

A vigorous *presto*, propelled by motoric three-note cells used melodically, begins the last movement. Bearing in mind the close relationship between *Partita* and *Chain 2*, some details are worthy of comparison. For example, in the latter part of stage 1, the violin plays harshly dissonant intervals and chords, derived from the semitone/tone pairing, which anticipate the *rude* passages in the second movement of *Chain 2* (see Ex. 7 : 10a). This effect contrasts strongly with a passage from the violin line earlier in the movement (Ex. 7 : 6), where the expressive quality of the line is determined by the 2 + 5 interval pairing that provides the *soave* passages in the second movement of *Chain 2* (see Ex. 7 : 10b). The other significant feature of the first stage is the reappearance of chords superimposing minor thirds and perfect fifths. They first enter at bar 13 against the 2 + 5 melodic interval pairing of the violin line, and re-enter between bars 35 and 39, where they alternate between minor thirds and major thirds (an effect of harmonic ambiguity exploited in the final bars of the work). The second stage is slower and more reposeful, with the violin mostly playing quietly in its highest register above arpeggiated six- and seven-note harmonies sustained by the piano. The third drives towards the climax of the work, which is the only stage within any of the three main movements to be played *ad libitum*. Pitch complementation in the final movement is here at its clearest, each instrument having a band of six pitches covering a perfect fourth: B–E (violin); F–B♭ (piano). The final stage is a fast coda which propels the work to a crisp, quasi-cadential ending. From bar 107 to the end the harmony fans out, with motoric three-note cells being transformed vertically into chords of superimposed minor thirds (Ex. 7 : 7), and an effect of instability is maintained by changing several times between chords of major and minor thirds. Close to the end we reach a chord of three minor thirds placed minor ninths apart. The final cadence resolves the intervallic conflict of this highly dissonant sound and decides in favour of the minor third F♯/A, with A/E played by the violin (yet again the 3 + 7 pairing).

EX. 7 : 7 *Partita*, fifth movement, reduction of bars 107–18

The harmony of *Partita* is distinctive. The vertical superimposition of minor thirds (and perfect fifths) creates a harmonic colour that is instantly recognisable at each reappearance and lends itself to contrast against other types of interval combination. The way this harmony is used illustrates the composer's general approach in the late works. As the chords usually only contain either four or six notes, the level of density is sufficiently transparent to allow complementary pitches to be perceived as a separate harmonic layer, but horizontally in the melodic plane.

Melody in *Partita* is both rich and varied. There are many examples of horizontal interval pairing, the most common being semitones/tones used to generate various types of line. The three-note cells appear in many guises, slow and lyrical, fast and motoric, quiet and scurrying. Although Lutosławski has always regarded himself as 'a composer of harmony' rather than melody, *Partita* has demonstrated that, faced with the prospect of writing for a chamber music medium that offers little opportunity for dense textural and harmonic effects, he is able to respond to that challenge as a master of line.

Ad libitum polyphony in *Partita* is severely limited, even by comparison with other late works. This is hardly surprising, as the original duo version provided little potential for the rhythmic effect of 'going astray' which is central to Lutosławski's purpose in exploiting the technique. Whether by design or accident, the result of restricting *ad libitum* polyphony to self-contained sections has been to give the main movements a regularity of pulse and generally faster harmonic pace that obviates the problem of harmonic stasis and infuses the work with rhythmic energy and forward propulsion. These differences between the mature and late styles become clear if one compares *Partita* with the composer's only other substantial chamber work composed since 1960, the String Quartet. The approach to large-scale form is different, the harmonic language and role of *ad libitum* technique radically so.

The orchestration of *Partita* evidently presented the composer with one major problem: how to translate the piano part of the *ad libitum* sections into orchestral terms without re-composing the aleatory counterpoint. His solution was to retain the duo partnership for these passages, hence the piano plays an important obbligato role in the orchestral version. Comparing the orchestral version of *Partita* with *Chain 2*, we find that the former has no oboes or untuned percussion, but unlike the latter it does require a harp. Otherwise, the instrumentation is similar, and neither piece includes horns. The use of tuned percussion (glockenspiel, xylophone, marimba, vibraphone, celesta and piano) to contribute brightly coloured embellishments and highlights to the harmony is common to both pieces and thoroughly characteristic of the composer. The scoring is mostly light and transparent, with little risk of the soloist's line being overpowered by density of orchestral texture.

Interlude

As is invariably the case with Lutosławski's dramatically conceived large-scale forms, both *Partita* and *Chain 2* are structured in relation to the drive towards a decisive climax. In marked contrast to this dynamic approach, the piece that now forms the central panel in a triptych, *Interlude*, links the other two together in concert performance and provides a central five-minute period of calm, repose and relaxation.[7] The absence of the violin soloist, for whom the melodic lyricism of both *Chain 2* and *Partita* was developed, ensures that the focus of attention is no longer directed towards expansive horizontal lines. Instead, Lutosławski concentrates on harmony. As there is no overriding necessity in this case for him to restrict the harmonic density in order to allow for the projection of melodic ideas, he is able to use the strings to provide a succession of slow-moving chords that are harmonically dense by comparison with those used in *Partita*. Against a subtly shifting harmonic texture of muted *pianissimo* string sound, other instruments enter sporadically to play fragmented embellishments in the foreground. The effect is not unlike *The Unanswered Question* by Charles Ives, one of the earliest examples (1908) of contrasted instrumental groupings that are coordinated in a way that anticipates Lutosławski's aleatory technique. In *Interlude*, however, there is no *ad libitum* playing; instead, the piece consists of eighty bars in conventionally notated, regular metre.

The strings are subdivided into eight parts: basses combine with the second group of cellos to form the lowest part. These eight parts provide a harmonic sonority of eight-note chord-aggregates. Each individual part alternates between two notes of the chord in one of four clearly defined harmonic strands: high, upper-middle, lower-middle, or low. As two parts are assigned to each strand, each alternating between their given notes, the whole chord can be sustained for much of the time, even though the individual parts are not static. The change from one chord to another is deliberately blurred by altering the notes very gradually, and at different moments in each part. Further harmonic blurring is caused by the use of auxiliary notes. Lutosławski's use of eight-note rather than twelve-note chord-aggregates is entirely in keeping with the general approach to pitch organisation revealed throughout his late works. If the string background contained all twelve pitches, the inevitable duplication between melodic and harmonic layers would produce the type of problem which led the composer to be dissatisfied with the first stage of *Mi-Parti*.

By the time the various parts have entered and the first eight-note chord is complete (bar 9), one hears a distinctive sonority which will reappear regularly throughout the piece as part of an underlying sequential progression. In the lowest of the four harmonic strands, cellos and basses combine to play the perfect fifth E–B. Above this, in the lower-middle harmonic strand, subdivided violas play another perfect fifth, G–D. The sum of these two strands is the minor-seventh chord E–G–B–D. In the upper-middle strand, subdivided second violins play the minor sixth A♯–F♯, while in the highest strand the subdivided first violins play another minor sixth, C♯–A; these give the major/minor chord A♯–C♯–F♯–A.

The combination of these four-note chords (types C and H) is encountered in many of Lutosławski's mature and late works, although usually as the chord-aggregate C–H–C (see Ex. 3 : 5). As the latter type of aggregate defines the main events in the dramatic scheme of *Chain 2* (see Ex. 7 : 15), it is entirely appropriate that the harmony of *Interlude* should prepare the ear for the types of chord and sonority that are to follow. Gradually the parts move, changing pitch at different times so that the change of harmony is so blurred as to be almost imperceptible. By bar 13 all parts have risen a semitone, to produce an exact upward transposition of the chord that was introduced in bars 1–10.

EX. 7 : 8   a) *Interlude*, harmonic reduction of 8-note chords;   b) *Interlude*, underlying bass line

The underlying harmonic progression in *Interlude* consists of fifteen eight-note chord-aggregates, each with four-note chords C and H in the low and high harmonic strands, respectively. Example 7 : 8a shows these chord-aggregates both with the layout as in the score (maintaining the original spelling of accidentals), and reduced to a compact format (with enharmonic changes to accidentals) showing the configuration of their constituent four-note chords. Horizontal progression between them is determined by a bass line (Ex. 7 : 8b) which ascends through a sequentially extended pattern of semitones and minor thirds (interval-pairing 1 + 3). This pattern grows from a three-note cell, extended with additional rising minor thirds to make groups of four, five, then six notes. Each group begins on the penultimate note of the preceding group. Bass notes always provide the root of a minor-seventh chord, except for the last three (B, D, F). By that time, as the piece nears its end, the separate harmonic strands have overlapped to such an extent that identification of individual chords would no longer be meaningful. The shape of *Interlude* is one of gradual convergence, from very widely spaced chords onto a central unison. As the number of pitches in each chord is reduced in the final bars, the harmony exposes the minor seconds and minor thirds that have provided the underlying progression for the whole piece, and this interval pairing leads inexorably towards a conclusion on the final F.

Curiously, the harmonic blurring achieved by changing the rhythmic values at different times in each of the eight parts, seems to show Lutosławski aiming for a polyphonic result more characteristic of *ad libitum* counterpoint than *a battuta* co-ordination; and yet the piece is metred throughout. He could easily have achieved a rhythmically complex texture by aleatory means, although this would have restricted the changes of harmony and led to the problem of harmonic stasis. *Interlude* shows Lutosławski confronting this problem, and deciding on a solution that produces a slow-moving but constant harmonic rhythm. In order to maintain control over the polyphony, he employs rhythmic canons involving all eight parts. His treatment of this method, however, is not strictly systematic. Instead of allowing it to generate all the rhythmic values with repetitive consistency, he overrides it, deliberately introducing discrepancies. His prime reason for doing this may be deduced from the result: a complex polyphonic texture of superimposed rhythmic layers whose synchronisation is avoided.

Melodic embellishments to the string harmony are provided by various combinations of the other instrumental tone-colours, grouped in pairs (apart from bar 8 where the harp assists the cellos and basses by strengthening the lowest note of the initial eight-note chord). These pairs each consist of wind instrument(s) and a percussive instrument. Lutosławski's choice of pitches for these embellishments is determined mainly by the principle of complementing the background harmony. Where the instrumental pairs coincide with one of the eight-note chords they add the four-note complement. Where they do not coincide, but occur midway between the gradual transition from one chord to another, they make use of notes from the complements of both the previous and the following chord. The effect conveyed to the listener is of a softly focused harmonic haze rather than harmonic clarity. The peculiar aural effect could be described in extra-musical terms as being similar to focus and field-depth in photography (it is worth noting that the title of Lutosławski's piece composed for Elliott Carter's eightieth birthday, *Slides*, is an intended photographic reference). By making the texture of eight-note chords rhythmically and harmonically 'blurred', Lutosławski sets the listener's aural focus to a field-depth that implies and requires something in the foreground. The colouristic highlights provided sporadically by the instrumental pairs enter and occupy this field-depth by supplying notes 'missing' from the background. In contrast with this approach of 'changing focus', the first stage of *Mi-Parti* might be described as 'fixed-focus'. For the listener, both treatments can be of equal validity, but the composer's preference is now clear. His late works demonstrate many different attempts to solve the problem of melodic and harmonic separation. *Interlude* is one of the most interesting, its simplicity constituting a study in this one issue.

Chain 2

In the preface to the published score of *Chain 2*, Lutosławski followed his brief remarks on the principle of chain technique with a revealing statement concerning the development of his approach to the all-important matter of pitch organisation:

I composed *Chain 2* during the years 1984–5. The title of the work relates to its form. Over the last few years I have been working on a new type of musical form, which consists of two structurally independent strands. Sections within each strand begin and end at different times. This is the premise on which the term 'Chain' was selected . . . In the *ad libitum* movements and in the *ad libitum* section of the fourth movement the element of chance plays a part within fixed parameters. This has been a feature of my style since 1960 and always offers new possibilities. However, in the last few years I have been preoccupied more by the shaping of pitch (i.e. melody, harmony and polyphony) than by the organisation of time. In my opinion the traditional scale, with its twelve notes, has not yet been fully exploited in terms of harmony. I believe that there are still many possibilities to be discovered, independently from Schoenberg's twelve-tone technique.

His attitude to the resources of twelve-note harmony had been steadily altering since *Mi-Parti*, with a decisive turning-point marked by *Epitaph*. Yet, of the late works, only the score of *Chain* 2 carries such a declaration, in which he draws attention to the evolution of his treatment of melody, harmony and polyphony. It is significant that he lists these three elements in an order that implies greater importance for melody.

Confidence in the potential of the chromatic scale to yield new and interesting results may explain why Lutosławski, unlike many other composers of the last decade, has not been tempted to flirt with references to the past through neo-Romantic forms of expression. The example of Penderecki must be considered here, particularly since his neo-Romantic works include several string concertos: the First Violin Concerto, Cello Concerto no. 2, the Viola Concerto, and a Second Violin Concerto currently in progress for Anne-Sophie Mutter. Whereas Penderecki reached an *impasse* at the end of the 1970s that caused him to turn towards the music of Bruckner (and Shostakovich), Lutosławski's continuing search for new methods of pitch organisation had led him, in *Chain* 2, to find fresh means of melodic expression without apparent stylistic reference to the past.

As is often the case in Lutosławski's music, the first movement is introductory, fragmentary, and hesitant (although this contrasts strongly with the rhythmically energetic beginning of *Partita*). *Ad libitum* ensemble co-ordination is used, except for ten metred bars. The solo violin plays the leading role throughout, with chordal rather than merely textural harmonic support from differentiated instrumental groups drawn from the orchestra, which does not play tutti in the first movement.

Structurally, there are five main stages in the unfolding of the violin line. The first extends from the opening tremolo between middle C/D to the equivalent tremolo between Db/C after Fig. 2. The second stage ends at Fig. 6, just before a passage of harmonics that begins the third stage and develops into rapid, motoric four-note patterns that drive towards the beginning of the fourth stage at Fig. 12. The fifth and final stage extends from Fig. 15 to the end of the movement. It must be stressed, however, that these structural subdivisions do not occur in an obviously sectional manner. The whole idea of the chain principle is to avoid a simple, sectional construction. Sections do not necessarily begin or end at the same moment but are deliberately overlapped, blurring the structural divisions of the form. One is confronted with a musical fabric woven from various ideas, rendering at best artificial, at worst invalid, any analytical approach based on drawing sectional divisions vertically through the whole score. Instead, one should view the solo violin line and the orchestra as two separate elements that engage in a dialogue, hence the subtitle: 'Dialogue for violin and orchestra'.

There are no chords of twelve notes in the first movement; most contain only four notes, and provide various kinds of harmonic support for the remaining eight pitches to be used in the melodic dimension. There are many examples of pitch complementation, but one passage illustrates both this technique and the use of melodic interval pairing. At Fig. 15, the strings and piano play a four-note chord which is sustained beneath a memorable, expansive and expressive phrase for the soloist generated by interval pairing 2 + 5 (Ex. 7 : 9). Here there is no duplication of pitch-classes between the melodic line and the harmony: the four-note chord contains B♭–B–C–C♯, complemented by the violin line which contains all eight remaining pitches between D and A, inclusive. Melodic pairing of interval-classes 2 + 5 is used by Lutosławski for some of the most lyrical passages in both *Chain 2* and *Partita*. Here it marks the beginning of the last formal stage in the movement.

EX. 7 : 9   *Chain 2*, first movement, Fig. 15

Chain technique is demonstrated by the first movement only in the most general sense. It is in the second movement that one finds the most striking example of the principle, where it operates in links forged by the soloist, that overlap and interlock with those of the orchestra. Whereas the first movement is co-ordinated almost entirely *ad libitum*, the second is mostly metred. Whereas the first is relaxed, meandering and introductory, the second is rhythmically energetic and goal-orientated. Whereas the first contains no twelve-note chord-aggregates, the second is planned around three harmonies of full chromatic density (see Ex. 7:15).

In the first stage of the second movement, successive violin links are differentiated by contrasting interval pairings associated with Italian terms that indicate their different modes of expression: the first, *rude*, is associated with harshly dissonant two- and three-note chords that emphasise three-note cells of adjacent semitones, and interval-classes 1 + 6, (Ex. 7 : 10a); the second, *soave*, is identified with melodic interval-pairing 2 + 5, major seconds and perfect fourths/fifths (Ex. 7 : 10b). These terms of expression have already been noted in the last of the Iłłakowicz songs, *Dzwony Cerkiewne* (see Ex. 3 : 9). Although the actual interval content of the chords used for the orthodox-church bells is not the same as in *Chain* 2, the principle of intervallic contrast is similar.

EX. 7 : 10   *Chain* 2, second movement: a) Violin line from Fig. 23;   b) Violin line from Fig. 29

The twelve-note chord-aggregate reached at Fig. 35 is the most important landmark so far, since it is the first twelve-note chord not only of the movement but of the work as a whole. Rhythmically, it is a continuation of the link begun by the orchestra just before Fig. 34, which in turn takes its triplet quavers from the violin line. We hear it twice, as rising arpeggiated figures lead to a repetition of the same harmony at Fig. 36. The structure of the chord-aggregate (C–H–C) is significant, as a similar harmony occurs both at Fig. 48, and as the climactic chord of the final movement. Such long-range harmonic planning is not unique in Lutosławski's music, but the role played by this harmony in both *a battuta* movements of *Chain* 2 (see Ex. 7 : 15) demonstrates the importance of recurring chord structures in his late works. The same type of chord-aggregate also plays an important role in the long-range harmonic organisation of *Chain 3*.

Stage 2, beginning at Fig. 37, introduces a feature strongly reminiscent of the second movement of the Concerto for Orchestra (see Ex. 2 : 11). The ends of four-note melodic cells played by the violins are highlighted by flutes and oboes playing major triads rooted successively on B♭, D♭, E, G, E♭, B, D, F, D♭ and A (Ex. 7 : 11a). Here there is a clear relationship between the vertical and horizontal planes of the pitch organisation: vertically the triads consist of a major and a minor third, while the horizontal progression consists of rising minor thirds and falling major thirds. When reduced to a single line within one octave, the manipulation of intervallic cells (sequential and inverted) is more clearly exposed as an example of melodic pairing in major and minor seconds (Ex. 7 : 11b).

EX. 7 : 11   *Chain 2*, second movement, Figs. 37–9:   a) Harmonic reduction;
b) Melodic reduction

Meanwhile the solo part re-enters at Fig. 38, to begin a long, lyrical line of thirty-five bars generated by melodic interval pairing 2 + 5 (Ex. 7 : 12), which extends through to Fig. 48 and the twelve-note chord-aggregate that stands as the destination point of this stage in the form. Although the composer marks the violin line *espressivo* and later *dolce*, rather than *soave*, it is clearly a development of the shorter, *soave* links that appeared earlier in the movement. From Figs. 47 to 48 the soloist plays together with piccolo, xylophone and subdivided first violins. Piccolo and xylophone chase each other in short canonic phrases, while the first violins repeat a C major triad. All play similar triplet patterns, and are united by the same interval pairing (the last four bars of Ex. 7 : 12 show a compression of the violin, piccolo and xylophone parts reduced to a single line). Triadic accompaniment continues throughout the entire passage, moving from glissando strings to arpeggios played by flute and clarinet with violins *pizzicato*, to piano, vibraphone, glockenspiel and strings, to three violins.

EX. 7 : 12   *Chain* 2, second movement, solo violin line Figs. 38–48

The beginning of the third stage returns to the abrasively dissonant sound of the *rude* passages, this time marked *pesante*. The intervallic character after Fig. 50 contrasts strongly with what has just gone before. From Fig. 53, two methods are employed in the orchestral parts to achieve a gradual build-up towards the climax of the movement at Fig. 59; first, a chromatically rising progression of four-note string chords, followed by five-note chords in the strings and woodwind; then, from Fig. 56, a rising chromatic scale that is passed around the orchestra covering all registers through octave displacement. Both techniques are simple, but none the less effective in conveying a sensation of continually rising pitch level with relatively fast harmonic pace. Meanwhile the soloist maintains an appropriate degree of rhythmic energy with fast, motoric three-note patterns that eventually lead to the climax.

Lutosławski is usually careful to ensure that mid-term points of culmination in the unfolding of a large-scale form do not undermine the climax of the work. *Chain* 2 is no exception. The twelve-note chord-aggregate that marks the highpoint of the second movement quickly subsides, both in dynamic intensity and harmonic density, so that the listener's appetite is only partially and temporarily satisfied; there is a sense of exhilaration but not exhaustion.

EX. 7 : 13 *Chain 2,* third movement, opening violin line

The third movement, like the first, is almost entirely *ad libitum*. Its construction is simpler than either the second or fourth movements, and is determined by the leading role of the solo violin line. The orchestra accompanies, providing various kinds of harmonic and timbral support that nearly always complement rather than duplicate the pitches used by the solo line. Three distinct types of melody are used in alternation, each moving naturally into the other to effect a smooth, yet changing melodic flow. The first is a *cantando* melody of the *dolente* type, moving in three-note cells of interlocking tones and semitones linked by grace notes. The initial phrase (Ex. 7 : 13), played *molto cantabile* on the G string, is followed by 'scurrying' three-note cells played *punta d'arco*. Melodic interval-pairing of semitones/tones is common between these phrases, hence they flow quite naturally from one to the other; yet there is a marked difference in character. Both kinds of melodic line can be found in other works by Lutosławski. A third type, however, can be found so far only in *Chain* 2 and the Third Symphony (see Ex. 6 : 10). It occurs three times during the course of this movement and is one of the most hauntingly memorable melodic ideas in the work. The first time it appears (Ex. 7 : 14a) there are just two phrases, each rising through minor thirds and perfect fifths, and falling through perfect fifths and major thirds. Although presented melodically, its true organisation is vertical, as diminished triads, superimposed to emphasise minor ninths in the line. Its second appearance has three phrases (Ex. 7 : 14b), the last of which extends to the violin's highest register. When the idea is heard for the third time (Ex. 7 : 14c) it has been transformed: the intervals have been contracted, flattening the melodic contour, so that successive phrases can open out until the melody regains its original interval structure at Fig. 89. The third movement ends with an expressively potent development of the opening *dolente* melody, played first by the soloist, who ascends to the upper register and is then joined by the other violins in unison as they gradually climb to the top E harmonic, *fortissimo*. The soloist concludes the movement alone.

The final movement, like the second, evolves through overlapping strands of melodic and harmonic material in dialogue between the soloist

The composer's summer house in Norway, near Skiptvet (about 80 km south of Oslo) overlooking the river Glomma.

The composer and his wife, after receiving a doctorate honoris causa at the Northwestern University, Evanston, Illinois (Chicago), on 15 June 1974.

Lutosławski in 1980.

The composer conducting.

The composer conducting.

The composer conducting.

The composer sailing on Lake Michigan, Chicago, at the time of the première of the Third Symphony (1983).

NAGRODA
ARTYSTYCZNA

NSZZ Solidarność
1983

dla   *Witolda
       Lutosławskiego*

KOMITET KULTURY NIEZALEZNEJ

The 1983 Solidarity Prize awarded to Lutosławski in 1984.

The composer with Paul Sacher and Anne-Sophie Mutter. (Photograph © Susesch Bayat.)

The composer with Krystian Zimerman during rehearsals in Salzburg for the première of the Piano Concerto (1988).

The composer and his wife at a post-concert reception at the Leeds Club, England, to celebrate his seventy-third birthday (25 January 1986, photograph by the author).

The composer with Charles Bodman Rae at the Royal Albert Hall, London, during rehearsals for the British première of the Fourth Symphony on 27 August 1993 (photograph © Malcolm Crowthers).

The composer at his Steinway, in the study of his home in Śmiała Street (1991, photograph © Malcolm Crowthers).

The composer at his desk, in his study in ul. Śmiała, Warszawa (1991, photograph © Malcolm Crowthers).

EX. 7 : 14   *Chain* 2, third movement: a) Violin line Figs. 67–9;   b) Violin line Figs. 72–4;   c) Violin line Figs. 86–90

and the orchestra, according to the principle of chain technique. As one expects with Lutosławski, the final movement drives towards the climax of the work. Propelling the music towards that point are three formal stages, each beginning with a tutti passage followed by several chain links (nine, seven, and six, respectively). Subdivision into formal stages is determined primarily by the strategic placing of certain chords. Of these, the eight-note chord that begins the second stage at Fig. 100 is similar to one at Fig. 60, in the succession of chords concluding the second movement. The third stage begins with a succession of ten nine-note chords. The placing of twelve-note chord-aggregates in the final movement is crucial to an understanding of the form: one at the beginning and the other at the climax, with no other twelve-note chord in between. The use of an eight-note chord-aggregate to mark the beginning of the second stage, shows the composer deliberately restricting the harmonic density so that the climax will not be pre-empted or undermined. Example 7 : 15 shows all five twelve-note chord-aggregates used in *Chain* 2: three from the second movement and two from the fourth.

EX. 7 : 15   *Chain* 2, all five 12-note chord-aggregates

All five aggregates are of the general type which uses similar four-note chords in two of the harmonic strands (see Ex. 3 : 5). The most important observation to make, however, is that the first twelve-note chord-aggregate of the work, from the second movement, is virtually the same as the one used at the climax in the final movement. Their different spelling of some accidentals confuses the relationship between them slightly, and the distribution of notes within each strand is not quite the same. But the sonority is similar, especially that there is no transposition involved. Acoustically, the decisive difference between the C–H–C chord-aggregates and the other two (D–D–J and B–K–B), is the presence of perfect fifths/octaves at the bottom, as opposed to a tritone (see also Ex. 2 : 2). Whether or not the listener's ear is acute enough to detect that the first and last chords are at the same pitch level, the harmonic timbre in each strand is distinctive and recognisable on its return.

In Lutosławski's works of the 1960s and 70s, the psychological effect on the listener of repeating a particular twelve-note chord or chord-aggregate that has been heard before is not particularly meaningful, because of the large number of such chord structures which pervade the music. In the late works, however, we find the composer using them sparingly, presumably because he recognises that the potency of their effect in any given work is likely to be in inverse proportion to the frequency of their use. It would be quite impossible, for example in the Second Symphony, for even the most sophisticated ear to recognise, remember or recall any particular twelve-note chord, the listener's aural memory being swamped by the amount of dense harmony.

Melodic richness is the most striking feature of *Chain 2* when this work is contrasted with Lutosławski's music of the 1960s and 70s. Projection of expressive melodic lines is made possible through the separation of horizontal and vertical planes by pitch complementation. Much of the work illustrates this partition into melodic and harmonic layers, or strands. Compared with works from the 1960s, such as the Second Symphony or *Livre pour orchestre*, or works such as *Mi-Parti* from the 1970s, this reduction in harmonic density constitutes a radical departure from Lutosławski's earlier manner of deploying twelve-note chords, and has made possible his return to chamber music as well as the late *concertante* works.

Finally, it is worth noting that when *Partita, Interlude* and *Chain 2* are performed together, as a triptych, they have a combined performance duration of at least forty minutes. If they were to be regarded as one work, rather than three separate pieces, this would be Lutosławski's longest composition (exceeding the duration of Preludes and Fugue). Even though the composer does regard them as a set of three separate pieces, the psychological effect on the listener (if there is no applause after *Partita*) is one of continuing drama that commands unbroken attention over the whole time-span. There is no comparable work in the repertory of music for violin and orchestra, and it is without doubt one of the finest achievements of Lutosławski's career.

In the year that elapsed between the première of *Partita* in January 1985 and the first performance of *Chain 2* in January 1986, Lutosławski was also able to undertake a project of a rather different kind. For a concert in London on 5 December 1985 he orchestrated seventeen of the Polish Carols drawn from the set of twenty that he had composed for voice and piano in 1946 (he orchestrated the remaining three carols in 1990, and the complete set was first performed in its new version that December). In most cases it proved to be merely an exercise in transcription, without the need for any recomposition, although a few settings received minor adjustments (e.g. *Bóg się rodzi, Z narodzenia Pana* and *Pasterze mili*), and *Hej, Hej, lelija Panna Maryja* gained a series of changes to the bass line that slightly affect the harmony.

Lutosławski also received two major awards in 1985. The Ferrer Salat Award was presented to him by Queen Sofia of Spain at a ceremony held in Madrid. The other award was specifically for the Third Symphony and took him back to the United States, to the University of Louisville in Kentucky. When Charles Grawemeyer established his prize for musical composition in 1984 (to be awarded for the first time the following year), his aim was to create an award of international scope, something that could be compared to a Nobel Prize. The monetary element of $150,000 makes the Grawemeyer Prize by far the most substantial in the field of composition and has succeeded in attracting nominations from all over the world, including submissions on behalf of eminent figures such as Elliott Carter and Michael Tippett.[8] In his acceptance speech Lutosławski announced his intention to use the prize money in order to establish a scholarship fund for young Polish composers to continue their post-graduate studies abroad.[9] Lutosławski kept to his word, and over the next few years all the money from this and other sources was used in support of the younger generation of composers then in their late twenties and early thirties (it is worth making the poignant observation that Lutosławski had been at this crucial stage in his own career prior to the outbreak of the Second World War, and that his plans to continue studying, in Paris, had been thwarted by events). The scholarship fund was later augmented in 1987 by a substantial donation made on behalf of the San Francisco Symphony Orchestra, at the composer's request, being in lieu of a commission fee for *Chain 3*.

Chain 3

Written for the San Francisco Symphony Orchestra, *Chain 3* received its première in that city on 10 December 1986, conducted by Lutosławski. Chain technique is used in the first stage of the piece, but as a means of travelling towards a destination rather than as the main purpose of the journey. The composer's aim in *Chain 3* was to feature the brass section, focusing on their ability to play *cantabile*, rather than the strident sounds he had exploited in earlier works such as the Cello Concerto. Hence the one-movement form is structured to achieve a sense of arrival at Fig. 37 where the brass section plays a section of collective *ad libitum* in a 'singing' manner. Table 15 summarises the formal scheme. Instrumentation is of significance, particularly in the first stage, where contrast between groups is one of the methods employed to differentiate the overlapping links of the chain.

The form subdivides into three stages. The first uses the chain principle in twelve overlapping links, almost all *ad libitum* apart from link 12. The

TABLE 15   *Chain 3*, formal scheme

Fig.	Stage	Section	Co-ordination	Instrumentation
[0]	1	introduction	*a battuta*	ww, str, bells
1		link 1	*ad libitum*	3 fls
1		link 2	*ad libitum*	4 dbs
2		link 3	*ad libitum*	3 vns/xyl
3		link 4	*ad libitum*	3 cls
4		link 5	*ad libitum*	4 vcs
5		link 6	*ad libitum*	celesta/harp/pf
6		link 7	*ad libitum*	2 tpts/2 trbns
7		link 8	*ad libitum*	b cl/3 bns
8		link 9	*ad libitum*	4 vns
9		link 10	*ad libitum*	3 tpts
10		link 11	*ad libitum*	3 vns
11		link 12	*a battuta*	harp/3 fls
12		extension	*ad libitum*	tutti
13	2	Presto 3/4	*a battuta*	tutti
17		9/4	*a battuta*	str (*uniti/divisi*) etc
23		3/2	*a battuta*	tutti
27		3/2	*a battuta*	str (*uniti/divisi*) etc
31		3/4	*a battuta*	tutti
37	3	*cantabile*	*ad libitum*	brass
38			*ad libitum*	str
43			*ad libitum*	str/brass/ww
44		climax	*ad libitum*	tutti
45–46		Presto	*a battuta*	tutti

static, introductory character of this opening section is comparable with the first movement of Symphony no. 2. The episodic nature of the overlapping links in *Chain 3* is similar to the seven episodes of *Hésitant*, and they perform a similar function, although the time-scale differs considerably. Another similarity lies in the contrasted instrumentation chosen for the links of one and the episodes of the other.

While the beginning and end of the first formal stage are both marked by a twelve-note chord-aggregate (C–H–C), the overlapping links of the chain show subdivision of the chromatic whole into complementary harmonic strands; pitch complementation is observed throughout, except where links 11 and 12 overlap. As the latter gradually accumulates notes,

building towards a twelve-note chord, it is inevitable here that duplication of notes between strands will occur. Melodic patterns used for the
twelve links are mostly derived from three-note cells of adjacent semitones, and the composer's chosen division of the chromatic whole assists
the emergence of such motifs. The dense chord that eventually results
from the gradual accumulation of woodwind, brass and tuned percussion
parts (Figs. 12–13) is basically of type C–H–C, although the presence of
octave doublings in arpeggiated patterns obscures the identity of the
four-note chords in each harmonic strand. The significance of this type of
chord-aggregate has already been noted in connection with *Chain 2*, and
a related type of eight-note chord-aggregate in *Interlude*. In *Chain 3*, as in
Chain 2, the C–H–C chord-aggregate is used as a structural signpost,
defining the long-range harmonic organisation and the form. Having
heard the sonority at the beginning (albeit briefly), and again at the end of
the first stage, the listener is unconsciously conditioned to recognise its
reappearance as the harmony that sustains the brass *cantabile* passage
from Fig. 37.

Stage 2 is marked *Presto* and gives an unbroken span of conventionally
metred *a battuta* writing. Whereas *ad libitum* ensemble co-ordination was
used for the hesitant, harmonically static character of the introductory
stage, the second moves with greater rhythmic energy and a faster harmonic pulse, two factors that invest this stage with the function of driving
towards the points of destination (the brass *cantabile* at Fig. 37) and
culmination (the *fortissimo* seven-note chord at Fig. 44). The second stage
is conceived primarily in terms of the gradual unfolding of a very long
melodic line, delivered by the first and second violins playing mostly in
unison, but with connecting phrases *divisi* in order to blur the line (Ex.
7 : 16). It unfolds in two phrases (Figs. 17–23 and 27–31), each of which
is supported by various six-note chords of superimposed minor thirds and
perfect fifths (3 + 7). Just as the use of the C–H–C chord-aggregate is
characteristic of the works of the mid-1980s, so the pairing of these

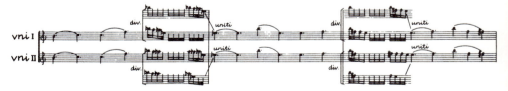

EX. 7 : 16   *Chain 3*, extract of string *cantilena*

intervals is typical of certain melodic phrases encountered in the Third Symphony and *Chain 2*, while their use in chords is typical of *Partita*. *Chain 3*, the Piano Concerto, and several of the *Chantefleurs et Chantefables*. The sonority of minor thirds and perfect fourths/fifths also tends to predominate in C–H–C aggregates.

In Lutosławski's earlier works the destination point of a large-scale form is usually synonymous with the point of climax. In the late works this is no longer necessarily so. The Third Symphony, for example, reaches its main point of destination in a unison string *cantando* line in the epilogue, only after an (abortive) attempt at a collective *fortissimo* climax. In *Chain 3* the point of destination to which the long *cantando* string line of the second formal stage leads is an expansive *cantabile* passage for the brass section, played *ad libitum* between Figs. 37 and 38. The climax, however, does not occur until the *fortissimo* chord at Fig. 44. Apparently mindful of matters concerning the psychological perception of the listener, the composer appears to have avoided treading exactly the same ground twice. Paths over the available ground criss-cross and it is hardly surprising to find that some of them are well worn, but this does not mean that he takes the same route each time.

Comparing the placing of the climax within their respective dramatic schemes, at first glance *Chain 1* and *Chain 3* appear remarkably similar. They each arrive at this point comparatively late in the form (0.9 and 0.95, respectively). This comparison suggests close correspondence, but it also masks the contrast that is the decisive difference between them. While the second stage of *Chain 1* moves inexorably towards its sole highpoint, in *Chain 3* the destination and culmination points are separate, and occur at different moments.

The climactic harmony of *Chain 3* is not a twelve-note chord, but a seven-note extended chord rooted very firmly on A. If described quasi-tonally, it would be a subdominant-thirteenth chord in E major (i.e. A–C♯–E–G♯–B–D♯–F♯). Here, however, it does not occur in the context of any tonal function. Its intervallic 'physiognomy' (to use the composer's expression for describing a harmonic *objet sonore*) is effectively that of a chord built from superimposed perfect fifths (A–E–B–F♯–C♯–G♯–D♯), but with the notes rearranged to give wider intervals at the bottom (which strengthens the acoustic sonority of the harmonic series projected upwards by the fundamental/root A) and closer intervals in the higher register. After this bright, open resonance emphasising perfect fifths, octaves and a major second, the work ends with divided cellos descending to a murky low register through slow glissandi, giving an oblique reference, perhaps, to the mood of resignation in which the Second Symphony ends.

1986 had begun with the première of *Chain 2* in Zurich and ended with the first performance of *Chain 3* in San Francisco. In the meantime, Lutosławski had received the International Record Critics' Award for his Philips recording of the Third Symphony with the Berlin Philharmonic Orchestra. In the autumn Lutosławski made a return visit to Louisville, in order to serve on the jury that selected the winner of the second Grawemeyer Prize. The award that year went to György Ligeti for his six *Etudes* for piano, first performed in January the previous year (one of the criteria for eligibility is that the submitted work should have received its première within the preceding five years).[10] Lutosławski also provided for his hosts a short ceremonial piece, simply entitled Fanfare for Louisville, that was played by the Louisville Orchestra on 19 September.[11] A few weeks later he was in London to receive the highest musical accolade in Britain, in the form of the Gold Medal of the Royal Philharmonic Society (commemorating the Society's commission of Beethoven's Ninth Symphony). This was presented to him by Michael Tippett (who had received the award in 1976) during a concert at the Royal Festival Hall on 8 October, at which Lutosławski conducted his Third Symphony with the Philharmonia Orchestra.[12] The following month he returned to England for a major retrospective of his work at the Huddersfield Contemporary Music Festival. There, in addition to presenting recent pieces (such as the Double Concerto, with the Holligers) Lutosławski attended the first concert performance of several of his Children's Songs from the 1950s.

Lutosławski's current preoccupations with the *concertante* medium and chain technique did not end with *Chain 2* and *3*, but continued through his work with the Piano Concerto, with which he was already engrossed by the end of 1986. By the spring of the following year his progress with the new piece was already sufficiently advanced for him to be able to give a detailed description of its form and content during the course of ten days of conversations with the present author conducted at his home in Warsaw.[13] These discussions were wide-ranging, and covered many details of his compositional technique, but one striking feature of them was the way in which *Chain 2* emerged as a kind of touchstone, a standard of compositional achievement against which previous and future pieces might be measured. Much of the composer's enthusiasm for the piece at that time can certainly be attributed to the impeccable playing of Anne-Sophie Mutter, and he readily acknowledges the inspiring quality of her performances of the work. But underlying its success is the synthesis of concerto and chain.

8

Catching up with Arrears

(1987–1994)

Having taken the decisive step in 1979 towards simplifying and refining his harmonic language, with the consequent shift in emphasis towards expressive melodic line, Lutosławski progressed to a stage in his career where he could bring to fruition pieces that he had felt unable to compose in earlier years. When recalling the difficult circumstances of post-war Poland he has often remarked 'I could not compose as I wished, so I composed as I was able'.[1] This statement is usually interpreted in the context of the political conditions and restraints of that time, but the composer was also referring to his awareness of limitations and lacunae in his compositional technique. By the mid-1980s, however, it appears that Lutosławski had found solutions to his remaining problems, particularly the techniques of pitch complementation that so often define the relationship between the vertical and horizontal dimensions of his music. Once this stage had been reached he was ready to catch up with some of the long-term unfinished business of his youth, such as the composition of *concertante* pieces for the violin and the piano. His own term for this phenomenon of making up for lost time is the idiomatic Polish expression 'odrabiac zaległości': 'to catch up with arrears'.[2]

Piano Concerto

After finishing the Symphonic Variations in 1938, Lutosławski had plans to compose two large-scale works: a symphony and a piano concerto. He was then twenty-five. Many works in the piano concerto repertory have been written by youthful composer–pianists wishing to perform their own music. Lutosławski's early plans conform to such a pattern, but he was dissatisfied with the sketches he assembled before the war and postponed work on the project.[3] The reasons for his dissatisfaction were primarily ones of style and language, rather than any problems with the tactile aspects of pianism. At that early stage in his career Lutosławski was still a skilled pianist with a solo repertoire that included pieces such as the Toccata, op.7, of Schumann, and Chopin's Fourth Ballade.[4] After the war, he again attempted to compose a piano concerto, but his main priorities at that time were to complete the First Symphony and to survive by writing functional pieces. During the period of redefinition of harmonic vocabulary and language that followed the completion of the First Symphony in 1947, temporary postponement became longer-term abandonment.

Throughout the years from 1960 to 1979, the piano was conspicuous by its absence from Lutosławski's work. Instead, he concentrated on applying and exploring his harmonic and polyphonic techniques in orchestral works. Only after solving the problem of how to compose without the dense harmony typical of the Second Symphony, *Jeux vénitiens* or the *Trois poèmes d'Henri Michaux*, did he find ways of using the piano again. The compositional breakthrough that enabled him to fulfil his youthful ambition, as with the other *concertante* works composed since 1979, was the projection of melodic line against simpler harmony. Another important factor, however, was the wish to provide a piece for Krystian Zimerman (to whom the work is also dedicated). Lutosławski had followed Zimerman's career with interest since the Chopin Competition of 1976 in which the young pianist had won the first prize, and he certainly found a degree of inspiration in Zimerman's beauty of tone that can be compared with his experience of working with Anne-Sophie Mutter. Even so, the Piano Concerto is not treated in the bravura tradition. Instead, there is a sense of equal participation in a dialogue, as suggested by the subtitle for *Chain 2*. In both cases there is a marked contrast with the confrontational treatment of the relationship between soloist and orchestra as exemplified by the Cello Concerto.

Lutosławski worked intensively on the Piano Concerto during 1987 and completed it early the next year. Commissioned by the Salzburg Festival, it was first performed there on 19 August 1988 by Zimerman with the Austrian Radio (ORF) Symphony Orchestra, conducted by the composer. For the first performance, Lutosławski provided a programme note that includes a brief commentary on the work and the character of its four movements:

My Piano Concerto consists of four movements which are played without any break, despite the fact that each of the movements has a clear ending. The first movement is comprised of four sections. In the first and third, the motifs presented are as if nonchalant, light, sometimes rather wayward, never over-serious. In contrast to the first and third, the second and fourth sections are filled with a broad *cantilena*, finally leading to the highpoint of the whole movement. The second movement is a kind of *moto perpetuo*, a quick chase by the piano against the background of the orchestra which ends by calmly subsiding in preparation for the third movement. The third movement opens with a recitative for the piano alone, which then intones, also without the involvement of the orchestra, a singing *largo* theme. The middle section, beginning with the entrance of the orchestra, contrasts against the first section with moments of a more sudden, dramatic character. The *cantilena*, without orchestral accompaniment, returns at the end of the movement. The fourth movement, by its construction, alludes to the Baroque form of the chaconne. Its theme (always played by the orchestra) consists of short notes separated by rests and not (as with the traditional chaconne) chords. This theme, repeated many times, provides only one layer of the musical discourse. Against this background the piano each time presents another episode. These two layers operate in the sense of chain-form, i.e. the beginnings and endings of the piano episodes do not correspond with the beginnings and endings of the theme. They come together only once, towards the end of the work. The theme appears again for the last time in a shortened form (without rests) played by the whole orchestra without the piano. There follows a short piano recitative, *fortissimo*, against the background of the orchestra, and a short coda (*presto*) concludes the work.[5]

Although the composer conceived the first movement as being in four sections, the listener is likely to perceive it in two main stages, determined by the entry of the strings at Fig. 20. In this respect the scheme is not unlike the first movement of the Double Concerto, which is divided into two stages marked 'Rapsodico' and 'Appassionato', respectively. As in the Double Concerto, the introductory stage is structured as episodes separated by an orchestral ritornello (a brief, quasi-cadential gesture that functions as a device for interrupting and punctuating the episodes, rather than as a section that could be termed a refrain). The scheme of episodes and ritornello/refrains has already been observed in *Jeux vénitiens*, the Second Symphony, *Livre pour orchestre*, the Double Concerto and the Third Symphony. Here, the ritornello comprises simply a single bar of $\frac{5}{4}$ in which a twelve-note chord (predominantly of minor seconds and minor thirds, with a perfect fourth at the bottom) collapses onto a semitone dyad. Each subsequent appearance of this gesture exploits the effect of symmetrical intervallic expansion and contraction from a three-note cell of adjacent semitones onto a chord of superimposed perfect fourths, and back onto a three-note cell.[6]

Each of the seven episodes is played *ad libitum*, whereas the six appearances of the ritornello device are conducted. The first section contains four episodes, including an introductory 'babble' for woodwinds, each terminated by the fast ritornello. Episode 2 has the piano playing against aleatory mobiles from a static bundle of three flutes that sustain a single three-note cell (Ab,G,F#). Here the piano part demonstrates the kind of chromatic voice-leading that governs the linear progression of harmony in many sections of the concerto and in the *Chantefleurs et Chantefables* (Ex. 8 : 1a). The third and fourth episodes (Exx. 8 : 1b and 8 : 1c, respectively) illustrate Lutosławski's practice of generating horizontal lines from the 2 + 5 interval-pairing of major seconds and perfect fourths/fifths. The second section begins with the fifth episode, for piano with two flutes and two oboes, but soon the woodwind instruments drop out, leaving the piano to play a decorated *cantilena*. The fifth appearance of the ritornello signals the beginning of the third section, which leads via the seventh and final episode (for piano and timpani), to the final section.

EX. 8 : 1   Piano Concerto, first movement, reduction of piano episodes

While the first three sections are predominantly static, the fourth is metred, is not interrupted by the ritornello, and builds cumulatively towards a highpoint, through a polyphonic texture of rhythmic layers provided by the strings. From Figs. 20 to 24 this rhythmic polyphony is in only five parts (four-note chords with the bottom doubled at the low octave), with the slowest-moving layer at the bottom and the quickest at the top (the soloist adds further rhythmic layers). From Fig. 28 until the culmination of the movement at Fig. 34, the polyphonic texture is thickened to seven parts with the rhythmic layers interchanging. At the beginning of each section of string polyphony, the harmony consists of two perfect fifths and a minor third (interval pairing 3 + 7). This combination of intervals has already been noted in connection with the Third Symphony, *Partita*, *Chain* 2 and *Chain* 3. Its use throughout these late works establishes the sonority as a harmonic characteristic of the late style. At Fig. 28 the five-note chord of pairing 3 + 7 is thickened by octave doubling, and the ensuing linear progression is defined by chromatic voice-leading (Ex. 8 : 2). The climax of the movement comes with a succession of six-note chords (some with doublings) played by the whole orchestra without the soloist. The first and fourth of these chords consist of super-imposed minor thirds (pairing 2 + 3) that emphasise minor ninths.

EX. 8 : 2   Piano Concerto, first movement, harmonic reduction from Fig. 28

The second movement is a fleet, whispering scherzo conveyed by pian-ism of Chopinesque delicacy. It opens, however, not with any gestural references to the Romantic period, but with motoric rhythmic figurations similar to those at the beginning of *Partita*, which the composer associates with allusion to Baroque keyboard music (Ex. 8 : 3). The movement owes its fast pace to the use of conventional metre throughout, including the cadenza-like passage for the soloist between Figs. 63 and 64. Much of the melodic and harmonic material in the second movement is derived from either three-note cells of interlocking tone/semitone, or the pairing of tritones and semitones. This can be observed, melodically, in the first section from the beginning to Fig. 38, and harmonically in the woodwind chords (of superimposed and interlocking tritones) that interrupt the perpetual motion later in the movement, before and after the piano cadenza.

The slow third movement epitomises Lutosławski's late style, and opens with a long, unaccompanied passage for the soloist. The String Quartet and the Cello Concerto each opened with a long solo, akin to a

EX. 8 : 3   Piano Concerto, second movement, opening piano figurations

dramatic monologue or soliloquy, but here if there is any valid theatrical analogy it must be to an operatic *scena*. The movement begins with a recitative, which prepares for the lyrical *cantabile* theme that Lutosławski marks Largo (Ex. 8 : 4). Dramatically and gesturally (although not stylistically) this could be compared with the opening of the third movement of Beethoven's Sonata in A flat, op. 110.

The typical combination of minor thirds and perfect fifths can be seen in the melodic contour of the opening recitative as well as bars 5–7 of the ensuing Largo. Initially the 3 + 7 pairing is used in a three-note pattern (F–A♭–E♭), transposed sequentially at the tritone as the line rises. The

EX. 8 : 4   Piano Concerto, third movement, recitative and Largo

221

pattern is inverted as the line falls (D–B–E; A♭–F–B♭; etc). Simple as this melodic shape may be, it carries a highly distinctive harmonic colour when sustained by the pedal. Similar sequential extension follows as the line becomes more expansive, ranging from low A (A–C–G; E♭–G♭–D♭; etc) to reach D in preparation for the beginning of the Largo theme. The individual character of the latter is determined largely by the minor-ninth sonority underpinning the line.

After the orchestra re-enters at Fig. 67, the piano part becomes more impassioned and declamatory and leads to a point of dramatic emphasis in a *fortissimo* eight-note chord-aggregate at Fig. 77, played by the whole orchestra together with the soloist. In keeping with the harmonic character of the movement, this chord superimposes only minor thirds and perfect fourths/fifths, with a notable absence of minor ninths between harmonic strands. The Largo theme then transfers to the violins and is developed in whole-tone scale segments. The movement ends as it began, with the soloist intoning the Largo theme in phrases that gradually subside to conclude with a low, four-note chord of two superimposed perfect fifths and one minor third (C–G–D–F), similar to the chords used at Figs. 20 and 28 in the first movement.

The finale is the easiest of the four movements to discuss in technical and structural terms, because there is a method of pitch and rhythmic organisation that extends up to and including the climax of the work. For this movement, Lutosławski returned to his earliest formal model for the chain principle: the Passacaglia that begins the finale of the Concerto for Orchestra. There, the eight-bar theme (see Ex. 2 : 12) was overlapped with contrasting episodes (unrelated to each other) so that phrases in each strand rarely coincided. In the Piano Concerto Lutosławski adopts another term that makes a similar allusion to compositional technique of the Baroque era: chaconne (although stressing that it is not strictly a chaconne in the traditional sense). The chaconne (Ex. 8 : 5) consists of two elements: a ten-bar rhythmic pattern, and a thirty-seven note melodic

EX. 8 : 5   Piano Concerto, fourth movement, 10-bar 'chaconne' theme

line (referred to here as *talea* and *color*, respectively, to borrow terminology from the medieval techniques of isorhythm).

Of the eighteen statements of the chaconne, seventeen preserve the *talea* in its original form, including rests, and the last compresses it into only five bars by deleting rests (Ex. 8 : 6). Twelve statements of the chaconne combine *talea* and *color*, and six use the *talea* without the *color* (five of these – nos. 6,13,15,16 and 17 – use the *talea* harnessed to chords rather than a horizontal line). Only the tenth version of the chaconne (for untuned percussion) uses the *talea* without any pitch element at all. Successive statements of the *color* are transposed, so that the last note of one corresponds with the first note of the next. Melodic interval-pairing of semitone/tritone (1 + 6) governs each of the twelve statements of the chaconne theme to preserve the *color*. Although the sixth statement has a different intervallic structure, because of its chordal framework, it nevertheless preserves some characteristics of the *color* and reproduces its general contour, albeit more expansively. Underlying the system of transposition, determining the first note of each *color* is a simple rotation anti-clockwise round the cycle of fifths (starting with C and ending with G).

EX. 8 : 6 Piano Concerto, fourth movement, compression of 'chaconne' theme

The orchestral climax of the last movement is reached with the final statement of the chaconne between Figs. 113 and 114. The soloist does not play at this point, but reaches a separate climax in the ensuing *ad libitum* section, which is the first aleatory section of the movement. Although the piano sonority here is harmonically dense, with *fortissimo* chords sustained by the pedal, there is no twelve-note chord, either played by the orchestra or by the soloist. In fact, the concerto contains few twelve-note chords (as distinct from the more general principle of twelve-note harmony). In this respect it is similar to *Partita*, which also exploits the resources of the chromatic whole, but partitioned between the melodic and harmonic dimensions. The Piano Concerto finishes with a fast, vigorous coda that drives to a crisp, cadential ending. The composer approaches the final cadence by means of a chromatically falling bass line, introduced at the beginning of the coda, that outlines the dominant–subdominant–tonic progression E♭–D♭–A♭. This pattern is repeated and extended, in order to stretch and delay the inevitable conclusion on a chord rooted to A♭ (Ex. 8 : 7).

EX. 8 : 7   Piano Concerto, fourth movement, cadential bass line

In the case of a piano concerto, it is likely that comparisons will be made with the existing repertory. In Lutosławski's case such comparisons must also take into account his own experience as a pianist, and the composers that influenced him in his youth. Ravel, Bartók and Prokofiev are the most obvious in this context, as each was influential at some stage in Lutosławski's career. The Piano Sonata of 1934, for example, displays many traces of Ravelian harmony and pianistic figurations strongly reminiscent of the Ravel Sonatine. This influence was never completely lost, although it is hardly apparent in Lutosławski's music of the 1960s. It resurfaces in the harmony of the late works, particularly those sonorities characterised by the pairing of perfect fifths and minor thirds. In the Piano Concerto such harmony plays an important role, and at those moments when it is emphasised perhaps an allusion to Ravel may be sensed by the listener. The music of Bartók has exercised a pervading influence on Lutosławski's musical vocabulary, for example, in the manipulation of intervallic cells; but there is little evidence of any direct influence from the pianism of Bartók's concertos on that of Lutosławski. A less obvious connection could be drawn with the pianism of Chopin, for example, in the use of melodic decoration in the high register drawn from patterns that curl around chromatic notes auxiliary to the supporting harmony (such as at Fig. 64, near the end of the second movement).

Of the connections that might be made, perhaps the most unexpected is with the music of Brahms, although in relation to form rather than content. There is a structural similarity between the chaconne technique used by Lutosławski in the finale of the Piano Concerto and the passacaglia that defines the last movement of Brahms's Fourth Symphony. The short unit of variation, the changing moods between sections, and the cumulative purpose of the whole are all reminiscent of the Brahms model. There is also a formal similarity between the four-movement design adopted by Lutosławski and the scheme of Brahms's Second Piano Concerto, particularly in the placing of the scherzo before the slow movement. One might even detect (or imagine) some traces of Brahms in the treatment of chromatic voice leading in thirds, harmonically thickened by the addition of octave doublings (due to the pianist's hand positioning and the role of the thumbs). But even if one can find tactile and gestural similarities of pianism, it does not necessarily follow that the musical language will convey any aural allusion. Lutosławski's harmony does not observe the diatonic functions that are integral to music of the nineteenth century, and the aesthetics of neo-Romanticism remain anathema to him.

Lutosławski's work on the Piano Concerto during 1987 was punctuated by his attendance at three ceremonies to receive honorary awards: the doctorate of music from the University of Cambridge on 11 June (he also provided a very brief fanfare for brass ensemble for this occasion); the fellowship of the Royal Northern College of Music in Manchester on 7 December; and on 18 December a doctorate from the University of Belfast.[7] Then, after completing the full score of the Piano Concerto on 20 January 1988, Lutosławski turned to the orchestral version of *Partita*, which he finished on 7 April. It is worth noting that the original score of *Partita* carries no dedication, hence the composer was able to dedicate the *concertante* version to Anne-Sophie Mutter, also presenting her with the autograph manuscript.

Soon after the première of the Piano Concerto in Salzburg, Lutosławski and Zimerman repeated the work at the Warsaw Autumn Festival. The programme for this concert on 25 September also included the Third Symphony, and although Lutosławski had already given numerous performances of the work in many different countries this was the first time he had conducted it in Poland. The timing of this gesture was significant. Since the imposition of martial law in 1981, although he remained on the programme committee of the Warsaw Autumn Festival, he had resolutely declined invitations to appear on the podium, in order to maintain solidarity with the artists' boycott of the state media. By

1988, however, the domestic political situation was beginning to change, and arrangements were already being made for the 'Round-Table' talks that would formalise a dialogue between the government and opposition groups.[8]

Between these performances of the Piano Concerto, Lutosławski composed a short piece 'for eleven soloists' as an eightieth birthday present for Elliott Carter (born on 11 December 1908).[9] He completed it on 13 September, and the première was given by the New York chamber ensemble Speculum Musicae, at a concert held in Carter's honour at the Merkin Concert Hall, New York, on 1 December. The Polish title, *Przezrocza*, translates into English as *Slides*, in the photographic sense of 'transparencies'. The main feature of the piece is the way in which the percussion player delivers a *fortissimo* signal (on two bongos and three tom-toms) to mark the divisions between short sections. The analogy here is of the abrupt, noisy change from one slide to another in a projector. The percussionist acts in lieu of a conductor and is positioned facing the ensemble so that the signals will operate visually as well as aurally. Characteristically, Lutosławski plays a little psychological trick with the listener's expectation. Towards the end, where the percussion player gives the tenth signal, still *fortissimo*, one expects another section to begin, but the ensemble does not respond and there are a few seconds of silence. Two more 'false' signals follow, but quieter and slower. The final entry of the percussionist, this time with the whole ensemble playing *fortissimo*, is fast and furious. Lutosławski had played a similar game at the end of the first movement of *Jeux vénitiens*, in which a percussive signal also marks the division between sections.

Although it was not apparent to observers at the time, since completing the Piano Concerto Lutosławski had been at work on a major orchestral piece that eventually realised his ambition to write a Fourth Symphony. Much of the piece was composed in an abbreviated score between 1988 and 1990, and the substance of it therefore predates the *Chantefleurs et Chantefables*. During 1989 he also composed *Interlude* to link *Partita* and *Chain 2*, as well as two short occasional pieces: an orchestral Prelude for the Guildhall School of Music and Drama, first performed in London on 11 May; and an orchestral Fanfare for Lancaster, played at the University of Lancaster on 12 October.[10]

In 1989 the pace of political change in Poland quickened as a result of the epoch-making Round-Table talks between the Communist government and Solidarity representatives, held from 6 February to 5 April. The direct outcome of these difficult negotiations was the round of 'semi-free' democratic elections to the Polish Sejm (Parliament) and Senate held on 4 June 1989. A controversial compromise had been reached whereby not all seats would be contested at once, hence whatever the verdict of the popular vote there would still be a substantial presence of Communist representatives in the Sejm. In the event, Solidarity representatives swept almost all the the seats that they had been allowed to contest, including 99 per cent of the seats in Senate. The political shock-waves of these elections were immediately felt in each of the neighbouring Eastern European states, and the Polish experience acted as the catalyst that activated the 'Year of Revolutions', of which the most potent visual symbol was the opening of the Berlin Wall on 7 November.

Among the reforms carried during 1989 was the restoration of the legitimate name of the Polish state, from its Communist identity as Polska Rzeczpospolita Ludowa (Polish Peoples' Republic), to the independent status of Rzeczpospolita Polska (The Polish Republic) that it had gained from the Treaty of Versailles in 1919. This re-baptism of Poland, which took effect from 1 January 1990, was a gesture of more than ritual significance. The potent national emblem of the crown was also reinstated on flags and insignia bearing the Polish white eagle.

After the installation of the first quasi-democratic government in Poland since 1947, comprising a volatile coalition of Solidarity and Communist members under the leadership of Tadeusz Mazowiecki, Lutosławski was invited to preside over a new forum to be known as the Polish Cultural Council, intended as a committee of the 'great and good'. At this stage, however, he declined to act as its president. Nevertheless, he was supportive of the idea, and after Lech Wałęsa's election to the Polish presidency in December 1990,[11] Lutosławski was invited by the new President's office to join a reconstituted Polish Cultural Council. This time Lutosławski accepted the invitation and also agreed to serve on a new committee for 'Reconciliation between Poles and Jews'.

Among the musical events in Poland during the heady atmosphere of 1990 were two that would not have occurred under the old regime. The first was the inauguration of the Lutosławski International Composers' Competition, held in Warsaw from 14 to 17 January. The second was the visit to Poland of Lutosławski's erstwhile piano-duo partner, Andrzej Panufnik, after thirty-six years of exile. It is conceivable that Panufnik could have visited Poland some years earlier, because his work had been 'rehabilitated' and performed during the 1970s; but he chose not to return while the Communist regime was still in power. Much of the 1990 Warsaw Autumn Festival was devoted to his music, and at the opening concert on 14 September he conducted the European première of his Tenth Symphony.[12]

Chantefleurs et Chantefables

It has already been observed that a feature of Lutosławski's career since 1960 has been the avoidance of duplicating certain types of piece; hence there has tended to be only one *concertante* work for each featured instrument, and only one large-scale work for each type of voice with orchestra. The idea of writing a large-scale piece for soprano and orchestra remained a challenge that awaited a suitable text, not only inspiring a musical setting through strength of poetic images, but also having a shape, a dramatic 'plot' that would lend itself to the composer's treatment of psychology and form. The texts of the *Trois poèmes d'Henri Michaux*, *Paroles tissées* and *Les espaces du sommeil* had all been selected because of their potential for formal development, dramatic growth and culmination. Throughout the early and mid-1980s, Lutosławski searched for another French text that might suit his purposes, but in vain. Eventually, he decided to approach the structure in an entirely different way, setting a cycle of short poems. At this point he turned once more to the verse of Robert Desnos.

In 1944, shortly before he was arrested by the Gestapo for his activities in the French Resistance, Desnos deposited with his publisher in Paris the manuscript for thirty 'Chantefables à chanter sur n'importe quel air' (Song-fables for singing to any tune). Tragically, the poet did not live to see these verses in print.[13] In 1952 a selection of sixty *Chantefables et Chantefleurs*, thirty of each, was published in a limited edition. The complete collection of eighty poems was not published, however, until 1955, when a further twenty 'Chantefleurs' were discovered and added.[14]

The verses are charming nonsense rhymes, in spirit somewhere between Hilaire Belloc and Ogden Nash. Against the background of his abstract concert works composed since 1960, it may appear odd that Lutosławski turned to such light-hearted poetry as his source of inspiration; yet this is not at all out of character. Although the forty-five Children's Songs composed during the late 1940s and throughout the 1950s were written purely as functional pieces, to fulfil commissions from Polish Radio and PWM, they nevertheless display a genuine sympathy for the simplicity of the medium, and reveal a side of the composer that remains open to the enchanting world of a child's imagination (the Iłłakowicz poems that he chose for the Five Songs of 1957 were also taken from a collection of children's verse). From the full set of eighty 'poems for wise children' by Desnos, Lutosławski selected four representing creatures, and five representing flowers:

1. *La Belle-de-Nuit*   (The 'Marvel of Peru')
2. *La Sauterelle*   (The grasshopper)
3. *La Véronique*   (The speedwell)
4. *L'Eglantine,*   (The wild-rose,
   l'Aubépine et la the hawthorn
   Glycine   and the wistaria)
5. *La Tortue*   (The tortoise)
6. *La Rose*   (The rose)
7. *L'Alligator*   (The alligator)
8. *L'Angélique*   (The angelica)
9. *Le Papillon*   (The butterfly)

As individual songs they are inevitably quite short, but the cycle as a whole is far from insubstantial, and lasts some twenty minutes in performance, slightly longer than either *Les espaces* or *Paroles tissées*. The cycle was written with a soprano of light vocal timbre in mind, although not for a particular singer. The songs had already been composed in 1990 when Lutosławski attended a gala recital in the recently renovated Royal Castle in Warsaw, given by the Norwegian soprano, Solveig Kringleborn.[15] Impressed by the lightness and purity of her vocal timbre, Lutosławski decided to request her as soloist for the first performance.

The instrumental requirements are modest by comparison with the large orchestra used for *Les espaces*, and were chosen partly for considerations of balance between soloist and orchestra, but also to suit the resources of smaller ensembles such as the London Sinfonietta. The work is scored for flute, oboe, clarinet (doubling piccolo and bass clarinets), bassoon (doubling contra-bassoon), trumpet, horn, trombone, percussion (timpani, xylophone, xylorimba, glockenspiel, tubular bells, snare drum), harp, piano (doubling celesta), and strings. Vivid use of instrumental tone-colours is one of the most striking features of the song cycle. Certain combinations are typical of Lutosławski: vibraphone, glockenspiel, piano and celesta are used for the nocturnal atmosphere of *La Belle-de-Nuit*; fragmented woodwind motifs and string *pizzicati* for the jumping of the grasshopper; and especially the arpeggiated patterns for woodwind and tuned percussion that represent the fluttering of the butterfly in the last song.

Comparing the *Chantefleurs et Chantefables* with the Iłłakowicz songs, one notices a marked difference in the treatment of harmony and melody, and particularly of the balance between these prime elements. While the earlier set concentrates on harmony, to the extent that it constitutes a study in the composer's methods of building twelve-note chords and chord-aggregates, the later cycle focuses primarily on the melodic dimension. In this respect it continues the process of development that can be traced through *Partita*, *Chain 2*, and the Piano Concerto. Although the Iłłakowicz songs were composed before Lutosławski had adopted techniques of aleatory counterpoint, the Desnos songs could have made full use of such rhythmic effects, but he opted for conventional ensemble co-ordination that assists the projection of line instead of dense harmonic or polyphonic textures.

La Belle-de-Nuit opens with a melodic line played by first and second violins in unison with motorless vibraphone. This line is produced by melodic pairing of semitones and tones ($1 + 2$), but blurred by rhythmic discrepancies between the two violin parts. The effect of this blurring is to establish a difference of aural focus between the instrumental line and the vocal melody. The latter is generated in the opening and closing sections by melodic pairing of major seconds and perfect fourths/fifths ($2 + 5$). Thus a clear distinction is made between both the intervallic character and the texture of these two melodic strands. Example 8 : 8 gives a reduction of the vocal line together with the instrumental countermelody, and also shows a reduction of the harmony in the middle section and at the end of the song. In the closing section, the countermelody slowly winds its way through the violins' upper register, this time joined by celesta. The four-note string chord on which the song comes to rest has a vertically symmetrical pattern of interval-classes $2 + 5$ that matches the character of the vocal line.

In contrast to the lyrical, nocturnal mood of the opening song, *La Sauterelle* depicts the jerky, leaping motion of a grasshopper. This is achieved with fragmented three-note cells of adjacent semitones from the woodwinds, with xylorimba and piano highlighting *pizzicato* chords from the strings. *La Véronique* marks a return to the mood of the first song, although no direct thematic connections are established. It also opens with a rhythmically blurred string line, this time blending with the

EX. 8 : 8   *La Belle-de-Nuit*

harp. The vocal line begins by twisting chromatically through tone/
semitone patterns. Later it becomes more expansive, but still emphasising
similar three-note cells. Much of the vocal line of the strophic fourth
song, *L'Eglantine, l'Aubépine et la Glycine* (Ex. 8 : 9), derives from
melodic pairing of semitones and minor thirds, although the setting of the
second part of each stanza combines 1 + 3 cells with the 2 + 5 pairing
where the poem refers to a bird singing in flight. The contour of the line
shows a gradual ascent to high B♭ within each verse, matched by the end
of the song where the soloist outlines a minor ninth by climbing in minor
thirds (and one major third) from A to B♭. Example 8 : 9 also shows the
accretion of intervals in the accompanying harmony as the voice ascends
to its highpoint. The final chord (E♭,F,G) strongly emphasises E♭ as its
root, thus creating a cadential effect (dominant to tonic) in relation to the
preceding B♭.

EX. 8 : 9   *L'Eglantine, l'Aubépine et la Glycine*

The two humorous songs of the cycle are the fifth and seventh: *La Tortue* and *L'Alligator*. The former begins with a slow, descending semitone motif that, together with plodding *pizzicati* from the strings, subtly mimics the deliberate gait of the tortoise, who remarks that he could imitate the swallows if only he had wings to fly (he also expresses

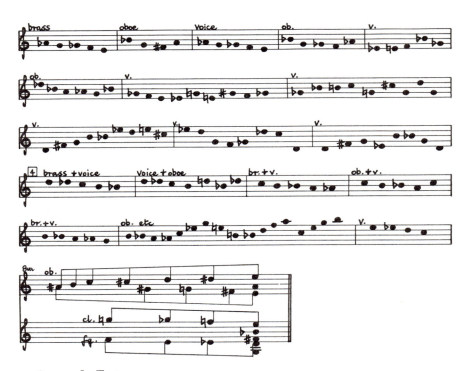

EX. 8 : 10   *La Tortue*

satisfaction that his elegant tortoise-shell waistcoat is cut exactly to his size). The vocal melody of *La Tortue* alternates with linking oboe phrases to form a continuous line (Ex. 8 : 10). The voice's initial five-note falling phrase remains undeveloped on repetition, while the intervening oboe links (of interval pairing 1 + 3) gradually expand and provide motifs for extension and development of the melody. A final, quasi-cadential flourish further extends the oboe line (diverging in contrary motion) to reach top E. The finality of this device is due not to any functional progression (either chordal or melodic) but to its semitone voice-leading.

La Rose, like *La Belle-de-Nuit*, *La Véronique* and *L'Angélique*, inhabits the sound world of Ravel's *Schéhérazade* (particularly the harmony of *Asie*). This is evident at the end, where the sensuous poetic image of 'son parfum m'endort' is accompanied by a minor-seventh chord underpinning the vocal line (note how this G♯ minor-seventh chord is placed above a C major triad as the final harmony). A reduction of the melodic line is shown in Example 8 : 11, together with significant details from the harmony. In the vocal line a falling gesture of semitone and minor third establishes a connection with similar phrase-endings in the slow movement of the Piano Concerto (particularly its conclusion). The song reaches a climax of expressive intensity as the vocal line climbs chromatically to top A.

EX. 8 : 11   *La Rose*

In *L'Alligator*, an apt combination of bass clarinet, bassoon and *pizzicato* cello, playing in irregular metres in the low register, succeed in suggesting the awkward gait of the creature along the mudbanks of the Mississippi. It has already been observed that Lutosławski tended to avoid obvious word-painting in serious vocal works such as *Paroles tissées* and *Les espaces du sommeil*, but here the rationale is entirely different. Intentionally lighthearted, the suggestions of the various creatures' characters and attributes are gently humorous without being unduly burlesqued (and therefore not banal). The implausible scenario, of an alligator addressing his intended (though not entirely unsuspecting) victim in the mode of human speech, is just the kind of situation that would appeal to Lutosławski were he ever to compose an opera. He has often quoted the example of Ravel's *L'enfant et les sortilèges* as his ideal opera, largely because of the surreal nature of Colette's characters, such as the singing teapot, the armchair and the clock. His view that, because it is ridiculous to think of a teapot speaking it is no more ridiculous when the teapot sings, provides a clue to his attitudes towards the personification of the tortoise and the alligator. It would appear that Lutosławski is now unlikely to embark on the composition of an opera, but the *Chantefleurs et Chantefables* give a taste of the kind of surreal images that he might have been tempted to explore.

The penultimate song, *L'Angélique*, is harmonically the warmest and melodically the most lyrically expressive of the set.[16] The vocal line (Ex. 8 : 12) is reminiscent of the end of the Largo theme in the slow movement of the Piano Concerto, particularly the way it eventually subsides onto the final E by means of the semitone and minor third pattern G♯–G–E. Similar 1 + 3 cells can be observed in the melody as it gradually ascends, sequentially, from F♯ to its highpoint on A. The supporting harmony also shows the characteristic sonority of minor thirds and perfect fifths. The final chord, arrived at by semitone voice-leading, is of a similar kind to that first encountered at the end of *Epitaph* (see Ex. 6 : 3), and contains two perfect fifths and a minor third (F♯,C♯,G♯,B).

The final song. *Le Papillon*, is the only one to make use of *ad libitum* playing. There are just three moments when the conductor is required to give a downbeat signalling the beginning of an aleatory section: at the beginning; at the end of the first verse; and just before the end of the song. These short *ad libitum* sections feature rapid, unsynchronised, arpeggiated patterns played by woodwinds, horn, harp, piano and xylorimba. They elaborate a nine-note chord that appears at the beginning and the

EX. 8 : 12   *L'Angélique*

end (at the same pitch level), and is transposed at Fig. 8 (up a minor third) to provide a harmonic, textural and gestural climax to the whole cycle. Although it is not surprising that Lutosławski chose to limit the extent of aleatory procedures in chamber pieces such as *Epitaph*, *Grave* and *Partita*, it comes as a surprise to find such a tiny proportion of an ensemble work devoted to *ad libitum* co-ordination.

In terms of compositional technique, the leading role in *Le Papillon* is taken, not by the vocal line, but by a strong *pizzicato* bass line divided between cellos and double bass.[17] Closely integrated with this melodic and harmonic feature in the low register there is a part for xylorimba that adds short insertions; the rhythmic result is almost perpetual motion in staccato quavers. In the upper register, the woodwinds play arpeggiated figures (similar to the intervallic patterns of the opening chord) that provide perpetual motion in semiquavers. The effect of combining these different rhythmic layers in metred counterpoint is to invest the piece with a fast pace that is due as much to the rapid delivery of changing pitch material as it is to the degree of rhythmic activity. This outcome would not have been possible with aleatory counterpoint.

Although humour is an essential aspect of this song cycle, it is not a feature that one associates with Lutosławski's other mature or late works (with the exception of the finale of the Double Concerto; see Ex. 6 : 5b). To a listener familiar with the *Trois poèmes d'Henri Michaux*, *Paroles tissées* and *Les espaces du sommeil*, it may come as a considerable surprise to find Lutosławski engaging in word-painting such as the irregular metres and motifs used for the lumbering gait of the alligator, or the repeated-note figure that suggests the gnashing of its numerous sharp teeth. But a listener familiar with his earlier children's songs, composed between 1945 and 1960, is likely to recognise in the *Chantefleurs et Chantefables* a return to some elements of the composer's earlier style and to personality traits of his youth.

At the first performance of *Chantefleurs et Chantefables*, given on 8 August 1991,[18] the programme for the Promenade Concert included another of Lutosławski's works to have had its world première in London: the Cello Concerto. The contrast between these works, composed twenty years apart, underlined the degree of refinement that has taken place in his musical language during this period. The intimate, enchanted world inhabited by the Desnos songs could not be at a further remove from the extrovert, confrontational drama that unfolds in the concerto. Yet both represent vital, complementary aspects of the composer's musical persona.

Eleven days after the première of the *Chantefleurs et Chantefables*, a sequence of events began in the Soviet Union that, in an astonishingly short period of time, accomplished the third Russian Revolution of Lutosławski's lifetime.[19] On Christmas Day 1991 the USSR ceased to exist and was succeeded by the CIS (Confederation of Independent States). Although these events did not affect Lutosławski or his family in any direct way, it is nevertheless worth noting (especially because his childhood had been so badly scarred by the loss of his father during the Bolshevik Revolution), that the politics running parallel with his life have turned full circle.

Symphony no. 4

Lutosławski's Fourth Symphony was commissioned by the Los Angeles Philharmonic Orchestra, with whom he gave the first performance, in Los Angeles, on 5 February 1993 (twelve days after his eightieth birthday). Although the full score of the symphony was not completed until the summer of 1992 (the autograph manuscript bears the completion date of

22 August), the intensive period of composition took place between 1988 and 1990. This places the genesis of the work between the Piano Concerto and *Chantefleurs et Chantefables*. Over the intervening two years Lutosławski laboured over the production of the full score, though this work was interrupted by the song cycle and his frequent concert engagements.

It is interesting to compare the dates when Lutosławski's symphonies were written. Whereas a period of nineteen years separated the completion of the First Symphony from the beginning of the Second, and fourteen years elapsed between finishing the Second and beginning intensive work on the Third (excluding the abortive attempt in the early 1970s), Lutosławski started to compose his Fourth Symphony only five years after completing the Third. It has already been noted in Chapter 4 that the application of *ad libitum* techniques after 1960 tended to make Lutosławski's progress with each new work very slow, while the 'least advantageous solutions' to ensemble problems were calculated and solved. This meant that the process of establishing a satisfactory page-image for scores employing *ad libitum* sections was very time consuming. The greater fluency with which Lutosławski produced his pieces of the 1980s, however, can largely be ascribed to the diminishing role of aleatory material, and a consequent easing of notational difficulty. Only fifteen of the eighty pages of the score of the Fourth Symphony are devoted, either entirely or in part, to *ad libitum* co-ordination.

The most obvious difference between the Fourth Symphony and each of the other three is the time-scale over which it operates in performance. Whereas the First, Second and Third all cover a time-span of thirty minutes or more, the Fourth is somewhat shorter (about twenty-two minutes). The listener may have a different experience of the unfolding of thematic ideas across this span.

Lutosławski conceived his Fourth Symphony as a two-movement structure that would function as a kind of Introduction and Allegro. As with the Second and Third, however, it is performed without any break between the sections. The division between the two movements occurs at Fig. 22, and is marked by a decisive change in tempo (from 55 crotchets to 85 dotted crotchets per minute).

Instead of employing for the first movement the scheme of refrains and episodes that he had used for both the Second and Third Symphonies, Lutosławski adopted a form similar to the first section of *Mi-Parti*, where each metred phrase is treated as inconclusive and dissolves into an *ad libitum* section, to be followed by a kind of new beginning (these fresh starts occur at Figs. 6 and 13). Unlike *Mi-Parti*, however, the solo lines that occupy the melodic foreground complement rather than duplicate the harmony.

The symphony opens, not with an introductory movement containing the relaxed, whimsical gestures that characterise many other works by Lutosławski, but with a slow, portentous passage of muted string harmony over which the clarinet develops an expressive solo line. This sombre opening is quite unlike the beginnings of the previous two symphonies, and conveys ideas of thematic and dramatic significance. There is a peculiar psychological effect, as if one is listening to a slow movement and the first movement has been omitted. The decision to begin in this way seems to reveal a darker side of the composer's personality, more akin to the intimate sound world of *Mi-Parti* and *Interlude* than to the extrovert world of the Double Concerto or the Third Symphony.

There is some similarity between this fourteen-bar opening (Ex. 8 : 13) and the first thirteen bars of the slow movement of *Partita*, even though the latter is louder and more assertive. The aural connections between these pieces are established by chromatically shifting chords in the middle register, the tension-building agent of slow, regular pulsation, and by the chord that punctuates the end of each passage (containing a C major triad contradicted by an octave on low C♯). The symphony contains other, melodic similarities to *Partita*, and this is not surprising when one considers that Lutosławski devoted the spring of 1988 to orchestrating the duo version of this earlier work. The style of the opening also evokes the mood of the Largo theme in the slow movement of the Piano Conceto.

The tension created by the opening bars is relaxed at Fig. 3, as regular pulsation gives way to the first aleatory section. The second beginning comes at Fig. 6, but this time with the low pedal note moved up a tone from E to F♯.[20] After only ten bars the tension once more dissolves into *ad libitum* playing. The third beginning, from Fig. 13, is considerably more extended, and develops into an orchestral tutti focused on an increasingly intense unison line carried by the violins. The progress of the movement is arrested by insistent repetition of chords, from the horns, brass and strings before it launches into the last aleatory passage of the first movement. Here the strings merely punctuate the downbeat, leaving woodwind and brass to elaborate, loudly, a vertically symmetrical twelve-note chord (two hexachords of alternate major and minor thirds, separated by a semitone), the first twelve-note chord of the work. The movement ends

EX. 8 : 13   Symphony no. 4, opening

by delivering three equally emphatic, staccato punches of this chord from the whole orchestra, separated by pauses of increasing length. At the point where one expects the same chord to be repeated again the music changes abruptly, and the second movement begins.

The rhythmic momentum of the second movement is carried by a faster basic pulse (*c.*85 dotted crotchets per minute), and by a constant triple metre (in ⅜) subdivided to give almost perpetual motion in motoric semiquaver patterns. Between Figs. 22 and 39 this momentum is broken in only a few places by interventions from the percussion section, but such disruption only serves to emphasise the strength of the underlying pulse. The choice of a triple metre is typical for Lutosławski; his predilection for such pulsation has already been noted in relation to the Concerto for Orchestra. Here the choice of a compound pulse unit further enhances the rhythmic powers of three, and enables the composer to obtain sub-divisions into groups of three and six semiquavers (he also makes much use of syncopated subdivisions into groups of four).

The prime function of the initial stage of the second movement is transitional rather than narrative (to invoke Maliszewski's terminology), but the twelve bars between Figs. 23 and 25 do carry a theme that is implanted in the memory to be recalled later, particularly in the aftermath of the climax. At Fig. 39 the momentum is broken by an *ad libitum* section that begins with a kind of fanfare for three trumpets, before featuring the piano against a babble of bassoons and trombones. The piano plays a succession of *fortissimo* chords in a declamatory way that invites comparison with several passages in the Piano Concerto, such as the solo that precedes the climax of the slow movement, and the accompanied solo that follows the climax of the finale. This is the only place in the symphony where the piano plays such an important obbligato role.

The fast, metred tempo resumes briefly at Fig. 42 before relaxing slightly for the introduction of a string *cantando* beginning at Fig. 43. The strings play in four parts, with the top line intensified by unison doubling of the first and second violins. Harmonically, this idea of potent narrative is static, underpinned by the dissonant sound of a major seventh between basses and cellos (B,A♯); but melodically it develops, climbing chromatically (from A to A). The point at which the ascent ceases is significant, because here Lutosławski consistently avoids duplicating notes between the melody and the supporting harmony. Hence the line can go no further and is obliged to subside. It does so, at Fig. 46, onto a chord that provides a harmonic background for a brief, lyrical flute phrase that recalls the violins' theme from Fig. 23, near the beginning of the movement (the motifs are also reminiscent of the whimsical gestures from the soloist at the end of the first movement of *Chain* 2). The fast tempo returns at Fig. 47, again briefly, before slowing to *lento* for a little interlude for clarinets, supported by bassoons, that plays on the earlier flute phrase. In the Third Symphony such woodwind interludes were treated according to *ad libitum* co-ordination, but here Lutosławski continues to maintain metred control. The rhythm pattern of the clarinet motif then transfers to timpani and is repeated, *pianissimo*, as the work enters a new and more intimate phase.

The ensuing passage that begins at Fig. 52 forms one of the most interesting and memorable episodes of the symphony. Here, Lutosławski appears to engage in a kind of experiment, achieving by conventionally conducted means a harmonic and rhythmic texture that would have been attempted by aleatory means in an earlier work. He begins by introducing a four-note chord (type E) in the top register, played in a rhythmically fragmented manner by piccolo, glockenspiel, a solo violin playing *arco*, the other first violins playing *pizzicato*, and the unpitched addition of a small cymbal. At Fig. 54 he then adds another four-note chord (type F) which becomes the middle harmonic strand of a twelve-note chord-aggregate when the remaining four notes (type G) are added in a lower register at Fig. 55. The middle and low strands are also associated with similar combinations of instrumental tone-colour, although successively lower in pitch: oboe, solo violin II (*arco*), violins II (*pizz*), vibraphone, and a medium sized cymbal; bassoon, solo cello (*arco*), cellos (*pizz*), harp I, and a large cymbal. Example 8 : 14 shows a harmonic reduction of the section from Figs. 53 to 59. The outcome is radically different from the technique of deploying a twelve-note chord-aggregate within an *ad libitum* section. The problem of harmonic stasis, endemic to many of Lutosławski's earlier works that make extensive use of aleatory technique, is here overcome. As a consequence of maintaining metred control over the orchestra the composer is able to regulate not only the rhythmic pulsation but, more significantly, the pace and precise moments of harmonic change. Having combined the component strands of the chord-aggregate, at Fig. 56 Lutosławski begins to thicken the harmonic texture further by introducing an additional strand that reproduces the top one, but doubled an octave below. Similar doubling of the middle and low strands occurs at Figs. 57 and 58, respectively, thus giving a twenty-four-note chord; other instruments join the ensemble with each of these doubled strands.

EX. 8 : 14   Symphony no. 4, harmonic reduction of Figs. 53–9

The most effective aspect of this section is the way the fragmented rhythm patterns of each harmonic strand gradually overlap and interlock in order to create a scintillating texture with perpetual semiquaver motion. The only suitable visual analogy for this aural effect would be with the *pointilliste* technique of painters such as Seurat and Pissarro; yet it is quite different to the compositional *pointillisme* of Webern's orchestral works, where the textures tend to remain sparse. Although its harmonic and rhythmic effects are memorable, the function of the passage from Figs. 52 to 63 is nevertheless transitional, and its purpose is to drive towards the main narrative element of the work at Fig. 64.

At Fig. 59 a foreground element is introduced in stark relief: a trumpet solo that recalls a featured phrase at Fig. 4 in the first movement. This line is cued rather than conducted, and the trio of trombones that follows is played as a polyphonic bundle, also in the aleatory manner. The disruptive nature of these interventions signals impending change, and this begins at Fig. 62 where the main body of strings draws the section to its conclusion with homorhythmic reiteration of a twelve-note chord-aggregate (of type D–J–D). The string harmony then gradually converges onto a powerful unison B♭ which acts as one of the focal points of the work. Here the extended *cantando* theme of the symphony begins.

Whereas the main movement of the Third Symphony moves towards its highpoint with material that is primarily textural and rhythmic, reserving its main thematic impact for the epilogue, in the Fourth Symphony the gradual build-up towards the climax is achieved by melodic and polyphonic means. This is the area of the piece where the centre of gravity lies. The use of a string *cantando* in this way invites comparison with *Livre pour orchestre* and especially *Chain 3*. The latter is perhaps too short a work for the psychology of this feature to be fully appreciated, at least by comparison with the broader canvas of the Fourth Symphony.

The *cantando* unfolds in three stages, the first two of which both rise and fall, while the third simply rises (Ex. 8 : 15). The power of the first stage (Figs. 64–8) derives from its unison delivery by all the violins together with the violas. The second stage (Fig. 68 until the third bar of Fig. 71) divides into two lines with a countermelody positioned below the main theme so that only interval-classes 2, 4 and 5 occur between them. Thus a distinctive harmonic character is maintained. The third stage (to Fig. 73) subdivides into three lines: the main theme and two subsidiary parts.

Lutosławski structures the melody sequentially (Ex. 8 : 16). The first stage (Ex. 8 : 16a) ascends through three phrases each containing only rising major seconds, a falling perfect fourth and a rising minor third (a falling semitone links the phrases by three-note, tone/semitone cells). There is a process of growth through each stage that determines its gradual ascent; this is achieved by the number of rising major seconds,

EX. 8 : 15   Symphony no. 4, *cantilena* Figs. 64–73

first three, then four and five with each successive phrase. Once the line has reached its apex it falls through three whole-tone scale segments which also grow from three to four, then five notes. The second stage (Ex. 8 : 16b) is generated in a similar way, although starting a tone higher, on middle C, and with the top line shadowed by the supporting part. The third stage (Ex. 8 : 16c) also rises in the same way, starting from D, but this time it does not subside.

EX. 8 : 16   Symphony no. 4, reduction of *cantilena*

While the *cantando* line unfolds through three stages it is accompanied by two other elements in order to produce counterpoint in three rhythmic layers. The slowest of these layers is the *cantando* itself. In the low register there is a faster, *pizzicato* line in quavers, played by cellos and basses, that dovetails with staccato chords from the woodwind and brass. In the upper register there is a strand running in semiquavers, played by flutes and oboes in alternation with various percussion instruments and the harp. Obviously, none of this could have been achieved by aleatory means, because it was necessary for the composer to regulate precisely the rapid delivery of pitch material. The idea for the texture of three-part counterpoint in different rhythmic layers came to Lutosławski via J. S. Bach, in whose music he found a model for this type of procedure. He adopted a similar technique for *Le Papillon*, the last of the *Chantefleurs et Chantefables*, but the *cantando* of the Fourth Symphony was actually written earlier and forms the prototype for the song.

Just as the *cantando* had begun by focusing on a powerful unison, so it ends with a *fortissimo* middle C from the strings at Fig. 73. There then follows a harmonically dense tutti carrying a developed recapitulation of the first string theme that appeared at Fig. 43. At the point where the orchestral texture simplifies and this theme becomes fully exposed, with trumpets doubling the violins from Fig. 80, the pace accelerates as the melodic line and its supporting parts converge. The destination of this process of convergence is an extremely powerful unison A♭ at Fig. 82, played *fortissimo* by all the strings (except basses) doubled by horns, trumpets and trombones. Instead of maintaining the faster speed as we are driven to the climax of the work, Lutosławski slows the tempo slightly to give an *allargando* effect as the unison line approaches the climax at Fig. 85.

Unlike the Third Symphony, where a climax is attempted but not fully attained, the Fourth reaches a decisive moment of culmination: a collective *fortissimo* on a ten-note chord consisting mainly of superimposed perfect fourths and tritones (thus rich in major sevenths). The chord is still metred and swells to the point where the conductor signals for it to end, leaving a *pianissimo* four-note chord. In the Third Symphony the most potent melodic idea came after the abortive climax, in an epilogue. Here, in the Fourth, the aftermath presents a series of wistful melodic gestures, played by solo violins, that seem to convey a sense of disappointment rather than fulfilment. These phrases are related to the first theme of the second movement, introduced at Fig. 23 and briefly recalled at Figs. 46 and 51. The intimate setting of these solo lines, particularly the delicate support given by *pianissimo* tremolos on the vibraphone and marimba, is also reminiscent of some moments in the slow movements of the Double Concerto and *Chain 2*.

A fast coda ends the symphony. It begins with a *pizzicato* line for cellos at Fig. 92, and gains momentum through the use of motoric triplet patterns. A loud, staccato twelve-note chord-aggregate (type D–J–D) is reached at Fig. 96, and is repeated by the whole orchestra in a composed rhythmic accelerando that drives to a quasi-cadential flourish. In terms of pitch focus, the symphony finishes as it began, rooted to E (the final harmony is an extended E major triad with major seventh and sharp eleventh – E, B, G♯ , A♯ , D♯). But in terms of mood there is a world of difference between the sombre way the work opened and the spirit of exuberance with which it ends.

It is inevitable that the Fourth Symphony will be compared with Lutosławski's previous symphonies, especially the Third. There are certainly interesting comparisons to be made, such as the varied treatments of a two-movement form; but there are also significant areas of contrast, such as the different amounts of aleatory material. Although the Third Symphony is typical of the late works in showing a reduction in the amount of *ad libitum* co-ordination used (by comparison with the Second Symphony, for example), there is still a substantial proportion of the work composed in this way. The Fourth Symphony shows an even greater reduction in the extent of aleatory procedures. This change is an effect rather than a cause, and has been brought about by Lutosławski's increasing concentration on the melodic dimension of his musical language.

The Fourth Symphony appears to be a more homogeneous work than the Third. The latter's long gestation, from the initial sketches in the early 1970s to the final period of composition ten years later, signified Lutosławski's search for a suitable relationship between the symphonic medium and his own technique. By the time he came to the Fourth, however, these problems had already been resolved, and the elements of his late style were securely in place. Consequently he was apparently able to proceed fairly quickly and encountered no major obstacles (although an early draft of the first movement was deemed unsatisfactory and discarded). The Fourth Symphony, therefore, lacks the hybrid quality of the Double Concerto or the Third Symphony.

If one tries to summarise Lutosławski's overall achievement as a symphonist, one must face the conundrum that, for a composer whose essential aesthetics were shaped by the Franco-Russian tradition of Debussy and Stravinsky, it is surprising that he chose to work in the symphonic medium at all. Several of the composers whom he most admired are often held to represent an alternative, non-symphonic, or in some cases anti-symphonic tradition. But this would be to ignore the peculiar dichotomy, in Lutosławski's case, between the group of influences concerning style and language on the one hand, and those relating to drama and form on the other hand. It has already been noted that this separation manifested itself very early in his career, and that his interest in the music of Albert Roussel was primarily as a result of what he saw as the reconciliation between a French approach to harmony as colour (rather than function) and a Germanic approach to form. Lutosławski's opinion that Roussel was 'a kind of French Brahms of the twentieth century' tells us much, not only about the influences on him during the period when the First Symphony was composed, but also about his subsequent approach to the symphonic medium.

The 'formalist' accusation raised against the First Symphony was prompted by malevolence and tells us more about the time when it was written than about the piece itself. But if we consider in broader musical terms the notion of 'elevation of form over content' (and if we jettison the heavy political baggage carried by the concept of formalism), this must surely bring us to the Second Symphony. In that work the form itself is the content; the content is the form. But this could not be said of either the Third or the Fourth symphonies, in which the melodic dimension is sufficiently focused for the music to operate as a more traditionally symphonic discourse based on the treatment of theme.

The Fourth Symphony was the last of Lutosławski's works to receive its première during his lifetime. But neither the symphony nor *Subito*, his final completed piece, was intended to be final.

Subito

During the spring of 1992, when he was still putting the finishing touches to the full score of the symphony, Lutosławski devoted some time to the composition of a short piece for violin and piano, to be used as the test piece for a competition scheduled for the autumn of 1994. *Subito* was composed at the request of Joseph Gingold, founding artistic director of the Indianapolis International Violin Competition (and former leader of the Cleveland Orchestra), and was commissioned with funds provided by the World Life and Accident Association of Richmond, Indiana. Once again, the composer chose not to receive his fee personally, but in this case asked the organisers of the competition to arrange for the entire amount to be paid direct, as a scholarship, to a young Polish composer then studying in the United States.

As is customary in such cases, where a new piece is to be used as a qualifying test for competitors, the terms of the commission stipulated that there must be a complete embargo on the work until after the competition, a restriction which extended to both of the publishers involved, PWM and Chesters. As a consequence of this embargo the work could not be published or performed until after it had been played by each of the competition's sixteen semi-finalists (the semi-finals took place over four days, from 16 to 19 September 1994).

The harmonic and melodic style of *Subito* is reminiscent of the first and final movements of *Partita*. Its mood is that of a scherzo, a playful tease of the listener's expectations effected through sudden, unexpected twists and turns. The title ('suddenly') is suggestive of the mood of changeability that results from the frequent, abrupt changes of rhythm, dynamic, and mode of attack.

In some respects the form of the four-minute piece is similar to *Epitaph*; each contains a recurring device with intervening episodes. Both pieces also observe the principle whereby the repeated idea contracts on repetition, while the successive episodes grow. But although they share these general features, the actual musical content is quite different. Whereas in *Epitaph* (and *Grave*) the refrains and episodes are defined and contrasted by means of identification with particular melodic interval-class pairings, *Subito* exploits sudden changes of performance gesture rather than systematic interval techniques. As we would expect, the piece is goal-orientated and drives towards a highpoint. The latter comes towards the end of the fourth episode, where the violin line reaches a high, ecstatic trill (on G♯) extending across thirteen bars. It is significant to note that this climax, in common with the rest of the piece, is conventionally metred; aleatory techniques are nowhere to be found.

Subito does not break new ground, either in terms of its structure or its harmonic, melodic or rhythmic style. It does demonstrate, however, that Lutosławski was more interested in continuing to explore the possibilities opened up by the style and technique of *Partita* than in revisiting the sound world of *Epitaph* or *Grave*. In any case, the sombre mood of those pieces reflects their function as memorial tributes, and the basic intention of *Subito* was to create a piece of vigour and virtuosity, exuberant rather than intense. There is one more intriguing aspect of *Subito* which establishes a curious parallel with the original, duo version of *Partita*. Both are chamber pieces for violin and piano conceived and completed while the composer was also working on a concertante piece for violin and orchestra. It has already been noted in previous chapters that each of the late chamber pieces was either subsequently turned into a concertante piece (i.e. *Grave* and *Partita*), or is closely related to a separate concertante work (i.e. *Epitaph* in relation to the Double Concerto, *Partita* in relation to both *Chain 2* and the Piano Concerto). Although it is not apparent from Lutosławski's catalogue of completed works, *Subito* was part of the same syndrome, whereby each chamber piece acted as a kind of compositional study for the bigger piece which followed.

Not long after completing the full score of the Fourth Symphony at the end of August, Lutosławski began to prepare himself for the task of conducting the première. It may seem strange to imagine him having to 'learn' his own piece, but he invariably approached the work of conducting in this way, almost as if he were performing music that he had not written.

Although the première of the symphony was not scheduled until February 1993, his work in preparing for this performance was helped greatly by having an opportunity to 'test' his realisation of the piece in a series of rehearsals in Katowice with the Polish Radio Symphony Orchestra. These were held in closed session over a three-day period just before Christmas (21–23 December) and they resulted in a studio performance which was recorded and stored for use at some time after the official, public première in Los Angeles.

1993 was an exceptionally busy (and exhausting) one for Lutosławski and his wife as they travelled all over the world, including Europe, North America and Japan, in order to fulfil a large number of conducting engagements and to receive various prizes and honours. Even though Lutosławski always professed that he attached no importance to the celebration of his birthday (preferring to feel that he was invited to conduct for purely musical reasons, rather than in connection with any kind of marketing exercise), there was to be no escaping the fuss made in his eightieth birthday year. In Poland his birthday was marked by a broadcast concert of his works played by the Polish Radio Symphony Orchestra from Katowice, but Lutosławski could not be present as he was committed to long-standing engagements in the United States. His birthday, on 25 January, was spent in San Francisco, where he had been invited to conduct a series of concerts with the San Francisco Symphony Orchestra. He and his wife then made the short journey to Southern

California for the première of the Fourth Symphony, which he conducted with the Los Angeles Philharmonic Orchestra on 5 February (repeated on 6th and 7th). He then flew to England for the 'Lutosławski Live' festival of his music in Manchester from 12 to 18 February, promoted by the BBC in association with the Royal Northern College of Music (of which he had been made an Honorary Fellow in December 1987), and the music department of Manchester University, with performances given by the BBC Philharmonic Orchestra and the London Sinfonietta. He participated in another retrospective festival in Paris during the first week of March, under the title 'Portrait de Lutosławski', and this was followed immediately by concerts in Helsinki.

The next visit, to Strasbourg from 19 to 22 April, combined concerts with receipt of the 'galet' medal of the Council of Europe (he had already received an honorary doctorate from the University of Strasbourg in 1990). In May he returned to Paris in order to serve on the jury of the Dutilleux Competition for composers. He then travelled to Stockholm to receive an award of very considerable financial value (one million Swedish crowns): the Polar Prize for Music, administered by the Swedish Royal Academy of Music on behalf of the Music Award Foundation established and endowed by Stig Anderson (producer of popular music, including the Swedish group ABBA). This was presented to him by King Carl Gustav XVI of Sweden at a ceremony held in the Swedish Royal Academy of Music on 18 May (the citation was read by Elisabeth Söderström). He returned once more to London to perform with the London Sinfonietta, and within a few hours was back in Warsaw on 23 May for an invitation concert of his works given in Studio S1 of Polish Radio. The programme for this broadcast included the first performance in Poland of the Fourth Symphony (and thus also the European première).[21]

June was a month for which Lutosławski invariably declined concert invitations, preferring to reserve this time for an annual holiday with his stepson and his family; 1993 was no exception. Hence the composer was unable to be present for the Italian première of several of his chamber pieces at the Festival Pontino held at the mediaeval Caetani Castle at Sermoneta, south of Rome.[22] An added significance of this concert on 4 June, however, was the world première (by Roland Diry of the Ensemble Modern, based in Frankfurt-am-Main) of a short piece for solo clarinet by Elliott Carter, *Gra*, composed in honour of Lutosławski's eightieth birthday, and thus reciprocating the gesture made by Lutosławski in 1988 with *Przezrocza* (*Slides*).

249

There were to be only three more concert engagements which Lutosławski was able to fulfil. On 27 August he conducted the Fourth Symphony with the BBC Symphony Orchestra (billed as the 'European première') in the series of Promenade Concerts at the Royal Albert Hall.[23] One month later, on 25 September, he conducted the closing concert of the 36th Warsaw Autumn Festival, in a programme devoted entirely to his music: Symphony no. 1, *Les espaces du sommeil* (with the baritone soloist François Le Roux), *Chain 3* and Symphony no. 4, with the Warsaw Philharmonic Orchestra. The Polish Composers' Union later issued a compact disc recording of this programme under the title 'Lutosławski: His Last Concert'. This was not quite true, although the Warsaw concert was to be his last in Poland and in Europe. The following month he visited Canada, and there, in Toronto on 24 October, he conducted what subsequently proved to be his final concert. The programme was another substantial one, this time consisting entirely of late works: *Chain 1*, *Slides*, *Chantefleurs et Chantefables*, *Partita*, *Interlude* and *Chain 2*. While in Canada he also received yet another doctorate of music *honoris causa*, this time from MacGill University in Montreal, on 27 October.

When the composer and his wife made their last journey together, to Japan, there was still no indication of any deterioration in the composer's health or any suggestion of the tragic sequence of events that would soon overtake both of them. He had been invited to Kyoto for a ten-day period (7–17 November) in order to receive the prestigious Kyoto Prize awarded by the Inamori Foundation. The prize took the form of a gold medal and a very substantial sum of money (fifteen million Yen), and was awarded on 11 November to three laureates representing different areas of achievement: Lutosławski received the prize in the category for Creative Arts and Moral Sciences; the other awards were for Advanced Technology and Basic Sciences.

On returning from Japan Lutosławski was suffering from fatigue, which did not seem surprising in view of the strenuous schedule he had accepted for that year. He made an appointment with his physician in Warsaw for a check-up, and this resulted in his admission, early in December, to the hospital of the Ministerstwo Spraw Wewnętrznych (Ministry of the Interior) in Emil Plater Street, for what was expected to be only minor skin surgery (zabieg), in order to investigate a growth under his left arm. An apparently benign growth was removed and sent for pathological tests. At this stage (and later) his admission to hospital was kept a closely guarded secret and no visitors were allowed. He was re-admitted to hospital for a second operation on 15 December, and then returned home once more two days before Christmas, whereupon he seemed to recover.

1994 began badly for Lutosławski. By the end of the first week of the new year his condition deteriorated as his system became progressively weaker. By this time he knew that the growth under his arm had not, in fact, been benign, and that cancer had begun to spread rapidly throughout his body. He was greatly touched, however, by news received via a telephone call from President Wałęsa's Office at the Belvedere Palace, informing him that on 19 January he had been awarded Poland's highest civil or military honour, the Order of the White Eagle. This order, which, significantly, was not awarded during the communist period, is in the personal gift of the President, and Lutosławski was only the second recipient, after Pope John Paul 11.[24] Because of his illness, Lutosławski was unable to receive the order in person.

Another accolade followed only two days later. In a ceremony at the Royal Albert Hall in London on 21 January, the present author received on his behalf the 1994 Classical Music Award for the best composition (of 1993), for the Fourth Symphony. Although he had requested that a minimum amount of public fuss be made about his condition, and had suggested that the short proxy-acceptance speech should convey a positive message that he was in the process of making a good recovery, this was the habitual smoke-screen of a man who had always valued and maintained privacy in personal matters such as health. Beneath this layer of civilised forms Lutosławski was already facing the private truth. He spent his eighty-first birthday at home, not in hospital, but there was no cause for celebration and his physician was called to the house in the evening. Lutosławski was once again re-admitted to the MSW hospital in Warsaw, where, in the company of his wife, he died at 10pm on Monday 7 February.[25]

He had expressed the wish to be cremated, and after this had been carried out, a simple funeral service was held on Wednesday 16 February at the Church of St Karol Boromeusz in Powązki cemetery, Warsaw. His ashes were then interred in sector 2, an area of the cemetery (by the corner of Powązkowska and Okopowa Streets) largely devoted to other distinguished musicians of his own generation. His grave is immediately adjacent to the tomb of his friends, the conductor Witold Rowicki and his wife, and close to the graves of other friends and colleagues including the critic Stefan Jarociński, and the composers Kazimierz Serocki and Tadeusz

Baird (in sector I). Although Lutosławski's family had carried out his wishes that the funeral should be private and modest, and they had strongly resisted all attempts for the occasion to be turned into a public affair of national mourning, nevertheless about two hundred people, from Poland and abroad, attended to pay their last respects. Two days before the funeral a representative of President Wałęsa had briefly visited Danuta Lutosławska at home to present her with the composer's Order of the White Eagle, consisting of a citation, the insignia and legitimacja. During the burial ceremony the Order was displayed on a velvet cushion, held by a single, uniformed soldier standing by the graveside. The whole occasion was one of private grief rather than public commemoration, and none present was more deeply stricken than the composer's devoted widow, who was heard to remark: 'Szczęśliwa Rowicka, że umarła zaraz po mężu' (How happy for Rowicka that she died straight after her husband).[26] This was to be an uncanny premonition of her own destiny.

9
Epilogue

When the text of the first edition of this book was completed Lutosławski was still alive. He appeared to be in good health and was accepting concert engagements well into the future. He was still composing. It was therefore inappropriate for me to try to present the kind of final assessment of his career and creative achievement that would only be possible some time after his death. No one, least of all the composer himself, had expected the end to come at the time and in the way that it did. Before attempting such assessment, however, it is necessary for me to continue the narrative a little beyond the composer's death.

Inevitably, the experience of nursing and losing her husband was a devastating blow for Danuta Lutosławska. They had been inseparable throughout their married life, and in the 'Indian summer' of their later years, they almost always travelled together and shared all aspects of his career. It had been evident for many years, to those close to them, that neither could contemplate outliving the other.

In the weeks that followed the composer's death, Danuta Lutosławska isolated herself at home, accepting only the support and company of her immediate family (her son, daughter-in-law and granddaughters), and avoiding contact with friends or acquaintances from the world of music who might intensify her grief by reminding her of her husband. Although she was undoubtedly acutely grief-stricken, she nevertheless kept busy. She was able to achieve some degree of solace by engaging in therapeutic, but nonetheless highly essential, practical tasks, such as sorting through her husband's papers, manuscripts and final sketches, so as to leave his affairs in an orderly state. For example, she systematically made copies of all his final sketches, before sending the originals to Paul Sacher in order to complete the Lutosławski Collection held by the Sacher Foundation's archive of music manuscripts in Basel (in accordance with an agreement made by Lutosławski in 1990).[1]

Although her family tried to persuade her to stay with them in Oslo, and to leave – for some time, at least – the sad atmosphere of the house in Żoliborz, she resolutely refused to leave Warsaw. Thus she maintained a vigil at home for the eleven weeks which separated her husband's death from her own, most of this time (day and night) spent in the large L-shaped study which she had designed for him twenty-five years before. It was there, in that room, that Danuta Lutosławska suffered a heart attack on the morning of Saturday 23 April. An ambulance was called and she was taken to the same hospital (MSW in Emil Plater Street) where she had shared her husband's last moments. She died there at 3pm, aged eighty-three. Like her husband, she was cremated, and then her ashes were interred with his in Powązki cemetery on Friday 29 April.[2]

It is such a well-worn and sentimentalised cliché to observe that someone 'died of a broken heart' that I feel I should resist explaining the cause of death in this way. But in her case it was absolutely true. Theirs was a genuine love story spanning fifty years, and if this book were intended to be a personalised biography (which it is not), then one would devote much space to the relationship between the composer and his wife. They were certainly aware that, at some point after their deaths, this most intimate aspect of their lives might well be invaded by the investigations of biographers, and therefore they agreed to destroy their letters to each other. It is not that they had anything sinister or embarrassing to hide, but simply that they valued privacy in their personal lives and realised that it would have to be protected.

I visited Danuta Lutosławska several times during those last few weeks. The first time was to deliver the bronze statuette which I had received on the composer's behalf at the Classical Music Awards in London. I also handed her a copy of the first edition of this book.[3] She received both items briskly yet graciously, but we did not discuss her husband; there was no need to do so, and I had no wish to provoke additional distress. On the subsequent occasions, however, she invited me to see the composer's final sketches (taken from his desk and his piano), on which he had been working until shortly before his death. Among the many pages of sketches outlining ideas for vertical and horizontal pitch organisation, there were several bundles of pages encapsulating ideas for a violin concerto which he had been composing for Anne-Sophie Mutter.

The final sketches amount to some sixteen bundles, containing music manuscript sheets (cut down to half-size, as was his custom) together with some ideas notated on plain or graph paper.[4] The overwhelming majority of these sketches is devoted to pitch organisation, and it would appear that he was still collecting ideas that could be used for several different projects, including the orchestral medium. Of the sketches that contain specific indications, such as instrumentation, the most highly developed are those for the violin concerto.

It is not known what design Lutosławski had in mind for the concerto, and there is no explicit reference to the number or order of movements. But there are three sections (perhaps movements): one is marked Presto (initially), and could represent the first movement of a three-movement scheme; another appears to be a slow movement, although the tempo marking is not shown; and a third is headed 'Danza' (perhaps a finale?). The latter is notated with the rhythmic structure of the solo part on plain, rather than music manuscript paper, and shows an outline of the melodic contours. But it is not clear which of the many sketches of pitch material relate to this section. The sketches for the other two sections are notated on music manuscript paper, partly in short score, but with some passages scored more fully, for subdivided strings and brass. (Taking into account all the sketches for the concerto, it would appear that Lutosławski was planning his instrumentation for the full symphonic complement of triple-woodwind/brass, four horns etc., and thus for larger resources than either *Chain 2* or the orchestral version of *Partita*.) In view of the fact that Lutosławski's last few works show a decline in the application of aleatory technique, it is also worth observing that the sketches for the violin concerto suggest that *ad libitum* co-ordination might have played as important a role as in the first and third movements of *Chain 2*.

The Presto movement begins with a loud stroke on a tuned gong which sets in motion a chromatic line in fast semiquavers (played by strings), leading to an aleatory section in which the brass predominate. The solo violin part then enters with a line marked appassionato (Ex. 9 : 1). The gestures are rhapsodic, with the orchestra (strings and brass at this point) accompanying the soloist, colla voce, until the gesture changes from appassionato to furioso. The style is similar to that of *Chain 2*, and this is not surprising since Lutosławski was drawing much of his inspiration from Anne-Sophie Mutter's performances of that work.[5]

Example 9 : 2 shows the solo violin line for what appears to be intended as the slow movement of the concerto, together with the harmonic support which the composer had notated only for the opening and closing phrases. Among the bundle of related sketches are many with details of chords that were presumably intended for the rest of the movement, but the cryptic nature of the notation is such that it is unclear how the vertical and horizontal dimensions of this jigsaw would be put together. The mere fact that he was able to sketch in this way, defining

EX. 9 : 1   Solo line from sketches for violin concerto: appassionato

the melodic dimension on its own, for a whole section or movement, is in stark contrast to his manner of working during most of the 1960s and 1970s, but it is similar to his approach in the *Chantefleurs et Chantefables*.

Familiar hallmarks of Lutosławski's style and technique are present. For example, the minor ninth interval between the first note in the violin line, and the sustained middle-C♯ at the top of the accompanying chord. The melodic idea is very simple: merely the repetition of a descending phrase that is gradually extended. The method of extension shows Lutosławski's characteristic preference for odd numbers (a constant aim in his approach to rhythm and phrasing was to avoid or to break the powers of 2. Thus the melodic line is extended downwards, by sequential repetition, increasing the number of crotchets from 3 to 5 and then 7). The decorative links in this phrasing (the demi-semiquaver patterns) are also in groups of 5 and 7.

EX. 9 : 2   Solo line from sketches for violin concerto: slow movt

It must be stressed that Lutosławski left strict instructions to the literary executors of his estate that no attempt should be made to produce 'completed' versions from any of the final sketches.[6] In any case, it would not be possible to establish a credible version for performance, because there are too many unknown factors. But even though the sketches for the violin concerto must remain as fragments they serve to confirm the importance of *Chain 2* as a touchstone for the works of Lutosławski's final decade.

Assessment of Lutosławski's creative achievement must inevitably consider the complex interlocking network of influences on him. Most of the influences on Lutosławski are now clear: Debussy (general approach to harmonic sonority); Ravel (can be heard in the harmony of the Piano Sonata of 1934, and again in late works such as the Piano Concerto and *Chantefleurs et Chantefables*); Szymanowski (an over-rated influence, less significant than Ravel); early Stravinsky (heard in early works such as the Symphonic Variations); Roussel (affecting aspects of form in the First Symphony); Prokofiev (can be seen in the wartime woodwind canons and interludes, and heard in various parody marches); Bartók (a pervading influence from the 1940s onwards, affecting intervals, goal-directed form, and placing of climax); Cage (an influence of ideas rather than music, conceptual rather than compositional, but acting as the catalyst for Lutosławski's adoption of chance procedures); Brahms (aspects of form); Varèse (aspects of sound texture); Chopin (chromatic harmony and voice-leading); Haydn and Beethoven (form rather than language, and including psychological principles of expectation and surprise).

There are also other composers whose work suggests a connection with the music of Lutosławski, but from whom there may have been no direct influence. The case of Berg is a curious one. Lutosławski expressed a certain lack of sympathy with the post-Romantic aesthetic and hybrid style of Berg, and yet there are some interesting similarities; for example, the deployment of carefully constructed twelve-note chords (e.g., the 'Todesschrei' chord in *Lulu*, which is almost vertically symmetrical and contains only three classes of interval – 1, 5 and 6; and the melodically expressive use of the kind of curling three-note cells of semitone/tone which are also associated with Bartók). Lutosławski certainly knew some of Berg's music from his student days, and recalled hearing Louis Krasner perform the Violin Concerto in Warsaw, in 1936, shortly after its première.

Comparison with Andrzej Panufnik is also an intriguing issue, not only because of their close association as fellow students at the Warsaw Conservatory before the war, but also because of their close collaboration during the war. There are clear similarities in some aspects of compositional technique, for example in the habitual manipulation of small intervallic cells; but this does not necessarily mean that one influenced the other. Instead, it reveals their common debt to Bartók, from whose music they each learned so much. Panufnik remains, unfortunately, a little known and hitherto undervalued figure, as much in his adopted country, England, as in Poland. In due course his career and reputation will inevitably be reassessed and this process may well shed further light on significant similarities between Panufnik and Lutosławski.[7]

When I first proposed to Lutosławski, in the mid-1980s, the idea of writing a detailed study about his compositional technique, I was pleased to receive his co-operation, but I was also surprised to learn that he had, for many years, considered trying to write something himself, comparable to Messiaen's *Technique de mon langage musical*. He explained to me that he had felt constrained from doing so for two reasons: firstly, because of an inherent resistance to producing something that could be regarded (and used, or misused) as a compositional 'system'; secondly, because he was constantly adding to his procedures and refining his methods, so there was never a time (until after *Chain 2*) when he felt he might be able either to codify his technique or explain his language.

There are more fundamental differences than similarities between Lutosławski's music (and aesthetics) and that of Messiaen, yet it must be acknowledged that Lutosławski had a very high regard for Messiaen, mainly because of his sensitivity to harmony (this, it must be remembered, was during an era when concern for harmony was often considered old-fashioned). But Lutosławski's respect for Messiaen should not be mis-construed and taken as justification for equating Lutosławski's technique of horizontal interval-class pairing with the modal technique of Messiaen; the two are not comparable.[8]

A more interesting, and more revealing avenue to explore in relation to Lutosławski and Messiaen, is to compare the ways in which they have each influenced others. Perhaps Messiaen's most potent influence has been in the field of rhythm. His modal, harmonic/melodic language is so distinctive, and so personal, that it tends to discourage imitation. Lutosławski has also had a strong influence in the rhythmic field, and his *ad libitum* technique has been very widely imitated. Yet the risks (of stylistic over-dependence) involved in adopting Lutosławski's techniques of aleatory polyphony are just as great as the risks in adopting Messiaen's techniques of modal harmony. It remains to be seen whether it will be possible for others to build on Lutosławski's achievements in the field of pitch organisation (as he, in turn, built on the example of Bartók) whilst still maintaining stylistic independence and originality.

Elliott Carter is another of Lutosławski's composer contemporaries who has made equally significant advances in the fields of pitch and rhythmic organisation. Although they differ in their approach to rhythm, there are significant similarities in some of their methods of pitch organisation. These similarities concern not only the use of twelve-note chords, but also the characteristic procedure of subdividing twelve notes into complementary pitch sets (often assigned to, and identified with, particular instruments or instrumental groups). It is not clear whether these connections indicate direct lines of influence, or whether each composer evolved his methods independent of the other. It is clear, however, that Lutosławski and Carter had mutual respect, even admiration, for each other's work, and this is confirmed by the gestures of genuine friendship shown in recognition of their respective eightieth birthdays; in 1988 Lutosławski composed *Slides* for Carter (the only living composer to whom he ever dedicated a piece); and Carter returned the compliment in 1993 by composing *Gra* for Lutosławski.[9] Apart from Carter, the other composer for whom he had a very high regard was György Ligeti. It is perhaps not coincidental that when Lutosławski returned to Louisville in 1986, as a member of the jury for the Grawemeyer Award (and former laureate), that year's prize went to Ligeti.

Lutosławski's creative achievement is obviously defined by an understanding both of the progress of his career, and, above all, of each individual piece. The question of influences on him is a primary concern and forms an integral part of that understanding. Comparison with his composer contemporaries is also an interesting issue, but only as a secondary consideration, tangential to the main purpose of this book. In any case, there are other means of comparison. One of my own tests is to draw an analogy between composers and writers, in order to establish if the majority of a particular composer's work corresponds to one (or more) of four basic types: a poet, evoking images in short, lyric forms (like Chopin); a philosopher, provoking thought by means of only a few words (like Webern); a dramatist, pacing events over a time span (like Brahms); or a novelist, narrating the progress of an epic (like Mahler). (Some composers seem to fulfil the requirements of all four categories; Beethoven, for example). Like all absurd over-simplifications this group of analogies lays itself open to criticism, yet it does sometimes expose a valid parallel.

According to these criteria, Lutosławski was rarely a novelist, and certainly not on an epic scale (his music tends to be fairly concise, and does not have the long-winded, discursive quality of an epic novel). He was not really a philosopher, except perhaps in a tightly argued piece like *Musique funèbre* (but even here the analogy is not convincing, because the piece is as dramatic as it is philosophical). He was occasionally a poet, for example, in miniatures such as *Epitaph* and the Iłłakowicz songs (perhaps also in *Paroles tissées*). But, judged on the majority of his works, he seems overwhelmingly to have been a dramatist.

The dramatic quality of works such as the Cello Concerto, the Second Symphony, and *Les espaces du sommeil*, is self-evident, but the underlying concern for pacing events through real performance time is common to nearly all his mature compositions, and even to several of the earlier ones. Lutosławski's treatment of music as abstract drama developed as a combination of inclination, influence and experience. The experience of working regularly in the theatre, over a period of some fifteen years or so, gave Lutosławski an intimate knowledge of the dramatist's art. The strongest influence was undoubtedly exerted by Maliszewski's ideas on the psychology of form, and the spectre of his teacher looms large over the formulation of Lutosławski's ideas on the treatment of large-scale forms. Neither the influence nor the experience would have had such a potent effect, however, had it not been for some natural inclination.

Another way of testing our assessment of Lutosławski's creative output can be to distinguish between two, polarised but complementary characters: the introvert and the extrovert. Silence and solitude are essential to enable a composer to inhabit the introverted, conceptual world from which creative ideas develop, and Lutosławski was no exception in this respect. But it must also be remembered that throughout his career he engaged in various types of performance activity (in his youth as violinist, for many years as pianist, and in his maturity as conductor). In particular works there is often a balance between the kinds of approach, but in other cases one side seems to predominate. Works exemplifying Lutosławski's strongly gestured, extrovert character include the Concerto for Orchestra, the Cello Concerto, the Double Concerto, the Piano Concerto and *Subito*. Works exemplifying his moody, introverted character include *Musique funèbre* (and the other memorial pieces, *Epitaph* and *Grave*), the String Quartet, *Paroles tissées*, the Second Symphony, *Mi-Parti*, *Les espaces du sommeil*, *Chain 3*, and perhaps the Fourth Symphony. Other works represent a mixture of both tendencies: *Trois poèmes d'Henri Michaux*; *Partita* and *Chain 2*.

When questioned about developments in his musical language, Lutosławski suggested that he had not changed direction, but had merely added compositional methods and techniques to the collection of means at his disposal, without discarding the previous ones. While this may have been true of his harmonic and melodic techniques, the evidence of his late works indicates that there was a fundamental reassessment of the role and importance of aleatory procedures. It was partly the dramatist in him who felt the need to re-examine ways of avoiding the problem of harmonic stasis and of achieving a faster pace in his music. But it was also the performer in him who had relayed back to the composer the experience and insight gained as conductor.

Lutosławski was undoubtedly the pre-eminent Polish composer born this century, but it is inappropriate merely to think of or categorise him in a narrowly nationalistic way. Although his character was shaped to a large degree by his experience living through the turbulent twentieth-century history of his mother country, it must be acknowledged that the literary and artistic culture of the man was more broadly European.

Conclusive assessment can be attempted but not easily attained, and the process of re-assessment will certainly continue for many years after his death. But it is already clear that Lutosławski must be considered one of the greatest European composers of the twentieth century since Bartók, to whom, in many respects, he was the natural successor. But perhaps the most telling observation of all is that he commanded an almost universal degree of respect and admiration from other composers of all generations and many nationalities. This was not merely the familiar ritual of veneration for an eminent creative artist, but showed a deep level of esteem earned over many years. His work is respected for its compositional rigour, its fastidious attention to detail, and its refinement of expression in the art of performance. Above all, he is admired for the musical and moral integrity of his long search, and often difficult struggle, for the personal language and consummate technique that served his individual voice.

Notes

Chapter 1

1. A comprehensive view of Polish history is given in the masterly two-volume study by Norman Davies: *God's Playground: A History of Poland* (Oxford, 1981).

2. Detailed profiles of five of the Lutosławski brothers can be found in *Polski Słownik Biograficzny*, vol. xviii/1, zeszyt 76 (Warsaw, 1973), 148–56. Only Stanisław, the second eldest, is not represented.

3. The English birth certificate of Jerzy (shown as 'George') gives his father's occupation as 'science student' and his residence as 227 Bascombe Avenue, Streatham Hill.

4. Steven Stucky states erroneously, 'When Józef went to Russia in August 1915 he left behind Maria and three sons'; *Lutosławski and his Music* (Cambridge, 1981), 3.

5. References to the Lutosławski family can be found in several accounts of the temporary Polish emigration to Russia during the First World War: for example, J. Spustek, *Polacy w Piotrogrodzie: 1915–1918* (Warsaw, 1966); W. Lednicki, *Pamiętniki* (London, 1967).

6. Roman Dmowski, 'Poland, Old and New', in *Russian Realities and Problems*, ed. J. D. Duff (Cambridge, 1917), 83–122. Norman Davies presents a virtuosic account of the politics and personalities of this period in 'The Duel: Dmowski versus Piłsudski', in Chapter 3 of *The Heart of Europe* (Oxford, 1984), 129–48.

7. An intimate account of this friendship was published after the war by one of the composer's cousins, the second daughter of his uncle Wincenty: Izabela z Lutosławskich Wolikowska, *Roman Dmowski: Człowiek, Polak, Przyjaciel* [Roman Dmowski: Man, Pole, Friend] (Chicago, 1961). The chapter titled 'Płomień Miłości' describes life at Drozdowo and includes photographic plates of the Dolny Dwór (192–3).

8. References to the political and military activities of Józef and Marian can be found in S. Kozicki, *Historia Ligi Narodowej* (London, 1964); Z. Oplustil, *Polskie formacje wschodnie 1918–19* (Warsaw, 1922); and in other accounts of the period.

9. Published posthumously (Warsaw, 1919).

10. The numerous scholarly publications of Wincenty Lutosławski include *The Origin and Growth of Plato's Logic with an Account of Plato's Style and the Chronology of his Writings* (London, 1905); *Über die Grundvoraussetzungen und Konsequenzen der individualistischen Weltanschauung* (Helsingfors, 1898); *Volonté et Liberté* (Paris, 1913); *The World of Souls* (London, 1924); *Preexistence and Reincarnation* (London, 1928); *Knowledge of Reality* (Cambridge, 1930).

11 See the extensive correspondence between Dmowski and Maria z Lutosławskich Niklewicz (and other family members) given in Mariusz Kułakowski, *Roman Dmowski w świetle listów i wspomnień*, 2 vols (London, 1968/72).

12 Wolikowska, op. cit.

13 See also Roman Dmowski, 'O księdzu Kazimierzu', *Myśl Naród* (1939, no. 10); H. Mościcki and W. Dzwonkowski, *Parlament Rzeczypospolitej Polskiej: 1919–1927* (Warsaw, 1928).

14 Norman Davies gives a full account of these events in *White Eagle, Red Star: The Polish–Soviet War 1919–20* (London, 1972), including detailed discussion of the Battle of Warsaw, which he assesses as one of the decisive battles of European history.

15 The première of Szymanowski's Third Symphony was given in St Petersburg on 20 January 1917. The performance in Warsaw which Lutosławski heard was presumably its Polish première. At about the same time, for Stravinsky's visit to Warsaw in 1924, Szymanowski wrote a celebratory article for the journal *Warszawianka* (1924, no. 7).

16 Tadeusz Kaczyński, *Conversations with Witold Lutosławski* (London, 1984), 33.

17 Conversation between composer and author (Warsaw, 12 April 1987).

18 Bálint András Varga, *Lutosławski Profile* (London, 1976), 22.

19 Conversation between composer and author (London, 1 May 1988).

20 Anatol Krakowiecki, *Książka o Kołymie* (London, 1950), chapter 18, 'Śmierć Henryka' [Henry's death], 124–32.

21 Conversation between composer and author (London, 7 November 1987).

22 Andrzej Panufnik, *Composing Myself* (London, 1987), 112–18.

23 i.e. the three films commissioned and produced by the Institut Spraw Społecznych (Institute of Social Affairs): *Gore, Zwarcie* and *Uwaga*.

24 Conversation between composer and author (London, 7 November 1987).

25 Stucky's numbering of these canons is incomplete.

26 At the end of the autograph score of these four-part canons there are some fascinating sketches of pitch organisation that include several of the types of four-note chord on which Lutosławski's method of constructing twelve-note chord-aggregates was to be based (see Chapter 3 and Ex. 3 : 4).

Chapter 2

1 Neither of these films has been shown publicly for many years. I saw them in a private screening at the Polish Film Archives in Warsaw on 23 April 1987.

2 Their marriage was dissolved at the end of the war.

3 See my background notes to the most recent edition of the composer's early piano works in Lutosławski, *Album for the Young* (London, Chester Music, 1991), 40.

4 An unpublished collection.

5 Anna Szweykowska, 'Z Dziejów Kolędy', in *Polskie Kolędy i Pastorałki* (rev. edn. Warsaw, 1982).

6 Michał Mioduszewski: *Śpiewnik kościelny* . . . (Kraków, 1838–53); and *Pastorałki i kolędy z melodyjami* (Kraków, 1843). Oskar Kolberg: *Lubelskie*, vol. 1/16 (Kraków, 1883); and *Łęczyckie*, vol. xxii (Kraków, 1889).

7 My rhyming English translations have been published with the score of the orchestral version (London, Chester Music, 1993).
8 Stucky overlooks the structural significance of this chord's reappearance and misplaces the recapitulation as beginning at bar 113: *Lutosławski and his Music*, 27.
9 Conversation between composer and author (London, 1 May 1988).
10 A profile of the life and work of Zofia Lissa, by Zofia Helman, was published (in English) in *Polish Musicological Studies*, vol. ii (Kraków, 1986), 7–24.
11 Curiously, 'Bierut' was apparently not his real name. A detailed account of these events is given by Norman Davies in *Heart of Europe: A Short History of Poland* (Oxford, 1984).
12 Penderecki's stance towards the Soviet Union and the Polish regime during this period was slightly different, one of several topics I addressed in a documentary for BBC Radio 3, 'An Affair with Romanticism', first broadcast on 20 March 1990.
13 My translation. His address to the Congress of Culture remains unpublished, except for an inaccurate transcript that appeared in an account of the proceedings circulated under martial law by the Solidarity underground.
14 Varga, *Lutosławski Profile*, 8.
15 Ibid., 8–9.
16 Texts and tunes are from Bystroń (ed.), *Pieśni ludowe z polskiego Śląska* (Kraków, 1927–34).
17 Folk melodies from the Kurpie region, collected by Władysław Skierkowski, *Puszcza kurpiowska w pieśni* (Płock, 1928–34).
18 Source of folk materials: Oskar Kolberg, *Mazowsze* vols. ii/v, *Lud*... vols. xxv/xxviii (Kraków, 1886, 1890). Zofia Lissa's detailed study of folk materials used in the Concerto for Orchestra was published in *Studia muzykologiczne*, 5 (1956), 196–299.
19 Stucky's account of the Concerto for Orchestra is generally good, and reworks some of Lissa's findings; nevertheless there are a few errors. For example, in his discussion of the last movement (pp. 54–5) he miscalculates the length of 'variations' 6 and 7, and states that the passacaglia theme coincides with variation 10 (in fact no. 11). His calculation of structural proportions in the first movement is not accurate (p. 51).
20 See Scarlett Panufnik, *Out of the City of Fear* (London, 1956), and the composer's autobiography, *Composing Myself*.
21 See note 13, above.

Chapter 3

1 For a more detailed analysis of these harmonic, melodic and polyphonic dimensions, with examples drawn from all periods of Lutosławski's career, see C. Bodman Rae, *Pitch Organisation in the Music of Witold Lutosławski since 1979* (PhD thesis, Leeds, 1992).
2 Conversation between composer and author (Warsaw, April 1987).
3 In some editions of the score there is misprint, showing D♭ rather than D♮ in the part for violins 21 and 22 at Fig. 44.

4 Conversation between the composer and author (Warsaw, April 1987).

5 Julian Krzyżanowski, *Dzieje Literatury Polskiej od początków do czasów najnowszych* (Warsaw, 1972); English edn entitled *A History of Polish Literature* (Warsaw, 1978).

6 I first drew attention to this mistranslation in a programme about music influenced by Russian Orthodox *zvon*-ringing, 'Kolokola', first broadcast by BBC Radio 3 on 6 February 1990.

7 C. Bodman Rae, 'The Voice of European Bells', *The Listener*, vol. cxxiii (18 Jan 1990), 44–5. Note that Russian bells do not swing.

8 Jean-Paul Couchoud, *La musique polonaise et Witold Lutosławski* (Paris, 1981), 76–7 (my translation).

9 Stucky suggests 'including as simultaneities interval classes 0, 1, 2, 5, and 6', *Lutosławski and his Music*, 71.

10 Couchoud, op. cit., 88 (my translation).

11 Wilfried Brennecke, 'Die Trauer musik von Witold Lutosławski', in Abert and Pfannkuch (eds), *Festschrift Friedrich Blume zum 70 Geburtstag* (Kassel, 1963), 60–73. This analysis was made with the composer's assistance.

12 John Casken, reviewing Stucky's book, correctly identified these chords which had been overlooked: *The Musical Times*, vol. cxxii, (December 1981), 822–3.

13 Ernö Lendvai: *Béla Bartók, an Analysis of his Music* (London, 1971); *The Workshop of Bartók and Kodály* (London, 1983). Also see the following by Roy Howat: 'Bartók, Lendvai and the Principles of Proportional Analysis', *Music Analysis*, vol. ii/1 (March 1981), 69–95; and *Debussy in Proportion* (Cambridge, 1983). It is also worth noting Lendvai's response to Howat: 'Remarks on Roy Howat's "Principles of Proportional Analysis" ', *Music Analysis*, vol. iii/3 (October 1984), 255–64.

14 For a more detailed discussion of structural proportions see Bodman Rae, *Pitch Organisation in the Music of Witold Lutosławski since 1979*, Part 1, Chapter 2, 'Archetypal Dramatic Shapes', 29–45.

Chapter 4

1 John Cage's Concert for Piano and Orchestra was composed in 1957–8, and received its première in New York on 15 May 1958 (not to be confused with his Concerto for prepared piano and chamber orchestra of 1951).

2 Varga, *Lutosławski Profile*, 12.

3 For example, the article by Pierre Boulez, 'Alea', in *La nouvelle revue française*, 59, reprinted in *Relevés d'apprenti* (Paris, 1966).

4 For example, the section on Indeterminate Notation in the entry for 'Aleatory' by Paul Griffiths, in *The New Grove Dictionary of Music and Musicians* (London, 1980) vol. 1, 239.

5 *Die Reihe*, vol. 1 (Vienna, 1955); my translation. A slightly different translation appears in 'Statistic and psychologic problems of sound', *Die Reihe*, vol. i (English edn, 1958). See also the following writings by Meyer-Eppler: 'Informationstheoretische Probleme der musikalischen Kommunikationen', *Die Reihe*, vol. viii (Vienna, 1962), and published in English as 'Musical

Communication as a Problem of Information Theory', *Die Reihe*, vol. viii (English edn, 1968); and *Grundlagen und Anwendungen der Informationstheorie* (Berlin, 1959).

6 Lutosławski, 'Rhythm and the organisation of pitch in composing techniques employing a limited element of chance'. This and subsequent extracts from the lecture are taken from the composer's original English text (a Polish translation was published in *Muzyka w kontekście kultury* [Music in the context of culture] (Kraków, 1978), and a version in English, unfortunately with many serious inaccuracies and omissions, appeared in *Polish Musicological Studies,* vol. ii (Kraków, 1986), 37–53.

7 A more detailed explanation of Lutosławski's methods of organising pitch in aleatory sections can be found in Bodman Rae, *Pitch Organisation in the Music of Witold Lutosławski since 1979*, Chapter 5, 'Oblique pitch organisation: polyphony'.

8 Lutosławski, 'Rhythm and the organisation of pitch . . .', op. cit.

9 Idem.

10 e.g. Griffiths, op. cit.

11 Varga, op. cit., 24.

12 Lutosławski, op. cit.

13 Idem.

14 Couchoud, *La musique polonaise et Witold Lutosławski,* 108–20. See also the article on Henri Michaux by Madeleine Fondo-Valette in *Dictionnaire des Littératures de langue française,* ed. Beaumarchais, Couty and Rey (Paris, 1987), 1600–04).

15 Couchoud, op. cit., 110–11.

16 Ibid., 109–10.

17 Ibid., 111–12.

18 Ibid., 114–15.

19 Kaczyński, *Conversations with Witold Lutosławski,* 1–2.

20 Edward Cowie, 'Mobiles of Sound', *Music and Musicians,* vol. xx (October 1971), 34–45.

21 Kaczyński, op. cit., 12.

22 A lengthy extract of the full text of Lutosławski's letter to Walter Levin is given as a supplement to the score published by Chester.

23 Idem.

24 Kaczyński, op. cit., 25–6.

25 My translation from Lutosławski's original Polish text published in *Res Facta*, 4 (1970), 6–13. There is also an unattributed English translation in Chapter 7 of *The Orchestral Composer's Point of View: Essays on Twentieth-Century Music by Those Who Wrote it,* ed. Robert Hines (University of Oklahoma Press, 1970), 128–51.

26 See Casken's excellent account of the pitch organisation in the first movement of the Second Symphony in 'Transition and transformation in the music of Witold Lutosławski', *Contact,* 12 (Autumn 1975), 3–12. The same article was later published in a Polish translation as 'Przejście i transformacja w muzyce Witolda Lutosławskiego', *Res Facta,* 9 (Kraków, PWM, 1982), 142–51.

27 The same example has been used in each of the following sources: Kaczyński's interview in Polish for *Ruch Muzyczny* (1967), 3–6, reprinted in an English translation in *Lutosławski*, ed. Owe Nordwall (London and Stockholm, 1968), 113–14, and reprinted again in the 1986 English edn of Kaczyński's interviews, 41–2; Varga's volume of conversations, op. cit., 25; Stucky, *Lutosławski and his Music* (Cambridge, 1981), 121–2; and the conversations in French with Couchoud, op. cit., 134.

28 Lutosławski, *Res Facta*, 4 (1970).

29 The structural proportions of all the major works since 1958 are discussed more fully in Bodman Rae, op. cit., Chapter 2, 'Archetypal dramatic shapes', 29–45.

30 Cowie, op. cit.

Chapter 5

1 'Notes on the construction of large-scale closed forms'. This and another lecture, 'Rhythm and the organisation of pitch in techniques employing a limited element of chance', were written in 1967 or 1968. In the event, the planned visit to Darmstadt did not take place. Both lectures have since been presented publicly on several occasions.

2 Lutosławski, 'Notes on the construction of large-scale closed forms'.

3 It is interesting to note that Rostropovich flew to Moscow within hours of the attempted *coup d'état* on 19 August 1991. He was among those defending the Russian Parliament building on 20 August, and joined the jubilant iconoclasts who celebrated the removal of the statue of the hated Cheka/KGB founder, Felix Dzierzyński (original Polish spelling), on Friday 23 August.

4 Kaczyński, *Conversations with Witold Lutosławski* (London, 1984), 60–61.

5 In *Lutosławski and his Music*, 175, Stucky incorrectly states that the *dolente* cello line contains only interval-classes 2 and 5.

6 Lutosławski explained the chronology of events interrupting his work on the Third Symphony in an interview published in *Polish Music*, vol. xviii/3–4 (1983), 4–5. In March 1973, during his conversations with Varga (*Lutosławski Profile*, London 1976, 36) he refers to work currently in progress on a Double Concerto for Heinz and Ursula Holliger (see also Chapter 6).

7 The surname is pronounced 'Deznoss' rather than 'Dayno'.

8 A brief profile of 'La vie et l'oeuvre de Robert Desnos' is appended to *Corps et biens* (Paris, 1953) 187–90. See also the article on Robert Desnos by Marie-Claire Dumas in *Dictionnaire des Littératures de langue française*, (Paris, 1987) 669–71; and the preface to the most recent edition of *Chantefables et Chantefleurs* (Paris, 1991).

9 Kaczyński, op. cit., 70.

10 Jean-Paul Couchoud, *La musique polonaise et Witold Lutosławski*, 183 (my translation).

11 A detailed study (in German) of *Mi-Parti* has been made by Martina Homma, 'Witold Lutosławski: *Mi-Parti*', *Melos*, 3 (1985), 22–57.

12 Kaczyński, op. cit., 81.

13 Stucky, op. cit., 118–19 and 190; he did not identify, however, the construction of these harmonies as chord-aggregates.

14 Conversation between composer and author (Warsaw, April 1987).
15 *Polish Music*, vol. xviii/3–4 (1983).
16 i.e. the eight piano pieces of op. 21 (1838).

Chapter 6

1 Whether this will be the last such development remains to be seen. Although the characteristics of the 'late works' and the 'late style' now appear to be clearly identifiable, at the time of writing these can only be interim, not final, assessments. Stucky prematurely deemed all the works from *Jeux vénitiens* onwards to represent the 'late style': *Lutosławski and his Music, passim*.
2 Kaczyński, *Conversations with Witold Lutosławski*, 88.
3 I first drew attention to the new harmonic thinking of the late works in an article for *The Musical Times*, 'Lutosławski's Golden Year', vol. cxxvii (October 1986), 547–51, and pursued the matter further in 'Lutosławski's Late Style?', *The Listener*, vol. cxxii (26 January 1989).
4 The expression 'An Affair with Romanticism' was used by Penderecki himself when I interviewed him on 13 March 1990 for a radio documentary on his recent work. It provided an apt title for the programme, first broadcast on BBC Radio 3, 20 March 1990.
5 My translation from the original Polish text (hitherto unpublished, except by the Solidarity underground press).
6 Varga, *Lutosławski Profile*, 36.
7 Stucky discusses the genesis of the work in 'Lutosławski's Double Concerto', *The Musical Times*, vol. cxxii (August 1981), 529–32, although he makes no mention of *Epitaph*.
8 A commemorative profile of Jarociński's life and work is given by Michał Bristiger (in English) in *Polish Musicological Studies*, vol. 2 (Kraków, 1986), 25–36.
9 Stefan Jarociński, *Debussy a impresjonizm i symbolizm* (Kraków, 1966; 2nd edn. 1976); also published in French as *Debussy, impressionisme et symbolisme* (Paris, 1970), and translated from French into English by Rollo Myers as *Debussy, Impressionism and Symbolism* (London, 1976).
10 Jarociński, *Witold Lutosławski: Materiały do monografii* [W.L.: materials for a monograph] (Kraków, 1967).
11 Jarociński, *Debussy, Impressionism and Symbolism*, 137.
12 Ibid., 147–8.
13 Stucky, *Lutosławski and his Music*, 195.
14 From an interview with the composer in *Polish Music*, vol. xviii/3–4 (1983), 4–5.
15 I drew this to the composer's attention in May 1988, with a suggested rewording. He agreed that the sense had been incorrect and did not correspond to his original intention.
16 From the interview in *Polish Music*, vol. xviii/3–4 (1983), 7.
17 For an explanation of Lutosławski's 'once-only conventions' see the introduction to Chapter 5.

18 There is a crucial misprint in the published score at Fig. 76, which shows low D for the basses. This should read low B thus sounding together with the bassoons, tuba and timpani.

19 Conversation between composer and author (London, 11 October 1992).

Chapter 7

1 Similar relationships between preparatory studies and certain major works can be found earlier in Lutosławski's career, for example the woodwind Trio, Canons and Interludes that assisted him with the First Symphony, and the various functional pieces that led to the Concerto for Orchestra.

2 Although a similar kind of passacaglia/chaconne approach had been adopted in the finale of the Concerto for Orchestra, in that piece there was no particular *concertante* focus. In the Piano Concerto's finale, however, one strand of the chain technique is identified with the soloist and the other with the orchestra.

3 I first drew attention to the significance of *Partita* in 'Lutosławski's Golden Year', *The Musical Times*, vol. cxxvii (October 1986), 547–51.

4 In 'Lutosławski's Late Violin Works', *The Musical Times*, vol. cxxi (October 1990), 530–33, I discussed the genesis of *Partita*, *Interlude* and *Chain 2*, and their bearing on the late style. This article was published in conjunction with the UK première of the complete triptych in London on 17 October 1990.

5 I conjectured on the possibility of influence from these and other pieces of Chopin on the harmonic language of Liszt, Wagner and Debussy in an illustrated talk for BBC Radio 3, 'Tristan Triangles', first broadcast in *Music Weekly* on 15 October 1989.

6 The only apparent deviation from this scheme is due to a misprint in the printed score: the fourteenth note on the third stave of the violin part should read A♭ rather than A♮.

7 Although *Interlude* was not composed until 1989, and is therefore discussed in Chapter 7 out of its chronological position, it is obviously desirable to consider the piece in its relationship to the two works it is designed to link.

8 In 1992 the School of Music of the University of Louisville published a catalogue of *The Grawemeyer Collection of Contemporary Music 1985–1991*, edited by the Head of the Anderson Music Library, Richard Griscom. It lists a unique collection providing 'a series of annual time capsules capturing the trends and styles of contemporary music composition'.

9 The group of young Polish composers that has received financial support from this source includes several who have graduated from the class of Włodzimierz Kotoński at the Chopin Academy of Music in Warsaw.

10 The difficulty of selecting a recipient for the Grawemeyer Prize (in any year) can be imagined if one considers that the numerous scores submitted in 1985 for the 1986 award included *Penthode* by Elliott Carter, the Third Symphony of Peter Maxwell Davies, *Il ritorno di Ulisse in patria* by Hans Werner Henze, and the *Scardanelli-Zyklus* of Heinz Holliger.

11 The Fanfare for Louisville lasts only about one minute in performance and is scored for triple woodwind and brass with timpani and light percussion. It begins

and ends on a unison A, and the ending is quasi-tonal with a root progression that defines a perfect cadence E–A.

12 Other composer recipients of the RPS Gold Medal include Brahms, Elgar, Vaughan Williams, Rakhmaninov, Sibelius, Strauss, Prokofiev, Stravinsky, Britten, Shostakovich, Kodály and Messiaen.

13 The account of the Piano Concerto given by Lutosławski at that stage (April 1987) corresponded exactly with the finished work.

Chapter 8

1 Lutosławski has made this observation in numerous interviews over the years.

2 The expression 'odrabiac zaległości' was used by the composer in conversation with the present author (Warsaw, April 1987).

3 I explained the genesis of the Piano Concerto in an article for *The Listener*, vol. cxxii (27 July 1989), 36–7.

4 A full list of the pieces that Lutosławski performed for his piano diploma from the Warsaw Conservatory is given in Chapter 1.

5 My translation from the composer's original programme note in Polish, prepared at the time of the first performance. This translation is also reproduced in the published score, together with the German translation by Martina Homma (used for the Salzburg première), and the composer's own translation into French.

6 For a more detailed analysis of the pitch material of the Piano Concerto see Bodman Rae, *Pitch Organisation in the Music of Witold Lutosławski since 1979* (Ph.D. thesis, Leeds, 1992), Chapter 10.

7 Lutosławski has received doctorates *honoris causa* from the Cleveland Institute of Music, and the universities of Warsaw, Kraków, Chicago, Lancaster, Glasgow, Toruń, Durham, Cambridge and Belfast.

8 In order to encourage moves towards democracy in Poland, a number of diplomatic gestures were made by the West during the latter days of the Jaruzelski regime, including the official visits by US Vice-President George Bush from 26 to 29 September 1987, and British Prime Minister, Margaret Thatcher, on 2 November 1988. There was also an official visit by Mikhail Gorbachev from 11 to 14 July 1988, a gesture that was taken to signify his personal approval and encouragement for the reform process within the Polish Communist administration.

9 It is worth noting that there are some interesting similarities between Lutosławski's and Carter's approach towards twelve-note pitch organisation, for example, their use of complementary sets.

10 Lutosławski had been made an honorary fellow of the Guildhall School in 1978, and returned there in the autumn of 1992 to present the Lutosławski Prize for composition. He had received an honorary doctorate of music from the University of Lancaster on 8 May 1975.

11 In the free elections for the Polish Presidency Lech Wałęsa received 74 per cent of the vote on the second ballot. He declined to receive his insignia of office from the outgoing (Communist) President, General Wojciech Jaruzelski. Instead, he was invested on 22 December 1990 with the legitimate pre-war insignia by the Polish President-in-exile, Ryszard Kaczorowski.

12 Andrzej Panufnik was knighted in the New Year's Honours List of 1991, but he died only a few months later, on 27 October.

13 See note 8 to Chapter 5.

14 See the commentary by Pierre-André Touttain in the Gründ edition (Paris, 1991).

15 At the time of the première of *Chantefleurs et Chantefables*, the soloist spelled her surname 'Kringlebotn'. It has since been changed to 'Kringleborn'.

16 *L'Angélique* was repeated as an encore at the première.

17 The bass line of *Le Papillon* was modelled on an example from Bach.

18 My review of the world première was given in *The Musical Times*, vol. cxxxii (October 1991), 524.

19 The attempted *coup d'état* in the Soviet Union took place on 19 August, but it collapsed only two days later. On 23 August President Yeltsin signed a declaration suspending all activities of the Communist Party throughout the Russian Federation. The following day President Gorbachev resigned as General Secretary of the Party which then formally dissolved itself. See also note 3 to Chapter 5.

20 In view of the fact that the Fourth Symphony, like the Third, both begins and ends with harmonies that are strongly 'rooted' to low E, one must consider whether there is any significance in this choice of note and whether the composer was thinking in terms of long-range connections of pitch. When questioned about this issue, however, the composer explained that his choice of bass notes in these cases (and others) was determined, not by any desire to establish quasi-tonal effects of pitch-centre, but, more mundanely, simply by the sonority of the lowest open string of the double basses.

21 Details (and photographs) of this occasion are given by Tadeusz Kaczyński in *Lutosławski: życie i muzyka* (Warsaw, Sutkowski Edition, 1994), pp. 139–40 and 228–30.

22 As Lutosławski was unable to be there himself, I was invited to deliver the pre-concert lecture which introduced and opened the Festival.

23 It is worth noting that this concert was televised, thus adding to the BBC's archive of Lutosławski's performances at the Promenade Concerts which also includes *Chain 2* (with Anne-Sophie Mutter) and the world première of *Chantefleurs et Chantefables*.

24 The citation reads: '. . . w uznaniu wybitnych osiągnięć w twórczości kompozytorskiej, za doniosły wkład w rozwój kultury polskiej, odznaczony zostaje ORDEREM ORŁA BIAŁEGO Witold Lutosławski s. Józefa . . . Prezydent Rzeczypospolitej Polskiej, Lech Wałęsa'. ('In recognition of great achievement in the art of composition, and an outstanding contribution to the development of Polish culture, the Order of the White Eagle is awarded to Witold Lutosławski (son of Józef) . . . President of the Polish Republic, Lech Wałęsa'.)

25 The following day I wrote a lengthy obituary which was published in the *Independent* newspaper (London, 9 February 1994).

26 Quoted in Tadeusz Kaczyński's personal tribute to the composer, *Lutosławski: życie i muzyka* (Warsaw, Sutkowski Edition, 1994), p. 234. Kaczyński also reproduces, in full, the text of the funeral oration by Ks. Wiesław Niewęgłowski, pp. 237–8. Witold Rowicki and his wife had died within a few weeks of each other in 1989.

Chapter 9

1 The Archive of the Paul Sacher Foundation (established in 1973) is located at the following address: Auf Burg, Münsterplatz 4, 4051 Basel, Switzerland. In addition to the Lutosławski materials, and Sacher's own extensive collection, the archive also contains collections of manuscripts and scores by Stravinsky, Webern, Pierre Boulez, Bruno Maderna, Luciano Berio, Frank Martin, Antoinette Vischer and Ina Lohr.

2 Danuta Lutosławska was born at Felin on 10 September 1911. On hearing of her death, only two weeks after I had last visited her, I wrote an obituary for the *Independent* newspaper, published in London (Thursday 28 April 1994), complementing the one I had already written for her husband. In spite of the widespread international coverage of Lutosławski's death, with numerous tributes, very little attention was given to his widow's death. This is a pity, because her practical contribution to his work was invaluable, and yet it was frequently overlooked or taken for granted.

3 Two other books (apart from my own) were published in 1994. Tadeusz Kaczyński has produced a personal tribute: *Lutosławski: życie i muzyka* (Warsaw, Sutkowski Edition, 1994). The other book, by Irina Nikolska, is a collection of conversations (although, confusingly, with exactly the same title as the English editions of Kaczyński's earlier book): *Conversations with Witold Lutosławski* (Stockholm, Melos Musiktidschrift, 1994). Nikolska's book was widely publicised prior to its publication as a biography of Lutosławski; it is not. Unfortunately the book presents some problems for the reader: it suffers from double translation (apparently from Polish into Russian, and then from Russian into English) which is regrettable, because Lutosławski expressed himself very clearly in English, and much better than this doubly translated text is able to convey; secondly, it seems to be an unedited, verbatim transcript of the composer's remarks; but the greatest problem is presented by the translation into English which has escaped the normal processes of proof-reading and verification (by a native speaker). The resulting text, therefore, is often rather comic, which is a shame, because it does not do full justice to the subject matter. Perhaps a subsequent edition will put these matters right.

4 Since he was a young man, Lutosławski had made his sketches on pieces of portrait-format score paper cut horizontally in order to give half-size sheets in landscape-format. Nearly all his musical sketches were notated on customised sheets of this sort, which he evidently found more comfortable to work on and to collect in bundles. He once told me that this method had been suggested to him by Panufnik (either during their student days, or during their wartime collaboration) who apparently also worked in this way.

5 I have already commented earlier on the extraordinary effect which Anne-Sophie Mutter's performance of *Chain 2* had on Lutosławski, but the issue is so important it can hardly be overstated. I recall, on one occasion, in the spring of 1987, accompanying Lutosławski to a performance of *Chain 2* at the Warsaw Philharmonic (he was not conducting it himself). Although the soloist was excellent (the Hungarian/British violinist György Pauk, who had given the British première with Lutosławski), the ensemble co-ordination was not secure. When we returned to his house after the concert, he invited me to his study in order to hear a tape of the first

performance, partly in order to erase the memory of the imperfect concert we had just attended, but also to share his intense enthusiasm for Anne-Sophie Mutter's beauty of tone and clarity of technique. It was evident then that her performance of *Chain 2* had had a profound effect upon him, and he derived great satisfaction from their subsequent performances together.

6   The literary executors are Marcin Bogusławski (the composer's stepson) and his wife Gabriela (née Zamoyska).

7   This process of re-evaluation has already been set in motion by Tadeusz Kaczyński: *Andrzej Panufnik i jego muzyka* (Warsaw, Wydawnictwo Naukowe PWN, 1994). Other research in this field is currently in progress.

8   This is a common error betraying misunderstanding of both Lutosławski's and Messiaen's techniques. For example, in a review of the first edition of this book (*Musical Times*, London, August 1994), the reviewer stated (incorrectly) that Messiaen had not been mentioned at all, and then went on to argue that the techniques of interval-class pairing which I had explained should have been compared with Messiaen's use of modes. Yet there is a fundamental difference of music theory between the two: Messiaen's modal technique defines specific pitch-classes, which can give rise to various combinations of intervals; Lutosławski's intervallic technique defines specific interval-classes, which can give rise to various combinations of pitches.

9   I first drew attention to the significant scope for comparison between Lutosławski and Carter in *Pitch Organisation in the Music of Witold Lutosławski since 1979* (PhD thesis, University of Leeds, 1992), pp. 5, 15–16, and 373.

List of Works

The following list of works is in chronological order, except for revisions,
arrangements or orchestrations of earlier work, which are listed immediately after the
original version. In some cases the period of composition was spread over several
years; for example, Symphony no. 1, the Concerto for Orchestra, and *Muzyka
żałobna*. The chronology of these works is taken from the date of completion; the
overlap of dates often sheds interesting light on other pieces composed at the same
time. Where the period of composition is known, the span of dates is given. Generic
titles are given in English. Others are given in either Polish or French, whichever was
the original language given by the composer.

Functional music composed by Lutosławski from 1945–60 falls broadly into two
categories: published and unpublished. The former is included here, but reference to
the latter is selective. Until April 1990, most of the sketches and manuscripts were
kept in the composer's study at his home in Warsaw. Since then, these have been
acquired by the Paul Sacher Stiftung in Basel. Others (including four scores/parts of
incidental music for the theatre) are held in the music manuscripts section of the Polish
Biblioteka Narodowa (National Library) at the Krasiński Palace in Warsaw.

Only three publishers hold copyright in Lutosławski's work: Polskie Wydawnictwo
Muzyczne (PWM); Chester Music; and Moeck Verlag. PWM (Al. Krasińskiego,
31–111, Kraków, Poland) cover all works in what was referred to until recently as the
'Soviet bloc', together with other socialist and former socialist countries (although this
demarcation may change in the light of continuing political and economic changes in
those countries). Moeck Verlag (Postfach 143, D–3100, Celle 1, Germany) have rights
in all other countries for only two works: the Five Songs to poems of Iłłakowicz; and
Jeux vénitiens. Since 1966 the leading publisher has been J & W Chester Ltd of
London, formerly part of the Wilhelm Hansen publishing group, since 1989 part of
the Music Sales group (8–9 Frith Street, London W1V 5TZ). Chesters also act as
sub-publishers for works composed prior to 1966.

In order to obviate the need for a separate discography, details of selected
recordings are included here. Recent issues on compact disc are listed, including the
Polskie Nagrania series (PNCD) which is largely drawn from performances of the
1960s previously issued on LP. Although the 1978 set of six LPs issued by EMI is
unfortunately no longer available (and sadly not issued on CD), its importance
requires it to be included.

Early pieces, no longer extant
> These and other manuscripts were destroyed in 1944 during the Warsaw Uprising
> Prelude for piano (1922)
> Other small piano pieces (1923–6)
> Two Sonatas for violin and piano (1927)

Poème for piano (1928)
Taniec Chimery [Dance of the Chimera] for piano (1930)
Scherzo for orchestra (1930)
Incidental music for *Haroun al Rashid* for orchestra (1931)
Double Fugue for orchestra (1936)
Prelude and Aria for Piano (1936)

Sonata for piano (1934)
Completed 'Warszawa, 29 XII 1934'
I. Allegro; II. Adagio ma non troppo; III. Andante – Allegretto – Andantino
PREMIÈRE : Polish Radio broadcast, Warsaw, 1935
PERFORMER : the composer
DURATION : *c.* 23'; (I: *c.* 9'; II: *c.*6'; III: *c.* 8')
MANUSCRIPT : unpubl. MS in the composer's collection

Two Songs for soprano and piano (1934)
  Wodnica [Water-nymph]
  Kołysanka lipowa [Linden lullaby]
TEXTS : poems by Kazimiera Iłłakowicz (1892–1983) from *Płaczący Ptak* (Warsaw, 1927)
PREMIÈRE : at a café concert in Warsaw, 1941
PERFORMERS : Ewa Bandrowska-Turska (sop), the composer (pf)
MANUSCRIPT : lost / destroyed in 1944 during the Warsaw Uprising

Three Short-Film Scores (*c.* 1935–36)
  1. *Gore* [Fire]
  2. *Uwaga* [Beware!]
  3. *Zwarcie* [Short-circuit]
COMMENTARY : All three made for Institut Spraw Społecznych ('Institute for Social Affairs', akin to Health and Safety Executive), and focusing on domestic or occupational hazards: danger of fires, safety at work, and safety with electricity, respectively. Nos. 1 and 3 directed by Eugeniusz Cękalski; no. 3 directed by Stefan and Franciszka Themerson.

Lacrimosa, for soprano (optional SATB chorus) and orchestra (1937)
Surviving fragment of a Requiem
PREMIÈRE : Warsaw, 1938
PERFORMERS : Helena Warpechowska, Warsaw PO, cond. Tadeusz Wilczak
DURATION : *c.* 3'
PUBLISHER : unpubl. MS in the composer's collection
  Transcription for soprano and org publ. by PWM, 1948.
  The other fragment, *Requiem aeternam* for chor and orch,
  was lost / destroyed in 1944 during the Warsaw Uprising.
RECORDING : (without chor) PNCD 040 (1988) Stefania Wojtowicz, Polish Radio SO / Lutosławski

Symphonic Variations (1936–8)
3. 3. 3. 3; 4. 3. 3. 1; timp, perc, cel, pf; harp; str
PREMIÈRE : (broadcast), Polish Radio, Warsaw, April 1939; (concert), Wawel
    Festival, Kraków, 17 June 1939
PERFORMERS : Polish Radio SO, cond. Grzegorz Fitelberg
DURATION : c. 9′
PUBLISHERS : PWM / Chester
RECORDINGS : EMI IC 165–03 236 Q (1978) Polish Radio SO / Lutosławski; EMI
    ED29 1172–2 Polish Radio SO / Lutosławski

Two Studies, for piano (1940–41)
I : Allegro; II : Non troppo allegro
PREMIÈRE : (I) Kraków, 26 January 1948
PERFORMER : Maria Bielińska-Riegerowa
DURATION : c. 4′20″ (I : 1′50″; II : 2′30″)
PUBLISHERS : PWM / Chester
RECORDING : PNCD 045 (1974) Marek Drewnowski

Variations on a Theme by Paganini for two pianos (1941)
    (Theme and twelve variations)
SOURCE : Caprice in A minor no. 24, for violin, by Paganini
PREMIÈRE : at a café concert in Warsaw, 1941
PERFORMERS : the composer and Andrzej Panufnik
DURATION : c. 6′
PUBLISHERS : PWM / Chester
RECORDINGS : numerous, e.g. PNCD 045 (1978) Jacek and Maciej Łukaszczyk.
ORCHD : (and slightly extended) by the composer in 1978 for solo pf and orch, 2. 2. 2.
    2; 4. 3. 3. 1; timp, perc; harp; str. First perf of this version in Miami on 18 November
    1979 played by Felicja Blumental with the Florida PO, cond. Brian Priestman.

Pieśni walki podziemnej, for voice and piano (1942–4)
Songs of the Underground Struggle
    1. *Żelazny marsz* [Iron march]
    2. *Do broni* [To arms]
    3. *Przed nami przestrzeń otwarta* [An open stretch before us]
    4. *Jedno słowo, jeden znak* [One word, one sign]
    5. *Wesoły pluton* [Merry platoon]
TEXTS : (1) Stanisław Dobrowolski, an officer of the Armia Krajowa (AK), the
    underground 'Home Army'; (2) Aleksander Maliszewski; (3, 4) Zofia Zawadzka;
    (5) anon
DURATION : c. 15′
PUBLISHER : PWM in vol. 1 of *Pieśni walki podziemnej* (1948)

Fifty Contrapuntal Studies for woodwind, etc (1943–4)
    Ten Interludes for oboe and bassoon (1943–4)
        1. Allegro giusto

2. Poco adagio
3. Tempo di Menuetto
4. Allegro vivace
5. Con moto
6. Vivo
7. Allegretto
8. Andante
9. Allegro giocoso
10. Allegro vivo

Ten Canons for two clarinets (1943–4)
Ten Canons in four parts
Eleven Miniatures in four / five parts
Nine Canons for three clarinets (2 B♭ cl and B♭ bass cl) (1944)
    1. Allegro non troppo (20.x.1944)
    2. Stesso movimento (22.x.1944)
    3. Stesso movimento (24.x.1944)
    4. Stesso movimento (28.x.1944)
    5. Adagio (30.x.1944)
    6. Adagio (31.x.1944)
    7. Stesso movimento (1.xi.1944)
    8. Stesso movimento (2.xi.1944)
    9. Stesso movimento (4.xi.1944)
MANUSCRIPTS : unpubl. MSS in the composer's collection

Trio, for oboe, clarinet and bassoon (1944–5)
I : Allegro moderato; II; III : Allegro giocoso
PREMIÈRE : Festival of Contemporary Polish Music, Kraków, September 1945
PERFORMERS : Seweryn Śnieckowski (ob), Teofil Rudnicki (cl), Bazyli Orłow (bn)
DURATION : *c.* 16′
MANUSCRIPT : original MS missing

Melodie Ludowe [Folk Melodies] (1945)
'Twelve easy pieces for piano'
    1. *Ach mój Jasieńko* [O, my Johnny] Sostenuto
    2. *Hej, od Krakowa jadę* [Hey, I come from Kraków] Allegretto
    3. *Jest drożyna, jest* [There is a path, there is] Andantino
    4. *Pastereczka* [The little shepherdess] Allegretto
    5. *Na jabłoni jabłko wisi* [An apple hangs on the apple tree] Moderato
    6. *Od Sieradza płynie rzeka* [A river flows from Sieradz] Allegretto
    7. *Panie Michale* [Master Michael] Poco sostenuto
    8. *W polu lipeńka* [The lime tree in the field] Sostenuto
    9. *Zalotny* [Flirting] Allegretto
   10. *Gaik* [The grove] Allegro vivace
   11. *Gąsior* [The gander] Andantino
   12. *Rektor* [The schoolmaster] Allegro
SOURCE : melodies from an unpubl. collection by Jerzy Olszewski

PREMIÈRE: Kraków, 1947
PERFORMER: Zbigniew Drzewiecki
DURATION: *c.* 10′
COMMISSION: from Polskie Wydawnictwo Muzyczne
PUBLISHERS: PWM/Chester. Transcription [of nos. 1–5, 8, 10, 12] for guitar by José de Azpiazu, PWM 1971
ARRANGED: by the composer, for (school) str orch in 1952 (nos. 1, 2, 10, 11, 12), and for 4 vns in 1954 (nos. 9–12)

Odrą do Bałtyku [Via the Oder to the Baltic], 35 mm documentary film (1945)
orchestral film score
DIRECTOR: S. Możdżeński
DURATION: 39′
LOCATION: Polish Film Archives at Wytwórnia Filmowa, ul. Chelmska, Warsaw; shown to present author in private screening on 23 April 1987.
COMMENTARY: With text, maps and voice-over narration throughout. Follows the route of the River Oder from Silesia to the Baltic Sea, via Bytom (etc), Kędra, Opole, Brzeg, Wrocław (Breslau), Lignice, Głogów, Ziemia Lubuska, and Szczecin (Stettin). Begins with maps of Poland's new boundaries, particularly the Oder-Neisse line forming the new border with the then DDR and Czechoslovakia. Propagandist narration relegates the music to a subordinate position.

Suita Warszawska [Warsaw Suite], 35 mm documentary film (1946)
scored for full symphony orch
I. *Klęska* [Disaster]
II. *Powrót do Zycie* [Return to life]
III. *Wiosna Warszawska* [Warsaw spring]
DIRECTOR: T. Makarczyński
DURATION: 20′ (I: 5′; II: 6′; III: 9′)
LOCATION: Polish Film Archives at Wytwórnia Filmowa, ul. Chelmna, Warsaw; shown to present author in a private screening on 23 April 1987.
COMMENTARY: There is no text, no subtitled captions, and no voice-over narration; only visual images and music. *Klęska* shows the utterly devastated, deserted capital. *Powrót do Zycie* gradually introduces scenes of human activity as the music becomes more active and 'warmer'. *Wiosna Warszawska* is atmospheric and colourful, both visually and musically. Vivid orchestration is used for images for trees blossoming.

Dwadzieście kolęd [Twenty Carols] for voice and piano (1946)
1. *Anioł pasterzom mówił*
2. *Gdy się Chrystus rodzi*
3. *Przybieżeli do Betlejem*
4. *Jezus malusieńki*
5. *Bóg się rodzi*
6. *W żłobie leży*
7. *Północ już była*

   8. *Hej Weselmy się*
   9. *Gdy śliczna Panna*
 10. *Lulajże, Jezuniu*
 11. *My też pastuszkowie*
 12. *Hej, w dzień narodzenia*
 13. *Hola, hola, pasterze z pola!*
 14. *Jezu, śliczny kwiecie*
 15. *Z narodzenia Pana*
 16. *Pasterze mili*
 17. *A cóż tą dzieciną?*
 18. *Dziecina mała*
 19. *Hej, hej, lelija Panna Maryja*
 20. *Najświętsza Panienka po świecie chodziła*
SOURCES : texts and melodies from: Father Michał Mioduszewski, *Śpiewnik kościelny* (Kraków, 1838 [nos. 1, 5, 6], 1842 [nos. 14, 15], 1853 [nos. 2, 16]); Mioduszewski, *Pastorałki i kolędy z melodyjami* (Kraków, 1843) [nos. 3, 4, 7, 8, 9, 10, 11, 12, 13, 16, 17, 18]; Oskar Kolberg, *Lubelskie* (Kraków 1883) [no. 19]; Kolberg, *Łęczyckie* (Kraków, 1889) [no. 20]
PREMIÈRE : [nos. 11, 15, 17, 18, 20, only] Kraków, January 1947
PERFORMERS : Aniela Szlemińska (sop), Jan Hoffman (pf)
DURATION : *c.* 45'
COMMISSION : from Polskie Wydawnictwo Muzyczne
PUBLISHERS : PWM / Chester
RECORDING : Veriton SXV-778P, Szostek-Radkowa (sop), Hiolski (bar), Witkowski (pf)

Twenty Polish Carols (1946, orch 1984–9)
S solo; female chor; 1. 1. 2. 1; 2. 1. 1. 0; timp, perc, pf; harp; str
   1. Angels to the shepherds came (*Anioł pasterzom mówił*)
   2. Hey! We rejoice now (*Hej! Weselmy się*)
   3. When the Christ to us is born (*Gdy się Chrystus rodzi*)
   4. Just after midnight (*Północ już była*)
   5. God is born (*Bóg się rodzi*)
   6. Our lovely Lady (*Gdy śliczna Panna*)
   7. Hurrying to Bethlehem (*Przybieżeli do Betlejem*)
   8. In a manger (*W żłobie leży*)
   9. Jesus there is lying (*Jezus malusienki*)
 10. We are shepherds (*My też pastuszkowie*)
 11. Lullaby, Jesus (*Lulajże, Jezuniu*)
 12. Hey, on this the day (*Hej, w dzień narodzenia*)
 13. Jesus, lovely flower (*Jezu, śliczny kwiecie*)
 14. Heyla, heyla, shepherds there you are (*Hola, hola, pasterze z pola!*)
 15. What to do with this child? (*A cóż z tą dzieciną ?*)
 16. Hey, hey, lovely Lady Mary (*Hej, hej, lelija Panna Maryja*)
 17. This is our Lord's birthday (*Z narodzenia Pana*)
 18. Shepherds can you tell? (*Pasterze mili*)

19. Infant so tiny (*Dziecina mała*)
20. Holy Lady Mary (*Najświętsza Panienka po świecie chodziła*)
TEXTS : English rhyming translations by Charles Bodman Rae, © 1988 / 9
PREMIÈRE : Aberdeen, 14 December 1990; Queen's Hall, Edinburgh, 15 December
   1990 (an incomplete selection of only 17 Carols was performed, in Polish, at the
   QEH, London, on 15 December 1985 by Marie Slorach (sop) with the London
   Sinfonietta and Chorus, cond by the composer).
PERFORMERS : Susan Hamilton (sop), with the Scottish Chamber Orchestra and
   Scottish Philharmonic Singers, cond by the composer
DURATION : *c.* 45'
PUBLISHER : Chester

Symphony no. 1 (1941–7)
3. 3. 3. 3; 4. 3. 3. 3. 1; timp, perc, cel, pf; str
I. Allegro giusto; II. Poco adagio; III. Allegretto misterioso; IV. Allegro vivace
PREMIÈRE : Katowice, 6 April 1948
PERFORMERS : Polish Radio SO, cond. Grzegorz Fitelberg
DURATION : *c.* 25'
PUBLISHERS : PWM / Chester
RECORDINGS : EMI IC 165–03 232 Q (1978) Polish Radio SO / Lutosławski;
   PNCD 040 (1964) Polish Radio SO / Lutosławski

Sześć piosenek dziecinnych [Six Children's Songs] for voice and piano (1947)
   1. *Taniec* [Dance]
   2. *Rok i bieda* [Year and trouble]
   3. *Kotek* [Kitten]
   4. *Idzie Grześ* [Here comes Greg]
   5. *Rzeczka* [Little river]
   6. *Ptasie plotki* [Birds' gossips]
TEXTS : Julian Tuwim (1894–1953)
PUBLISHER : PWM
ARRANGED : by the composer, for children's choir and orch in 1952 (concert
   performance, Warsaw, 29 April 1954), and for mezzo-sop and orch in 1953
   (broadcast by Polish Radio). Both remain in MS.

Two Children's Songs for voice and piano (1948)
   Spóźniony słowik [The overdue nightingale]
   O Panu Tralalińskim [About Mr Tralaliński]
TEXTS : Julian Tuwim
PREMIÈRE : Kraków, 26 January 1948
PERFORMERS : Irena Wiskida(sop), Jadwiga Szamotulska (pf)
PUBLISHERS : PWM / Chester
ARRANGED : by the composer for voice and chamber orch in 1952; this version first
   performed by Maria Drewniakówna with the Polish Radio SO, cond. Stefan
   Rachoń

Lawina [The Snowslide] for voice and piano (1949)
TEXT : poem by Alexander Pushkin (1799–1837), *Obval* (1829)
PREMIÈRE : Lesław Finze (T), Kraków, 26 September 1950
PUBLISHER : PWM
PRIZES : Second Prize in a competition of the Polish Composers' Union for songs to celebrate 150th anniversary of Pushkin's birth

Overture for Strings (1949)
PREMIÈRE : Prague, 9 November 1949
PERFORMERS : Prague Radio SO, cond. Grzegorz Fitelberg
DEDICATION : to Mirko Očadlik
DURATION : *c.* 5'
PUBLISHERS : PWM / Chester

Selection of extant incidental music for the theatre (1948–50)
Cyd (1948) *El Cid*, by P. Corneille
for small instrumental ensemble
PRODUCTION : Teatr Polski, Warsaw; première 8 January 1948
SOURCE : autograph score and parts in Biblioteka Narodowa (Mus. 3611)

Fantazy (1948), by Juliusz Słowacki
ENSEMBLE : 1. 0. 1. 0; 0. 2. 1. 0; GC; pf; 2vn, vc, db; female chor
PRODUCTION : Teatr Polski, Warsaw; première 10 July 1948
SOURCE : autograph score and 12 parts in Biblioteka Narodowa (Mus. 3612)

Wesołe kumoszki z Windsoru (1949)
Merry Wives of Windsor, by William Shakespeare
ENSEMBLE : 1. 0. 1. 0; 0. 1. 1. 0; perc; vn, va, vc, db
PRODUCTION : Teatr Polski, Warsaw; première 28 October 1949
SOURCE : set of 9 parts in Biblioteka Narodowa (Mus. 3613)

Bóg, cezarz i chłop (1950)
God, Caesar and Peasant, by Julius Hay
ENSEMBLE : 0. 0. 1. 0; 1. 1. 1. 0; perc; harp; 2vn, va, vc, db
PRODUCTION : Teatr Polski, Warsaw; première 5 April 1950
SOURCE : autograph score and 11 parts in Biblioteka Narodowa (Mus. 3610)

Little Suite, for chamber orchestra (1950)
I. *Fujarka* [Fife], Allegretto; II. *Hurra polka*, Vivace; III. *Piosenka* [Song], Andante molto sostenuto; IV. *Taniec* [Dance], Allegro molto
SOURCES : Folk melodies from Machów in the Rzeszów region
PERFORMED : on Polish Radio by a light-music chamber orchestra
REVISED : in 1951 for symphony orch (2. 2. 2. 2; 4. 3. 3. 1; timp, perc; str). Première, Warsaw, 20 April 1951, Polish Radio SO / Fitelberg
DURATION : *c.* 11'
PUBLISHERS : 1950 version, unpubl. MS; 1951 version, PWM / Chester

Słomkowy łańcuszek i inne dziecinne utwory (1950–51)
Straw chain and other children's pieces

Cycle of children's songs for sop, mezzo-sop, fl, ob, 2 cl, bn
 1. *Wstęp instrumentalny* [Instrumental introduction]
 2. *Chałupeczka niska* [Low hut]
 3. *Była babuleńka* [There was an old woman]
 4. *Co tam w lesie huknęło* [What went bang in the woods?]
 5. *Rosła kalina* [A guelder rose grew]
 7. *Chciało się Zosi jagódek* [Sophie wanted blueberries]
 8. *Słomkowy łańcuszek* [Straw chain]
TEXTS : nos. 2, 3, 4, 7, traditional material collected by Oskar Kolberg; no. 5, text by
   Janina Porazińska (1888–1971); no. 6, text by Teofil Lenartowicz (1822–93); no.
   8, text by Lucyna Krzemieniecka (1907–55)
PREMIÈRE : Polish Radio, Warsaw, 1951
DURATION : *c.* 10'
PUBLISHERS : PWM / Chester

Tryptyk Śląski [Silesian Triptych], for soprano and orchestra (1951)
 sop; 3. 2. 3. 2; 4. 3. 3. 1; timp, perc, cel; harp; str
SOURCES : Silesian folk texts and melodies from Bystron (ed) *Pieśni ludowe z
   polskiego Śląska* (Kraków, 1927–34)
PREMIÈRE : Warsaw, 2 December 1951
PERFORMERS : Maria Drewniakówna, Polish Radio SO, cond. Grzegorz Fitelberg
DURATION : *c.* 9'
PRIZES : First Prize at the Festival of Polish Music, Warsaw, 16 December 1951; State
   Prize class II, 17 July 1952
PUBLISHERS : PWM / Chester

Recitative e arioso for violin and piano (1951)
PREMIÈRE : Eugenia Umińska (vn), Kraków, *c.* 1952
DURATION : *c.* 3'
PUBLISHER : PWM (written for its director, Tadeusz Ochlewski)
ARRANGED : by Bronisław Eichenholz for violino grande and pf, this version first
   performed at Malmö in Sweden, 30 September 1966

Wiosna [Spring] (1951)
Cycle of children's songs for mezzo-soprano and chamber orch
 1. *Już jest wiosna* [Already it's spring]
 2. *Piosenka o złotym listku* [Song of the golden leaf]
 3. *Jak warszawski Woźnica* [Like a Warsaw coachman]
 4. *Majowa nocka* [May night]
TEXTS : (1) W. Domeradzki; (2) Jadwiga Korczakowska; (3) Januszewska; (4)
   Lucyna Krzemieniecka (1907–55)
PREMIÈRE : Polish Radio, Warsaw, 1951
PERFORMERS : Janina Godlewska, Warsaw Radio SO, cond. the composer
MANUSCRIPT : unpubl.
ARRANGED : Nos 2 and 4 arr. in 1952, publ. by PWM in 1954. No. 4 arr. SSA
   chor / pf, publ. Chester in 1977.

Jesień [Autumn] (1951)
Cycle of children's songs for mezzo-soprano and chamber orch
  1. *W listopadzie* [In October]
  2. *Świerszcz* [The cricket]
  3. *Mgła* [Fog]
  4. *Deszczyk jesienny* [Light autumn rain]
TEXTS : Lucyna Krzemieniecka (1907–55)
PREMIÈRE : Polish Radio, Warsaw, 1951
PERFORMERS : Janina Godlewska, Warsaw Radio SO, cond. by the composer
MANUSCRIPT : unpubl.

Ten Polish Folksongs on soldiers' themes (1951) for unacc. male chor
  1. *Pod Krakowem czarna pola* [A black field near Kraków]
  2. *Nie będę łez ronić* [No tear will be shed]
  3. *A w Warszawie* [And in Warsaw]
  4. *Zachodzi słoneczko* [The sun is setting]
  5. *Oj, i w polu jezioro* [Oh, and a lake in the field]
  6. *Jam kalinkę łamała* [I broke the guelder rose]
  7. *Gdzie to jedziesz, Jasiu?* [Where are you going, Jack?]
  8. *A na onej górze* [And on that mountain]
  9. *Już to mija siódmy roczek* [Already passed the seventh year]
  10. *Małgorzatka* [Maggie]
SOURCES : 1, 2, 4, 7–10 texts and tunes from collections by Oskar Kolberg; nos. 2, 4,
  9 from *Krakowskie* vol. 2 / 6 (Kraków, 1873); no. 7 from *Mazowsze* vol. 3 / 26
  (Kraków 1887); no. 8 from *Mazowsze* vol. 4 / 27 (Kraków, 1888); no. 10 from
  Mazowsze vol. 1 / 24 (Kraków, 1885). Sources for nos 1, 3, 5, 6 unknown
COMMISSION : from the Polish Ministry of Defence
PUBLISHER : Ministry of Defence Press, Polish Army series

Seven Songs for voice and piano (1950–52)
Mass songs for unison chorus
  1. *Zwycięska droga* [The road to victory]
  2. *Wyszłabym ja* [. . .] [I would marry]
  3. *Nowa Huta* [The post-war 'new foundry' town near Kraków]
  4. *Służba Polsce* [Service to Poland]
  5. *Żelazny marsz* [Iron March; from Songs of the Underground Struggle]
  6. *Najpiękniejszy sen* [The most beautiful dream]
  7. *Naprzód idziemy* [Forward we go]
TEXTS : nos. 1 and 6 by Tadeusz Urgacz; no. 2 by Leopold Lewin; nos. 3 and 4 by
  Stanisław Wygodzki; no. 5 by Stanisław Ryszard Dobrowolski; no. 7 by Jan
  Brzechwa
PUBLISHER : PWM, in the series 'Festiwal Muzyki Polskiej'
ARRANGED : by the composer in 1951, for unaccompanied male chorus (no. 4), and
  for unaccompanied mixed chorus (nos. 2, 4, 5)

Children's Songs for voice and piano (1952)
  Srebna szybka [Silver window-pane)
  Muszelka [Cockle-shell)
TEXTS : Agnieszka Barto
PUBLISHERS : PWM / Chester
ARRANGED : by the composer in 1953, for mezzo-soprano and chamber orch

Bukoliki (Bucolics) for piano (1952)
I. Allegro vivace; II. Allegretto sostenuto, poco rubato; III. Allegro molto;
IV. Andantino; V. Allegro marciale
PREMIÈRE : Warsaw, December 1953
PERFORMER : the composer
DURATION : 5'15" (I : 57"; II : 45"; III : 41"; IV : 1'28"; V : 1' 14")
PUBLISHERS : PWM / Chester
ARRANGED : by the composer in 1962 for va and vc (first perf in the 1970s by Stefan
  Kamasa, va, and Andrzej Orkisz, vc)

Three Songs for voice and piano (1953)
Soldiers' songs
  1. *Kto pierwszy* [Who first?] *Żywo* [briskly]
  2. *Narciarski patrol* [Ski patrol] *Umiarkowanie* [restrainedly]
  3. *Skowronki* [Skylarks] *Żywo* [briskly]
TEXTS : (1) Stanisław Czachorowski; (2) Aleksander Rymkiewicz: (3) Mieczysław
  Dołega
PUBLISHER : PWM, in the series *Pieśni Dziesięciolecia* (1954–5)

Miniatura [Miniature] for two pianos (1953)
DURATION : *c.* 1'50"
PUBLISHER : PWM

Three Pieces for the Young, for piano (1953)
  1. Four-finger exercise, Allegro
  2. Melody, Andante con moto
  3. March, Allegro
COMMISSION : from PWM
PUBLISHERS : PWM / Chester

Children's Songs for voice and piano (1953)
  Pióreczko [Little feather], text Janina Osińska
  Wróbelek [Little sparrow], text Lucyna Krzemieniecka
  Pożegnanie wakacji [Goodbye to holidays], text Krzemieniecka
  Wianki [Wreaths], text Stefania Szuchowa
Children's Songs for voice and chamber orchestra (1954)
  Spijże, śpij [Sleep, sleep] (1954), text Krzemieniecka
  Idzie nocka [Night is falling] (1954), text Osińska

Warzywa [Vegetables] (1954), text Julian Tuwim
Trudny rachunek [Difficult sums] (1954), text Tuwim

All written for Polish Radio; all unpubl.

Concerto for Orchestra (1950–54)

3. 3. 3. 3; 4. 4. 4. 1; timp, perc, cel, pf; 2 harps; str
I. Intrada : Allegro maestoso; II. Capriccio notturno e arioso : Vivace; III. Passacaglia, toccata e corale : Andante con moto – Allegro giusto.
SOURCES : folk melodies from Kolberg, *Mazowsze, Lud* (Kraków, 1886, 1890)
PREMIÈRE : Warsaw, 26 November 1954
PERFORMERS : Warsaw National PO, cond. Witold Rowicki
DEDICATION : to Witold Rowicki
SCORE : autograph MS in Biblioteka Narodowa (Mus. 533 Cim), available on microfilm (no. 30448). Shows completion date 'l. viii. 1954'
DURATION : *c.* 30′
PRIZES : State Prize class I and Order of Labour class II, 22 July 1955
PUBLISHERS : PWM / Chester
RECORDINGS : EMI IC 165–03 234 Q (1978) Polish Radio SO / Lutosławski; PNCD 040 (1962) Warsaw National PO / Rowicki; Philips 412 377–2 Warsaw National PO / Rowicki; ERATO 4509–91711–2 (1993) Chicago SO / Barenboim

Dance Preludes, for clarinet and piano (1954)

I. Allegro molto; II. Andantino; III. Allegro giocoso; IV. Andante; V. Allegro molto
PREMIÈRE : (original version) Warsaw, 15 February 1955
PERFORMERS : Ludwik Kurkiewicz (cl), Sergiusz Nadgryzowski (pf)
ORCHESTRATED : 1955, for cl and chamber orch (timp, perc, pf; harp; str 8. 8. 6. 6. 4.). Concert première of this (second) version, Aldeburgh Festival, June 1963, by Gervase de Peyer, with the English Chamber Orchestra, cond. Benjamin Britten.
ARRANGED : 1959, for 9 instruments (1. 1. 1. 1; 1. 0. 0. 0; str 1. 1. 1. 1.). Première of this (third) version at Louny (NW of Prague), 10 November 1959, by the Czech Nonet
DURATION : *c.* 7′
PUBLISHERS : PWM / Chester
RECORDINGS : (1955 version) Hyperion A66 215 King / ECO / Litton; Philips 416 817–2 Brunner / Bavarian Radio SO / Lutosławski

Five Songs, for soprano and piano (1957)

1. *Morze* [Sea]; 2. *Wiatr* [Wind]; 3. *Zima* [Winter]; 4. *Rycerze* [Crusaders];
5. *Dzwony Cerkiewne* [Orthodox-Church bells]
TEXT : poems by Kazimiera Iłłakowicz (1892–1983) from *Rymy dziecięce* (1922)
PREMIÈRE : Katowice, 25 November 1959
PERFORMER : Krystyna Szostek-Radkowa (sop)
DEDICATION : (1) to Marya Freund, (2, 3, 4, 5) to Nadia Boulanger
DURATION : *c.* 10′
PUBLISHERS : PWM / Moeck Verlag
ORCHESTRATED : by the composer in 1958 (timp, perc; pf; 2 harps; str 9. 4. 4. 4), this

version first perf. in Katowice on 12 February 1960, by Krystyna Szostek-Radkowa
and the Polish Radio SO, cond. Jan Krenz
RECORDINGS : PNCD 045 (1967) Łukomska/Warsaw National PO /
  Markowski; EMI IC 165–03 234 Q (1978) Łukomska / Polish Radio SO /
  Lutosławski

Muzyka żałobna [*Musique funèbre*] (1954–58) for str orch:
  vn I (6–8), vn II (6–8), vn III (6–8), vn IV (6–8), va I (4–6), va II (4–6), vc I (4–6),
  vc II (4–6), db I (3–5), db II (3–5)
Prologue – Metamorphoses – Apogeum – Epilogue
PREMIÈRE : Katowice, 26 March 1958
PERFORMERS : Polish Radio SO, cond. Jan Krenz
DEDICATION : *à la mémoire de Béla Bartók*
SCORE : autograph MS in Biblioteka Narodowa (Mus. 532 Cim), available on
  microfilm (no. 30447). Dedication shown in French.
DURATION : *c.* 13'30"
PRIZES : Prize of the Polish Composers' Union [ZKP], 15 January 1959; joint first
  prize, Tribune Internationale des Compositeurs (UNESCO), Paris, 12–15 May
  1959 (with Tadeusz Baird)
PUBLISHERS : PWM / Chester
RECORDINGS : EMI IC 165–03 234 Q (1978) Polish Radio SO / Lutosławski;
  PNCD 040 (1959) Warsaw National PO / Rowicki; Philips 412 377–2 Warsaw
  National PO / Rowicki

Three Children's Songs for voice and piano (1958)
  Na Wroniej ulicy w Warszawie [On Wronia Street in Warsaw]
  Kuku, kuku [Cuckoo, cuckoo]
  Piosenka na prima aprilis [Song on April Fools' Day]
TEXTS : Roman Pisarski (1912–69)
MANUSCRIPT : unpubl.

Piosenki dziecinne [Children's Songs] (1958)
  1. *Siwy mróz* [Hoar-frost]
  2. *Malowane miski* [Painted bowls]
  3. *Kap, kap, kap* [Drip, drip, drip]
  4. *Bajki iskierki* [Sparkling tales]
  5. *Butki za cztery dudki* [Little shoes for fourpence]
  6. *Plama na podłodze* [A stain on the floor]
TEXTS : Janina Porazińska (1888–1971)
MANUSCRIPT : unpubl.

Trzy piosenki dziecinne [Three Children's Songs] (1959)
  1. *Trąbka* [Little trumpet]
  2. *Abecadło* [ABC]
  3. *Lato* [Summer]
TEXTS : Benedykt Hertz (1872–1952)

MANUSCRIPT : unpubl.

Three Postludes for orchestra (1958–63)
3. 3. 3. 3; 4. 3. 3. 1; 4 perc, pf; 2 harps; stri 16. 14. 12. 12. 8
I. m.m. = 80; II. m.m. = 160; III. m.m. = 150
PREMIÈRE : (I only) Grand Theatre, Geneva, 1 September 1963
PERFORMERS : Orch of the Suisse Romande, cond. Ernest Ansermet
PREMIÈRE : (all 3) Kraków, 8 October 1965
PERFORMERS : Kraków PO, cond. Henryk Czyż
DEDICATION : (I only) for the centenary of the Red Cross
DURATION : (I, 3′30″; II, 4′50″; III, 8′40″)
PUBLISHERS : PWM / Chester
RECORDINGS : (I only) PNCD 042 (1964) Polish Radio SO / Krenz; EMI IC 165–03
    236 Q (1978) Polish Radio SO / Lutosławski; EMI ED29 1172–2 Polish Radio
    SO / Lutosławski

Jeux vénitiens [Venetian Games] for chamber orchestra (1960–61)
2. 1. 3. 1; 1. 1. 1. 0; timp, perc, cel, pf (2); 2 harps; str 4. 3. 3. 2
I: [ad libitum]; II : m.m. = 150; III : m.m. = 60; IV : m.m. = 60
PREMIÈRE : (incomplete, without III), Teatro la Fenice, Venice Biennale, 24 April
    1961
PERFORMERS : Kraków Philharmonic Chamber Orch, cond. Markowski
PREMIÈRE : (complete, including III and slight revision of the other mvts) Warsaw
    Autumn Festival, 16 September 1961
PERFORMERS : Warsaw National PO, cond. Rowicki
COMMISSION : from Andrzej Markowski and the Kraków Philharmonic Chamber
    Orch
DURATION : c. 13′
PRIZE : First Prize, Tribune Internationale des Compositeurs (UNESCO), Paris, May
    1962
PUBLISHERS : PWM / Moeck Verlag
RECORDINGS : EMI IC 165–03 236 Q (1978) Polish Radio SO / Lutosławski;
    PNCD 041 (1962) Warsaw National PO / Rowicki

Trois poèmes d'Henri Michaux for chorus and orchestra (1961–3)
    [Three Poems of Henri Michaux]
Chor: twenty solo v (5 S, 5 A, 5 T, 5 B)
Orch: 3. 2. 3. 2; 2. 2. 2. 0; timp, 4 perc, 2 pf; harp [NB no str]
I. Pensées; II. Le grand combat; II. Repos dans le malheur
TEXT : poems by Henri Michaux (1899–1984). I, III from Plume (Paris, 1938); II
    from Qui je fus (Paris, 1928)
PREMIÈRE : Zagreb Music Biennale, 9 May 1963
PERFORMERS : Zagreb Radio Orch / Lutosławski; Zagreb Radio Choir / Zlatić
COMMISSION : from Slavko Zlatić and the Zagreb Radio Choir
SCORE : autograph in Biblioteka Narodowa (Mus. 534 Cim), available on microfilm
    (no. 30449). Shows completion date '17.iv.1963'.

DURATION : *c.* 20'
PRIZE : First Prize, Tribune Internationale des Compositeurs (UNESCO), Paris, May 1964
PUBLISHERS : PWM / Chester
RECORDINGS : EMI IC 165–03 235 Q (1978) Polish Radio Chor / Michniewski, Polish Radio SO / Lutosławski; PNCD 041 (1964) Polish Radio Chor / Lutosławski; Polish Radio SO / Krenz

String Quartet (1964)
I. Introductory Movement; II. Main Movement
PREMIÈRE : Stockholm, 12 March 1965
PERFORMERS : LaSalle Quartet
COMMISSION : from Swedish Radio for the 10th anniversary of 'Nutida Musik'
DURATION : *c.* 23'30" (I, *c.* 8'30"; II, c. 15')
PUBLISHERS : Chester / PWM
RECORDINGS : DG 423 245–2 (1968) LaSalle Quartet; PNCD 045 (1965) LaSalle Quartet

Paroles tissées [Woven words] for tenor and chamber orchestra (1965)
T soloist; perc, harp, pf; str (10. 3. 3. 1)
TEXT : 'Quatre tapisseries pour la Châtelaine de Vergi', by Jean-François Chabrun, from *Poésie 47*
PREMIÈRE : Aldeburgh Festival, 20 June 1965
PERFORMERS : Peter Pears, Philomusica of London, cond. the composer
DEDICATION : to Peter Pears
DURATION : *c.* 15'
PUBLISHERS : Chester / PWM
RECORDINGS : PNCD 042 (1968) Louis Devos, Polish Radio SO / Lutosławski; EMI IC 165–03 235 Q (1978) Devos, Polish Radio SO / Lutosławski

Symphony no. 2 (1965–7)
3. 3. 3. 3; 3. 3. 3. 1; 3 perc groups; harp; pf (2); str (16. 14. 12. 6. 6)
I. *Hésitant*; II. *Direct.*
PREMIÈRE : (II only) Hamburg, 15 October 1966
PERFORMERS : NDR [North German Radio] Symphony Orch, cond. Boulez
PREMIÈRE : (complete) Katowice, 9 June 1967
PERFORMERS : Polish Radio Symphony Orch, cond. the composer
DURATION : *c.* 30'
COMMISSION : from Norddeutscher Rundfunk for their 100th concert in the contemporary music series 'Das Neue Werk'
PRIZE : First Prize of the Tribune Internationale des Compositeurs (UNESCO) at Paris, 20–24 May 1968
PUBLISHERS : Chester / PWM
RECORDINGS : PNCD 041 (1968) Warsaw National PO / Lutosławski; EMI IC 165–03 232 Q (1978) Polish Radio SO / Lutosławski

Invention, for piano (1968)
DURATION : *c.* 50″
DEDICATION : for the 71 st birthday of Stefan Śledziński
PUBLISHERS : PWM / Chester (1991)

Livre pour orchestre (1968)
[NB no valid translations of the French title in use]
3. 3. 3. 3; 4. 3. 3. 1; timp, 3 perc, cel, pf; harp; str
1er Chapitre [Chapter 1]; 1er Intermède [Intermezzo 1]; 2me Chapitre [Chapter 2]; 2me
Intermède [Intermezzo 2]; 3me Chapitre [Chapter 3]; 3me Intermède et chapitre final
[Intermezzo 3 and final chapter]
PREMIÈRE : Hagen, 18 November 1968
PERFORMERS : Hagen City Orch, cond. Berthold Lehmann
COMMISSION : from the City of Hagen, Federal Republic of Germany
DEDICATION : to Berthold Lehmann
DURATION : *c.* 22′
PUBLISHERS : Chester / PWM
RECORDINGS : PNCD 042 (1969) Warsaw National PO / Krenz; EMI IC 165–03
   233 Q (1978) Polish Radio SO / Lutosławski

Concerto for Cello and Orchestra (1969–70)
Solo vc; 3. 3. 3. 3; 4. 3. 3. 1; timp, 3 perc, cel, pf; harp; str
PREMIÈRE : RFH, London, 14 October 1970
PERFORMERS : Rostropovich, Bournemouth SO, cond. Edward Downes
COMMISSION : Royal Philharmonic Society and the Gulbenkian Foundation
DEDICATION : to Mstislav Rostropovich
DURATION : *c.* 24′
PUBLISHERS : Chester / PWM
RECORDINGS : PNCD 042 (1976) Jabłoński, Polish Radio SO / Lutosławski; EMI
   IC 165–03 233 Q(1978) Jabłoński, Polish Radio SO / Lutosławski; Philips 416
   817–2 (1986) Schiff, Bavarian Radio SO / Lutosławski; EMI CDC7 49304–2
   (1975) Rostropovich, Orchestre de Paris / Lutosławski

Preludes and Fugue for 13 solo strings (1970–72)
for 13 solo strings (7.3.2.1)
COMPOSER'S NOTE : 'The work can be performed whole or in various shortened
   versions. In the case of performances of the whole, the indicated order of the [seven]
   Preludes is obligatory. Any number of the Preludes in any order can be performed
   with or without a shortened version of the Fugue.'
PREMIÈRE : Graz, 12 October 1972, Styrian Autumn Festival
PERFORMERS : Zagreb Radio / TV Chamber Orch, cond. Mario di Bonaventura
DEDICATION : to Mario di Bonaventura [who commissioned the work]
DURATION : *c.* 34′ [without omissions]
PUBLISHERS : Chester / PWM
RECORDINGS : PNCD 043 (1974) Warsaw National Chamber Orch / Lutosławski;
   EMI IC 165–03 231 Q (1978) Polish Chamber Orch / Lutosławski

Les espaces du sommeil, for baritone and orchestra (1975)
[The spaces of sleep; NB the title is given only in French]
3. 3. 3. 3; 4. 3. 3. 1; timp, perc, cel; pf; harp; str
POEM : by Robert Desnos (1900–45) from *Corps et Biens* (Paris, 1930)
PREMIÈRE : Philharmonie, [West] Berlin, 12 April 1978
PERFORMERS : Fischer-Dieskau, Berlin PO, cond. the composer
DURATION : *c.* 15′
PUBLISHERS : Chester / PWM
RECORDINGS : CBS IM 42203 (1985) Shirley-Quirk, Los Angeles PO / Salonen;
    Philips 416 387–2 (1986) Fischer-Dieskau, Berlin SO / Lutosławski

Sacher Variation, for solo cello (1975)
PREMIÈRE : Zurich, 2 May 1976
PERFORMER : Mstislav Rostropovich
DEDICATION : to Paul Sacher on his 70th birthday
DURATION : *c.* 5′
PUBLISHERS : Chester / PWM

Mi-Parti (1975–6)
3. 3. 3. 3; 4. 3. 3. 1; timp, perc, cel, pf; harp; str
PREMIÈRE : Concertgebouw, Amsterdam, 22 October 1976
PERFORMERS : Concertgebouw Orchestra, cond. the composer
COMMISSION : from the City of Amsterdam for the Concertgebouw Orchestra
DURATION : *c.* 15′
PUBLISHERS : Chester / PWM
RECORDINGS : PNCD 043 (1976) Polish Radio SO / Lutosławski; EMI IC 165–03
    236 Q (1978) Polish Radio SO / Lutosławski

Novelette (1978–9)
3. 3. 3. 3; 4. 3. 3. 1; timp, perc cel, pf; 2 harps; str
I, Announcement; II, First Event; III, Second Event;
    IV, Third Event; V, Conclusion
PREMIÈRE : Washington DC, 29 January 1980
PERFORMERS : National SO, Washington, cond. Rostropovich
DEDICATION : for Mstislav Rostropovich and the National SO, Washington
DURATION : *c.* 17′ 30″
PUBLISHERS : Chester / PWM
RECORDINGS : PNCD 043 (1984 Warsaw Autumn) Junge Deutsche Phil. / Holliger;
    DG 431 664–2 (1992) BBCSO / Lutosławski

Epitaph, for oboe and piano (1979)
PREMIÈRE : Wigmore Hall, London, 3 January 1980
PERFORMERS : Janet Craxton (ob), Ian Brown (pf)
DEDICATION : in memory of Alan Richardson
DURATION : *c.* 5′30″
PUBLISHERS : Chester / PWM

RECORDING : PNCD 045 (1980 Warsaw Autumn) Holliger/Esztényi

Double Concerto for oboe, harp and chamber orchestra (1979–80)
solo ob, solo harp; 2 perc; str 7. 2. 2. 1
I, Rapsodico; II, Dolente, III, Marciale e grotesco
PREMIÈRE : Lucerne, 24 August 1980
PERFORMERS : Heinz and Ursula Holliger, Collegium Musicum, cond. Sacher
DEDICATION : to Paul Sacher
COMMISSION : from Paul Sacher
DURATION : *c.* 20′
PUBLISHERS : Chester / PWM
RECORDING : Philips 416 817–2 (1986) Holligers / Bavarian SO / Lutosławski

Grave, Metamorphoses for cello and piano (1981)
PREMIÈRE : The National Museum, Warsaw, 22 April 1981
PERFORMERS : Roman Jabłoński (vc), Krystyna Borucińska (pf)
DEDICATION : *in memoriam* Stefan Jarociński (1912 – 8 May 1980)
ORCHESTRATED : by the composer in 1982 for vc and 13 str (4. 3. 3. 2. 1). First perf
  of this version at the Festival Estival in Paris on 26 August 1982, played by Mischa
  Maisky with the Polish Chamber Orch, cond. Jerzy Maksymiuk
DURATION : *c.* 7′
PUBLISHERS : Chester / PWM
RECORDING : PNCD 045 (1981 Warsaw Autumn) Jabłoński / Esztényi

Mini-Overture, for brass ensemble (1982)
hn, 2 trpts, trbn, tuba
PREMIÈRE : Lucerne Festival, Kunsthaus, Lucerne, 11 March 1982
PERFORMERS : Philip Jones Brass Ensemble
DEDICATION : to Dr Walter Strebi
DURATION : *c.* 3′
PUBLISHERS : Chester / PWM
RECORDING : Chandos ABRD 1190 Philip Jones Brass Ensemble

Symphony no. 3 (1981–3)
3. 3. 3. 3; 4. 4. 4. 1; timp, 3 perc, cel, pf (2); 2 harps; str
PREMIÈRE : Chicago, 29 September 1983
PERFORMERS : Chicago SO, cond. Solti
DEDICATION : for Sir Georg Solti and the Chicago Symphony Orchestra
COMMISSION : from the Chicago SO
DURATION : *c.* 30′
PUBLISHERS : Chester / PWM
RECORDINGS : Philips 416 387–2 (1985) Berlin PO / Lutosławski; CBS IM 42203
  (1985) Los Angeles PO / Salonen; PNCD 044 (1988) Polish Radio SO / Wit

Chain 1, for chamber ensemble (1983)
1. 1. 1. 1; 1. 1. 0; perc; cemb; str (1. 1. 1. 1. 1)
PREMIÈRE : QEH, London, 4 October 1983
PERFORMERS : London Sinfonietta, cond. the composer
DEDICATION : to Michael Vyner and the London Sinfonietta
DURATION : *c.* 9'
PUBLISHERS : Chester / PWM
RECORDING : PNCD 044 (1984 Warsaw Autumn) Junge Deutsche Phil. / Holliger

Partita for violin and piano (1984)
1. Allegro giusto, 2. Ad libitum, 3. Largo, 4. Ad libitum, 5. Presto
PREMIÈRE : Saint Paul, Minnesota, 18 January 1985
PERFORMERS : Pinchas Zukerman (vn), Marc Neikrug (pf)
ORCHESTRATED : by the composer in 1988 (solo vn; 2. 0. 2. 2; 0. 2. 2. 0; timp, perc,
    cel, pf solo; str). This version written for and dedicated to Anne-Sophie Mutter.
    First performed in Munich on 10 January 1990 by Mutter with the Munich PO,
    cond. the composer (NB. her recording of August 1988 predates this performance).
DURATION : *c.* 15'
PUBLISHERS : Chester / PWM
RECORDINGS : PNCD 045 (1988) Kulka (vn), Knapik (pf); DG 423 696–2 (1988)
    Mutter / BBCSO / Lutosławski

Chain 2 , Dialogue for violin and orchestra (1984–5)
Solo vn; 2. 2. 2. 2; 0. 2. 2. 0; timp, 2 perc, cel / pf; str (6. 6. 4. 4. 2)
1. *ad libitum*, 2. *a battuta*; 3. *ad libitum*, 4. *a battuta – ad libitum – a battuta*
PREMIÈRE : Zurich, 31 January 1986
PERFORMERS : Anne-Sophie Mutter, Collegium Musicum, cond. Paul Sacher
DEDICATION : to Paul Sacher
COMMISSION : from Paul Sacher for the Collegium Musicum
DURATION : *c.* 18'
PUBLISHERS : Chester / PWM
RECORDINGS : DG 423 696–2 (1988) Mutter / BBCSO / Lutosławski; PNCD 044
    (1988 Warsaw Autumn) Jakowicz / Warsaw National PO / Kord

Chain 3 for orchestra (1986)
3. 3. 3. 3; 4. 3. 3. 1; timp, 4 perc, pf, cel; 2 harps; str
PREMIÈRE : Davies Hall, San Francisco, 10 December 1986
PERFORMERS : San Francisco SO, cond. the composer
DURATION : *c.* 10'
PUBLISHERS : Chester / PWM
RECORDINGS : PNCD 044 (1988) Polish Radio SO / Lutosławski; DG 431 664–2
    (1992) BBCSO / Lutosławski

Fanfare for Louisville (1986)
3. 3. 3. 3; 4. 4. 3. 1; timp, perc
PREMIÈRE : Louisville, USA, 19 September 1986

PERFORMERS : Louisville Orch, cond. Lawrence Leighton Smith
DURATION : *c.* 2'
PUBLISHER : Chester

Fanfare for CUBE (1987)

for brass quintet (1. 2. 1. 1)
PREMIÈRE : the honorary degree ceremony, Cambridge, 11 June 1987
PERFORMERS : Cambridge University Brass Ensemble
DURATION : *c.* 30"
PUBLISHER : Chester

Concerto for Piano and Orchestra (1987–8)

solo pf; 3. 3. 3. 3; 4. 2. 3. 1; timp, perc; harp; str
I. m.m. = 110; II. presto, m.m. = 160; III. Largo, m.m. = 40–45; IV. m.m. = *c.* 84
PREMIÈRE : Kleines Festspielhaus, Salzburg, 19 August 1988
PERFORMERS : Krystian Zimerman, Austrian Radio SO, cond. the composer
COMMISSION : from the Salzburg Festival
DURATION : *c.* 27'
PUBLISHERS : Chester / PWM
RECORDING : DG 431 664–2 (1992) Zimerman / BBCSO / Lutosławski

Slides, for chamber ensemble (1988)

[*Przezrocza*; 'slides' in the sense of photographic transparencies]
1. 1. 1. 1. 1; 0. 0. 0. 0; perc, pf; vn, va, vc, b
PREMIÈRE : Merkin Concert Hall, New York, 1 December 1988
PERFORMERS : Speculum Musicae
DEDICATION : for the 80th birthday of Elliott Carter (b. 11 December 1908)
DURATION : *c.* 4'
PUBLISHERS : Chester / PWM

Prelude for G. S. M. D. (1989)

2. 2. 2. 2; 2. 2. 2. 1; timp, perc; str
PREMIÈRE : Guildhall School of Music and Drama, London, 11 May 1989
PERFORMERS : Guildhall SO, cond. the composer
DURATION : *c.* 2'
PUBLISHER : Chester

Fanfare for Lancaster (1989)

for brass ensemble (4. 3. 3. 1) and side drum
PREMIÈRE : University of Lancaster, 11 October 1989
DURATION : *c.* 1'
PUBLISHER : Chester

Interlude, for orchestra (1989)

1. 2. 2. 1; 0. 1. 1. 0; perc, cel, pf; harp; str
(composed to link *Partita* and *Chain 2*)

PREMIÈRE : Munich, 10 January 1990 (together with the orch version of *Partita*)
PERFORMERS : Munich PO, cond. the composer
DEDICATION : to Paul Sacher
COMMISSION : from Paul Sacher
DURATION : *c.* 5'
PUBLISHERS : Chester / PWM

Tarantella, for baritone and piano (1990)
TEXT : poem by Hilaire Belloc (1870–1953) 'Do you remember an inn, Miranda?'
PREMIÈRE : Purcell Room, London, 20 May 1990
OCCASION : gala concert for the AIDS charity 'CrusAid'
PERFORMERS : David Wilson-Johnson (Bar), David Owen Norris (pf)
DEDICATION : to Sheila MacCrindle
DURATION : *c.* 3'
PUBLISHERS : Chester / PWM

Chantefleurs et Chantefables (1989–90)
Sop solo; 1. 1. 1. 1; 1. 1. 1. 0; perc, harp; pf; str
   1. La Belle-de-Nuit [Marvel of Peru]
   2. La Sauterelle [Grasshopper]
   3. La Véronique [Speedwell]
   4. L'Églantine, l'Aubépine et la Glycine [Wild-rose, Hawthorn and Wistaria]
   5. La Tortue [Tortoise]
   6. La Rose [Rose]
   7. L'Alligator [Alligator]
   8. L'Angélique [Angelica]
   9. Le Papillon [Butterfly]
TEXTS : Robert Desnos (1900–45), selected from the full collection of *Chantefables et Chantefleurs* (Paris, 1955)
PREMIÈRE : Henry Wood Promenade Concert, London, 8 August 1991
PERFORMERS : Solveig Kringleborn (sop), BBCSO, cond. Lutosławski
DURATION : *c.* 20'
PUBLISHERS : Chester / PWM

Symphony no. 4 (1988–92)
3. 3. 3. 3; 4. 3. 3. 1; harp; cel, timp, perc; str
PREMIÈRE : Los Angeles, 5 February 1993
PERFORMERS : Los Angeles PO, cond. the composer
COMMISSION : from the Los Angeles PO
DURATION : *c.* 22'
PUBLISHERS : Chester / PWM

Subito, for violin and piano (1992)
written as a test piece for the Indianapolis Violin Competition
PREMIÈRE : Indianapolis, September 1994

Bibliography

1. Books: Monographs

Homma, Martina: *Witold Lutosławski: Zwölfton-Harmonik – Formbildung 'aleatorischer Kontrapunkt'* (Köln, Bela Verlag, 1996). 758pp. [Reprint of thesis]

Jarociński, Stefan: *Witold Lutosławski. Materiały do monografii* [Materials for a monograph] (Kraków, PWM, 1967). 91pp.

Kaczyński, Tadeusz: *Lutosławski. Życie i muzyka.* [L. Life and music] (Warsaw, Sutkowski Edition, 1994). 255pp.

Nordwall, Owe (ed.): *Lutosławski* (Stockholm/London, Wilhelm Hansen, 1968). 148pp.

Paja-Stach, Jadwiga: *Witold Lutosławski* (Kraków, Musica Iagellonica, 1996), 123pp.

Paja-Stach, Jadwiga: *Lutosławski i jego styl muzyczny* [L. and his musical style] (Kraków, Musica Iagellonica, 1997). 224pp.

Pociej, Bohdan: *Lutosławski a wartość muzyki* [L. and the value of his music] (Kraków, PWM, 1976). 133pp.

Rae, Charles Bodman: *The Music of Lutosławski* (London/Boston, Faber and Faber, 1994). 288pp.

Rae, Charles Bodman: *Muzyka Lutosławskiego*, revised/expanded (second) edn, trans. Stanisław Krupowicz (Warsaw, Wydawnictwo Naukowe PWN, 1996). 306pp.

Skowron, Zbigniew (ed.): *Lutosławski Studies* (Oxford, OUP, 1999). Contains chapters by: John Casken, Steven Stucky, Martina Homma, Charles Bodman Rae, Adrian Thomas, Arnold Whittall, Irina Nikolska, Jadwiga Paja-Stach, Andrzej Tuchowski, Peter Petersen, Anna-Maria Harley, James Harley.

Stucky, Steven: *Lutosławski and his music* (Cambridge, CUP, 1981). 252pp.

2. Books: Conversations

Couchoud, Jean-Paul: *La musique polonaise et Witold Lutosławski* (Paris, Stock Musique, 1981).

Kaczyński, Tadeusz: *Rozmowy z Witoldem Lutosławskim* [Conversations with W.L.] (Kraków, PWM, 1972). Second, revised and expanded edition (Wrocław, Tau Edition, 1993).

Kaczyński, Tadeusz: *Conversations with Lutosławski*, trans. Yolanta May (London, Chester Music, 1980). Second, revised and expanded edition, trans. Dorota Kwiatkowska-Rae (London, Chester Music, 1996).

Nikolska, Irina: *Conversations with Witold Lutosławski (1987–92).* (Stockholm, Melos, 1994).

Varga, Bálint András: *Lutosławski Profile* (London, Chester Music, 1976).

3. Symposia

Metzger, Heinz-Klaus, and Reihn, Rainer (eds): 'Witold Lutosławski', *Musik-Konzepte*, vols 71/72/73 (Munich, 1991). 229pp. Includes articles by: Lutosławski; Martina Homma; Aloyse Michaely.

Polony, Leszek (ed.): *Witold Lutosławski. Sesja naukowa poświęcona twórczości kompozytora. Kraków 24–25 kwietnia 1980. Wybór materiałów.* [W.L. Conference devoted to the composer's work. Kraków 24–25 April 1980. Collected materials.] (Kraków, Academy of Music, 1985). 189pp. Includes articles by: Danuta Gwizdała; Tadeusz Kaczyński (on trope techniques); Maciej Negrey; Bohdan Pociej; Krzysztof Szwajgier; Krystyna Tarnawska-Kaczorowska; and Lutosławski.

Tarnawska-Kaczorowska, Krystyna (ed.): *Witold Lutosławski. Materiały sympozjum poświęconego twórczości. Prezentacje, interpretacje, konfrontacje.* [W.L. Materials from a symposium devoted to his work. Presentations, interpretations, confrontations] (Warsaw, Polish Composers' Union, 1985), 208pp. Includes articles by: Andrzej Chłopecki; Krzysztof Szwajgier; Andrzej Tuchowski; Krystyna Tarnawska-Kaczorowska; Joanna Wnuk-Nazarowa; Witold Lutosławski [on Symphony no. 3]; Bohdan Pociej and Mieczysław Tomaszewski.

Morawska, Katarzyna (ed.): *Witold Lutosławski: 25 I 1913 – 7 II 1994*, commemorative double issue of *Muzyka*, vol. 40, nos. 1–2 (Warsaw, Institute of the Arts, Polish Academy of Sciences, 1995). 236pp. Contains articles by: Krzysztof Baculewski; Charles Bodman Rae; Martina Homma; Jadwiga Paja-Stach (and Maria Stanilewicz-Kamionka); Krzysztof Meyer; Irina Nikolska; Dorota Krawczyk; Alicja Jarzębska. Also contains two book reviews: by Zbigniew Skowron (on *The Music of Lutosławski*, by Charles Bodman Rae); and Dorota Krawczyk (on *Conversations with Witold Lutosławski*, by Irina Nikolska).

4. Doctoral Theses

Bietti, Giovanni Battista: *Forma e funzione nelle opere di Lutosławski (1961–76).* (PhD, University of Rome 'La Sapienza', 1992).

Gantchoula, Philippe: *Hésitant-Direct: l'oeuvre de Witold Lutosławski* (PhD, Paris Conservatoire, 1985).

Homma, Martina: *Witold Lutosławski: Zwölfton-Harmonik – Formbildung 'aleatorischer Kontrapunkt'; Studien zum Gesamtwerk unter Einbeziehung der Skizzen* (PhD, University of Köln, 1995).

Klein, Michael Leslie: *A Theoretical Study of the Late Music of Witold Lutosławski: New Interactions of Pitch, Rhythm and Form* (PhD, New York State University at Buffalo, 1995).

Paja [Paja-Stach], Jadwiga: *System w muzyce Witolda Lutosławskiego.* [System (i.e. 'Systems theory') in the music of W.L.] (PhD, Jagiellonian University of Kraków, 1982).

Rae, Charles Bodman: *Pitch Organisation in the Music of Witold Lutosławski since 1979* (PhD, University of Leeds, 1992).

Russavage, Kathy Ann: *Instrumentation in the works of Witold Lutosławski* (DMA, University of Illinois at Urbana-Champaign, 1988).

Rust, Douglas: *A Theory of Form for Lutosławski's Late Symphonic Work* (PhD, Yale University, 1994).

Skolnic, Vladimir: *Pitch Organisation in Aleatoric Counterpoint in Lutosławski's music of the Sixties* (PhD, Hebrew University of Jerusalem, 1993).

Stucky, Steven: *The Music of Witold Lutosławski: a Style-Critical Survey.* (DMA, University of Cornell, 1978).

5. Articles by the Composer (selected)

See also: Jarociński (1967); Nordwall (1968); Kaczyński (1972/1993; and 1980/1996); Jean-Paul Couchoud (1981).

Lutosławski, Witold: 'Tchnienie wielkości' [Breath of greatness], *Muzyka Polska* 1937/3, pp. 169–70 [on Szymanowski].

'O Grzegorzu Fitelbergu' [On Grzegorz Fitelberg], *Muzyka* 5 (Warsaw, Polish Academy of Sciences, 1954/7–8), pp. 26–33.

'Kompozytor a odbiorca', *Ruch Muzyczny* IV, 1964/4, pp. 3–4; English version, 'The Composer and the Listener', in *Lutosławski* ed. Owe Nordwall (Stockholm, Hansen, 1968), pp. 119–24.

'O roli elementu przypadku w technice komponowania' [On the role of the element of chance in compositional technique], *Res Facta* 1, 1967, pp. 34–8; English version, 'About the Element of Chance in Music', in *Ligeti, Lidholm and Lutosławski: Three Aspects of New Music* (Stockholm, 1968), pp. 45–53; German version, 'Über das Element des Zufalls in der Musik', *Melos* 36, 1969/11, pp. 457–60.

'O rytmice i organizacji wysokości dźwięków w technice komponowania z zastosowaniem ograniczonego działania przypadku' [c. 1968], in *Spotkania muzyczne w Baranowie* [1976]. *Muzyka w kontekście kultury*, ed. L. Polony (Kraków, 1978), pp. 76–87; English version, 'Rhythm and the organisation of pitch in composing techniques employing a limited element of chance', *Polish Musicological Studies* 2, 1986, pp. 37–53 [contains errors of proof-reading]; German version, 'Über Rhytmik und Tonhöhenorganisation in der Kompositionstechnik unter Anwendung begrenzter Zufallswirkung', *Musik-Konzepte* 71/72/73 (Munich, 1991), pp. 3–32.

'Notes on the construction of large-scale forms', unpubl. MS of lecture written *c.* 1969 (in English), and originally intended for presentation at Darmstadt.

'Nowy utwór na orkiestrę symfoniczną' [A new work for symphonic orchestra (Symphony no. 2)], *Res Facta* 4, 1970, pp. 6–13; English version in *The Orchestral Composer's Point of View: essays on twentieth-century music by those who wrote it*, ed. R. Hines (University of Oklahoma Press, 1970), pp. 128–51.

'Kilka problemów z dziedziny rytmiki' [Some problems in the area of rhythm], *Res Facta* 9 (Kraków, 1982), pp. 114–28.

6. Other Articles and Books (selected)

Baculewski, Krzysztof: 'Lutosławski: jedna technika, jeden styl?' [L.: one technique, one style?], *Muzyka,* 40/1–2 (Warsaw, Polish Academy of Sciences, 1995), pp. 25–39.

Baculewski, Krzysztof: *Polska twórczość kompozytorska 1945–1984* [Polish composers' work 1945–84] (Kraków, 1987).

Balázs, Istvan: 'Macht und Ohnmacht der Musik. Witold Lutosławskis Cellokonzert und seine gesellschaftlichen Zusammenhänge', *Neue Zeitschrift für Musik* CXLVII (1986/7–8), pp. 40–7.

BIBLIOGRAPHY

Brennecke, Wilfried: 'Die Trauermusik von Witold Lutosławski', in *Festschrift Friedrich Blume zum 70 Geburtstag*, eds A. A. Abert and W. Pfannkuch (Kassel, 1963), pp. 60–73.

Bristiger, Michał: 'Stefan Jarociński' [commemorative profile of his life and work], *Polish Musicological Studies* 2 (Kraków, 1986), pp. 25–36.

Bystron, Jan Stanisław, *et al.* (eds): *Pieśni ludowe z polskiego Śląska* [Folksongs from Polish Silesia] (Kraków, 1927–34).

Casken, John: 'Transition and Transformation in the Music of Witold Lutosławski', *Contact* (Autumn 1975), no. 12, pp. 3–12. Also publ. in Polish as 'Przejście i transformacja w muzyce Witolda Lutosławskiego', *Res Facta* 9 (Kraków, PWM, 1982), pp. 141–51.

Casken, John: review of Steven Stucky's *Lutosławski and his music* (Cambridge, CUP, 1981), in *The Musical Times*, vol. 122 (December 1981), pp. 822–3.

Chłopecki, Andrzej: 'The Structure of a Crystal, and All for Sale. On Witold Lutosławski's and Krzysztof Penderecki's Works', *Polish Art Studies*, vol. 3 (1982), pp. 261–6.

Chłopecki, Andrzej: ' "Tombeau" einer Epoche. Witold Lutosławski – eine Würdigung', *MusikTexte* 54 (June 1994), pp. 47–50.

Chłopecki, Andrzej: 'Zeugnis zerfallender Werte. Witold Lutosławskis Abschied von der Moderne', *MusikTexte* 42 (November 1991), pp. 45–50. Also publ. in Polish as 'Witolda Lutosławskiego pożegnania z modernizmem' [W.L.: farewell to modernism], in *Muzyka, słowo, sens: Mieczysławowi Tomaszewskiemu w 70 rocznicę urodzin* [Music, Word, Meaning: to Mieczysław Tomaszewski on the occasion of his 70th birthday], ed. Anna Oberc (Kraków, Music Academy of Kraków, 1994), pp. 101–12.

Cowie, Edward: 'Mobiles of Sound', *Music and Musicians*, vol. XX (October 1971), pp. 34–40.

Davies, Norman: *White Eagle, Red Star: The Polish-Soviet War 1919–20* (London, 1972).

Davies, Norman: *God's Playground: A History of Poland*, 2 vols (Oxford, OUP, 1981).

Davies, Norman: *The Heart of Europe* (Oxford, OUP, 1984).

Davies, Norman: *Europe: A History* (Oxford, OUP, 1996).

Desnos, Robert: *Corps et biens* (Paris, 1930).

Desnos, Robert: *Chantefables et Chantefleurs* (Paris, 1991).

Dmowski, Roman: 'Poland, Old and New', in *Russian Realities and Problems*, ed. J. D. Duff (Cambridge, 1917), pp. 83–122.

Dmowski, Roman: 'O księdzu Kazimierzu' [About Father Kazimierz (Lutosławski)], *Myśl Naród* (1939/10).

Dumas, Marie-Claire: 'Robert Desnos', in *Dictionnaire des Littératures de langue française*, ed. Beaumarchais, Couty and Rey (Paris, 1987), pp. 669–71).

Dziębowska, Elżbieta: 'Pieśń masowa w twórczości Witolda Lutosławskiego' [The mass song in the work of W.L.], *Muzyka* 5 (Warsaw, Polish Academy of Sciences, 1954/7–8), pp. 38–44.

Fondo-Valette, Madeleine: 'Henri Michaux', in *Dictionnaire des Littératures de langue française*, ed. Beaumarchais, Couty and Rey (Paris, 1987), pp. 1600–4.

Gantchoula, Phillipe: 'La 3ème Symphonie de Lutosławski: Synthèse d'un itinéraire créateur', *Analyse musicale* 10, (January 1988), pp. 68–74.

Gieraczyński, Bogdan: 'Witold Lutosławski in Interview', *Tempo* 170 (September 1989), pp. 4–10.

Helman, Zofia: *Neoklasycyzm w muzyce polskiej XX wieku* [Neoclassicism in Polish music of the 20th century] (Kraków, PWM, 1985).

Helman, Zofia: 'Zofia Lissa' [a commemorative profile of her life and work], *Polish Musicological Studies* vol. 2 (Kraków, 1986), pp. 7–24.

Homma, Martina: 'Witold Lutosławski: *Mi-Parti*', *Melos* 47 (1985/3), pp. 22–57.

Homma, Martina: 'Horizontal-vertikal. Zur Organisation der Tonhöhe bei Witold Lutosławski', and 'Materialen zur Arbeit von Witold Lutosławski', *Neuland-Jahrbuch* V (1985), pp. 91–112.

Homma, Martina: 'Unerhörtes Pathos. Witold Lutosławski: III Sinfonie' [Unprecedented pathos. W.L.: 3 Symphony], *MusikTexte* 13 (February 1986), pp. 7–12.

Homma, Martina: 'Vogelperspective und Schlüsselideen' [Bird's-eye views and key ideas], in *Witold Lutosławski*, ed. Heinz-Klaus Metzger, *Musik-Konzepte* vol. 71/72/73 (Munich, Riehn, 1991), pp. 33–51.

Homma, Martina: 'Chronologisches Werkverzeichnis. Auswahlbibliographie. Auswahldiskographie', in *Witold Lutosławski*, ed. Heinz-Klaus Metzger, *Musik-Konzepte* vol. 71/72/73 (Munich, Riehn, 1991), pp. 198–223.

Homma, Martina: 'Nostalgie des Aufbruchs? Witold Lutosławskis Klavierkonzert – ein Spätwerk', *MusikTexte* 42 (November 1991), pp. 27–34.

Homma, Martina: 'Gleichzeitigkeit des Ungleichartigen. Witold Lutosławskis Vierte Sinfonie – Synthese seines Schaffens', *MusikTexte* 54 (June 1994), pp. 51–6.

Homma, Martina: 'O przestrzeni muzycznej w harmonice dwunastotonowej W. Lutosławskiego' [On musical space in W.L.'s 12-note harmony], *Muzyka*, 40/1–2 (Warsaw, Polish Academy of Sciences, 1995), pp. 85–110.

Jarociński, Stefan: *Polish Music* (Warsaw, PWN, 1965), pp. 168–90.

Jarociński, Stefan: *Debussy a impresjonizm i symbolizm* (Kraków, PWM, 1966; 2nd edn, 1976). Also published in French as *Debussy, impressionisme et symbolisme* (Paris, Editions du Seuil, 1970), and in English as *Debussy, Impressionism and Symbolism*, trans. Rollo Myers (London, Eulenburg, 1976).

Jarzębska, Alicja: 'Problem kształtowania kontinuum formy w IV Symfonii W. Lutosławskiego' [The problem of building a form continuum in the Fourth Symphony by W.L.], *Muzyka*, 40/1–2 (Warsaw, Polish Academy of Sciences, 1995), pp. 135–54.

Kaczyński, Tadeusz: 'Na tropach systemu Lutosławskiego' [On L.'s trope techniques], in *Witold Lutosławski. Sesja naukowa poświęcona twórczości Kompozytora. Kraków 24–25 kwietnia 1980. Wybór materiałów*, ed. Leszek Polony (Kraków, Music Academy of Kraków, 1985), pp. 51–80.

Kaczyński, Tadeusz: *Andrzej Panufnik i jego muzyka* [A. P. and his music] (Warsaw, Wydawnictwo Naukowe PWN, 1994).

Kaczyński, Tadeusz: 'Witold Lutosławski vu à travers sa correspondance', *Mitteilungen der Paul Sacher Stiftung* 9 (March 1996), pp. 11–13.

Kaczyński, Tadeusz: 'Witold Lutosławski w świetle korespondencji', *Ruch Muzyczny*, vol. 40 (1996/3), pp. 6–7.

Kozicki, Stanisław: *Historia Ligi Narodowej* [History of (Polish) national legions] (London, 1964).

Krakowiecki, Anatol: *Książka o Kołymie* [Book about Kolyma] (London, 1950) [Contains an account of the death of Henryk Lutosławski, pp. 124–32].

BIBLIOGRAPHY

Krawczyk, Dorota: 'Koncepcja czasu Witolda Lutosławskiego' [W.L.'s conception of time], *Muzyka*, 40/1–2 (Warsaw, Polish Academy of Sciences, 1995), pp. 111–33.

Krawczyk, Dorota: 'Irina Nikolska: *Conversations with Witold Lutosławski*', *Muzyka* 40/1–2 (Warsaw, Polish Academy of Sciences, 1995), pp. 234–6.

Krzyżanowski, Julian: *Dzieje Literatury Polskiej od początków do czasów najnowszych* (Warsaw, PWN, 1972); English edition published as *A History of Polish Literature* (Warsaw, PWN, 1978).

Kułakowski, Mariusz: *Roman Dmowski w świetle listów i wspomnień* [R.D. in the light of letters and recollections], 2 vols (London, 1968/1972).

Lednicki, Wacław: *Pamiętniki* [Memoirs] (London, 1967).

Ligeti, György: 'Ligeti über Lutosławski', *Musica* 22 (1968/6), p. 453. [Letter from Ligeti to Owe Nordwall.]

Lissa, Zofia: '*Mała Suita i Tryptyk* Witolda Lutosławskiego' [The Little Suite and the (Silesian) Triptych by W.L.], *Muzyka* 3 (1952/5–6), pp. 7–56.

Lissa, Zofia: 'Koncert na orkiestrę Witolda Lutosławskiego' [W.L.'s Concerto for Orchestra], *Studia muzykologiczne* 5 (1956), pp. 196–299.

Lutosławski, Józef: *Chleb i ojczyzna* [Bread and fatherland], publ. posth. (Warsaw, 1919).

Lutosławski, Wincenty: *Über die Grundvoraussetzungen und Konsequenzen der individualistischen Weltanschauung* (Helsingfors, 1898).

Lutosławski, Wincenty: *The Origin and Growth of Plato's Logic with an Account of Plato's Style and the Chronology of his Writings* (London, 1905).

Lutosławski, Wincenty: *Volonté et Liberté* (Paris, 1913).

Lutosławski, Wincenty: *The World of Souls* (London, 1924).

Lutosławski, Wincenty: *Preexistence and Reincarnation* (London, 1928).

Lutosławski, Wincenty: *Knowledge of Reality* (Cambridge, 1930).

Marek, Tadeusz: 'Witold Lutosławski: *Mi-Parti*', *Polish Music* 12 (1977/2), pp. 3–4.

Marek, Tadeusz: 'Symphony no. 3 by Witold Lutosławski – conversation with the composer', *Polish Music* 108/3–4 (1983), pp. 3–8. Followed by a profile of the composer by Tadeusz Zieliński, pp. 9–20. Polish version in *Ruch Muzyczny* xvi (August 1983).

Markiewicz, Leon: 'II Symfonia Witolda Lutosławskiego' [W.L.'s Symphony no. 2], *Muzyka* 13 (1968/2), pp. 67–76.

Meyer, Krzysztof: 'O muzyce Witolda Lutosławskiego' [On the music of W.L.], *Res Facta* 9 (Kraków, PWM, 1982) pp. 129–40 [Written in 1978].

Meyer, Krzysztof: 'Kilka uwag na temat organizacji wysokości dźwięków w muzyce Witolda Lutosławskiego' [Some observations on the subject of pitch organisation in the music of W.L.], *Muzyka*, 40/1–2 (Warsaw, Polish Academy of Sciences, 1995), pp. 3–24.

Meyer-Eppler, Werner: 'Statistische und psychologische Klangprobleme', *Die Reihe* vol. 1 (Vienna, Universal Edition, 1955). English version as 'Statistic and Psychologic Problems of Sound', *Die Reihe* vol. 1 (London, Universal Edition, 1958).

Meyer-Eppler, Werner: *Grundlagen und Andwendungen der Informationstheorie* (Berlin, 1959).

Meyer-Eppler, Werner: 'Informationstheoretische Probleme der musikalischen Kommunikationen', *Die Reihe* vol. 8 (Vienna, Universal Edition, 1962). English version as 'Musical Communication as a Problem of Information Theory', *Die Reihe* vol. 8 (London, Universal Edition, 1968).

Michaely, Aloyse: 'Lutosławskis III Sinfonie', *Musik-Konzepte* 71/72/73 (Munich, 1991), pp. 63–92.

Michalski, Grzegorz: [interview with Lutosławski, particularly concerning the Piano Concerto], *Polish Music*, vol. 23/2–3 (1988), pp. 3–22.

Mioduszewski, Michał: *Śpiewnik kościelny* . . . [Church Songbook] (Kraków, 1838/1842/ 1853).

Mioduszewski, Michał: *Pastorałki i kolędy z melodyjami* [Pastoral songs and Christmas carols with melodies] (Kraków, 1843).

Mościcki, Henryk, and Dzwonkowski, Włodzimierz (eds): *Parlament Rzeczypospolitej Polskiej: 1919–1927* [The Parliament of the Polish Republic: 1919–1927] (Warsaw, 1928).

Nikolska, Irina: 'Symfonizm Witolda Lutosławskiego' [The Symphonism of W.L.], *Muzyka* 37/3 (Warsaw, Polish Academy of Sciences, 1992), pp. 37–51.

Nikolska, Irina: 'Niektóre zasady konstruowania melodii w twórczości W. Lutosławskiego z lat 1960–80' [Some principles for constructing melodies in Lutosławski's works from the years [1960–80], *Muzyka*, 40/1–2 (Warsaw, Polish Academy of Sciences, 1995), pp. 59–84.

Oplustil, Zdzisław: *Polskie formacje wschodnie 1918–19* [Polish formations in the East] (Warsaw, 1922).

Paja, [Paja-Stach] Jadwiga: 'The Polyphonic Aspect of Lutosławski's Music', *Acta Musicologica* 62/2–3 (1990), pp. 183–191.

Paja-Stach, Jadwiga: 'Witold Lutosławski: Dokumentacja' [W.L.: documentation], *Muzyka* 40/1–2 (Warsaw, Polish Academy of Sciences, 1995), pp. 155–222. Contains: chronicle of life and work, pp. 157–74; comprehensive list of works, including marginal pieces, pp. 175–91; complete list of the composer's writings and published interviews, pp. 191–200; comprehensive bibliography (to 1995), including books, theses/dissertations, articles, and journalistic writings, pp. 201–22. The author credits Maria Stanilewicz-Kamionka for the work which she left incomplete and unpublished on her death in 1984.

Panufnik, Scarlett: *Out of the City of Fear* (London, 1956).

Panufnik, (Sir) Andrzej: *Composing Myself* (London, 1987); Polish version, trans. Marta Glińska, *Panufnik o sobie* (Warsaw, Niezależna Oficjna Wydawnicza, 1990).

Petersen, Peter: 'Über die Wirkung Bartóks auf das Schaffen Lutosławskis', *Musik-Konzepte* 22 (Munich, 1981), pp. 84–117.

Petersen, Peter: 'Bartók-Lutosławski-Ligeti: einige Bemerkungen zu ihrer Kompositionstechnik unter dem Aspekt der Tonhöhe', Hamburger Jahrbuch der Musikwissenschaft 11 (Laaber, 1991), pp. 289–309.

Piotrowska, Maria: 'Aleatoryzm Witolda Lutosławskiego na tle genezy tego kierunku w muzyce współczesnej' [W.L.'s aleatorism in the context of this trend in contemporary music], *Muzyka*, 14/3 (Warsaw, Polish Academy of Sciences, 1969), pp. 67–86.

Rae, Charles Bodman: 'Lutosławski's Golden Year', *Musical Times*, vol. cxxvii, no. 1723 (October 1986), pp. 547–51.

Rae, Charles Bodman: 'Lutosławski's Late Style?', *The Listener*, vol. 121, no. 3098 (January 1989), pp. 36–7.

Rae, Charles Bodman: 'Lutosławski's Piano Concerto', *The Listener*, vol. 122, no. 3124 (July 1989), pp. 36–7.

Rae, Charles Bodman: 'Lutosławski's Late Violin Works', *Musical Times*, vol. cxxxi, no.
1772 (October 1990), pp. 530–3.

Rae, Charles Bodman: 'Witold Lutosławski' [obituary], *The Independent* (London, 9
February 1994).

Rae, Charles Bodman: 'Danuta Lutosławska' [obituary], *The Independent* (London, 28
April 1994).

Rae, Charles Bodman: 'Organizacja wysokości dźwięków w muzyce Witolda
Lutosławskiego' [Pitch organisation in the music of W.L.], *Muzyka*, 40/1–2 (Warsaw,
Polish Academy of Sciences, 1995), pp. 41–58.

Skierkowski, Władysław: *Puszcza kurpiowska w pieśni* [Folksongs from the Kurpie
region] (Płock, 1928–34).

Skowron, Zbigniew: 'Charles Bodman Rae: *The Music of Lutosławski*', *Muzyka* 40/1–2
(Warsaw, Polish Academy of Sciences, 1995), pp. 223–33.

Smoleńska-Zielińska, Barbara: 'Łańcuch 2 Witolda Lutosławskiego [W.L.'s *Chain 2*], *Ruch
Muzyczny* 30/15 (July 1986), pp. 3–4.

Spustek, Irena: *Polacy w Piotrogrodzie: 1915–1918* [Poles in St Petersburg: 1915–1918]
(Warsaw, PWN, 1966).

Stanilewicz, Maria: 'Organizacja materiału dzwiękowego w *Muzyce żałobnej* Witolda
Lutosławskiego' [Pitch organisation in *Musique funèbre* by W.L.], *Muzyka* 20/4
(Warsaw, Polish Academy of Sciences, 1975), pp. 3–27.

Stucky, Steven: 'The String Quartet of Witold Lutosławski' (M.F.A. diss., Cornell
University, 1973).

Stucky, Steven: 'Lutosławski's Double Concerto', *The Musical Times* vol. cxxii, no. 1662
(August 1981), pp. 529–32.

Szweykowska, Anna: 'Z Dziejów Kolędy' [On the history of carols], in *Polskie kolędy i
pastorałki* [Polish Christmas carols and pastoral songs] (rev. edn, Warsaw, 1982).

Thomas, Adrian: 'A Deep Resonance: Lutosławski's *Trois poèmes d'Henri Michaux*',
Soundings no. 1 (Autumn 1970), pp. 58–70.

Thomas, Adrian: '*Jeux vénitiens*: Lutosławski at the crossroads', *Contact* 24 (Spring 1982),
pp. 4–7.

Thomas, Adrian: 'Your Song is Mine', *Musical Times* vol. 136, no. 1830 (August 1995),
pp. 403–9. [Including information on the popular songs/dances which Lutosławski
published under the pseudonym 'Derwid']

Whittall, Arnold: *Music Since the First World War* (London, 1977; rev. edn, 1988).

Whittall, Arnold: review of Steven Stucky's *Lutosławski and his music* (Cambridge, CUP,
1981), in *Music Review*, vol. 13 (August–November 1982), pp. 280–2.

Wolikowska, Izabela z Lutosławskich: *Roman Dmowski: Człowiek, Polak, Przyjaciel*
[R.D.: Man, Pole, Friend] (Chicago, 1961).

Wolikowska, Izabela z Lutosławskich: *Bolszewicy w polskim dworze* (Łomża, 1990).

Zieliński, Tadeusz: 'Witold Lutosławski's *Chain 1*', *Polish Music* 1–2 (1985), pp. 17–24.

Lutosławski's Family

The following genealogical table was first presented as an appendix to the second edition. Much of the information was collated from various entries in the *Polski Słownik Biograficzny* [Polish Biographical Dictionary], vol. 18/1(76) (Warsaw, 1973), pp. 148–56. A few further details (e.g., on the eighteenth-century generations) have been collated from Jadwiga Paja-Stach's study: *Lutosławski i jego styl muzyczny* (Kraków, Musica Iagellonica, 1997), p. 17.

I **Franciszek Saryusz Lutosławski** (*c.* 1755–*c.* 1793)
(the composer's great-great-grandfather)
= **Antonina Burska** (heiress to the Drozdowo estate)

I.1 **Wincenty Jakób Lutosławski** (1793–1855)
(The composer's great-grandfather)
= **Józefa Grabowska**

I.1.1 **Franciszek Lutosławski** (1830–91)
(the composer's grandfather)
= (1) Maria Szczygielska   died 9 May 1869

I.1.1.1		Wincenty Lutosławski	born Warsaw, 6 June 1863
			died Kraków, 28 December 1954
		= (1) Zofia Perez Eguia y Casanova	marr. Madrid, 19 March 1887
			born Almeria, 30 September 1861
			died Poznań, 16 January 1958
	I	Maria Lutosławska	born Drozdowo, 1888
			died Drozdowo, 5 January 1948
		= Mieczysław Niklewicz	born 1880
	2	Izabela Lutosławska	born Drozdowo, 1889
			died Chicago
		= (-) Wolikowski	
	3	Jadwiga Lutosławska	born 1891; died 1895
	4	Halina Lutosławska	born 1897
		= Czesław Meissner	born 1879; died 1950
		= (2) Wanda Peszyńska	
	5	Tadeusz Lutosławski	
	6	Janina Lutosławska	born Kraków 1922

I.1.1.2 Stanisław Lutosławski (1864–1937)
= Maria Jabłońska

= (2) **Paulina Szczygielska** (d. 30 Jan 1922), sister of Maria Szczygielska
(the composer's grandmother)

I.I.I.3	Marian Lutosławski	born Drozdowo, 1 April 1871
		died Moscow, 5 September 1918
	= Maria Zielińska	
	I Franciszk Lutosławska	born 1899; died 1944
	2 Hanna Lutosławska	born 1901
	= (-) Zalewski	
	3 Zbigniew Lutosławski	born 1904
	4 Zofia Lutosławska	born 1905
I.I.I.4	Władysław Lutosławski	born c. 1872; died 1876
I.I.I.5	Jan Lutosławski	born Drozdowo, 20 January 1875
		died Kraków, 21 November 1950
	= Wanda Korybut-Waszkiewicz	
	I Bohdan Lutosławski	died Auschwitz, 1942
	2 Ewa Lutosławska	
	= (-) Wiszniewski	
I.I.I.6	Maria Lutosławska	born 1876; died 1877
I.I.I.7	(Father) Kazimierz Lutosławski	born Drozdowo, 4 March 1880
		died Drozdowo, 5 January 1924
I.I.I.8	**Józef Lutosławski**	born Drozdowo, 28 March 1881
	(the composer's father)	died Moscow, 5 September 1918
I.I.I.8a	**= Maria Julia Olszewska**	married 1904
	(the composer's mother)	born Kursk, 15 June 1880
		died Warsaw, 18 October 1967
I.I.I.8.1	Jerzy Lutosławski	born London, 27 December 1904
		died Warsaw, 1973
I.I.I.8.2	Aniela Lutosławska	born 1906
		died 1908
I.I.I.8.3	Henryk Gabriel Lutosławski	born 1909
		died Kolyma (Siberia), 7 October 1940
I.I.I.8.4	**Witold Roman Lutosławski**	born Warsaw, 25 January 1913
		died Warsaw, 7 February 1994
		bur. Powązki, 16 February 1994
I.I.I.8.4a	= Maria Danuta Bogusławska	marr. Warsaw, 26 October 1946
	(née Dygat)	born Felin, 10 September 1911
		died Warsaw, 23 April 1994
		bur. Powązki, 29 April 1994

305

'Derwid'

Mention has already been made of the 'functional' music which Lutosławski composed during the post-war period, including his music for two films, incidental music for the theatre and for radio plays, and pieces such as his songs for children. But there is another aspect (albeit a marginal one) of Lutosławski's post-war work in this field which was omitted from earlier editions of this book: the popular songs and dances which he composed under the pseudonym 'Derwid'. Initially, it seems rather odd that a composer of such an inherently serious nature as Lutosławski should have tried his hand at popular dance forms, especially when one considers that they were written during years when he was composing pieces such as *Musique funèbre*, and (most extraordinarily) perhaps even as late as his work on the *Trois poèmes d'Henri Michaux*. Yet if one considers the equally perplexing contrast between his wartime activity as café pianist (mostly with Panufnik, but before that, with cabaret singers) and his work on the First Symphony, then an intriguing pattern re-emerges.

There is also a link between 'Derwid's' activity as a songwriter and Lutosławski's activity as a composer of incidental music for the theatre. In Poland there is a long established tradition of what one might best call 'actors' songs'. The closest musical parallel outside Poland – moving somewhat westwards – would be with the French popular chanson (of Edith Piaf, *et al.*), with its 'acted' characterisation and often declaimed style of delivery. In spite of the current ubiquity in Poland (as elsewhere) of Anglo-American contemporary 'pop' song forms and styles, the genuinely popular appeal of the actor's song is as strong now as ever. It was (and is) perfectly natural for well known actors of the main Warsaw theatres to perform popular songs, both in the theatre (either as an element of a theatrical production or in specially designated musical evenings) and via the broadcast media. Perhaps the most famous examples of these actors' songs are now those immortalised in the repertory of the 'Kabaret Starszych Panów', and they make highly inventive (and extremely amusing) use of all the various popular song-forms of their day. Not only was Lutosławski regularly working (during the 1950s and early 1960s, via his instrumental music for the theatre) with actors who had such parallel careers, but his wife was related (as sister-in-law) to the famous cabaret singer Kalina Jędrusik (the wife of her brother, Stanisław Dygat), who was an established member of the Kabaret Starszych Panów. Once these significant connections are made, it does not require such a great leap of the imagination for one to understand how a serious composer such as Lutosławski could be drawn to this medium, especially in view of his freelance status and the ever-pressing need to provide for his wife, step-son, mother and mother-in-law.

The information in the listing given below is collated from two sources: the latter part of an article by Adrian Thomas ('Your Song is Mine', *The Musical Times*, August 1995, pp. 407–9), and a book by Jadwiga Paja-Stach (*Lutosławski i jego styl muzyczny*, Kraków

1997). Thomas, in particular, has done detailed research (for example, in the archives of Polish Radio) into Lutosławski's post-war activities as a composer of 'mass' songs together with Derwid's activities as a writer of popular songs and dances. In his article he comments on the nature of the lyrics (noting their sometimes poignant qualities for expressing some of the ironies of life in post-war Poland), and makes a generally sympathetic appraisal of Derwid's compositional skill in writing within rather than beyond the musical medium. It is worth noting, however, that Derwid does not seem to have experimented in his dance songs in the way that Lutosławski did in some of his children's songs (e.g., the melodic interval pairing technique used in *Piosenka o złotym listku*).

Most of the pieces were published in PWM's fortnightly magazine *Śpiewamy i tańczymy* [Let's sing and dance], although some were published in their other popular-music series *Biblioteka Orkiestr Tanecznych* [The dance orchestra library]. A few were also published (but just as top line and lyrics) in the magazine *Radio i Świat*, then the Polish equivalent of *The Radio Times*. The songs were written for voice and piano, although several were also arranged for dance orchestra (but not by the composer himself). The forms adopted by Derwid include the tango, the waltz, the beguine, a putative blues, the foxtrot, and the slow foxtrot (curiously, in Polish, known as the 'slow-fox').

Of the pieces listed below, only the first, 'Zimowy walc', was not written under the Derwid pseudonym. This is significant, because it is the earliest, dating from 1954 (according to Paja-Stach). The others date from about 1957 through to 1963 (or even 1964). It would seem, therefore, that Lutosławski had 'tested the water' before deciding to make a clear separation between the different personae.

Zimowy walc [Winter waltz]
    Dated 6 February 1954
    Arranged for dance orchestra by T. Kwieciński
    Publ.: *Biblioteka Orkiestr Tanecznych* (PWM, 1954)

Cyrk jedzie [The circus is coming]
    Waltz, for voice and piano
    Lyrics by Tadeusz Urgacz
    Publ.: Śpiewamy i tańczymy (PWM, 1958)
        Radio i Świat XIII/45 (638), 10 Nov. 1957, p. 21 [melody and lyrics]

Czarownica [The witch]
    Foxtrot, for voice and piano
    Lyrics by Tadeusz Urgacz
    Publ.: *Śpiewamy i tańczymy* (PWM, 1957)

Daleka podróż [Distant journey]
    Tango, for voice and piano
    Lyrics by Mirosław Łebkowski and Tadeusz Urgacz
    Publ.: *Śpiewamy i tańczymy* (PWM, 1957)

Milczące serce [Silent heart]
Tango, for voice and piano
Lyrics by Tadeusz Urgacz
Publ.: *Śpiewamy i tańczymy* (PWM, 1957)

Zielony berecik [Little green beret]
Foxtrot, for voice and piano
Lyrics by Mirosław Łebkowski
Publ.: *Śpiewamy i tańczymy* (PWM, 1957)
Radio i Świat XIII/29 (622), 22–8 July 1957, p. 21 (melody and lyrics)

Jak zdobywać serduszka [How to win hearts]
Tango, for voice and piano
Lyrics by Tadeusz Urgacz
Publ.: *Śpiewamy i tańczymy* (PWM, 1961)

Kapitańska ballada [The captain's ballad]
Tango, for voice and piano
Lyrics by Tadeusz Urgacz
Publ.: unpubl. MS

Miłość i świat [Love and the world]
Waltz, for voice and piano or accordeon
Lyrics by Eugeniusz Żytomirski
Publ.: *Śpiewamy i tańczymy* (PWM, 1958)

Nie chcę z tobą się umawiać [I don't want to date you]
Slow-foxtrot, for voice and piano
Lyrics by Zbigniew Kaszkur and Zbigniew Zapert
Publ.: unpubl. MS

Szczęśliwy traf [Good Fortune]
Foxtrot, for voice and piano
Lyrics by Jerzy Miller
Publ.: *Śpiewamy i tańczymy* (PWM, 1958)

W lunaparku [At the funfair]
Tango, for voice and piano
Also known as 'Nie kupiłeś mnie na własność' [You don't own me]
Lyrics by Jerzy Miller
Publ.: unpubl. MS

Warszawski dorożkarz [The Warsaw Cabbie]
Waltz, for voice and piano
Lyrics by Jerzy Miller
Publ.: PWM, 1958
Śpiewamy i tańczymy (PWM, 1962)

Zakochać się w wietrze [To fall in love with the wind]
Tango, for voice and piano
Lyrics by Jerzy Miller
Publ.: *Śpiewamy i tańczymy* (PWM, 1958)

Kiosk na Powiślu [Kiosk by the Vistula]
Waltz, for voice and piano
Also known as 'Kiosk inwalidy' [Kiosk of the invalid]
Lyrics by Jerzy Miller
Publ.: unpubl. MS

Nie oczekuję dziś nikogo [I'm not expecting anyone today]
Slow-foxtrot, for voice and piano or accordeon
Lyrics by Zbigniew Kaszkur and Zbigniew Zapert
Publ.: *Radio i Świat* XVI/1 (750), 3 Jan 1960 (melody and lyrics)
PWM, 1960
    Śpiewamy i tańczymy (PWM, 1963)
    Dzisiaj, jutro, zawsze. Piosenki dwudziestolecia (PWM, 1965)

Tabu [Taboo]
Foxtrot, for voice and piano
Lyrics by Tadeusz Urgacz
Publ.: *Śpiewamy i tańczymy* (PWM, 1959)

Telimena [Telimena]
Slow-foxtrot, for voice and piano
Lyrics by Tadeusz Urgacz
Publ.: *Kramik nowości tanecznych*, vol. 3 (PWM, 1959)

Filipince nudno [The bored Filipina]
Slow-foxtrot, for voice and piano
Lyrics by Jerzy Miller
Publ.: *Śpiewamy i tańczymy* (PWM, 1960)

Serce na wietrze [Heart on the wind]
Little waltz, for voice and piano
Lyrics by Z. Kierszysz
Publ.: *Śpiewamy i tańczymy* (PWM, 1960)

Moje ptaki [My birds]
Blues [*sic*], for voice and piano
Lyrics by Jerzy Miller
Publ.: *Śpiewamy i tańczymy* (PWM, 1960)

Po co śpiewać piosenki [Why sing songs?]
Tango, for voice and piano
Lyrics by Karol Kord
Publ.: *Śpiewamy i tańczymy* (PWM, 1961)

Złote pantofelki [Golden Shoes]
Slow-foxtrot, for voice and piano
Lyrics by Adam Hosper
Publ.: *Śpiewamy i tańczymy* (PWM, 1960)

Jeden przystanek dalej [One stop further]
Tango, for voice and piano
Lyrics by Jerzy Miller
Publ.: *Śpiewamy i tańczymy* (PWM, 1963)

Plamy na słońcu [Sunspots]
Slow-foxtrot, for voice and piano
Lyrics by Jerzy Miller
Publ.: *Śpiewamy i tańczymy* (PWM, 1961)

Rupiecie [Odds and ends]
Waltz, for voice and piano
Also known as 'Wędrowny czas' [Wandering time]
Lyrics by Jerzy Ficowski
Publ.: *Śpiewamy i tańczymy* (PWM, 1961)

Tylko to słowo [Only this word]
Beguine, for voice and piano
Also arranged for dance orchestra (not by the composer)
Lyrics by Adam Hosper
Publ.: *Śpiewamy i tańczymy* (PWM, 1961)
     Biblioteka Orkiestr Tanecznych (PWM, 1962)

W pustym pokoju [In an empty room]
Tango, for voice and piano
Also arranged for dance orchestra (not by the composer)
Lyrics by Artur Międzyrzecki
Publ.: *Śpiewamy i tańczymy* (PWM, 1961)
     Biblioteka Orkiestr Tanecznych (PWM, 1962)

I cóż dalej będzie [What's going to happen next?]
Slow-foxtrot, for voice and piano
Lyrics by Adam Hosper
Publ.: *Śpiewamy i tańczymy* (PWM, 1962)

Na co czekasz [What are you waiting for?]
Tango, for voice and piano
Also arranged for dance orchestra (not by the composer)
Lyrics by Jerzy Miller
Publ.: *Śpiewamy i tańczymy* (PWM, 1962)
     Biblioteka Orkiestr Tanecznych (PWM, 1963)

Wędrowny jubiler [The wandering jeweller]
Slow-foxtrot, for voice and piano
Lyrics by Aleksander Rymkiewicz
Publ.: *Śpiewamy i tańczymy* (PWM, 1962)

Z lat dziecinnych [From childhood years]
Slow-foxtrot, for voice and piano
Also arranged for dance orchestra (not by the composer)
Lyrics by Jerzy Miller
Publ.: *Śpiewamy i tańczymy* (PWM, 1962)
        Biblioteka Orkiestr Tanecznych (PWM, 1962)

Nie dla nas już [No longer for us]
Waltz, for voice and piano
Lyrics by Jerzy Miller
Publ.: *Śpiewamy i tańczymy* (PWM, 1964)

Znajdziesz mnie wszędzie [You'll find me everywhere]
Tango, for voice and piano
Lyrics by Zbigniew Kaszkur and Zbigniew Zapert
Publ.: *Śpiewamy i tańczymy* (PWM, 1963)

Index

317